KANT ON SELF-KNOWLEDGE AND SELF-FORMATION

As the pre-eminent Enlightenment philosopher, Kant famously calls on all humans to make up their own minds, independently from the constraints imposed on them by others. Kant's focus, however, is on universal human reason, and he tells us little about what makes us individual persons. In this book, Katharina T. Kraus explores Kant's distinctive account of psychological personhood by unfolding how, according to Kant, we come to know ourselves as such persons. Drawing on Kant's Critical works and on his Lectures and Reflections, Kraus develops the first textually comprehensive and systematically coherent account of our capacity for what Kant calls 'inner experience'. The novel view of self-knowledge and self-formation in Kant that she offers addresses present-day issues in philosophy of mind and will be relevant for contemporary philosophical debates. It will be of interest to scholars of the history of philosophy, as well as of philosophy of mind and psychology.

KATHARINA T. KRAUS is Assistant Professor of Philosophy at the University of Notre Dame, Indiana. She has published numerous articles on Kant's theoretical philosophy in journals such as *Studies in History and Philosophy of Science*, *European Journal of Philosophy* and *Noûs*.

KANT ON
SELF-KNOWLEDGE
AND SELF-FORMATION

The Nature of Inner Experience

KATHARINA T. KRAUS
University of Notre Dame

CAMBRIDGE
UNIVERSITY PRESS

CAMBRIDGE
UNIVERSITY PRESS

University Printing House, Cambridge CB2 8BS, United Kingdom

One Liberty Plaza, 20th Floor, New York, NY 10006, USA

477 Williamstown Road, Port Melbourne, VIC 3207, Australia

314-321, 3rd Floor, Plot 3, Splendor Forum, Jasola District Centre, New Delhi - 110025, India

103 Penang Road, #05-06/07, Visioncrest Commercial, Singapore 238467

Cambridge University Press is part of the University of Cambridge.

It furthers the University's mission by disseminating knowledge in the pursuit of education, learning and research at the highest international levels of excellence.

www.cambridge.org
Information on this title: www.cambridge.org/9781108812757
DOI: 10.1017/9781108874304

© Katharina Teresa Kraus 2020

This publication is in copyright. Subject to statutory exception
and to the provisions of relevant collective licensing agreements,
no reproduction of any part may take place without the written
permission of Cambridge University Press.

First published 2020
First paperback edition 2022

A catalogue record for this publication is available from the British Library

Library of Congress Cataloging in Publication data
Names: Kraus, Katharina T., 1983– author.
Title: Kant on self-knowledge and self-formation : the nature of inner experience / Katharina T. Kraus.
Description: Cambridge, United Kingdom ; New York, NY : Cambridge University Press, 2020. |
Includes bibliographical references and index.
Identifiers: LCCN 2020026286 (print) | LCCN 2020026287 (ebook) | ISBN 9781108836647 (hardback) |
ISBN 9781108874304 (ebook)
Subjects: LCSH: Kant, Immanuel, 1724–1804 – Criticism and interpretation. | Self-knowledge, Theory of.
| Self (Philosophy)
Classification: LCC B2799.S37 K73 2020 (print) | LCC B2799.S37 (ebook) | DDC 126.092–dc23
LC record available at https://lccn.loc.gov/2020026286
LC ebook record available at https://lccn.loc.gov/2020026287

ISBN 978-1-108-83664-7 Hardback
ISBN 978-1-108-81275-7 Paperback

Cambridge University Press has no responsibility for the persistence or
accuracy of URLs for external or third-party internet websites referred to in
this publication, and does not guarantee that any content on such websites is,
or will remain, accurate or appropriate.

Für meine Mutter und dem Andenken meines Vaters (1948–2000)

To my mother and in memory of my father (1948–2000)

Ich lebe mein Leben in wachsenden Ringen,
die sich über die Dinge ziehn.
Ich werde den letzten vielleicht nicht vollbringen,
aber versuchen will ich ihn.

Rainer Maria Rilke, 'Ich lebe mein Leben
in wachsenden Ringen'

CONTENTS

FIGURES

viii

TABLE

PREFACE

Modern life is full of change and transition. We constantly undergo new experiences or even actively seek them, and with those new experiences we ourselves change. All these changes become manifest in some way or other in our conscious mental life, which consists, most basically, of a constant stream of passing thoughts, perceptions, desires, joys, hopes, and fears, as well as various other mental states. Reflecting upon this seemingly endless flow of experiences, we may notice – once in a while and perhaps often to our own surprise – that many of these changes are profound, even if slow. They concern long-held beliefs, core commitments, and even character traits. And yet we have a sense of *still being me*, unmistakably and distinctively. We almost unavoidably think of ourselves as being the same unique individual persons throughout all these changes. We are rarely willing to accept that our lives may just consist in single experiential episodes strung loosely together. Rather, we even may find ourselves trying to make sense of our lives as a whole, perhaps hoping that all our experiences may add up to an overall character, aim, or purpose towards which we unswervingly strive.

This book aims to enhance our understanding of the intricate relationship between becoming a unique individual person and knowing oneself as such by exploring Immanuel Kant's distinctive account of psychological personhood. For this purpose, it expounds, in accordance with the tenets of his transcendental philosophy, Kant's account of empirical self-knowledge as the knowledge that one has of oneself as a unique psychological person. The resulting account of personhood, I shall argue, is able to explain both the experience of psychological change and the sense of personal identity.

By focusing on the structural conditions of human mental life and retrieving Kant's conception of inner experience, this book will tackle two puzzling questions that lie at the heart, not only of Kant's philosophy, but of any philosophical account of self-knowing subjects. Firstly, how, if at all, can we become the objects of our own experience and, if so, what kind of objects are we for ourselves? Secondly, how, if at all, can we know ourselves objectively? That is, how can the subjective contents of our minds become items of knowledge meeting the standards of objective validity? Kant's philosophy, I argue, provides an exceptionally productive framework to resolve the baffling tension that arises between the self-consciousness that one has of oneself qua *thinking subject* and the self-knowledge that one has of oneself as *object of knowledge*.

Kant's solution, I shall argue, draws centrally on his conception of *the soul as an idea of reason*, which he takes to serve as the "guiding thread of inner experience" (*Critique of Pure Reason*, A672/B700). While Kant denies that there is (at least that we can know of from experience) any Cartesian mental substance that underlies all inner change, he nonetheless assigns a crucial role to the idea of the soul. As a regulative idea of reason, it shapes how we conceive of ourselves as enduring psychological persons, providing the unity that enables us to experience our own mental states and more general psychological properties as varying across time. The individual person will be understood as evolving through self-formation in the course of realizing mental capacities under the normative guidance of the idea of the soul. In consequence, Kant's notion of the soul will turn out – perhaps surprisingly to many readers – to be much closer to an *Aristotelian soul-form* than to a *Cartesian mind-substance*. To be a person, for Kant, just means to live one's life according to the form of an integrated mental whole.

This book is, if anything, only the *sketch of a whole*. In the years working on this project, I have been fortunate to have invaluable teachers, colleagues, and friends. I am especially grateful to all my colleagues at the University of Notre Dame for offering me an extraordinarily productive as well as cooperative atmosphere. Above all, I thank Karl Ameriks for his philosophical guidance and encouragement, and just for seemingly knowing the answers to all my questions. Moreover, I thank in particular Robert Audi, David Cory, Therese Cory, Sam Newlands, Fred Rush, Jeff Speaks, and Meghan Sullivan for supporting me in numerous ways.

Eric Watkins was exceptionally kind to organize a workshop on an early draft of the book at the University of California San Diego in February 2018, which was extremely helpful for clarifying and developing my view. I thank all those who participated in the discussions and in particular those who prepared comments: Lucy Allais, Rosalind Chaplin, Max Edwards, Clinton Tolley, Brian Tracz, and Eric Watkins. Beyond that, Eric repeatedly provided me with detailed written comments on several chapters.

My work has greatly benefited from the numerous helpful comments and suggestions that I have received at conferences and workshops. I owe special thanks for valuable feedback on drafts of individual chapters to Angela Breitenbach, Yoon Choi, Alix Cohen, Silvia DeBianchi, Corey Dyck, Sacha Golob, James Hebbeler, Peter McLaughlin, Thomas Land, Amy Levine, Béatrice Longuenesse, Michael Oberst, Thomas Sturm, Jens Timmermann, and Marcus Willaschek. Numerous other people have engaged with me in a productive dialogue about self-knowledge and psychology in Kant. To name but a few: Matthew Boyle, Andrew Chignell, Janelle DeWitt, Patrick Frierson, Gideon Freudenthal, Ido Geiger, David Hyder, Patrick Kain, Jessica Leech,

Jacqueline Mariña, Samantha Matherne, Sofie Møller, Sasha Newton, Karin Nisenbaum, Konstantin Pollok, Carl Posy, Ursula Renz, Tobias Rosefeldt, Janum Sethi, Daniel Sutherland, Udo Thiel, and Rachel Zuckert. I thank in particular Julia Peters for co-organizing the workshop "Kant on the Self: Moral and Psychological Dimensions" at Notre Dame in September 2019, as well as all speakers and discussants who participated in it. I am especially grateful to Wolfgang Freitag for his refreshing "analytic" challenges to my Kant scholarship and for developing together with me an expressivist reading of Kant's "I think". I also thank him, as well as Maik Niemeck and other colleagues at the University of Freiburg, for co-organizing several workshops on issues concerning the *first person* in Freiburg and Mannheim. These workshops and my research on the *first person* more generally were kindly supported by a generous grant of the Elite Programme for Postdocs of the Baden-Württemberg Stiftung (2016–19). Moreover, I thank Marcus Willaschek for hosting me at Goethe University in Frankfurt for two fruitful summers in 2017 and 2018. I am especially indebted to Brigitte Falkenburg and Peter McLaughlin for their invaluable academic mentorship over many years.

I kindly thank Cambridge University Press for letting me reuse material from my paper "The Parity and Disparity between Inner and Outer Experience in Kant" (*Kantian Review* 24(2): 171–95); and the publisher De Gruyter for permitting me to reprint parts of my paper "Rethinking the Relationship between Empirical Psychology and Transcendental Philosophy in Kant" (*International Yearbook of German Idealism* 15: 47–76).

This work would not have been possible without the guidance, trust, and encouragement of my supervisors at the University of Cambridge, Marina Frasca-Spada, Nick Jardine, and Onora O'Neill, who helped me plant the seeds of this book. I am deeply grateful for their enduring support and generosity, which they have still shown me long after I had finished my dissertation.

Special thanks must also go to Aaron Wells, who read numerous drafts of this manuscript, gave meticulous and acute comments, and helped me in various other ways in preparing this manuscript for submission. I also thank Hilary Gaskin and the staff at Cambridge University Press for their generous assistance and advice.

Last but not least, I am blessed with the loving support of my family, close friends, and especially of Julian. I dedicate this book to my parents, who taught me how to be a person long before I had any theoretical grasp of this notion.

INTRODUCTION

From Inner Experience to the Self-Formation of Psychological Persons

i.1   Two Theses

As the pre-eminent Enlightenment philosopher, Immanuel Kant is famous for emphasizing that each and every one of us is called to "make use of one's own understanding without direction from another" (*Enlightenment* 8:35). We are all called to make up our own minds, independently from the external constraints imposed on us by others. In the face of this Enlightenment calling, much of Kant's philosophy, then, reads as a manual for how to employ one's mental faculties in the proper way – faculties that are supposed to be universally realized by all human beings. Given his focus on a universal conception of the human mind, Kant tells us surprisingly little about what makes us the unique individual persons we are and how we come to know ourselves as such.

This book explores Kant's distinctive account of *psychological personhood* by unfolding, in accordance with the tenets of his Critical Philosophy, his account of *empirical self-knowledge* as the knowledge that one has of oneself as a unique psychological person. A central role is played by the capacity to judge one's own psychological features, that is, the capacity for what Kant calls *inner experience*. Primarily, inner experience concerns a person's conscious mental states, such as occurrent sensory perceptions, thoughts, memories, imaginations, feelings, and desires. Moreover, inner experience also concerns general psychological properties such as personality traits and character dispositions, standing attitudes, commitments, and values. Although inner experience has been neglected in the contemporary literature on Kant, I argue that, for Kant, it is a primary means by which persons not only gain knowledge of a range of psychological phenomena that make up their mental lives, but also determine who they are. So in this book I defend two central theses.

First, for Kant, *inner experience is empirical cognition of oneself, not as a mere object, but as a psychological person.*[1] On my reading, Kant conceives of inner

---

[1] Throughout this work, I employ the term *experience* in this Kantian sense, which I introduce in i.2. Moreover, I use the terms *capacity* and *faculty* interchangeably, if not stated otherwise.

experience as analogous to the experience of mind-independent objects in some respects, yet as fundamentally different from it in other crucial respects. On the one hand, a person should be construed by analogy with external objects of experience insofar as the person's specific psychological features are embedded in the spatio-temporal, causally structured world and therefore give rise to a particular kind of experience, namely inner experience. On the other hand, a person fundamentally differs from *mere* objects of experience in that a person must also be construed as a mental being endowed with particular faculties for representation and a distinctive representational perspective, as well as with the ability for self-determination.

My second thesis is, then, that *psychological persons form themselves in the course of realizing their mental capacities under the guidance of a unifying idea, the idea of the soul.* So this book defends what I call the *self-formation view* of the psychological person. On this view, a psychological person is understood not as a self-contained entity that exists prior to the particular happenings of one's mental life, but rather as an entity that first emerges through self-formation in the course of mental activity. An individual person is precisely the unique mental whole that progressively evolves through exercising mental capacities under the normative guidance of a unifying idea, viz. the idea of the soul. The central task of such an interpretation is to discern the conditions that make the formation of oneself as a psychological person possible.

I focus primarily on the experiential, rather than the agential, side of personhood. That is, I explore the nature of psychological persons insofar as they can know themselves through inner experience, rather than insofar as they act as rational agents in the world. Therefore, I examine the conditions of self-formation with regard to the conditions of inner experience, rather than with regard to the conditions of agency. For the former, I draw mainly on the resources of Kant's theoretical philosophy, whereas the latter would involve a close examination of Kant's practical philosophy. Despite confining myself primarily to the experiential side, I firmly believe that the conception of psychological personhood I am offering here is compatible with Kant's theory of agency and can be expanded in this direction in the future.

In sum, my interpretation has the following three characteristics:

(1) It remains agnostic regarding the intrinsic nature of that which appears in inner experience, such as an underlying pre-existing soul or non-material substance.
(2) It takes the idea of the soul – as the concept of a unified mental whole – to be a regulative guideline for determining one's psychological features in time.
(3) It takes the idea of the soul to define normative demands both for acquiring self-knowledge and for realizing oneself as a unified person.

The starting point from which I develop this interpretation is the puzzle of self-reference, to which I now turn.

i.2   The Puzzle of Self-Reference: Parity or Disparity?

Empirical self-knowledge raises an intricate puzzle – a puzzle that is indeed a problem for any philosophical or scientific theory addressing it. On the one hand, self-knowledge is *reflexive* in that it points back to the representing subject who has such knowledge. On the other hand, self-knowledge *refers* to a particular individual "object", namely oneself, with specific psychological features. The puzzle thus concerns the issue of how actively thinking subjects can represent themselves as passively given objects without distorting themselves or becoming estranged from themselves. That is, how can self-knowledge be *self-referential* at all?

Let me expand on this thought. Self-knowledge seems to involve two ways of representing oneself: representing oneself *as subject* and representing oneself *as object*. In contemporary philosophy of mind, this issue has been reflected in the distinction between two kinds of self-consciousness, between "consciousness of oneself *as subject*" and "consciousness of oneself *as object*".[2] Contemporary philosophers of language often appeal to Wittgenstein's famous distinction between two uses of the first-person pronoun "I": the use of "I" as subject and the use of "I" as object.[3] While this terminology is certainly helpful, it leaves the following two questions unanswered. Firstly, if I were to become the object of my own experience, what *kind of object* would I be for myself? Would I be a mind endowed with mental capacities, an embodied human being, a collection of mental states, or rather something else? Secondly, if my self-knowledge is primarily concerned with the subjective contents passing through my consciousness, can these contents ever become items of knowledge meeting the standards of *objective validity*? That is, can I objectively know myself?

This study is driven by the belief that Kant's Critical Philosophy – as an enquiry into the necessary conditions of the possibility of experience – provides an exceptionally productive framework for examining these questions. In his *Critique of Pure Reason* (1781/1787; henceforth, first *Critique*), Kant assigns a central role to the thinking subject in the constitution of experience of objects and thereby conceives of experience as *empirical theoretical cognition of objects*, rather than as merely subjective sensation.[4] A detailed analysis of Kant's account of mental faculties offers, I shall

---

[2] For example, Cassam (1997), Carl (2014), Frank (2007), Longuenesse (2017).

[3] Wittgenstein (1958); see also, for example, Shoemaker (1968), Perry (1979), Lewis (1979), and, more recently, García-Carpintero and Torre (2016).

[4] In this study, I confine myself to empirical theoretical cognition of objects, which I will just call *cognition*, if not stated otherwise.

argue, crucial resources for resolving the puzzle of self-reference. Such an analysis will reveal the distinctive ways in which we relate to ourselves as objects, while at the same time acknowledging our nature as thinking subjects.

According to Kant's transcendental philosophy, *experience* (*Erfahrung*) is a kind of *empirical cognition* (*empirische Erkenntnis*), that is, experience consists in sensation-based judgements about an object or an objective reality. Experience results from the mind's activity of bringing a multitude of sensations under empirical concepts and of combining those concepts into judgements. The two main faculties involved in experience are the faculty of sensibility and the understanding as the faculty to judge. *Sensibility* (*Sinnlichkeit*) immediately relates to objects and yields sensory *intuitions* (*Anschauungen*) of them according to the forms of time and space. The *understanding* (*Verstand*) applies general *concepts* (*Begriffe*) and yields *judgements* (*Urteile*) about objects of experience in accordance with its basic forms, the so-called categories such as unity, substance, and causality. Both the forms of sensibility and the forms of the understanding are conditions of the possibility of experience that are universally shared by all humans.

The paradigmatic case of experience that Kant considers throughout the first *Critique* is the cognition of material objects in space. The notion of inner experience is nonetheless a ubiquitous theme in the first *Critique*, and in other works from the same period.[5] Kant construes inner experience – by and large – by analogy with outer experience. By "observing" ourselves through inner sense, as opposed to observing outer objects through outer sense, we are able to become aware of our mental states, such as perceptions, feelings, and passing thoughts. On the basis of this awareness, we are then able to make judgements about these states and their temporal relations, and arguably about more general psychological properties, such as character traits, moods, passions, and standing attitudes. Inner experience consists in such empirical judgements about one's psychological features.[6]

This conception of inner experience raises precisely the puzzle that I have stated above. In light of Kant's account of experience in the *Critique*, we can now ask: firstly, if inner experience concerns the subjective states of consciousness, can it then be understood as the representation of an object and, if so, of what kind of object? Secondly, can inner experience fulfil the conditions of objective validity necessary for empirical cognition of myself? Kant is aware of the intricate puzzle that is raised by the fact that "the I that I think is to differ from the I that intuits itself ... and yet be identical with the latter as the same

---

[5] For example, B277–9, A672/B700; *Anth* 7:141–2, 7:161–2.
[6] He also uses other phrases, each emphasizing a different aspect, such as *determining my existence in time* (see Bxl, A35/B53, B157n, B430–1), *cognizing myself as I appear to myself* (see B68, B155, B157–8, A337/B394), and *connecting my inner appearances and actions* (see A672/B700, A683/B711).

subject" (B155–6). But unfortunately Kant does not offer a clear account of his solution to the puzzle.

Despite its frequent recurrence in the *Critique* and other texts, the theme of inner experience has mostly aroused suspicion and perplexity among commentators regarding its nature and epistemic status, and only little interpretive consensus about it has been achieved. Most notably, there is a striking lack of discussion of it in the Anglophone literature, and also a surprisingly small amount of discussion in German or in other languages.[7] When it is discussed, various commentators are sceptical about whether inner experience is able to play a significant role in Kant's Critical Philosophy, and some even deny that inner experience can be theoretical cognition of an object at all.[8]

There are two main rival lines of interpretation of inner experience within Kant scholarship and beyond. One line of interpretation construes inner experience as cognition of a mental object on a par with the construal of outer experience as cognition of physical objects. Another denies that such an objectual or objectified grasp of oneself is in any way possible and claims that self-knowledge, if one can speak of it at all, must be knowledge of an entirely different kind. In the history of the reception of Kant's thought, both these approaches have had persuasive defenders and both are still alive today. The tendency towards the objectification of the mental has been pursued predominantly by neo-Kantian and naturalist interpretations of Kant's philosophy; the subjectivist line of interpretation has been defended mainly by German idealists, phenomenologists, and existentialists.[9] This leads me to distinguish, in a more systematic way, two interpretive approaches to Kant's conception of inner experience, both of which are problematic: the *parity view* and the *disparity view*.

According to the *parity view*, inner experience is construed in the same way as outer experience and so, like the latter, as empirical cognition of an object. This view appeals to an alleged structural parallel between inner and outer sense and holds that inner and outer experience are determined through the same set of formal conditions, despite some specific differences, such as the non-spatiality of mental states and the lack of the attractive and repulsive forces of matter in the case of inner experience.[10]

---

[7] The notion of inner experience is rarely discussed or altogether absent from studies of Kant's accounts of the mind, the self, and empirical psychology, such as Ameriks (2000), Kitcher (1990, 2011), Wuerth (2014), and Longuenesse (2017). Exceptions include some neo-Kantians, such as Meyer (1870), and, more recently, Mohr (1991), Emundts (2007), Frierson (2014), and Dyck (2014).

[8] For references, see my discussion of the disparity view later in this section.

[9] For the former, see Wundt (1888, 1902), Cohen (1885), Natorp (1912); for the latter, see Fichte (1794/1997), Husserl (1900/1975, 1931/1988), Heidegger (1929/1990).

[10] A strong tendency towards the parity view can be found in Vogel (1993), Frierson (2014), Chignell (2017); for discussion, see Kraus (2019a).

In contrast, another diverse set of interpretations emphasizes the disparity between inner and outer experience and therefore rejects the identification of inner experience with the empirical cognition of an object in the proper sense. Although these interpretations come in a wide variety of flavours, I subsume them under the common label *disparity view*. Some defenders of the disparity view argue that inner experience amounts not to cognition of a mental object but to some sort of empirical awareness of one's own mental activity, which is conditioned only by the features of reflexive thought.[11] Others detect an apparently insurmountable disparity between inner and outer experience on the grounds that inner experience allegedly lacks a referent, since no object is given to inner sense that could be determined by the category of substance.[12] For a third group, Kant's notion of inner experience can be meaningfully discussed only as an aspect of practical deliberations in the context of agency.[13] Furthermore, Kant's apparent denial of proper scientific status to empirical psychology in the *Metaphysical Foundations of Natural Science* (1786; henceforth *Foundations*) has led many commentators to think that Kant must reject the very possibility of any theoretical knowledge of psychological phenomena and hence of inner experience as empirical cognition.[14]

The novel account that I develop in this study proposes a more nuanced understanding of inner experience as empirical cognition, which is able to answer the worries of the disparity theorists. In line with the parity view, I shall argue that inner experience is empirical cognition of a person's psychological features. Yet the special nature of persons, which gives rise to some of the disparities pointed out above, will warrant a crucial qualification: inner experience is only *analogous* to experience of spatio-material objects. The most important difference is that inner experience is not cognition of a persistent substance given to inner sense; rather, the object of inner experience is first formed in the course of one's mental activity under the guidance of the unifying idea of the soul. Hence, the account of inner experience offered here – in combination with the self-formation view of psychological personhood – preserves conceptual coherence with Kant's notion of outer experience and yet remains sensitive to the distinctive systematic concerns that arise from the puzzle of self-reference.

---

[11] For example, Henrich (1994) and Keller (1998); see also Kitcher (2011), Brook (1994), Hatfield (2006), Schmidt (2008), Longuenesse (2017).

[12] For example, Strawson (1966), Mischel (1967), Gouaux (1972), Washburn (1976), Nayak and Sotnak (1995), Westphal (2004), Friedman (2013).

[13] For example, Sturm (2001, 2009:205–60) and Emundts (2017); see also Makkreel (2001) and Cohen (2009).

[14] See *MFNS* 4:471. For example, Mischel (1967), Gouaux (1972), Washburn (1976), Leary (1978), Schönrich (1991), Friedman (2013), Hudson (1994), Klemme (1996), Makkreel (2003). For discussion, see Kraus (2018).

i.3   The Argument of the Book: Varieties of Objects and Varieties of Self-Consciousness

What is at stake in the dispute between parity and disparity views is whether we can discern an "object" of which inner experience could achieve empirical cognition. The central question is then: what, if anything, do we cognize in inner experience? Reading Kant's texts, the following candidates may recommend themselves: the thinking subject (*denkendes Subjekt*), the self (*Selbst*), the mind (*Gemüth*), the soul (*Seele*), a mere collection of inner appearances (*innere Erscheinungen*), or the whole embodied human being (*Mensch*). A central element of inner experience is the term "I" (and its cognates), as Kant himself states in a note: "All my inner experience is a judgement in which the predicate is empirical and the subject is *I*" (*Refl* 5453, 18:186, my translation). Accordingly, inner experience typically consists in what one may call *I-judgements*, that is, judgements that can typically be expressed by statements of the basic form "I φ" (and derivations thereof), where the subject term is always the first-person pronoun "I", and "φ" a mental predicate. Examples include the self-ascription of occurrent mental states, such as "I see a red rose", "I believe that the sun is shining", or "I feel joy", as well as the self-ascription of more general, temporally extended properties such as "I am a generous person" or "I aim to become a successful piano player". What, if anything, does the term "I" refer to in such I-judgements?

What exactly, on Kant's view, the "I" of inner experience denotes can be understood only within his more comprehensive theory of representation, which spells out the basic relation of a subject towards an object in terms of a variety of mental faculties and their characteristic forms. Based on this account of mental faculties, Kant distinguishes several kinds of objects and, as I shall argue, several corresponding kinds of self-consciousness, some of which involve the use of the term "I". Given Kant's account of empirical cognition as involving both sensibility and the understanding, we can distinguish at least three fundamental ways in which a human subject can relate to an object, corresponding to the following three types of representation:

(R-i) via sensible representations, viz. *intuitions*, through which a particular object is given;

(R-ii) via intellectual representations, viz. *concepts*, through which an object is thought;

(R-iii) via *empirical cognition*, through which an object is cognized on the basis of (R-i) and (R-ii).

Corresponding to these three types of representation, we can now distinguish three kinds of object:

(O-i) the *object of the senses* (commonly called *appearance, Erscheinung*);[15]

(O-ii) the *object of thought* (sometimes called *thought-entity, ens rationis, Gedankending*);[16]

(O-iii) the *object of experience*, that is, an *object of empirical cognition* (commonly called *object, Gegenstand*).

Kant provides complex arguments for how these fundamental ways of relating to objects can be integrated into a single account and in particular for how intuitions are amenable to the conceptual conditions of thought and judgement. Some of these arguments will be relevant to the course of my later analysis. Important at this stage is the insight that taking something as an object does not necessarily mean representing it as an object of experience. The necessary conditions of the possibility of cognition – or what Kant calls its *transcendental conditions* – include time and space as the forms of sensibility and the categories as the forms of the understanding.[17] If a representation satisfies these transcendental conditions, then it is objectively valid, that is, it can be assessed as to its truth regarding the object and independently of the particular representing mind. We can now ask whether inner experience satisfies these transcendental conditions for theoretical cognition of an object. If this were not the case, then the inner domain for Kant would only amount to a merely subjective awareness of mental states in a more or less indeterminate manner, and not to experience in his distinctively demanding sense. Unfortunately, Kant remains ambivalent with regard to the existence and status of the object of inner experience. He appears to subscribe to two seemingly conflicting claims:

(K1) *No object* is *given* to inner sense that corresponds to an empirical inner intuition and that subsequently can be cognized in inner experience.[18]

(K2) In inner experience, I cognize myself *as an object*.[19]

The former claim appears to support the disparity view, whereas the latter claim seems to support the parity view.

In order to resolve this conflict, the book sets out to examine which types of representations and which kinds of objects are involved in inner experience.

---

[15] For example, Bxxvi, A20/B34.

[16] A thought-entity, strictly speaking, is an object of *mere* thought to which no intuition corresponds (see A290/B347).

[17] See A51/B75–6 and A92/B125.

[18] For example, A22/B37, A107, B275, A350, A381, B412.

[19] "Cognition of myself" is mentioned, for example, at Bxl, B139, B155, B158, B277–9, B400, B431; *Anth* 7:142, 7:161; *Prol* 4:336. The "object of inner sense" is specifically mentioned at A342/B400, A357, A368, A385, B403, B415, A443/B471, A846/B874; *CpracR* 5:95; *MFNS* 4:467, 4:542; *Refl* 6313, 18:614; *Anth* 7:142.

The main argument of the book thus consists in discerning the conditions of different types of self-consciousness, that is, of types of representations a subject can have of itself. Corresponding to the notions of object defined above, I distinguish the following types of self-consciousness:

(SC-i) consciousness of one's inner appearances, received by inner sense;

(SC-ii) consciousness of oneself as an object of thought, referred to by the term "I";

(SC-iii) consciousness of oneself through inner experience, expressed in empirical I-judgements.

All these types of self-consciousness – as I will show – have to be classified as *consciousness of oneself as object*. They have to be distinguished from another, still more fundamental type, namely:

(SC-0) consciousness of oneself as thinking subject, via transcendental apperception.

I will call this also *transcendental self-consciousness*, since it defines – as I will argue – the general form of reflexivity that any conscious representation must display, regardless of its specific type. Transcendental self-consciousness is thus a condition of the possibility of *all* empirical consciousness.

Let me add a further note of clarification with respect to Kant's doctrine of transcendental idealism. The notion of object is ambiguous in yet another way in that it can "be taken in a twofold meaning, namely as appearance or as thing in itself" (Bxxvii). Only appearances can be determinable objects for a subject, whereas things-in-themselves transcend the bounds of our senses and cannot be determined through experience. My aim here is neither to defend an interpretation of Kant's transcendental idealism, nor to give an account of inner experience in terms of the thinking thing-in-itself (or noumenon) that may be believed to appear in inner experience. Rather, I focus on those notions of object that are relevant for an analysis of inner experience. In the most general sense, an object is understood as something that can be represented and to some extent determined by a subject – *an object for a subject.*[20]

i.4 The Novel View of the Book: Self-Formation under the Idea of the Soul

As a solution to the puzzle of self-reference, this book argues that in inner experience we cognize ourselves *not* as *mere* objects of experience, since we are

[20] Etymologically, "object" (*Objekt*) is derived from *objectus* (Lat.), meaning "that which is thrown or put before or up against" the subject. Similarly, *Gegenstand* literally translates as "that which stands up against".

not given to ourselves as such objects in the first place. Rather, our inner experience is fundamentally shaped by our nature as human subjects who – endowed with mental faculties and the ability for self-determination – have an individual representational perspective on ourselves and the world. As such subjects, we must conceive of ourselves in inner experience, despite the fact that we cannot intuit ourselves as such. As a result, this book not only develops a novel account of the very "object" of inner experience, which accommodates parities as well as disparities between inner and outer experience, but also offers a novel account of psychological personhood per se.

The account of personhood this book defends, which I call the *self-formation view*, is crucially based on the Kantian idea of the soul. As an idea of reason, no corresponding intuition can be given to it. That is, we cannot intuit ourselves as souls, though we may very well conceive of ourselves as such. Reason, for Kant, is the highest intellectual faculty, whose primary function is the capacity for inferring conclusions that go beyond that which is immediately given in experience. Assigning a central role to the idea of the soul within Kant's Critical theory of experience may sound perplexing to many readers. The Paralogisms in the first *Critique* are commonly read as a devastating criticism of the metaphysical theories of his day, including rationalist theories of the human soul. In consequence, Kant is often taken to deny us any theoretical knowledge of the human soul, including properties such as substantiality, simplicity, and non-materiality. Yet there is ample evidence that Kant never abandons the notion of the soul altogether, nor does he outright reject all meaningful employment of it. Even in his most mature published works, such as the three *Critiques*, and in his late lectures on metaphysics and anthropology, Kant still makes some positive use of this notion in the context of theoretical reason and psychology – a fact that is rarely discussed in contemporary Kant scholarship or appreciated as an interesting and illuminating aspect of his Critical Philosophy.[21] The self-formation view of psychological personhood recovers the idea of the soul by showing it to be not only compatible with Kant's Critical Philosophy, but also extraordinarily philosophically productive for accounts of personhood and self-knowledge.

The crucial point is that the idea of the soul – as the concept of a mental whole – defines the unity of a person. It defines the context within which we can first make sense of inner appearances in consciousness as the states of our own mind. Moreover, it defines the guiding principle by which we come to unify all aspects of our mental life as belonging to the same person. The idea of the soul is thus the unifying form of a person's mental life.

This interpretation is inspired by a claim that Kant puts forward in the Appendix to the Dialectic in the first *Critique*. After having diagnosed the

---

[21] Exceptions include Klemme (1996), Heßbrüggen-Walter (2004), Serck-Hanssen (2011), Goldman (2012), Dyck (2014), Wuerth (2014), and Falduto (2014:24–33).

misuse of reason common to many rationalist philosophies, Kant proposes a positive use of reason in terms of the "guiding thread of inner experience" (*Leitfaden der inneren Erfahrung*) (A672/B700).[22] The notion of a "guiding thread" indicates a certain regulative – rather than constitutive or determining – status. Kant spells out the function of the guiding thread by appeal to an *as-if* claim. The idea of the soul unfolds its function precisely by considering all inner appearances "*as if* the mind (*Gemüth*) were a simple substance that, with personal identity, persistently exists (*beharrlich existiert*)" (A672/B700). I will argue that this claim should be understood neither as an assertive claim about the existence of a preconfigured soul that cannot be empirically proven, but must be rationally believed, nor as a working hypothesis that might be true about the mind, but could equally turn out to be false. Rather, in presupposing this *as-if* claim, reason itself becomes productive through human individuals: reason first produces the context within which we first become intelligible as psychological beings, and hence sets the stage within which we can determine our inner appearances in cognition. In turn, in order to be psychological persons at all, we have to realize our mental activities such that they can be meaningful to us and hence be made sense of as the inner reality of a person.

The idea of the soul, I shall thus argue, serves two roles. With regard to inner experience, the idea of the soul defines transcendental presuppositions that are indispensably necessary to first understand oneself as a psychological person and to determine one's inner appearances, without thereby determining a mental unity as such (for instance, as a persistent mental substance). With regard to the self-formation of an individual person, the idea defines prescriptive principles that are practically efficacious in normatively governing all first-order mental acts through which we realize ourselves as persons. The novel interpretation of Kant's account of psychological personhood that this book offers will, I believe, eventually foster a better understanding of Kant's account of practical personhood, as well.[23]

i.5 Outline of the Chapters

This book consists of three parts, each investigating a different *kind of representation* through which human subjects can relate to themselves in

---

[22] The importance of the idea of the soul for inner experience is rarely acknowledged in the literature. Two recent exceptions are Wuerth (2014), who tries to restore an ontological interpretation of the soul, and Dyck (2014:199–225), who recognizes a methodological role of the idea for investigations of inner appearances.

[23] The self-formation view shares similarities with *self-constitution* accounts, such as that of Korsgaard (2008, 2009). The main difference is that the self-formation view derives a normative account of psychological personhood from the regulative principles of inner experience, whereas Korsgaard's self-constitution view derives an account of practical personhood specifically from the constitutive principles of morality.

accordance with the three major faculties of cognition – sensibility, understanding, and reason: through *sensible intuitions* of which we become conscious in perception (Part I), through *concepts of the understanding* combined in thoughts (Part II), and finally through inner experience, construed as a kind of empirical cognition and guided by an *idea of reason* (Part III). In Part I, "The Appearing Self", Chapters 1 and 2 are devoted to developing accounts of inner sense and of inner perception. In Part II, "Self-Consciousness and the 'I' of the Understanding", Chapter 3 offers an interpretation of transcendental self-consciousness as the general form of reflexivity, and Chapter 4 carves out a distinction between two uses of the term "I": the logical "I" and the psychological "I". In Part III, "The Human Person and the Demands of Reason", Chapter 5 explores the idea of the soul as the regulative "guiding thread" for inner experience, and Chapters 6 and 7 explore reason's normative demands of self-knowledge and of self-formation, respectively.

I specifically use the *Critique of Pure Reason* as a conceptual framework for explicating my systematic interpretation and mainly draw on the primary works from Kant's Critical period (c.1781–98). Moreover, I consider relevant Reflections from this period and his lectures on metaphysics, logic, and anthropology, as well as the *Anthropology from a Pragmatic Point of View* (1798; henceforth, *Anthropology*). As the lectures do not have the same systematic and authoritative status, I treat them with special caution in their historical context. In what follows, I offer a brief outline of each chapter.

Chapter 1, "Inner Sense as the Faculty for Inner Receptivity", sets the stage by introducing Kant's basic model of representation and by defining two pairs of concepts that will guide my analysis: reflexivity and referentiality, on the one hand, and objective and subjective validity on the other. Through an examination of the historical context, the chapter develops an account of inner sense as a transcendental faculty of sensibility, and gives preliminary accounts of central concepts, including *affection, sensation, appearance, intuition, perception,* and *experience.* As a result, the chapter suggests that – on analogy with outer sense – inner sense receives inner appearances and yields distinctively inner intuition according to its specific form, that is, time. The full argument for this claim will be put forward only in Chapter 2. Finally, by considering insights concerning the faculties for desire and feeling from the *Critique of the Power of Judgment* (1790; henceforth, third *Critique*) and the *Anthropology*, the chapter develops a broader notion of inner receptivity as susceptibility to all mind-internal causes.

Chapter 2, "Temporal Consciousness and Inner Perception", offers an interpretation of inner perception as the perception of distinctively inner appearances by drawing on resources from the Transcendental Aesthetic and the Transcendental Analytic (mainly the A-Deduction) of the first *Critique.* The chapter develops an interactional model of perception with three constitutive aspects: (1) affection through outer sense, (2) synthesis of apprehension through the active faculties of the mind, viz. imagination and understanding, and (3) self-affection through inner sense. Each of these constitutive aspects is shown to define a formal and a material condition of perception. By carving out the notion of transcendental self-affection, that is, the a priori determination of the form of inner sense through the understanding, the chapter derives the a priori temporal conditions of perception. Applying the general model to the inner case, inner perception is construed as empirical consciousness of inner appearances, based on empirical self-affection.

Chapter 3, "The Form of Reflexivity and the Expression 'I think'", explores the role of transcendental apperception for inner experience according to the Transcendental Deduction (B) of the first *Critique*. By showing the insufficiencies of two alternative views defended in the literature, namely the psychological view and the logical view, the chapter argues that transcendental apperception is the *capacity for reflexive consciousness* in general. Its characteristic form, the general form of reflexivity, is the most general condition on any conscious representation and can be expressed by the phrase "I think". The chapter concludes by arguing that the phrase "I think", if in fact attached to a representation in thought, is an *expression of self-presence*: it expresses that I myself as an individual thinker am present to the mind, without determining, or *re*presenting, myself as such.

Chapter 4, "The Conditions of Self-Reference", examines two ways in which one can conceptually represent oneself in judgements, in light of the results of the Paralogisms (in the Transcendental Dialectic of the first *Critique*). The logical "I" defines the way in which any thinking subject must represent itself in thought, and hence its logical predicates are conditions of I-judgements in general. The psychological "I" is used to represent oneself in empirical I-judgements, viz. inner experience, and under the temporal conditions of perception (which were derived in Chapter 2). Yet a close reading of the Paralogism of Personal Identity, and other passages, reveals that the principle of persistence cannot be applied in inner experience. The category of substance, therefore, requires a different kind of sensible explication to capture the trans-temporal unity of persons.

Chapter 5, "The Guiding Thread of Inner Experience", explores the regulative use of the idea of the soul with regard to inner experience (as discussed in the Appendix to the Transcendental Dialectic of the first *Critique*). The chapter argues that the idea of the soul provides a *presentation* (*Darstellung*) of a mental whole in relation to which we can first determine inner appearances, without cognizing the whole as such. Employed as an "analogue of a schema" (A665/B693), the idea substitutes for all those schemata that cannot be applied to inner appearances, including the schema of persistence, and outlines the domain within which inner experience can be operative as empirical cognition of inner appearances. The chapter thus establishes my first central thesis, namely that inner experience is empirical cognition of oneself. I develop my view in contrast to two rival interpretations: the noumenal view, which conceives of the soul as a noumenal substance, and the fictional view, according to which the soul is a mere fiction.

Chapter 6, "The Demands of Theoretical Reason and Self-Knowledge", completes Kant's account of empirical self-knowledge – the theoretical knowledge I have of myself as a psychological person. Following Kant's general theory of knowledge, I argue that self-knowledge requires – in addition to a cognition of myself – an attitude of *assent* towards this cognition and an *epistemic ground* for holding this cognition to be true. By laying out different types of epistemic grounds, I distinguish corresponding levels of self-knowledge. The highest level is a complete comprehension of myself based on an a priori idea of myself as a whole. While this highest level can never be attained, it sets the normative standard for all lower levels of self-knowledge. Hence, we are bound to conceptualize all psychological phenomena in accordance with a *system of psychological predicates*, the highest genus concept of which is the idea of the soul. Moreover, the idea of the soul can be understood as a template for approximating one's *complete individual self-concept*, which, if available, would completely and fully adequately describe the individual person. Finally, I outline possibilities of error, such as *self-blindness* and *self-deceit*, and revaluate the doctrine of *transparency* that is often ascribed to Kant.

Chapter 7, "The Demands of Practical Reason and Self-Formation", completes Kant's account of psychological personhood by showing that the idea of the soul defines the unifying form of a person's mental life. It finally establishes the self-formation view via my second central thesis, namely that psychological persons first form themselves in the course of realizing their mental capacities under the normative guidance of a unifying idea. The idea of the soul demands, for instance, that we realize ourselves as *unified across time* (according to the presupposition of substantiality), as the *self-efficacious* common cause of all mental activity (according to the presupposition of a fundamental power), and as *self-directing* towards a rational personality (according to the presupposition of personal identity). The chapter explicates the intrinsic normativity of personhood in terms of a demand for inner systematicity across three distinct, though interrelated spheres: the epistemic, the practical, and the affective. This demand is finally articulated in the form of two imperatives: the *imperative of self-formation* and the *imperative of self-knowledge*.

PART I

The Appearing Self

1

Inner Sense as the Faculty for Inner Receptivity

1.1   Introduction

Our inner experience concerns, most basically, our momentary state of consciousness that results from some ongoing mental activity, such as thinking, perceiving, remembering, judging, imagining, desiring, and feeling. More generally, it also concerns past states we underwent and future states we expect, as well as more stable psychological properties, such as our standing attitudes, moods, and character traits. All experience of these psychological features is centrally based on some sort of awareness of our own state. For Kant, this awareness is tied to a particular mental faculty, namely to *inner sense*. Only through inner sense can contents be taken up into consciousness and contribute to our momentary state, and hence be attributable to ourselves in inner experience. Inner sense belongs, together with outer sense, to the faculty of sensibility (*Sinnlichkeit*), by which we receive sensory contents. An account of inner sense is, therefore, central for understanding the sensible aspects of inner experience, and in particular the conditions under which we become aware of the contents that feature in inner experience.[1]

By appealing to the notion of inner sense, Kant follows a long tradition of inner-sense theories, which probably originates with Aristotle's account of psychological faculties.[2] The British empiricist John Locke famously defended an inner-sense theory, which was hugely influential among empiricist-minded German philosophers in the eighteenth century such as Johann Nikolaus Tetens, but which was also appropriated by some German rationalists, such as Alexander Baumgarten.[3] An interpretation of Kant's account of inner sense is complicated by several factors. Firstly, Kant drastically changes his account from his pre-Critical to his Critical Philosophy. These changes concern especially the intricate relationship between inner sense and

---

[1] Throughout this work, I use the English term *sensible* as a translation of Kant's term *sinnlich*, that is, as pertaining to the senses or resulting from sense affection (*Sinnesaffektion*).

[2] Aristotle (350 BCE/2016); see Heller-Roazen (2007).

[3] Locke (1690/1975), Baumgarten (1739/2011), Tetens (1777). See Thiel (1997, 2011).

our capacity for self-consciousness, that is, transcendental apperception – a notoriously difficult and controversial subject.[4] Secondly, Kant himself never provided a thoroughgoing explication of inner sense, but rather treated this topic occasionally in the context of his transcendental theory of experience in the first *Critique* or in his practical writings and lectures, in relation to issues concerning anthropology and empirical psychology. Thirdly, inner-sense theories have faced sustained criticism for being at best obscure, but for the most part implausible and incoherent.[5] Unsurprisingly, there are various interpretative controversies attached to Kant's notion of inner sense and it is difficult to discern its systematic role.[6]

My aim in this first chapter is not to offer a comprehensive interpretation of inner sense, nor to examine Kant's account of it in the historical context. Rather, my goal is to highlight what is distinctive for Kant's *transcendental* account of inner sense and to develop an interpretation of inner sense specifically with a view to its role for inner experience. While certainly influenced by the early modern empiricist tradition, Kant develops a distinctively *transcendental* account in that, for him, inner sense not only passively receives sensible contents, that is, sensible *matter* (*Materie, Stoff*), as the empiricists have it, but also imposes its specific *form* (*Form*) on these contents. As a transcendental faculty, inner sense contributes a specific formal condition, that is, *time*, to experience, and fulfils specific functions for empirical cognition in general and for inner experience in particular.[7] Three aspects of inner sense are especially relevant for the current study. These are, firstly, its relation to *outer sense*, secondly, its distinction from other faculties that mediate *self-consciousness*, and finally its role for *empirical consciousness* in general. None of these issues can be fully addressed in this chapter, but will be further explicated in Chapters 2 and 3.

In what follows, I develop an interpretation of Kant's transcendental account of inner sense, firstly, by embedding this account within his basic theory of representation (1.2) and, secondly, by situating it within the historical context (1.3). I then outline the details of my interpretation specifically with respect to the *Critique of Pure Reason* (1.4). I conclude with a note on

---

[4] On the transition from the pre-Critical to the Critical account, see Carl (1989) and Kitcher (2011).

[5] Inner-sense theories are commonly interpreted as higher-order perceptual theories of self-consciousness (see Carruthers 2001/2016). A common critique of such theories is that they inevitably lead to an infinite regress of mental contents, for example, Shoemaker (1994).

[6] For detailed discussions, see Hölder (1873) and Reininger (1900), and, more recently, Kitcher (1990, 2011), Mohr (1991), Powell (1990), Klemme (1996), and Green (2010).

[7] Throughout this study, I use the notion of *cognition in the proper sense* (A78/B104), which requires both intuitions and concepts; see Kant's definition at A78/B104 and also A51/B75–6, A92/B125. Occasional exceptions to this definition can be found, for example, at A320/B377. For discussion, see Watkins and Willaschek (2017a).

a broader account of inner receptivity that emerges from the *Anthropology* and the *Critique of the Power of Judgment* (1.5).

1.2 Kant's Basic Model of Representation

1.2.1 Reflexivity and Referentiality

Kant's account of inner sense is embedded in his general theory of representation. *Representation* (*Vorstellung*) is indeed a central notion of Kant's Critical Philosophy. All of one's mental life is made up of some representation or other; and inner sense is crucial for becoming conscious of one's own representations. As a first approach to the study of inner experience, I therefore introduce what I call Kant's basic model of representation, alongside two crucial distinctions: the distinction between *reflexivity* and *reference*, and the distinction between *subjective* and *objective validity*. I take this model to apply not only narrowly to his theory of experience and a priori cognition in the first *Critique*, but to his Critical Philosophy in general, which concerns various other aspects of human mental life, such as practical cognition, aesthetic judgements, and feelings.

The fundamental feature of representation is its relational nature. A representation, for Kant, characteristically has a dual relation: a relation to the representing subject and a relation to the represented object.[8] The basic model of representation just states that a subject relates to an object *via* representation. It does not assume any specifics regarding the nature and existence of the subject or of the object, nor regarding the type or mode of representation. Insofar as a representation is *about something*, that is, directed at an object in the generic sense, it has some *representational content* in the generic sense. The representational content concerns the mode under which the object is represented. As we shall see, not all representations have content that is strictly speaking representational. For instance, sensation and feeling by themselves may not have content. Kant, nonetheless, subsumes them under the generic notion of representation because they have some representational function. Sensation, for instance, contributes to the representational content of intuition, and feelings – as I shall argue – to the representational content of inner intuition.

An important feature of Kant's basic model of representation is that each of the three basic notions – *subject, representation* (with *representational content*), and *object* – can be understood only in relation to the others. Someone is a subject only in virtue of representing some object or content. Something is an object only for some – individual or type of – subject, for example, an object for

---

[8] See "what is universal in every relation that our representations can have is (1) the relation to the subject, (2) the relation to objects, and indeed either as appearances, or as objects of thinking in general" (A334/B391; see also A320/B376; *L-Log/Jäsche* 8:33; *CJ* 5:188–9).

me or for humans more generally. A representation has some content only in virtue of being had by a subject and of being related to some object. Later I will call representations with representational content *significant representations*: broadly construed, these are representations that are "not nothing for me" (B132), but that mean something for me. They pick out something distinct or make a discernible representational difference for me.[9] What exactly this amounts to will become clear in my discussion of transcendental apperception in Chapter 3 (see Sections 3.2 and 3.4).

For the current purpose, it is crucial to discern two different senses of the distinction between the *subjective* and the *objective*. Primarily, the notions of *subjective* and *objective* concern the distinction between the two kinds of *relation* in the basic model: the relation to the subject and the relation to the object. Yet to be sure Kant more often uses these notions to denote a distinction between two kinds of *validity*, which I will introduce below.

In the basic model, *subjective* denotes whatever concerns the relation to the subject of representation (e.g., B70n, *CJ* 5:188, *Prol* 4:555). I call this relation *reflexivity*. Each representation is in a weak sense reflexive, insofar as it can be had by some subject and can hence contribute to the subject's state of consciousness (and is then commonly called a *mental state*). In the course of this study, I will discern the general form of reflexivity as a universal condition of any potentially conscious representation (see Chapter 3).

By contrast, *objective* denotes whatever concerns the relation to the object (e.g., A146/B185, A334/B391, *Prol* 4:282, 313, *CJ* 5:188). Here things are more complex because there are various kinds of objects and various corresponding kinds of object-dependencies. The central case in the first *Critique* is the object of experience: it is an object that appears in space and time through the senses (i.e., an appearance) and that is also thought through concepts (see, e.g., A92/B125). Yet there are other kinds of objects to which a representation can relate. To name a few other examples: mathematical objects, such as geometrical figures or numbers, are referred to via mathematical cognition; objects of mere thought, such as the world-whole and God, via non-experiential judgements; imaginary objects, such as a fictional character in a novel, via products of the imagination. Moreover, mental states themselves, such as thoughts, perceptions, desires, and feelings, may be regarded as belonging to an "inner object" of some sort, which is related to via inner experience (see A189–90/B234–5). Finally, things-in-themselves could, arguably, be seen as "objects" of transcendental philosophy.[10]

---

[9] Kant uses the notion of *significance* for representations with relation to a sensible object (e.g., A146/B185; see also "sense and meaning", *MFNS* 4:478). My notion of *significant representation* is inspired by, though also broader than, Keller's notion of *semantic significance* (Keller 1998:36–44).

[10] On different kinds of object, see i.3 and 4.2.

I call the relation to an object (in the generic sense) *reference*. Note, however, that reference in this generic sense does not necessarily involve the existence of the object referred to, nor should it necessarily be understood as a semantic reference that requires a concept. With respect to concepts, one could call the class of objects referred to by the concept its extension, or what Kant calls *domain* (*Umfang*) (e.g., A71/B96) or *sphere* (*Sphäre*) (e.g., A654/B682). The concept's representational content would then be the mode under which the object is represented and could be called its intension, or what Kant calls *content* (*Inhalt*) (e.g., A51/B75, A58/B83, A62/B87, A71/B97).

Kant's basic model of representation may be illustrated as shown in Figure 1.1.

1.2.2 Subjective and Objective Validity

Much more often, Kant uses the notions of *subjective* and *objective* to denote the broadly epistemic distinction between two kinds of validity, namely *merely subjective validity* and *objective validity*. In this respect, Kant calls a representation "merely subjective" to indicate some lack of objective validity (e.g., A49/B66, B140); in turn, he uses the notions "necessary and universal validity" (e.g., A48/B65, B140) and "logical objectivity" (*CJ* 5:189) to indicate that a representation is valid in a sense that is independent of the subject. While this distinction is certainly related to the distinction between reflexivity and reference, it should not be confused with the latter. In the *Prolegomena*, Kant elaborates on his definition of *thinking* as follows:

> To think, however, is to unite representations in a consciousness. This unification either arises merely relative to the subject and is contingent and subjective, or it occurs without condition and is necessary or objective. ... Judgments are therefore either merely subjective, if representations are related to one consciousness in one subject alone and are united in it, or they are objective, if they are united in a consciousness in general, i.e., are united necessarily therein.   (*Prol* 4:304–5)

This passage suggests that subjective and objective validity concern more specifically the *mode* under which a subject represents an object. The subject can do so either merely subjectively, or objectively.

For a merely subjective representation, the mode of representation depends on the contingent conditions under which a particular subject has or produces the representation and may be influenced by its empirical vagaries and sensory

Figure 1.1   Kant's basic model of representation

impairments. Sensible representations, such as sensation and intuition, are primarily merely subjective representations since they depend on the way in which the particular subject is affected (e.g., B68, B72, B129). For instance, my perception of this chair in front of me is influenced by my visual perspective and my wearing of red glasses, which gives it a red tint. To be sure, Kant's aim in the *Critique* is to show that sensible content can be taken up into objectively valid representations, if it is apprehended according to the logical forms of judgement, or so Kant argues in the Transcendental Deduction of the Categories.[11] In consequence, merely subjective sensations can be said to contribute objectively valid content to intuitions.

In turn, if the mode of representation is necessary with respect to the object and universal with respect to all possible subjects (of a particular type), then the resulting representation is objectively valid.[12] The representational content is then exclusively due to the features of the object, rather than to the specific contingent conditions of a particular subject. For instance, the chair that I perceive, objectively taken, has particular spatio-temporal determinations, which are in principle accessible to all perceivers of the same kind. The chair possesses a back side, even though I may not currently perceive this side, and the chair's colour is in fact brown, rather than displaying a red shimmer, which I perceive due to my red glasses. In general, a complex representation is objectively valid if all its partial "representations are combined in the object, i.e., regardless of any difference in the condition of the subject" (B142). It represents the object in a mode that is valid "for everyone", that is, for all subjects of the same type (*Prol* 4:299).

Note, however, that this sense of objective validity as independence from a particular contingent epistemic situation does not rule out that the representational content may still depend on some general features of the type of subject. According to Kant's transcendental theory of experience, the objective content of experience depends precisely on the forms by which subjects like us humans apprehend sensory content, namely in accordance with the forms of space and time, as well as with the categories of the understanding. The former are specifically human modes of representation, whereas the latter are more universally valid for all thinking subjects.[13]

The distinction between subjective and objective validity is often cashed out in terms of the *first-personal standpoint* and the *third-personal standpoint*, but this terminology should be used with caution. A first-personal standpoint is often taken to be the standpoint of a particular subject, for example, my

---

[11] In what follows, "Deduction" denotes the Transcendental Deduction of the Categories, while the letters "A" and "B" indicate, respectively, the first and second editions of the *Critique of Pure Reason*.

[12] See "Objective validity and necessary universal validity (for everyone) are therefore interchangeable concepts" (*Prol* 4:298); also A48/B65, B140.

[13] See, for example, B138–9.

particular geometrical perspective on the chair. It could be called the subject's private view, since at this moment only this particular subject has this view of some subject matter. By contrast, a third-personal standpoint is the standpoint of "everyone", that is, the public view that is in principle accessible to everyone who shares the same kind of mental apparatus. Yet this notion of a first-personal standpoint should not be confused with the general characteristics of *having a perspective* (or being a subject) at all, which, as we will see, are independent of particular viewpoints, and to some extent even of the temporal nature of human minds.

The distinction between subjective and objective validity is commonly understood as an epistemic distinction, since it is often related to the truth-aptness of representations. Only an objectively valid representation can be adequately assessed as to its truth or falsity. A merely subjective representation, by contrast, is not necessarily intended to represent an object in a truthful way, and therefore an assessment of its truth-value seems inadequate. Knowing an object requires us to represent the object in an objectively valid way since knowledge is supposed to be valid for everyone. In this sense the distinction is epistemic.

But Kant does not only apply this distinction in his theoretical philosophy (which is primarily concerned with the conditions of cognition and knowledge). Rather, he applies this distinction also in his practical philosophy. For instance, a maxim is primarily merely subjectively valid, since it is "a *subjective* principle of action, a principle which the subject himself makes his rule" (*MM* 6:225). The goal of a moral theory is to discern which types of maxims are "in conformity with universal ends", that is, ends as they are viewed from the standpoint of "an impartial rational spectator" (*Groundwork* 4:393). Only those maxims that are "free from all influences of contingent grounds", and can hence be valid "for everyone", can be principles of morality (*Groundwork* 4:426). Only by fulfilling "the condition of universal validity" can a maxim count as a moral law (*Groundwork* 4:458).[14]

In Kant's texts, these two distinctions – the distinction between *reflexivity* and *reference* and the distinction between *subjective* and *objective validity* – are often intertwined in various ways that must be carefully discerned. A representation can even be said to be both subjective and objective. For instance, Kant claims that a sensation is both merely subjectively valid, insofar as it concerns a particular subject's state of sensory affection, and yet has some objective purport, insofar as it immediately relates to a sensible object. If apprehended according to the forms of experience, it can even contribute objectively valid content to experience.[15] By contrast, feelings of pleasure and pain are said to be subjective in both senses – feelings are the states of

---

[14] See Engstrom (2009:104–8).
[15] For discussion of objective content, see Jankowiak (2014).

a particular subject that do not directly relate to an object and hence do not contribute to objectively valid content, at least with respect to *spatio*-temporal objects. I will discuss the case of feelings in more detail in Section 1.5.[16]

With these two distinctions at hand, we can now restate the puzzle of inner experience from the Introduction (i.2). As with any other representation, inner experience is related to the subject, that is, reflexive, and is related to some object, that is, referential. More specifically, inner experience is about the particular individual subject who possesses it. Employing my terminology, inner experience can now be said to be *self-referential*: inner experience refers to the subject itself as its object. The goal of this book is to examine how this *self-referentiality* can be understood as a specific kind of *reflexivity* and how it can be understood as a specific kind of *referentiality*. Following Kant's tenet that experience is empirical cognition of objects, one may initially assume that inner experience involves both empirical intuitions, through which an object is given, and concepts, through which an object is thought.[17] This assumption immediately raises the following fundamental questions: in which sense am I given to myself in inner sense, and what, in turn, are the conditions under which I can determine myself in an objectively valid way, if at all?

While this question primarily pertains to Kant's narrow theory of cognition, it cannot be fully answered without taking into account his broader theory of representation. Not only do my cognitive states such as perceptions, beliefs, and conjectures contribute to my mental life, but so first and foremost do my desires, dreams, hopes, fears, intentions, pleasures, and pains – in short, all representations that have some significance for me and of which I can be conscious. Inner experience, thus, can concern *all* my significant representations. In this chapter, I begin to examine the conditions under which I can be given to myself in inner sense and under which I can yield inner intuitions of myself. While I first focus on Kant's treatment of inner sense in the context of experience, I eventually broaden my interpretation and develop a more general account of *inner receptivity*. Let me add one final piece to my account of Kant's basic model: the distinction between transcendental and empirical faculties.

1.2.3 Transcendental and Empirical Faculties

A centrepiece of Kant's Critical Philosophy is the division of mental faculties. While Kant's view is broadly in line with the prevailing faculty psychology that

---

[16] See *CJ* 5:189.
[17] On the two conditions of cognition – intuition and concept – see A92/B125. In most places, Kant fully identifies *experience* with *empirical cognition* (e.g., Bxvii, B147, B161, B166, B277). In a few places, "experience" seems to denote the subject's state of experiencing an object, whereas "empirical cognition" always denotes the judgement made on the basis of such experiential state (e.g., Bxvii, Bxxvi(n), B1–2). I use "experience" and "empirical cognition" synonymously.

was held by many of his rationalist and empiricist predecessors, Kant crucially departs from their views in developing a *hylomorphic* account of mental faculties.[18] This account distinguishes between transcendental (or formal) and empirical (or in a broad sense "material") aspects of mental faculties. So Kant frequently introduces both a transcendental and an empirical variant of the major faculties, for example, "*a priori* sensibility" (A21/B35) and the "empirical sense(s)" (A29/B35, see *Anth* 7:153ff.); the "transcendental faculty of imagination" (A102) (or "productive imagination", B152) and the "reproductive imagination" (which "belongs to psychology", B152); and finally "transcendental apperception" and "empirical apperception" (A107). According to this hylomorphic account, a faculty is still seen as carrying out a mental operation upon given representational (e.g., sensory) data and thereby generating representations. For Kant, not only do these mental operations work upon such given representational *matter*, but each faculty has its characteristic *form* by which it informs such matter such that it becomes representational content for the subject. The forms of sensibility, for instance, are space and time; the forms of the understanding are the so-called categories (e.g., substance and causality), which are derived from the pure forms of judgement (e.g., categorical and hypothetical judgement). In general, matter constitutes the content of a representation only if it is apprehended according to a particular form, which then determines the type of representation. Any significant representation thus requires a union of both form and matter.[19]

Kant identifies three basic mental faculties and several derivative ones. The basic faculties are the *faculty of cognition* (*Erkenntnisvermögen*), the *faculty of desire* (*Begehrungsvermögen*), and *feeling* (*Gefühl*). The derivative faculties include: the senses, memory, understanding, and (speculative) reason, all of which belong to the faculty of cognition; the higher desires (e.g., rational motives) and lower desires (e.g., instincts, basic inclinations); the feeling of respect and the feelings of pleasure and pain; and so on. This tripartite division features prominently in Kant's lectures on rational and empirical psychology, which were closely modelled on a textbook by Alexander Baumgarten, a resolute proponent of rational psychology.[20] In his Critical Philosophy, Kant offers a transcendental justification for this tripartite structure in terms of three basic dependence relations that a faculty can have to its objects. Firstly, the faculty of cognition is

---

[18] Many seventeenth- and eighteenth-century philosophers endorsed some version of faculty psychology, both the empiricist-minded, such as Locke (1690/1975) and Hume (1740/1978), and the rationalist-minded, such as Wolff (1732/1968) and Baumgarten (1739/2011). For the historical context, see Heßbrüggen-Walter (2004) and Falduto (2014).

[19] On Kant's transcendental hylomorphism, see Pollok (2017:117–96).

[20] Baumgarten (1739/2011). For discussion of Kant's pre-Critical account of mental faculties, see Hatfield (2006), Kitcher (2011), and Dyck (2014).

directed at given objects in the world that are commonly existentially independent from the subject. Secondly, the faculty of desire aims for the realization of an object or state of affairs in the world and seeks to bring about the existence of the object that is represented by a desire. Thirdly, feelings of pleasure and displeasure are not directed at objects at all, though they may themselves be the effect of a subject's having a cognitive or conative relation to an object.[21]

According to Kant's transcendental hylomorphism, a mental faculty can be described either transcendentally qua its *form* or empirically qua the particular *representational content* that it actually produces in time. The former gives us "transcendental definitions" (*CJ* 5:177–8n; see also *CpracR* 5:9n; *CJ First Intro* 20:205–6, 230n).[22] Such transcendental definitions give functional accounts of each mental faculty in terms of the type of representation it produces. For instance, sensibility's function is to receive sensory content in the form of space and time, the understanding's function is to generate judgements in accordance with the logical forms of judgement, and so on.

The transcendental definition of a faculty applies universally to all human beings, or all beings that are assumed to have the same mental faculties.[23] A transcendental faculty can be understood as a *type* of faculty that, characteristically, gives rise to a particular *type* of representation according to the faculty's characteristic form. Transcendental philosophy enquires into the necessary conditions for a faculty to fulfil its characteristic function and, therefore, examines each faculty and its interrelations with other faculties with respect to form. In the first *Critique*, which focuses on the faculties of cognition, Kant argues that the characteristic forms of the cognitive faculties determine the transcendental conditions of experience: these conditions *must* be fulfilled in order for the resulting cognition to be *able* to truthfully represent an object of experience.

In turn, an empirical faculty can now be understood as the concrete realization or implementation of the corresponding transcendental faculty in a human individual. An empirical faculty is a particular *token* of a transcendental faculty, which operates within an individual mind and which produces the representations occurring in the individual's empirical consciousness.[24] The operations of empirical faculties can be observed primarily in terms of the states in empirical

[21] See *CJ* 5:189 and *CpracR* 5:9n. See also Engstrom (2009:119).
[22] Kant's transcendental definitions are supposed to provide a neutral basis for ethical disputes (see *CpracR* 5:9n). Although these definitions borrow concepts, such as "desire" and "feeling", from psychology, psychology cannot provide such transcendental definitions. For an opposite view, see Frierson (2014:2); for discussion, see Kraus and Sturm (2017).
[23] I leave aside any speculations about the existence of non-human beings with similar rational faculties, such as angels.
[24] Schmidt (2008) interprets a transcendental faculty as providing the "configuration" or "structure" of an empirical faculty, whereas the empirical faculty carries out mental operations defined by this configuration. I take her account to be broadly in line with mine.

consciousness they produce, or what Kant calls *inner appearances* (*innere Erscheinungen*). By actively attending to these states we can become conscious of them in *inner perception* (*innere Wahrnehmung*). The empirical faculties thus provide content for inner experience.

1.3 Inner Sense in Historical Context

1.3.1 *The Empiricist Tradition: Inner Sense as Perception of Mental Acts and Contents*

To highlight the salient features of Kant's mature view of inner sense, I first situate it in the historical context of the eighteenth century. This will reveal that Kant incorporates both empiricist and rationalist strands in his account of inner sense, while he remains crucially critical of both of them. The development of the spatial metaphor of the *inner self* has been decisively shaped by Saint Augustine. For Augustine, the inner self is the "inner space" that we find once we turn our gaze inward and which is "filled" with our temporary states and acquired dispositions, such as occurrent images, desires, memories, beliefs, and skills.[25]

John Locke takes up this notion of the mind as a private inner room containing one's past and present ideas, which one can perceive by means of a specific sense, which he calls *internal sense*.[26] Stripping the substantial theological and metaphysical implications from this notion, Locke construes internal sense as on a par with outer sense, and so as the "*Perception of the Operations of our own Mind*".[27] While outer sense yields "ideas of sensation" that pertain to external objects, internal sense yields ideas of the mind's internal operations, such as "[external] *Perception, Thinking, Doubting, Believing, Reasoning, Knowing, Willing*, and all the different actings of our own Minds", which Locke also calls *ideas of reflection*.[28] Moreover, Locke indicates that not only mental operations, but also mental contents such as feelings and passions, can be observed through internal sense.[29]

---

[25] Augustine of Hippo (397–8/2008, esp. I:8, X:12). See Cary (2000).

[26] Locke (1690/1975 II.1.4:105). For the metaphor of the "dark room", see Locke (1690/1975 II.11.1); also Cary (2000:122–4).

[27] On *sensation*, see Locke (1690/1975 II.1.24:117–8). On *internal sense*, which Locke also calls *reflection*, see Locke (1690/1975 II.1.4:105). To pre-empt a terminological confusion, note that, for the German rationalists (and for Kant), "reflection" denotes the capacity to draw comparisons between ideas, which involves general representations (i.e., concepts), for example, Wolff (1720/1997:§272, §733), Baumgarten (1739/2011:§626), Tetens (1777:§284). For discussion, see Thiel (1997:61–2).

[28] Locke (1690/1975 II.1.4:105; see also II.1.24:118 and II.6.1:127). For discussion, see Thiel (2011).

[29] See Locke (1690/1975 II.1.4:106). Feelings and passions, such as pleasure and pain, are simple ideas originating from both sources, from sensing and reflection (see Locke 1690/1975 II.7.1:128).

Although Locke's view involves some ambiguities, there is compelling evidence that internal sense should not be identified with the consciousness that accompanies thinking and perception in general. Rather, in addition to some ongoing mental activity that yields conscious mental contents, internal sense requires special attention towards this mental activity and the resulting ideas.[30] Overall, Locke's account suggests a perceptual model, according to which internal sense is a kind of *inner perception* that tracks both mental operations and the occurrence of mental contents resulting from these operations in consciousness. Locke has therefore often been interpreted as offering an account of what has later been called *introspection*, that is, a higher-order mental act of perceiving one's own lower-order mental operations and contents.[31]

Locke acknowledges a close relation between inner sense and time: the ideas of duration and of succession, which are needed for the temporal determination of outer things, are ideas of reflection derived through internal sense.[32] Internal sense, in cooperation with the faculty for recalling past ideas and actions, also plays a crucial role for being conscious of one's personal identity through time, which, for Locke, is not grounded in an underlying persistent substance.[33] This, however, raises the concern how Locke can avoid a merely subjective account of temporal determination, if such determination is based on the perception of one's mental operations.[34]

Empiricist-minded German philosophers of the eighteenth century take inspiration from Locke and develop accounts of inner sense through which they try to discern various kinds of self-relation. These self-relations include, for instance, the feeling of one's existence and the feeling of one's personality (i.e., of one's diachronic and synchronic unity).[35] Tetens, among others, defends the notion of a "feeling of the self" (*Selbstgefühl*), by which we become aware of the "modifications of the soul", that is, "of any kind of inner states . . ., as they exist in us" (Tetens 1777, Preface).[36] It is an immediate feeling of one's

---

[30] On the distinction between consciousness and internal sense, see Thiel (1994:102–5, 1997:60–1) and Weinberg (2008).

[31] Introspection was an accepted method in psychology in the nineteenth century, for example, Wundt (1888, 1902). In philosophy of mind, it is still popular as a model for understanding self-consciousness (e.g., Armstrong 1968, Lycan 1996). Not only has introspection received much criticism as a scientific method, but it has also been rejected as an adequate model to explain self-consciousness, for such models leave unexplained (or render implausible) the specific self-relation required for self-consciousness (e.g., Shoemaker 1968, 1994).

[32] See Locke (1690/1975 II.14.3–5:181–3).

[33] See Locke (1690/1975 II.27:328–48).

[34] For discussion, see Longuenesse (1998:237).

[35] For accounts of inner sense in eighteenth-century Germany, see Thiel (1997, 2011, 2018). Thiel considers in particular Michael Hißmann, Christoph Meiners, and J. G. H. Feder.

[36] For translation, see Watkins (2009:357).

existence, as opposed to the perceptual consciousness (*Gewahrnehmen* or *Apperzeption*) of one's past mental states that is derived from the consciousness of objects. Only the latter can give rise to the consciousness of one's personal identity through time. Tetens also incorporates some Wolffian rationalist elements, such as the notion of a unified self that is grounded in the rationalist idea of a substantial soul.[37]

Kant's account of inner sense is certainly inspired by Locke's perceptual model, as well as by Tetens' *Selbstgefühl*.[38] While Kant praises Locke for his impressive "physiology of human understanding" (Aix, also A86/B118), he also criticizes Locke for overlooking the important distinction between inner sense and a faculty for self-consciousness, viz. (transcendental) apperception, as I explain in 1.3.2.[39] Kant's main worry is that the empiricist methodologies lead to *merely subjective* accounts of human nature, which cannot properly ground the cognition of objects.[40]

1.3.2 The Rationalist Tradition: Empirical Consciousness Requires Self-Consciousness

Appropriations of Locke's concept of internal sense can also be found among eighteenth-century German rationalists, especially with respect to their view of empirical psychology. For the rationalists, the function of Locke's internal sense is more closely associated with *empirical consciousness* and the capacity to cognize objects, but is also more clearly distinguished from *self-consciousness*. Alexander Baumgarten construes "internal sense" as the faculty by which I represent the "state of my soul", as opposed to the "external sense" by which I represent my body (Baumgarten 1739/2011:§535). He explicitly identifies internal sense with "consciousness, more strictly considered" (Baumgarten 1739/2011:§535). Although the notion of inner sense is less prominent with other rationalists, Christian Wolff, for instance, acknowledges some sort of immediate consciousness of one's perceptions (see Wolff 1720/1997:§728) and Georg Friedrich Meier endorses a notion of the consciousness of one's own modifications (see Meier 1755 III:87f.). Rationalist accounts of such inward-directed consciousness certainly differ from empiricist ones in that they are commonly combined with metaphysical assumptions concerning

---

[37] See Dyck (2014:54–60), Thiel (2017).

[38] On the influence of Locke's theory of inner sense on Kant, see Carl (1989:105–14), Longuenesse (1998:235–40), Kitcher (2011:15–26). For the influence of German empiricists on Kant, see Wunderlich (2005:69–114) and Dyck and Wunderlich (2017). On Kant's pre-Critical account of inner sense, see Dyck (2016).

[39] For Kant's critique of Locke, see B127, A217/B327. On the relationship between Tetens and Kant, see Thiel (2017).

[40] See "Tetens examines the concepts of pure reason merely subjectively (human nature), I objectively" (*Refl* 4901, 18:23).

the existence and nature of souls as simple substances with representational forces. Following Leibniz, most rationalists accept that not all perceptions are conscious, but only those that in addition to being perceived are also *apperceived*.

For Wolff, to become conscious of an object requires one to distinguish (*unterscheiden*) the object both from other objects and from oneself. The mental act of distinguishing is accompanied by an immediate consciousness of this act and of the perceptions involved. Following Leibniz, Wolff calls this consciousness of one's perceptions *apperception*.[41] Importantly, for Wolff, object-consciousness and self-consciousness are mutually dependent.[42] We can obtain a conscious representation of an object only if our perceptions of the object are accompanied by apperception. In turn, the apperception of one's perceptions inevitably leads to the consciousness of one's own self as a mental substance with representational powers, that is, to self-consciousness proper. Furthermore, for Wolff, all consciousness is necessarily temporal – a feature that is also central for Wolff's account of *personality*: the essential character-istic of a person is the capacity to be conscious of one's own identities through time.[43] For Wolff, unlike Locke, this capacity presupposes that personal identity is already given on the basis of a continuous underlying mental substance.[44]

Many German philosophers followed Wolff's views of consciousness, apper-ception, and self-consciousness in the eighteenth century, and Wolffian ration-alism became hugely influential. Most Wolffian rationalists accepted that the consciousness of objects is based on the discrimination between objects and oneself. Object-consciousness therefore requires both some sort of conscious-ness of one's inner state (often construed as apperception or second-order perception) and proper self-consciousness (construed as the consciousness of one's existence or of one's substantiality). Hence, for most German rationalists, some sort of inward-directed consciousness is constitutive of the empirical consciousness of objects.

Kant himself is strongly influenced by Wolffian rationalism. In a *Reflection* on Meier's *Metaphysics*, he explicitly specifies that "[c]onsciousness is *sensus internus*" (*Refl* 1680, 16:80). In his lectures on metaphysics, Kant mainly follows Baumgarten's *Metaphysics* in distinguishing between inner and outer sense as the two faculties for inward and outward sensation, respectively. For

---

[41] Wolff (1720/1997:§§728–30). For Leibniz's concept of apperception, see 3.2.

[42] Wolff (1720/1997:§§728–30). For detailed discussions, see Blackwell (1961), Thiel (1996, 2011:304–11), Wunderlich (2005:19–31), Dyck (2014:19–42).

[43] On the requirement of time, see Thiel (2011:309).

[44] Wolff (1720/1997:§§741, 921–7). Note that, although Locke rejects that personal identity is grounded in an underlying substance, it is frequently argued that Locke, too, presup-poses a "continuant" that is already given, for instance, in terms of a continuous "subject of experience" (see, for example, Strawson 2011:136).

instance, in the much-discussed *Pölitz-Lecture* (*Metaphysics L₁*) from the mid-1770s, inner sense is defined as the faculty to be conscious of oneself as "thinking subject" (*L-MP/L₁* 28:222), as "soul" (*L-MP/L₁* 28:224), as "intelligence" (*L-MP/L₁* 28:224), or as "I in the strict sense <sensu stricto> or only selfhood alone" (*L-MP/L₁* 28:265). Although the *Pölitz-Lecture* already indicates some transcendental considerations, for instance in defining time as "the form of inner sense" (*L-MP/L₁* 28:202), it still mainly endorses a pre-Critical understanding of inner sense. Accordingly, inner sense still has a double function: it is the faculty for becoming sensibly aware of a particular *object*, namely one's own soul with its changing states, and the faculty for *self-consciousness*, that is, for thinking oneself by means of the concept "I".[45] So, in his pre-Critical writings, Kant himself, like other German rationalists, conflates two distinct mental activities, namely the sensible intuition of one's own inner states in time, on the one hand, and the representation of oneself in thought or conceptual self-consciousness, on the other hand.[46]

A decisive step for Kant towards his Critical Philosophy is therefore the discovery of the *paralogisms*. Paralogisms for Kant are errors that inevitably arise from the conflation of these two mental activities. The central insight of this discovery, namely that neither inner sense, nor a purely conceptual self-consciousness, is able to yield a representation of oneself as persistent thinking substance, is already apparent in the *Duisburg Nachlaß*, as a close analysis shows.[47] In the *Duisburg Nachlaß*, Kant begins developing his Critical concept of transcendental apperception by considering "the consciousness of thinking, i.e., of the representations as they are placed in the mind", which centrally concerns their "relation to the subject", as distinct from the consciousness of one's diverse inner states in time (*Refl* 4674, 17:647). Thus, Kant now starts to separate the two functions formerly attributed to inner sense and distinguishes inner sense as the faculty for intuiting one's own state from transcendental apperception as the faculty for self-consciousness in thought.[48]

---

[45] For example, *L-MP/L₁* 28:265. Throughout his lectures on metaphysics and on anthropology, as well as in some Critical texts, Kant identifies the soul as the object of inner sense, for example, *L-MP/Mrongovius* 29:875, *L-MP/L₂* 28:541, 584, *L-MP/Dohna* 28:670.

[46] On the relationship between *Metaphysics L₁* and the *Critique*, see Carl (1989:115–26), Kitcher (2011:35–8), and Dyck (2016). Kant also characterizes inner sense as the faculty for "making one's own representations the objects of one's thought" (*Subtlety* 2:60).

[47] *Duisburg Nachlaß*: *Refl* 4674–84, 17:643–73. In the *Critique*, Kant criticizes the rationalist metaphysics of the soul, that is, rational psychology, since it inevitably falls prey to what he calls paralogisms of pure reason (see A341–405/B399–431 and Chapter 4). For discussions of the discovery of the paralogisms and the transition to the concept of transcendental apperception, see Carl (1989) and Kitcher (2011:66–77).

[48] See A107, B152–56, *Anth* 7:134n. In the *Duisburg Nachlaß*, Kant already develops an argument for the unity of the thinking subject as a presupposition of thinking in general – an argument that later becomes central for the Transcendental Deduction of the Categories (esp. §16 of the B-Deduction, B131–6). See 3.2.

1.4   Kant's Transcendental Account of Inner Sense in the *Critique*
of Pure Reason

After this brief outline of the historical context, I introduce the salient features of Kant's mature Critical view of inner sense, for which I shall provide detailed arguments only in Chapter 2. In developing a distinctively *transcendental* account of inner sense, Kant radically reconceptualizes inner sense, though he retains both an empiricist and a rationalist strands. Following the empiricist strand, Kant defines inner sense as part of sensibility, which provides the mind with suitable *matter* for cognition. As the faculty for intuiting one's inner state, inner sense is to some extent on a par with outer sense. Its specific *matter* concerns all representations "passing before the mind" and, hence, all mental activities from which these representations originate. Following the rationalist strand, inner sense plays a constitutive role for empirical consciousness in general. As I shall argue in Chapter 2, inner sense is involved in any conscious representation of spatio-temporal objects, as well as of one's inner states in time. This constitutive role of inner sense is due to its specific a priori *form*, that is, time, which is a form not only of inner appearances, but of all appearances in general. Let us consider these two aspects of inner sense in turn, as they are discussed in the *Critique*.

1.4.1   *Inner and Outer Sense as the Two Parallel Faculties of Sensibility*

Kant introduces inner and outer sense as the two aspects of sensibility in the Transcendental Aesthetic, a move that is broadly in line with empiricist-perceptual models of inner sense. Sensibility (*Sinnlichkeit*) is our receptive capacity to acquire sensible representations by way of being affected (*affiziert*) through objects. Through being affected, the senses receive manifolds of sensation (*Mannigfaltigkeiten der Empfindung*) and yield *empirical intuitions* (*empirische Anschauungen*), that is, singular representations of particulars that immediately relate to objects.[49] Only together with an a priori *form* does a manifold of sensation provide the *matter* (*Materie*) of an *empirical intuition*.[50] For the human kind of sensibility these forms of intuition are *space* and *time*.

Kant primarily defines inner sense in parallel with outer sense:

> By means of outer sense ... we represent to ourselves objects as outside us, and all as in space. ... Inner sense, by means of which the mind intuits itself, or its inner state, gives to be sure, no intuition of the soul, as an object; yet it is still a determinate form, under which the intuition of its

---

[49] For example, A19/B33, A68/B93, A320/B377, *Prol* 4:281–2. The German term *affizieren* would be better translated, more neutrally, as "having an effect on".

[50] On the form of intuition, see A23/B37, A38/B55, B67, B140, B154, B160.

inner state is alone possible, so that everything that belongs to the inner determinations is represented in relations of time.   (A22–3/B37)[51]

This passage suggests the following parallel: outer sense is concerned with *outer objects* and represents them as something outside oneself and in space, whereas inner sense is concerned with *inner states* and represents them as something inside oneself ("in me") and in time. In the remainder of the Transcendental Aesthetic, Kant goes on to argue that space (as the form of outer sense) and time (as the form of inner sense) are the a priori forms of intuition, and as such are transcendental conditions under which an object must be intuited.

The parallel between the senses thus concerns three aspects: outer and inner sense each involve:

- *sensation* (*Empfindung*), which arises from sensory affection (*Sinnesaffektion*) and which corresponds to the *matter* of the resulting intuition;
- *something given* (or immediately related) to the senses, that is, outer objects and inner states, respectively;
- a distinctive *form*, that is, space and time, respectively.[52]

Note that in the passage above, Kant appeals not to the object of inner sense, but only to inner states. Nonetheless, Kant occasionally still invokes the notion of an "object of inner sense" in the first *Critique* (and other Critical writings), especially in the context of his critique of rational psychology.[53] Yet the lack of a proper object given to inner sense will turn out to be a fundamental disparity between the two senses (see 4.4).

The parallelism between inner and outer sense observed above seems to suggest a view on which two mutually exclusive faculties operate independently from each other.[54] This view finds support in various passages in the first *Critique*, for instance, in passages in which Kant contrasts the notions of

---

[51] The German term *Gemüth* is commonly translated as "mind". It denotes the whole of mental faculties, including both passively receptive and spontaneously active faculties (e.g., A50/B75, also *L-Anth/Parow* 25:247, *L-Anth/Philippi* B1.4).

[52] See general definition of sensibility at A19/B33f.

[53] For example, A345/B403, A361, A362, A368, A385, B415, B427, A443/B471, A683/B711, A846/B874; also *Prol* 4:334–6; *MFNS* 4:467, 542–3; *Progress* 20:269, 281, 308. See also his lecture on metaphysics, delivered during the Critical period: *L-MP/Mrongovius* 29:875; *L-MP/L₂* 28:541, 584; *L-MP/Dohna* 28:670.

[54] Reininger (1900:23) calls this the *coordination view* of the two senses, but criticizes it as systematically and textually inconsistent. Cohen (1885/1987:423–4), Hölder (1873:9), and Vaihinger (1892:125) seem to endorse this view as an adequate interpretation of Kant's account of sensibility; as do, more recently, Rosenberg (2005:70) and Bennett (1966:15). Ameriks (2000:249) discusses the coordination thesis under the heading of the "independent stream theory" and eventually rejects it. For critical discussion, see also Mohr (1991:97–105), Schmitz (2015), and Indregard (2018).

inner and outer appearance.[55] Moreover, Kant clearly accepts the idea of being "internally affected *by our selves*" (B156), as opposed to being externally affected by objects (or things).[56] The former then, arguably, results in some sort of *inner sensation*, as opposed to outer sensation.[57] In line with this parallelism, Kant occasionally distinguishes an *inner intuition* (of myself) – the type of representation that is characteristic of inner sense – explicitly from an *outer intuition* (of a spatial object).[58]

This parallelism seems to obtain at the level of form, as well. Kant characterizes time as the form of inner sense independently of space as the form of outer sense:

> Time can no more be intuited externally than space can be intuited as something in us.   (A23/B37)

> Time is nothing other than the form of inner sense . . .. For time cannot be a determination of outer appearances; . . . but on the contrary determines the relation of representations in our inner state.   (A33/B49–50)

These passages suggest that *only* inner intuition is determined according to the form of time and *only* outer intuition according to the form of space. Yet this strict parallelism between the two senses creates a severe problem already for the cognition of physical objects in motion. It is indisputable that Kant thinks that physical objects are given in space *and time*, and that an essential feature of physical matter is *motion*.[59] Yet "the concept of motion (as alteration of place) is only possible through and in the representation of time" (B48). For physical objects to be representable as moveable in space, they must also be intuited according to the form of time and hence subject to inner sense. This problem of the temporality of physical objects leads Kant to grant inner sense a universal role with regard to empirical consciousness and to acknowledge certain interdependencies between the two senses.[60]

---

[55] "Inner appearance": A107, A478/B56n, A492/B520, B673/B701, A691/B719, A772/B800; "outer appearance": A24/B39, A28/B44, A33–4/B50–1, A37/B53, A106, A163, A264/B320, A357–60, A367–80, A672/B700, A840/B868.

[56] See also A34/B51, B67–9, B152–6, 158–9; *Anth* 7:140, 153. I will remain neutral as to whether outer sense is affected by sensible objects, or by things-in-themselves, or by both. For discussion, see Allison (2004).

[57] The notion of *inner sensation* occurs nowhere in the *Critique*, but is used in the *Anthropology* at 7:142 and 162 (see also *Groundwork* 4:451 and *Dreams* 2:350). Kant, moreover, uses phrases such as "the impressions of inner sense" (*Anth* 7:142) and "inner representations (pain . . .)" (*Prol* 4:309). See 2.3.

[58] For example, Bxl, A33–4/B50, A37/B54, B68, B72, A115, A124, B156, B157n, B158, B163, B224, B227, A362, A380–1, B407, B412, B420; also *Anth* 7:142, 161. Furthermore, Kant distinguishes between *pure* inner intuition of time and *empirical* inner intuition of my inner state (see 2.3).

[59] For example, A41/B58, B277, *MFNS* 4:496, *L-MP/L₁* 28:222, *L-MP/Mrongovius* 29:841.

[60] This problem has been extensively discussed, for example, by Reininger (1900:42–62), Ameriks (2000:241–52), Mohr (1991:87–105), and Schmitz (2015).

1.4.2   Inner Sense and Empirical Consciousness in General

In his conclusions from the expositions of space and time, Kant tackles the problem of moveable objects in space by arguing that time is the *universal form* of appearances in general. His argument involves two premises, which are contained in this passage: "all representations, whether or not they have outer things as their object, nevertheless as determinations of the mind themselves belong to the inner state, while this inner state belongs under the formal condition of inner intuition, and thus of time" (A34/B50).

According to this passage, firstly, all representations, regardless of their content, are determinations of the mind and therefore belong to the mind's inner state. Secondly, since inner sense is the faculty for intuiting one's inner state, it receives all representations that belong to this state and subjects these representations to its specific form, viz. time. In consequence, Kant concludes that time is a universal condition of appearances in general, as he explicitly states a few lines below:[61] "time is an *a priori* condition of all appearance in general, and indeed the immediate condition of the inner intuitions (of our soul), and thereby also the mediate condition of outer appearances" (A34/B50).[62]

The idea that time is an a priori condition of both inner and outer appearances is reinforced, for instance, in the Transcendental Deduction of the Categories (A). There, Kant further clarifies what may belong to one's "inner state" as follows: "Wherever our representations may arise, whether through the influence of external things or as the effect of inner causes, whether they have originated a priori or empirically as appearances – as modifications of the mind they nevertheless belong to inner sense, and as such all our cognitions are eventually subject to the formal conditions of inner sense, namely time" (A99). In this passage, Kant refers to several kinds of representations, all of which can be "modifications of the mind" and hence make up the mind's inner state. This state includes all representations regardless of their causal origin, that is, whether they arise either from affection through external things or from "inner causes". It also includes all representations regardless of their source of justification, that is, whether they are empirical representations, such as

---

[61] Reininger (1900:23) calls this claim the thesis of the "subordination" of outer appearances under inner sense. Various interpreters have endorsed this thesis, such as Cohen (1885/1987:440) and Vaihinger (1892:396), who both additionally maintain a coordination thesis, apparently without noticing the tension between the two theses. Reininger (1900:42–62) himself criticizes these positions on the grounds of *psychologizing* outer appearances, and argues that Kant's position can be rescued only by introducing an additional form for *outer time*. Mohr (1991:87–105, esp. 92–8) develops a cogent critique of both Vaihinger's and Reininger's accounts and eventually – to my mind rightly – rejects both of them.

[62] See also A124, A155/B194.

perceptions, or a priori representations, such as geometrical figures. All these representations become modifications of the mind only insofar as they *appear* in inner sense and as *inner appearances* are subject to the condition of time. These considerations call for a refined account of the relationship between inner sense and consciousness.

In the first *Critique*, Kant distinguishes empirical consciousness from transcendental (or pure) consciousness.[63] In line with Kant's hylomorphic account of transcendental and empirical faculties, I submit that transcendental consciousness concerns the pure form of representing something with consciousness, whereas empirical consciousness concerns those representations that actually occur in an individual mind. In several places, Kant explicitly argues that the former is an a priori condition of the latter.[64] Kant introduces two distinct faculties, and associates transcendental consciousness primarily with transcendental apperception, as the faculty for self-consciousness in thinking, and empirical consciousness with inner sense, as the faculty for intuiting one's inner state. So Kant discerns two distinct a priori conditions, or a priori forms, of consciousness in general. The form of apperception concerns the relation to the subject and defines the general form of reflexivity of all conscious representation, as I will argue in Chapter 3 (see 3.4). The form of inner sense, viz. time, concerns the relation to the specific object or "matter" of which one is conscious. This recalls the Wolffian account of consciousness, which requires that each conscious representation of an object be accompanied by a consciousness of the act of distinguishing it from other objects and from oneself, and by an awareness of its specific representational content (viz. Wolffian–Leibnizian *apperception*).[65] For Kant, the consciousness of the act of distinguishing takes the specific form of *transcendental* apperception, whereas inner sense mediates the apprehension of representational contents into empirical consciousness.

In the current context, it is important to note that inner sense plays a more fundamental role for empirical consciousness than outer sense. Empirical consciousness is construed as the "consciousness that accompanies different representations" (B133). This accompanying consciousness is mediated by inner sense as the faculty for intuiting one's own representations. While outer sense certainly provides most of the "material with which we occupy

---

[63] See A117n, B133, B139–40, and B144. See also the distinction between "a psychological (applied) consciousness, and ... a logical (pure) consciousness" in *Anth* 7:142, also 7:134n, 7:140, and *L-MP/L₁* 28:227.

[64] See A115–6, A122–3, B133, B144, A177/B220, also *Anth* 7:134n, 142.

[65] Like Wolff, Kant at times identifies *clear*, as opposed to obscure, representations with empirical consciousness (e.g., A117n, *Anth* 7:135–7). Yet, unlike Wolff, Kant accepts indefinitely many degrees of empirical consciousness down to the unconscious (e.g., A176/B217, B414n, *MFNS* 4:542). For an illuminating discussion, see Indregard 2018:178–82.

our mind", it is inner sense that defines the "formal condition" under which representations occur in empirical consciousness (B68). In consequence, *all* empirical consciousness requires both Kantian transcendental apperception and Kantian inner sense, and can occur only according to relations of time, as Kant explicitly states, "For the original apperception is related to inner sense (the sum of all representations), and indeed related *a priori* to its form, i.e., the relation of the manifold empirical consciousness in time" (A177/B220; see also B68). Hence, inner sense, through providing the universal form of time, plays a fundamental role in the constitution of empirical consciousness. In turn, all contents of empirical consciousness can be considered as inner appearances that are intuited in inner sense, though not necessarily actively attended to, as I will argue in Chapter 2.

In various places, empirical consciousness is directly identified with perception, for instance in the following passages:

> perception, i.e., empirical consciousness of [an empirical intuition] (as appearance), becomes possible. (B160)

> all possible perceptions, hence everything that can ever reach empirical consciousness, i.e., all appearances of nature. (B164)

> Perception is empirical consciousness, i.e., one in which there is at the same time sensation. (A165/B207)

These passages suggest that perceptions (*Wahrnehmung*) are the primary candidates for states of empirical consciousness. Given Kant's focus, in the first *Critique*, on external nature, the perception of spatio-material objects seems the most plausible item of empirical consciousness. The passages above then suggest the following picture: outer sense yields empirical, that is, sensation-based, intuitions of outer appearances, which are then "taken up into empirical consciousness" (B202) and turned into the perception of an outer object. The latter, I shall argue in Chapter 2, requires an awareness of one's own representations through inner sense. Yet I shall also argue that empirical consciousness is not confined to the perception of outer intuitions only, but that Kant also allows for an equivalent notion of inner perception.[66] An intuition in general is a representation that – whether yielded by either outer or inner sense – merely belongs to one's inner states. A perception, by contrast, is an intuition of which one is conscious.[67] Thinking a perception by means of concepts then yields experience (see B160, B219).

---

[66] For the notion of *inner perception*, see B68, B156, A343/B401, A368, A379.

[67] See "the first thing that is given to us is appearance, which, if it is combined with consciousness, is called perception" (A119–20). For an excellent discussion of intuition and perception, see Tolley (2017). On the distinction between *having a representation* and *being conscious of a representation*, see Anth 7:135 and 3.4.

So I submit that, despite the constitutive role of inner sense for empirical consciousness, we can distinguish the following levels of analysis for each sense:[68]

(1) *Affection* through external objects or through oneself;
(2) *Sensation* arising from affection and corresponding to the *matter* of intuition;
(3) *Empirical intuition*, a sensible representation that is apprehended according to the forms of space (for outer intuition) and time (for inner intuition);
(4) *Perception*, as an empirical intuition of which we are conscious;
(5) *Experience*, as an empirical cognition of an object based on perception.

The initial parallelism of inner and outer sense would suggest that at each level there is an equivalent concept:[69]

(1) *Inner affection – outer affection*
(2) *Inner sensation – outer sensation*
(3) *Empirical inner intuition – empirical outer intuition*
(4) *Inner perception – outer perception*
(5) *Inner experience – outer experience*

What complicates matters is, as the previous discussion has shown, that the two senses are not neatly separable from one another, but are thoroughly intertwined and, therefore, have to be analysed in conjunction.[70] Moreover, Kant's emphasis on outer sense, in the second edition of the first *Critique*, has indeed led many commentators to deny that there is an inner equivalent at some or all of these levels.[71] In Chapter 2, I will argue in favour of a qualified parallelism that allows for an equivalent concept at each level of analysis. My argument will involve a combined analysis of the interdependencies between outer and inner sense, as well as between the senses and the understanding.

In sum, in his Critical Philosophy, Kant construes inner sense as a transcendental faculty of sensibility by which a subject intuits the representations belonging to its inner state according to its distinctive form, that is, time. Kant accommodates both empiricist and rationalist insights in this account.

---

[68] Kant himself distinguishes these levels in the discussion of the principles of the understanding (see, e.g., A180/B223). I thank Clinton Tolley for pointing out to me the importance of these distinctions.

[69] Note that while all representations belong to the mind and are in this sense "inner", the adjectives "inner" and "outer" here denote whether a representation arises from inner or from outer sense, respectively.

[70] Several commentators have suggested models of inner and outer sense that take their specific interdependencies into account, such as Mohr (1991), Longuenesse (1998), Heidemann (2001), Melnick (2009), and Schmitz (2015) (see 2.3).

[71] For example, Allison (2004:277), Collins (1999), and Schmitz (2015).

The empiricist strand is most visible in the construal of inner sense as a sensible faculty for the reception of what is internal to the mind and in the initial parallelism between inner and outer sense. This parallelism, however, has to be qualified by the fact that inner sense has a universal character in defining the general form of empirical consciousness. In consequence, outer appearances are subject to the forms of both outer and inner sense, that is, space and time, respectively. This universal character of inner sense is a sign of the rationalist strand in Kant's Critical account. For Kant, as for the Wolffian rationalists, empirical consciousness fundamentally involves a consciousness that is directed inwardly at one's own representations. Yet, unlike the Wolffians, Kant recognizes two distinct faculties involved in consciousness: transcendental apperception as the faculty for mediating the formal relation to the subject by unifying all mental contents that belong to one and the same mental act; and inner sense as the faculty for mediating an empirical awareness of specific mental contents. This separation of transcendental apperception and inner sense offers Kant, as we will see in Chapter 3, a plausible explanation of how empirical consciousness, despite its fundamental reliance on inner sense and potentially on merely subjective inner sensation, can nonetheless yield objectively valid cognition.[72]

1.5   Inner Receptivity in the *Anthropology* and the *Critique of the Power of Judgment*

Let me conclude with a remark on a broader notion of inner receptivity. So far, inner sense has been considered as part of sensibility and thus as part of the faculty of cognition that aims at the veridical representation of sensible objects. In this context, inner sense is conducive to perception, primarily perception of external objects. Yet perceptions are only one of many kinds of representation of which we can be conscious. Representations that may appear in empirical consciousness include desires, inclinations, and intentions, as well as affects, moods, and aesthetic feelings. For those representations to be conscious requires them to be received by a faculty that mediates an inward-directed awareness, as inner sense does for intuitions. In what follows, I indicate how the previous account of inner sense can be expanded so as to accommodate *inner receptivity*, more broadly construed.

Recall that Kant defines three basic faculties – the faculty of cognition, the faculty of desire, and the faculty of feeling. The *faculty of feeling*, I submit, involves receptiveness towards a subject's inner state and complements inner

---

[72] Kant can thus escape the criticism of *psychologizing* outer objects by turning them into contents of empirical consciousness and hence mere appearances of inner sense – a problem that has, for instance, been raised by Strawson (1966:57, also 237).

sense as a kind of inner receptivity in practical and in aesthetic respects.[73] To argue for this thesis, it is not sufficient to examine the first *Critique*, which mostly focuses on the faculty of cognition, but relevant material in Kant's practical and anthropological texts must be consulted. In these texts, Kant considers the faculty of feeling as the basic "capacity for having pleasure (*Lust*) or displeasure (*Unlust*) in a representation", which he also calls the *susceptibility* towards pleasure or pain (*MM* 6:211).[74] The faculty of feeling has only recently become a subject of significant interest in Kant scholarship. Yet here I will ignore ongoing discussions regarding its exact relation to the faculties of cognition and of desire, as well as whether feeling itself has an a priori structure or a rational side to it.[75] Rather, I focus on the kind of inward-directed receptivity that is involved in feeling.

In the *Critique of the Power of Judgment*, Kant construes "feeling" as a sensible faculty by which "the mind becomes conscious in the feeling of its state" (*CJ* 5:204). He contrasts this faculty with inner sense: feeling supplies merely "subjective sensations", which cannot contribute to the cognition of objects (*CJ* 5:206), whereas inner sense "as a receptivity belonging to the faculty of cognition" affords "objective sensation" (*CJ* 5:206). By means of feeling, Kant writes,

> nothing at all in the object is designated, but in which the subject feels itself as it is affected by the representation   (*CJ* 5:204)

> [feeling] is related solely to the subject, and does not serve any cognition at all, not even that by which the subject *cognizes* itself.   (*CJ* 5:206)

I do not take these passages to exclude our eventually judging about our feelings in inner experience and gaining cognition of ourselves. Rather, Kant's point here is to distinguish two kinds of inner receptivity. Inner sense is construed as the receptivity that mediates the relation of an object of intuition to empirical consciousness and thereby makes possible objective judgements about the object's temporal relations. By contrast, feeling is construed as the receptivity that mediates the relation of the subject's inner state to empirical consciousness and thereby makes possible *subjective judgements of value*.[76] In consequence, feelings present us, not with an object of cognition, but with "an object of satisfaction" (*CJ* 5:205n). Feelings evaluate what a particular representation means for the subject. They concern the internal evaluation of "the relation of the representation to the subject" itself (*CJ* 5:229) – regardless of the nature of this representation. A feeling is thus frequently characterized as an empirical "effect of a representation . . . upon

---

[73] For insightful accounts of feeling as practical receptivity, see DeWitt (2018) and Wood (2018).

[74] See *CJ* 5:196–7, *Anth* 7:153.

[75] For insightful discussions, see Frierson (2014) and Sorensen and Williamson (2018).

[76] See DeWitt (2018:74) and Wood (2018:98).

a subject" by which the subject becomes conscious of the value this representation has for the subject (*MM* 6:212n).[77]

Pleasure and pain, as the two basic feelings, are then understood as subjective sensations of *agreeableness* and *disagreeableness*, respectively, which typically lead to subjective judgements of taste. As such, pleasure and pain can promote or hinder a certain activity.[78] A "practical pleasure" is, specifically, the feeling that results from judging an action as *good* and that motivates the execution of this action (see *MM* 6:212 and *CJ* 5:209–10). Aesthetic pleasures are commonly not related to desires or interests, but result from the disinterested "harmonious play of . . . imagination and understanding" in light of experiencing something as beautiful (*CJ First Intro* 20:224).[79] Moreover, the basic feelings of pleasure and pain are evaluative constituents of various emotional states, including short-term affects, such as anger, surprise, sadness, and anxiety; as well as moods, that is, affective states that last longer than momentary emotions and are typically more diffuse.[80] For example, a state of anxiety typically involves some sort of displeasure that is felt in response to a mental state, such as the perception of a wild animal, the expectation of an impending deadline, or diffuse thoughts about financial matters. Anxiety typically results from a negative evaluation of this mental state and leads me to avoid a certain situation. These considerations suggest that the faculty of feeling involves an inward-directed receptivity that concerns all evaluative matters of practical and aesthetic relevance.

In the *Anthropology*, we indeed find an explicit acknowledgement of two kinds of inner receptivity – inner sense as a sensible faculty of cognition and feeling as susceptibility to an internal relation or effect of a representation. There, Kant states:

> It should be noted that the latter [*sc., inner sense (sensus internus)*], as mere faculty of perception (of empirical intuition), is to be thought of differently than the feeling of pain and pleasure; that is, from receptivity of the subject to be determined by certain ideas for the preservation or rejection of the conditions of these ideas, which one could call *interior sense (sensus interior)*.   (*Anth* 7:153)

---

[77] On *empirical* feelings as the "effect" of other representations, see A28; *CJ* 5:189, 204, 295; *MM* 6:211–2n; *L-Log/Jäsche* 9:36–37; *L-Anth/Mrongovius* 25:1315–16; *L-MP/L₁* 28:245–7; *L-MP/L₂* 28:586. By contrast, *rational* feelings are *self-caused* by the higher intellectual faculties (see Wood 2018:103–6).

[78] On the feelings as the "promotion" or the "hindrance" of life, see *CJ* 5:278 and *Anth* 7:231–2.

[79] On the "feeling of the free play" of the faculties, see *CJ* 5:217, 238, 240, 258, 314, 331.

[80] On feelings of pleasure and pain and subordinated emotions, see *CJ* 5:226 and *Anth* 7:230–50; on passions and long-term emotional dispositions, see *Anth* 7:251–82. For detailed discussions, see Sorensen (2002) and Frierson (2014).

Although Kant never systematically explores this distinction, there is some evidence that he regards these two inward-directed senses as two subspecies of a generic faculty of inner receptivity. Later in the *Anthropology*, he construes inner sense, more broadly than in the first *Critique*, as a "faculty of [both] feeling and thinking", which yields "the consciousness of what [a human being ...] undergoes, insofar as he is affected by the play of his thoughts" (*Anth* 7:161). Here "thoughts" may be taken to stand for all kinds of theoretical and practical representations, and the "play of thoughts", again, indicates the internal interaction of various mental faculties. In line with the *Critique*, inner sense rests "on the relations of ideas in time" and presents its material in the form of time. So Kant concludes "There is then only *one* inner sense, because the human being does not have different organs for sensing himself inwardly" (*Anth* 7:161).

This suggests that Kant endorses a more inclusive account of inner sense as a general faculty of inner receptivity that yields mental contents of all kinds for empirical consciousness. Support for such a general faculty can also be found, for instance, in the A-Deduction, where Kant grants that the "effect[s] of inner causes" are "modifications of the mind [that ...] belong to inner sense" (A98–9). In the Paralogisms, Kant then cites further examples of "inner causes", such as "thoughts, feelings, inclinations, or decisions" (A358).[81] This may also include those "self-caused" feelings that arise as effects of the higher intellectual faculties, such as the feeling of respect in light of a morally worthy action.[82]

In sum, inner sense should be broadly construed as a general faculty of inner receptivity towards all internal modifications of a particular mind. Inner sense – as the faculty for responding to what is internal to one's individual mind – is thus the starting point for understanding how Kant's transcendental philosophy can explain issues of *individuality* and personal identity, given Kant's rejection of the traditional rationalist metaphysics of individual souls.

---

[81] "Inclinations" are generally defined as "habitual sensible desires" (*Anth* 7:251; see also *MM* 6:212).

[82] See *Groundwork* 4:401n and Wood (2018:103–6).

2

Temporal Consciousness and Inner Perception

2.1 Introduction

My inner experience concerns, first and foremost, the mental contents that constitute my state of mind and that occur in my empirical consciousness in time. Consider, for instance, the following mental episode. Looking at the snow-covered garden outside my window, I ponder whether I should go cross-country skiing later today. While doing so, I find myself remembering how much I enjoyed cross-country skiing in the past, desiring some distraction from my work, believing that some exercise in fresh air would do me well, and hoping that the skiing trails are in good condition today. In this mental episode, several partly interrelated mental activities generate a set of mental contents arising in my empirical consciousness. The current state of my mind, then, includes perceptions of external objects, memories of past events, feelings of joy and excitement, desires, beliefs, hopes, and eventually an intention to act. All these mental contents, I submit, can contribute content to my inner experience such that, given normal psychological conditions, I am able to judge what the current state of my mind is. In this example, I am able to judge *that I see* a snow-covered garden, *that I remember* myself skiing in the past, *that I feel excited* about the prospect of skiing later today, *that I believe* that exercise in fresh air is healthy, and so on.

The current chapter examines the *sensible conditions* under which mental contents occur in empirical consciousness and hence can become the content of inner experience.[1] Alternatively, one could describe these conditions as the sensible conditions under which a subject has *mental states* of which it can be conscious at all. Yet using the term *mental state* calls for some caution, as it appears to imply that there is an underlying mental substance in which these states inhere, as many rationalists would have it.[2] It is at least doubtful whether,

---

[1] *Sensible conditions* here refers to conditions that are due to the senses, rather than to the understanding or other nonsensible faculties.

[2] In Wolffian rationalism, the soul is conceived of as an immaterial substance in which thoughts inhere as accidents, or states, that change in time (e.g., Wolff 1734/1994:§§44–55).

for Kant, we are able to cognize a mental substance with varying states, and in fact, as I shall argue, he denies that we do so in inner experience. For current purposes, I nonetheless assume that we can make good sense of the notion of *mental states* as denoting particular, well-defined "inner determinations of our mind", as well as of the notion of an *inner state* (or "*state of mind*") as denoting the totality of these inner determinations at a particular time (A197/B242).[3] I will fully justify the usage of these notions only in Chapter 5. By then, I will have examined the full set of conditions that explain how there can be a (distinctively human) mind with mental states at all, and how the under-standing's concept of substantiality can be applied in the case of inner experience.[4]

The current chapter focuses on the sensible conditions under which it is possible for us to have distinctively *inner perceptions*: that is, to be empirically conscious of our mental states in a way that can underwrite inner experience.[5] The previous chapter has already introduced inner sense as the faculty for intuiting one's inner state and its constitutive role for empirical consciousness in general, as well as the relevant levels of analysis. This chapter explores the formal and material conditions of inner sense, as well as its relation to both outer sense and the understanding in the generation of perception. The under-standing comes into play in perception, since the apprehension of intuition into empirical consciousness requires a mental activity of synthesis. Synthesis cannot be accomplished by passive faculties that merely receive data, but requires active faculties that bring forth representations, such as the imagina-tion and the understanding. For most recent interpretations of experience in Kant, inner perception is not a central issue, and some commentators even deny that inner intuition and hence inner perceptions are possible at all.[6] My aim here is therefore to show, firstly, that Kant's transcendental theory of

---

[3] I use the term *mental state* roughly in line with contemporary philosophy of mind, to denote a particular token-representation of a general type, such as belief, hope, or desire. Kant frequently employs the singular terms *inner state* and *state of mind* to denote the sum total of representations present in the mind at a certain time (e.g., A23/B37, A34/B50, A272/B330, A197/B242, A20/B316, *MM* 6:228).

[4] I thank Clinton Tolley for making me aware of the significance of discerning the condi-tions of the possibility of a mind having mental states. These conditions may apply – in some generic form – for other creatures, such as non-human animals, which for Kant have inner sense, but lack higher intellectual faculties and the concept of "*I*" (e.g., *Anth* 7:127, 141n, 196).

[5] On inner perception, see, for example, B68, B155–6, A343/B401, A368, A379.

[6] The concept of *inner perception* is rarely explored in recent works on Kant's accounts of the mind (e.g., Brook 1994, Ameriks 2000, Dyck 2006, Valaris 2008, Melnick 2009, Kitcher 2011, Wuerth 2014) or of empirical psychology (e.g., Sturm 2009, Frierson 2014). It is also absent in interpretations of Kant's general theory of experience (e.g., Paton 1936, Longuenesse 1998, Collins 1999, Van Cleve 1999, Bird 2006). Some commentators deny that Kant allows for the possibility of inner perceptions (e.g., Allison 2004, Schmitz 2015). Two recent exceptions are Stephenson (2017) and Indregard (2017).

experience accommodates the possibility of inner perception and, secondly, that inner perception is best understood as first-order sensible awareness of one's mental states.

To this effect, I develop an account of perception in general based on the interaction between the senses and the active faculties, first with a view to the perception of mind-external objects. I call this account the *interactive model of perception* and will discern three constitutive aspects of it: (1) *outer affection* through outer sense, (2) *synthesis of apprehension*, and (3) *self-affection* in inner sense. From this model, I then derive conditions for the possibility of perception in general. I show that each aspect contributes a distinctive set of two conditions, containing one formal condition, and one material. In contrast to other "inter-dependence" models that have been suggested in the literature, my model focuses on accommodating the possibility of distinctively inner perception.[7]

Next, I turn to applying my model to the case of inner perception, so as to discern more clearly both the formal and the material condition contributed by inner sense. This leads me to distinguishing between two kinds of *self-affection*, that is, two ways in which inner sense can be affected. Firstly, what I call *transcendental self-affection* concerns specifically the effect of the understanding on inner sense. In this case, both faculties are considered as transcendental faculties and the results of such self-affection are the general forms of time that condition perception in general, that is, transcendental time-determinations. Secondly, what I call *empirical self-affection* concerns the effect that any productive faculty, including the imagination and the faculty of desire, *in fact* has on inner sense and which leads to an inner appearance in empirical consciousness. In this case, all faculties involved are viewed as empirical faculties that operate (or that receive data) in an individual's mind. This second kind of self-affection can be properly understood as *inner affection* through which inner perceptions are generated, as opposed to outer affection through which outer perceptions are generated.

I proceed as follows. Firstly, I briefly contextualize the role of the *synthesis of apprehension*, also called *sensible synthesis*, within Kant's theory of experience (2.2). Then I introduce the interactive model for outer perception and derive the conditions that follow from each of the three constitutive aspects (2.3). I then explore the *temporal forms* of perception in general. These forms result from the interaction between the understanding and inner sense in the so-called *figurative synthesis*, which in turn can be understood as transcendental self-affection (2.4). Finally, I apply the interactive

---

[7] Commentators who have argued for an *interdependence* of sensibility and understanding include Mohr (1991), Longuenesse (1998), Heidemann (2001), Melnick (2009), Grüne (2009), and Schmitz (2015). Their accounts focus on what I call transcendental self-affection such that most of them miss, and some even reject, the material condition of inner sense and, therefore, cannot accommodate the possibility of inner perception.

model to the case of inner perception and carve out an account of empirical self-affection (2.5).

2.2   Perception and Synthesis

The cornerstone of the *interactive model of perception* that I propose is the thesis that perception involves the interaction of passive-receptive and active-productive faculties of the mind. The role thereby assigned to the under-standing marks a fundamental difference between Kant's theory of perception and those of his predecessors. Unlike the empiricists such as Locke and Hume, Kant denies that perception is accomplished through the senses alone and in particular through the brute association of sensations, without guidance through higher intellectual faculties. Unlike Leibniz and the Wolffian ration-alists, Kant does not assume that the senses provide a myriad of unconscious perceptions, which become conscious only through additional acts of apper-ception, distinction, and attention. Rather, for Kant, perception necessarily involves empirical consciousness. The crucial novelty of Kant's account is that perception requires an activity of *synthesis* that is governed by rules of the understanding. Since this interpretation of Kant is still controversial, I first contextualize it within Kant's theory of experience, and then, in Section 2.4, address the particularly controversial role of the understanding.[8]

Recall the levels of analysis from Chapter 1, according to which perception lies above the levels of affection, sensation, and intuition, and below the level of experience. Perception has already been defined as the empirical consciousness of empirical intuitions. Recall, furthermore, Kant's distinctive conception of experience as sensation-based empirical cognition. Experience consists in empirical judgements with two components: empirical intuitions, through which an object is given, and empirical concepts, through which an object is thought.[9] Its representational content is formally conditioned by the cognitive

---

[8] There is a debate as to whether *intuition* can be accomplished without involving the under-standing. On the one hand, there are those commentators who endorse a *non-conceptualist* reading of intuition, according to which intuitions are accomplished by the senses alone (e.g., Hanna 2005, Allais 2009, 2015, Tolley 2013, McLear 2014, 2015). To the extent that these commentators distinguish between intuition and perception, none of them explicitly denies that *perception* involves synthetic activity. On the other hand, there are those who hold that the understanding can only be used in acts of judgement, whereas intuitions are not instances of judgement and therefore cannot involve the understanding (e.g., Paton 1936, Bennett 1966, Pippin 1982). These commentators rarely discuss the case of perception. While I take it that recent accounts of the relation between sensibility and understanding have made a compelling case for my reading (especially Longuenesse 1998, Grüne 2009, and Land 2015a, 2015b), I indicate below the extent to which my reading is compatible with a non-conceptualist reading of intuition.

[9] See A50–1/B74–5 and A92/B125. There is an ambiguity as to whether "experience" denotes the resulting *empirical cognition*, its *representational content*, or the *act* or *state*

faculties, which are shared by all humans. These formal conditions concern the sensible forms of space and time under which we receive intuitions and the logical forms of judgements by which we combine concepts into a judgement.[10] These forms are, therefore, necessary conditions of the possibility of experience.

This conception of experience calls for an explanation as to why (and how) intuitions and concepts correspond to one another in cognition, that is, why (and how) intuitions provide the right kind of content to be subsumed under concepts and then cognized in objectively valid judgements. While the Transcendental Aesthetic emphasizes the assumption of two distinct, heterogeneous faculties of sensibility and understanding, the Transcendental Analytic, and therein especially the Deduction (both A and B), focuses on the systematic relationship of these two faculties.[11] There, Kant presents an explanation of this relationship in terms of the *synthesis of apprehension*, by which a manifold of intuition is combined and taken up into consciousness. This synthesis is already necessary for the possibility of perception, as Kant states most explicitly in the B-Deduction: "by synthesis of apprehension I understand the composition of the manifold in an empirical intuition, through which perception, i.e., empirical consciousness of it (as appearance), becomes possible" (B160).[12]

Although this sensible synthesis operates with sensible representations, it involves the understanding, which – as we will see – supplies the rules for this synthesis. Kant's idea is, roughly, that only if intuitions are synthesized according to rules provided by the understanding, can they contribute sensible content to cognition. Hence, the synthesis of apprehension combines a manifold of intuition into a perception, not only according to the forms of sensibility, but also according to the forms of judgement. Several promising interpretations of this sensible synthesis have recently been proposed, according to which the understanding is conceived, not only narrowly as the capacity to judge, but more broadly as a capacity for synthesis.[13]

---

of experiencing. There is good evidence that experience is mostly identified with empirical cognition (e.g., Bxvii, B147, B161, B166, B277). In some places, Kant indicates that for empirical cognition an object must first be "given in experience", which suggests that experience concerns rather the act or state of experiencing (e.g., Bxvii, Bxxvi(n), B1–2). I use "experience" and "empirical cognition" interchangeably.

[10] For example, B161.

[11] For discussion of this heterogeneity, see Land (2015b).

[12] Note that I appeal to the broader notion of apprehension found in the B-Deduction, rather than the narrow definition at A99.

[13] See Longuenesse (1998), Ginsborg (2006, 2008), Grüne (2009), Land (2015a, 2015b). Since the details of their accounts differ considerably, I will elaborate on how exactly the understanding can be understood as capacity for synthesis in my view in 2.4.

Synthesis in the most general sense is the action of bringing unity to a representational multiplicity. It is "the action of putting different representations together with each other and comprehending their manifoldness in one cognition", or, more broadly, in one representation (A77/B103). The broad reading of the understanding is supported by passages in which it is defined as "the faculty of combining *a priori* and bringing the manifold of given representations under unity of apperception" (B135). There are different types of synthesis, depending on the elements that are synthesized. A synthesis can, for instance, yield the "combination of the manifold of intuition or of several concepts" (B130). The former results in perception, the latter in judgement.

While sensible synthesis is commonly understood as an empirical synthesis, it is mainly discussed in terms of the transcendental synthesis that it presupposes: namely the synthesis by which the understanding determines sensibility a priori, which Kant also calls the *figurative synthesis* or *synthesis speciosa* (see B151–3).[14] The figurative synthesis results in the a priori determination of the forms of intuition according to the categories.[15] In turn, Kant characterizes the result of this synthesis as an a priori "determination" of inner sense and as the "synthetic influence of the understanding on inner sense" (B154). I, therefore, construe figurative synthesis as a *transcendental self-affection* of inner sense through the understanding, both of which are viewed as transcendental faculties. Such self-affection is transcendental in the sense that it must be presupposed in any intuitions that *can* underwrite empirical cognition. It defines specifically the a priori temporal forms that must obtain for a series of intuitions to amount to the perception of an object, such as persistence and succession.[16] Transcendental self-affection is thus a key aspect of the interactive model of perception proposed here, and I explore it further in Section 2.4.

What is rarely explored is the empirical side of sensible synthesis and in particular the question whether sensible synthesis also involves an empirical

---

[14] For example, Longuenesse (1998), Valaris (2008), Land (2015a), Schmitz (2015). These commentators take a *prejudgemental* synthesis to be involved in the formation of intuition. My reading allows for the possibility of unsynthesized intuitions, though not that of unsynthesized perceptions.

[15] In the B-Deduction, Kant's account of the figurative synthesis is a major step in the argument for the objective validity of the categories, that is, for their applicability to sensible objects (§24). This account is supposed to show that appearances can be judged according to the categories.

[16] Note that this does not necessarily exclude the possibility of intuitions that are not subject to these conceptual conditions. Yet those intuitions would not be amenable to judgement and cognition. I take my account to capture the distinctively *human* kind of perception, and so I remain neutral on the question whether (and if so, how) *non-rational animals* can enjoy perceptual representations of objects (see also Keller 1998:35). For a discussion of animal perception, see McLear (2011).

effect on inner sense, which would properly be called *empirical self-affection*.[17] This issue is especially important for understanding the possibility of distinctively inner perceptions. In Section 2.5, I argue that self-affection is more complex than commonly assumed because it involves both formal-transcendental aspects and material-empirical aspects. The latter concern the way in which inner sense is affected – as an empirical faculty – by the representations that are in fact apprehended in empirical consciousness and that constitute conscious mental states, such as outer perceptions, past memories, passing thoughts, occurrent desires, and feelings. Hence, I will extend (and partly revise) the existing accounts of sensible synthesis by arguing that this synthesis involves, in addition to transcendental self-affection, *empirical self-affection* (or what one may also call *inner affection*).[18] Some commentators explicitly deny that empirical self-affection is possible at all for Kant, and reject the possibility of an inner sensible manifold, and hence the possibility of distinctively inner intuitions; others grant these possibilities, but deny that they could give rise to inner perception and empirical cognition.[19] My goal is therefore twofold: firstly, to demonstrate the very possibility of inner perception based on inner intuitions and, secondly, to discern the specific sensible conditions of such perception. I consider the conditions due to the understanding only insofar as they have an influence on sensible conditions as the rules of sensible synthesis. Let me start with the interactive model for perception in general.

2.3   The Interactive Model of Perception

The goal of developing the interactive model of perception is to discern the distinctive set of conditions that results from each of the faculties involved. I derive the model first from a close reading of a passage that Kant adds to the Transcendental Aesthetic in the B-Edition (§8). There, Kant introduces the idea of self-affection, which he later refines in §24 of the B-Deduction. Although the A-Deduction does not explicitly make use of the idea of self-affection, it retains a more explicit account of the notion of perception. My detailed discussion of this model therefore draws on both the A- and the B-Deduction.

---

[17] This issue is neglected in accounts of sensible synthesis, such as Mohr (1991) and Longuenesse (1998), and even denied in others, such as Allison (2004) and Schmitz (2015).

[18] This distinction is barely ever mentioned in the secondary literature. Exceptions include Grünewald (2009:211) and Indregard (2017, 2018). Suggestions for such a distinction are loosely indicated by Michel (2003:239–43) and Düsing (2010). Kant himself draws this distinction most explicitly in *Refl* 5661, 18:319.

[19] Commentators who deny the possibility of inner intuition include Collins (1999:133) and Schmitz (2015); those who deny the possibility of distinctively *inner cognition* include Wolff (2006) and Emundts (2007).

Let me begin with citing the relevant passage from §8 of the Transcendental Aesthetic. The specific purpose of this passage, with which I am not concerned here, is to provide another "confirmation" of the "transcendental ideality" of outer and inner sense: that is, the claim that the senses provide "mere appearances", but no insight into things-in-themselves (B67). The part of the argument that concerns inner sense divides into two parts: the first part deals with the consciousness of outer intuitions in time, that is, outer perception; the second with inner intuition, that is, intuition of one's inner state, and inner perception. I first focus on the former, which runs as follows:

> It is exactly the same in the case of [inner intuition].[20] [1] It is not merely that *the representations of outer sense* make up the proper material with which we occupy our mind, but also [that] *the time in which we place these representations*, which itself precedes *the consciousness of them* in experience and grounds the way in which *we place them in mind* as *a formal condition*, already contains relations of succession, of simultaneity, and of that which is simultaneous with succession (of that which persists). [2] Now that which, as representation, can precede any act of thinking something is intuition, and, if it contains nothing but relations, it is the form of intuition, which, since it does not represent anything except insofar as something is posited in the mind, can be nothing other than the way in which the mind is affected by its own activity, namely this positing of its representations, thus the way it is affected through itself, that is, it is an inner sense as far as regards its form.   (B67–8, emphasis and numbering added)

The first sentence [1] identifies three constitutive elements necessary for the perception of outer objects: it requires (1) "representations of outer sense", which (2) "we place in the mind" (3) under the "formal condition" of "time", in order to yield "the consciousness of [these representations]", that is, perception that is suitable for the experience of outer objects. The second sentence [2] then elaborates on this formal condition and traces it back to "an inner sense" that is "affected" through the mind itself. This passage suggests an interactive model of perception consisting of the following three aspects:

(P1) *Outer affection* yielding representations of outer sense, that is, a manifold of outer intuitions;

(P2) *Apprehension* as the synthetic activity of "positing" (or "placing") these outer representations in empirical consciousness;

(P3) *Self-affection*, through which time becomes a formal condition of such consciousness.

These three aspects should not be understood as three consecutive steps in time, but rather as three logical aspects of a single mental action. This is crucial

---

[20] The German text states "innere Anschauung".

because – in line with the transcendental ideality of time – a temporal order cannot be assumed as given at the outset, but first arises through this mental action as a condition of consciousness. In what follows, I discuss each aspect of the model in turn and discern for each the distinctive set of a material and a formal condition. For easier reference, I will call the passage above the *model passage*.

2.3.1   Outer Affection

Let us consider the following example. Imagine that you are observing two cats playing with a red ball of wool. In this perceptual episode, you receive various multisensory impressions of shapes, colours, sounds, etc. Based on these impressions, you have perceptions of the cats' bodies, their black-and-white fur, their meowing, their motions, the red ball rolling away, etc. It is indisputable that, for Kant, we receive sensation through outer sense being affected by the objects we observe. As finite, sentient creatures, we depend on sensory material being given to us in order to set our minds "into motion", as Kant aptly puts it in the opening remark of the B-Introduction:

> There is no doubt whatever that all our cognition begins with experience; for how else should the cognitive faculty be awakened into exercise if not through objects that stimulate our senses and in part themselves bring forth [*bewirken*] representations, in part bring the activity of our understanding into motion ... to work up the raw material of sensible impressions into a cognition of objects that is called experience?
>
> (B1, translation amended)

Hence, all experience begins with the affection and stimulation of the senses through objects.

Being affected by an object basically means that the object has a suitable relation to our sensibility to bring about an "effect", namely a sensation (A20/ B34). It is not immediately clear what exactly this relation consists in and what those objects of the senses are. Importantly, sensation entails an immediate relation to some objects or, we may say, "puts us in touch with" objects. Many commentators deny that we can properly speak of objects at the level of sensation and prefer to assume that affection yields a chaotic, undifferentiated manifold of sensation without relating to particulars.[21] Some argue that there are good reasons to conceive of these objects at least at the level of intuitions as bare spatio-temporal particulars.[22] Despite specific differences, there is some consensus that the primary role of *outer* affection can be understood in terms of a *material condition*: outer affection brings forth sensation as the "raw

---

[21] For example, Pippin (1982:31), Falkenstein (1995:71), Ginsborg (2008:75).

[22] Non-conceptualists hold that intuition gives us spatio-temporal particulars, for example, Hanna (2005), Allais (2009, 2015), Tolley (2013).

material" of intuition. In the *Critique of* the Power of *Judgment*, Kant states: "*Sensation* (in this case external) . . . expresses the merely subjective aspect of our representations of things outside us, . . . it expresses the material (the real) in them (through which something existing is given)" (*CJ* 5:189). Sensation – while a *merely subjective* state of the mind – delivers some "material (the real)" through which "something existing is given". It "expresses (*drückt . . . aus*)" primarily the fact that something mind-external (that actually exists) has had an effect on the mind.[23] Hence, only on the basis of sensation can an intuition relate to an existing object.

This may raise the sceptical worry that we can never be sure whether something external exists at all that affects us, rather than only figments of our own mind. While this worry is important, it should not occupy us here. For Kant, scepticism about the external world is the "scandal of philosophy" (Bxli; also Bxxxiv), and he makes great efforts to undermine this stance. Moreover, he rules out idealistic conceptions of perception according to which it would be at least doubtful whether we can ever be justified in perceiving existing external objects. In the Refutation of Idealism, he aims to prove that we can have an "immediate consciousness of the existence of other things outside me" (B276). Although it is controversial whether Kant's argument for this claim is successful, the Refutation gives further evidence for his view that something mind-independent must exist in order for *outer* sense to be affected and that sensation requires the presence of an object to the mind.[24] Now, one may still think of the possibility of *outer* sensation where no object is present, such as in hallucinations. While Kant certainly does not exclude the possibility of such cases, he insists that they do not involve what he calls sensation. They may involve retrieving some images from memory or inventing them through imagination without affection through something external. They may even result in empirical intuition without an object being present. Yet none of these cases involves proper sensation through outer sense.[25]

Kant himself draws a sharp distinction between appearance (*Erscheinung*) of the senses and mere illusion (*bloßer Schein*).[26] A few lines below the passage

---

[23] See 1.2, and Jankowiak (2014:500). Note that this is one instance of Kant's systematic distinction between "*expressing (ausdrücken)*" (also "*exhibiting (darstellen)*") and "*representing (vorstellen)*". I will explore this distinction with respect to the faculty of apperception (see 3.5), and to the schemata of the imagination and ideas of reason (see 5.5 and 5.6).

[24] It is controversial whether the Refutation proves the existence of outer objects in space or of things-in-themselves (see Allison 2004:300, Keller 1998:210). Various commentators have regarded Kant's argument as not being compelling (e.g., Guyer 1987, Longuenesse 2007). I cannot pursue this issue here.

[25] For Kant, "taking imaginings for sensations" is a state of illusion (*Anth* 7:161). For an insightful discussion of hallucination, see Stephenson (2015). On the object-dependence of intuition, see the debate between Watkins and Willaschek (2017a) and Grüne (2017).

[26] See *Prol* 4:314; A38/B55, B69–70, A293/B350.

TEMPORAL CONSCIOUSNESS AND INNER PERCEPTION   53

from which I derived the model of perception, he states, "[to say that some-thing] *appears* . . . is not to say that these objects would be a mere *illusion*. For in the appearance the objects . . . are always regarded as something really given" (B69).[27] An appearance requires that something is "really given" to the senses and hence that the subject stands in a suitable relation to an existing object, which in turn appears to the senses. By contrast, an illusion occurs if "subjective causes . . . are falsely regarded as objective" (*Anth* 7:142, also A294/B351), that is, if mind-internal conditions, such as imaginings, are themselves falsely regarded as something given to the senses and hence as appearing objects. Of course, hallucinations and other illusions may arise from causes within the mind, or from bodily causes, such as the ingestion of drugs or a malfunctioning physiological sense. Therefore, I shall later argue that hallucinations should be understood as resulting from affection, though of *inner*, rather than of outer sense. In consequence, hallucinations can be seen as an *inner* appearance in empirical consciousness.[28]

Hence, it seems safe to say that sensations are possible on the basis of outer affection through external objects, and that their actuality indicates the exis-tence of something real that affects or stands in a suitable, that is, efficient-causal, relation to outer sense.[29] From these considerations regarding outer affection, we can derive the first material condition of the interactive model as follows:

(P1-M) Perception requires a sensation-based immediate relation to a given object, which is an *appearance* that corresponds to a sensation.

For the case of *outer* affection and *outer* sensation, we may say more specifi-cally that it requires a suitable relation to a given object that exists in some sense independently of the mind. We will come back to the required sense of

[27] Recall that this passage occurs within a discussion of transcendental idealism, according to which time and space as the forms of intuition are transcendentally ideal, and as relational properties of appearances empirically real.

[28] While Kant confines himself, in the first *Critique*, to the two technical notions of *outer* and *inner* sense, he offers a more fine-grained account of sensation in the *Anthropology*, including the five physiological senses, "*vital sensation (sensus vagus)*", and "*organic sensations (sensus fixus)*" (see *Anth* 7:153–4). These kinds of sensation can be subsumed under the two technical notions, though it may be unclear under which one (see Cassam 1993).

[29] Affection has been interpreted in terms of an efficient-causal relation according to which the causal powers of an object have some causal impact on the sense (e.g., Watkins 2005 and Frierson 2014). Yet a word of caution is in order if one applies the notion of causality to the elements of Kant's transcendental philosophy, since this theory is supposed to first establish the applicability of the category of causality and the conditions of causal experience. Kant more cautiously talks of a *correspondence relation* between sensations and objects (or appearances) (see, e.g., A20/B34, A166, B207, A143/B182). See Stephenson (2015:494).

independence in Section 2.5, in the context of *inner* affection and *inner* sensation.

Sensations are essential for establishing an immediate relation to objects and *express* (or *exhibit*) this immediate relation, but by themselves do not have *representational content*. Affection yields a *manifold* (*Mannigfaltigkeit*) of sensation, which only together with an appropriate *form* of representation can be said to represent objects. It is hard to tell what a sensible manifold is, because we cannot be conscious of it as such. Kant employs this term in a counterfactual manner to denote the "raw material" that logically precedes its *informing* according to the forms of intuition, viz. space and time.[30] Only by being ordered in accordance with these forms can a sensible manifold become the sensible content (i.e., *matter*) of an intuition.[31] The resulting intuition then represents (*vorstellen*) the object that affects the senses and brings about sensation.

Space – as the form of outer sense – can be regarded as the first ordering function that is performed on a manifold of sensation. In the Transcendental Aesthetic, space is introduced as the form that makes possible the representation of "something outside me" and the representation of objects "next to one another".[32] This suggests that the form of space primarily imposes a primitive ordering onto a sensible manifold, which I call *sheer adjacency*, that is, *being sheerly one-next-to-the-other*. Space imposes a representational array on the manifold such that the manifold's diverse items are arranged according to the relation of being next to one another. Such an array does not display more complex spatial structures, as does a geometrically well-defined Euclidian space. It is also a further question whether the resulting outer intuition represents the diverse items *as* being one next to the other or whether this requires a synthesis according to the categories.[33]

In the example above, the observer obtains spatial intuitions of the whole scene of the two playing cats as representations that contain multiple visual impressions in a primitive spatial ordering. Each intuition might be pictured as a snapshot of the whole scene from the distinctive visual perspective of the viewer, covering a certain visual field from a particular angle. These snapshots

---

[30] See Ginsborg (2008:75) on Kant's "counterfactual" way of speaking.
[31] The "form of appearance" "allows the manifold of appearance to be (intuited as) ordered in certain relations" (A20/B34).
[32] For example, A23/B38, A27/B43, A40/B56.
[33] It is controversial whether the form of space represents a non-conceptual unity by itself (see, e.g., Land 2014, McLear 2015) and whether the intuition of spatial particulars requires a synthesis according to the categories (see, e.g., Longuenesse 1998:35, Allison 2000, Allais 2009). I take my proposal of "sheer adjacency" to be so minimal that it does not require synthesis, yet also does not suffice for the *perception* of spatial particulars. While remaining neutral on whether intuitions represent spatial particulars, I maintain that without synthesis, we cannot be conscious of spatial particulars.

may not yet represent distinct particulars without the employment of the categories as generic descriptions of sensible particulars. They may not yet represent the two cats as distinct from one another and from the red ball, or may not differentiate the cats' heads, tails, and torsos. The resulting outer intuitions are merely subjectively valid, that is, for the particular viewer only, although their representational content relates to empirically real objects.[34] The formal condition concerning outer perception can then be obtained as follows:

(P1–F) Outer perception requires outer intuition according to the mere form of space as the primitive ordering function of one-next-to-the-other.

In sum, outer affection results in two conditions, both of which concern the referentiality of outer perception: the material condition concerns the perception's immediate relation to a given object, viz. *reference*, and the formal condition concerns the representation of the object as primitively spatially structured.

The material condition has been interpreted so as to exclude the possibility of inner sensation, since inner sense would not be able to yield a manifold of sensation on its own without involving outer affection. Kant's claim that "the representations of outer sense make up the proper material with which we occupy our mind" (in the model passage) has been read as evidence that what counts as the "proper" material of intuition for Kant must be received through outer sense.[35] Allison, for example, claims that the sensible content of intuition is fully exhausted by sensations acquired through outer sense and that inner sense is merely a "reflective reappropriation of the contents of outer experience".[36] Since such a reorganization of data from outer sense would not amount to a "manifold of its own", Allison excludes the possibility of distinctively inner intuition.[37] While it may be true that some outer affection is needed to initiate mental activity in the first place, this is not tantamount to limiting all sensation to outer sense only and hence all empirical intuition to the intuition of outer objects. In Section 2.3.3, I shall argue that we cannot even explain how we can have perceptions of outer objects moving in space without granting inner sense a manifold of its own.

The model passage points out that the having of representations of outer sense calls for the activity of "placing" these representations in the mind, that is, in consciousness, in order for them to become perception. I now turn to this active component in sensory perception.[38]

---

[34] I focus on the visual case only for reasons of simplicity. By "outer intuition" I always mean the intuition of *outer* objects.

[35] Allison (2004:277), Collins (1999:109), Valaris (2008:2), Serck-Hanssen (2009), Schmitz (2015). Similar remarks by Kant can be found in *LB-Leningrad* 1.19–22, 2.9–10.

[36] Allison (2004:278).

[37] Allison (2004:277). For discussion, see Kraus (2019a:177–80).

[38] Melnick (2009:14) accounts for an active component in perception by characterizing outer sense as the faculty for "shifting or repositioning of outer-directed attention". While

2.3.2   Apprehension

When we observe the cats playing with the red ball of wool, we do not just have a set of static, unrelated snapshots of a spatial scene, but we see the cats chasing the ball (and each other) and the ball unwinding its red thread. So we perceive objects moving in space, changing their location and speed with time. In what follows, I argue that the perception of spatial objects in motion requires a synthetic activity of the mind, which I identify with the *synthesis of apprehension*.[39] As with the previous aspect, I discern a material and a formal condition of apprehension. In this case, these conditions concern specifically the *relation to the subject*, that is, the *reflexivity* of representations.

Recall from the model passage that Kant describes the activity exercised by the mind as "positing representations in the mind", as "placing representations in time", and as "occupying the mind with representations". One might wonder in which sense empirical intuitions are not yet "in the mind". The model passage states that this activity "precedes the consciousness of [the representations of outer sense] in experience". That is, this activity is required for being conscious of outer intuitions, that is, for perception, which can then underwrite the experience of outer objects. While Kant's use of the notion of *apprehension* is not entirely consistent throughout the first *Critique*, he generally associates it with the activity of taking up representations into consciousness, yielding perception.[40] Most explicitly, the B-Deduction offers a definition: "by the synthesis of apprehension I understand the composition of the manifold in an empirical intuition, through which perception, i.e., empirical consciousness of it (as appearance), becomes possible" (B160).[41] This suggests that apprehension fulfils a basic function of unifying, which Kant also calls *synthesis*. So I take it that the terms *positing, placing*, or *occupying* are spatial metaphors for one and the same synthesizing activity within the "inner space" of the mind, namely for the *synthesis* of *apprehension*.

In the Deduction, synthesis is defined with a view towards cognition, as "the action of putting different representations together with each other and comprehending their manifoldness in one cognition" (A77/B103). It is attributed to the faculty of imagination, yet the goal of the Deduction is to show that the imagination must operate in accordance with the understanding if it is to yield cognition (see A78/B103–4). Abstracting for a moment from this goal of

---

I am generally sympathetic to his dynamic account, I think it is misleading to attribute the active component to the senses.

[39] For example, A98–9, A119, B160–2.

[40] Kant borrows the idea of apprehension from Tetens (see, e.g., De Vleeschauwer 1976:289–90). Tetens conceives of an "apprehension of sensations" as an "aftersensation" (*Nachempfindung*) that first gives a noticeable sensory representation of a certain duration and intensity (Tetens 1777:31–40). By contrast, Kant construes "apprehension" as a synthesis that first generates the temporal determinations of appearances.

[41] See also B162, B202; moreover, A119, A166/B208, A191/B236, A499/B527.

cognition, we can enquire into the general conditions for representing intuitions in consciousness. Empirical intuitions – as we have seen – are composed of a primitively ordered manifold, and for the perception of moving objects we require a multitude of such empirical intuitions. To represent even a single intuition as being composed of multiple elements requires an activity of *differentiation*. What exactly differentiation involves is described in the account of apprehension offered in the A-Deduction.

In the A-Deduction, Kant portrays the synthesis of apprehension as an aspect of the so-called *threefold synthesis* and defines apprehension more specifically:[42] "Now in order for unity of intuition to come from this manifold (as, say, in the representation of space), it is necessary first to run through and then to take together this manifoldness, which action I call the *synthesis of apprehension*" (A99). On this account, apprehension denotes two inseparable activities, namely (1) running through, by means of which separate items of the manifold are distinguished, and (2) taking together those differentiated items such that they can be represented "as contained in *one representation*" (A99). Only if both of these activities are completed, can we represent manifold representations *as a multitude* of *different* representations. By these two activities we may differentiate either a multitude of elements within one intuition, for example, distinct parts within the scene of the playing cats, or a multitude of intuitions, for example, a temporal series of spatial intuitions that represent the motion of the chasing cat.[43]

In other places, Kant explicitly adds the activity of *taking up into consciousness*: a "manifold first [needs to] be gone through, taken up, and combined in a certain way" (A77/B102).[44] This phrase gives a hint at the material condition of apprehension. Apprehension – in the broader sense of the B-Deduction – does not only operate on given representations, but actively produces new ones. In the A-Deduction, this activity is assigned to the imagination in its reproductive function.[45] There, Kant argues that the

---

[42] The threefold synthesis consists in the syntheses "of the *apprehension* of the representations, as modifications of the mind in intuition; of the *reproduction* of them in the imagination; and of their *recognition* in the concept" (A97). It is controversial whether this is one synthesis with three aspects or three consecutive syntheses. Non-conceptualists often argue that the first two syntheses can yield empirical intuition without involving concepts, for example, Waxman (1991:11–36, 73–102, 183–248), Hanna (2001:31–54, 2005), Allais (2009). I remain neutral on this issue, since my argument draws on the broader notion of apprehension in the B-Deduction, which is required for perception. Grüne (2009:149–192) offers an excellent analysis of the threefold synthesis.

[43] Kant explicitly allows for both the "successive synthesis in apprehension" (A163/B204) and for an "apprehension [that . . .] fills only an instant" (A167/B209). On differentiation, see Grüne (2009:158–166) and Indregard (2018).

[44] Also, A116, B135, B202.

[45] See A99–102, also A119, A190/B235. For accounts of the synthesis of imagination, see Longuenesse (1998), Grüne (2009), and Horstmann (2018).

synthesis of apprehension (in the narrow sense of the A-Deduction) is "inseparably combined with the synthesis of reproduction", by which the imagination reproduces the representations given through the senses such that they can then be combined. This strongly suggests that for Kant, becoming conscious of one's intuitions requires us to *reproduce* them (or to sensibly exhibit their contents) in consciousness. The synthesis of apprehension (B-Deduction), if viewed materially (or empirically), just is the sensible production of *empirical consciousness*.

Hence, I conclude that the synthesis of apprehension (in the broader sense of the B-Deduction) is necessary for a human subject to have empirical consciousness at all. So the second material condition of the interactive model that follows from apprehension can be described as follows:

(P2-M) Perception requires the activity of reproducing representations in the empirical consciousness of a particular subject.

To be sure, the material condition of apprehension does not add to the perception's relation to the represented object. Rather, it concerns "the material [*das Materielle*] of consciousness" itself (*Anth* 7:141), that is, the representational matter that arises from the subject's own mental activity, as opposed to sensation as the "matter [*Stoff*]" arising from the affection through objects. It concerns what is empirically real with regard to the mind's own activity and the resulting state of consciousness. As we will see below, this "material" of consciousness is precisely the kind of matter that we intuit in inner sense.[46]

If we acknowledge a material aspect of empirical consciousness, then Kant's hylomorphism calls for a formal aspect, too. The formal aspect is more complex, since it involves conditions that are due to the intellectual faculties and in particular the faculty for transcendental apperception. Only by the end of Chapter 3 will we be able to formulate the formal condition of empirical consciousness. To round off the current discussion, I here offer only a few remarks.

Two main considerations concern the formal aspect of consciousness. Firstly, there is the question of the role of concepts, and in particular the categories, that is, the pure concepts of the understanding, in the synthesis of apprehension. In Section 2.4, I will argue that the categories must serve as the rules of synthesis if perception is to underwrite experience. Secondly, there is Kant's worry regarding an empirically disjointed and temporally dispersed consciousness that may follow from an empiricist account of synthesis. He aims to diffuse this worry with his account of transcendental apperception, on which I briefly comment.

---

[46] This material aspect of consciousness and synthesis is rarely acknowledged. An important exception is Indregard (2018).

Empiricist accounts of perception, such as Locke's and Hume's, also rely on the idea that sensory impressions must be run through and taken together, yet they commonly appeal to a principle of mere association, which at best leads to customary conjunctions, but never to necessary unities.[47] Kant, too, appeals to the "empirical rule of association" (A112), especially in the A-Deduction, and attributes it to the imagination. Given that Kant's goal in the Deduction is to explain the possibility of cognition, he argues that a merely subjective association of sensory impressions can never lead to objectively valid judgements about objects, and that neither can the empirical principle of association be proven to be necessarily and universally valid. If a sensible manifold is to underwrite experience, then its synthesis cannot be "at pleasure or arbitrarily", but must be "determined a priori" (A104). Hence, for a synthesis to establish a necessary unity, it must have "a transcendental condition as its ground" (A106).[48]

The ultimate transcendental condition of unity is defined by "transcendental apperception" (A107). Apperception yields a unity of consciousness in which all representations are unified as belonging to one and the same subject. The transcendental condition of apperception guarantees a priori the identity of the subject across all consciousness and is therefore an a priori condition of cognition. Kant's arguments for the unity of consciousness will be addressed in Chapter 3 (3.2 and 3.4). For now, we need only note the important claim that "the transcendental unity of apperception is related to the pure synthesis of the imagination, as an a priori condition of the possibility of all composition of the manifold in a cognition" (A118). That is, if the synthesis of apprehension, exercised by the imagination, is to yield perceptions that can underwrite cognition, then it must be subject to the transcendental unity of apperception. Therefore, the a priori condition of self-consciousness that guarantees the identity of the subject "must necessarily enter into the synthesis of all the manifold of appearances" (A113). In consequence, the "synthesis (of apprehension) must be in thoroughgoing accord" with the a priori condition of self-consciousness (A113).

In Chapter 3, I will argue, more broadly, that all representations of which we can be conscious, even those that do not lead to objectively valid judgements, must be subject to transcendental apperception. Therefore, the transcendental unity of apperception is a necessary condition of all empirical consciousness and hence of perception per se, as Kant himself states: "The objective unity of all (empirical) consciousness in one consciousness (of original apperception) is thus the necessary condition even of all possible perception" (A123).

---

[47] Locke (1690/1975 II.23: 295–317), Hume (1740/1978 I.1.1). For Kant's critique of Locke and Hume, see A95/B127.

[48] For the relation of Kant's theory to empiricist accounts of perception, see Wunderlich (2005), Kitcher (1990, 2011), Brook (1994).

In light of these remarks, we can formulate the second formal condition of perception as follows:

(P2-F) Perception requires a relation to the subject in accordance with the general form of consciousness.

In Chapter 3, the general form of consciousness will be identified with the general form of *reflexivity* that is defined by the transcendental unity of apperception.

In sum, the activity of apprehension results in two conditions concerning the relation of perception to the subject: the material condition requires the generation of conscious representations that constitute the empirical state of an individual's consciousness, and the formal condition stipulates the general form of consciousness as the transcendental unity of apperception.

2.3.3   Self-Affection

The model passage mentions a further formal condition of consciousness, namely *time*, which "grounds the way in which we place [representations of outer sense] in mind as a formal condition" (B67). To have a perception of the cats chasing each other and of the ball unwinding its red thread, I must represent these objects not only in space, but also in time. In the model passage, Kant identifies time with the "form of intuition" that belongs to inner sense and associates it with a second kind of affection, namely with "the way in which the mind is affected by its own activity", that is, self-affection (B68).[49] In what follows, I argue that empirical consciousness necessarily involves self-affection and that through self-affection time first arises as a determination of empirical consciousness and hence as a determination of sensible objects. As with the two previous aspects, I specify a material and a formal condition of self-affection, yet I will only fully lay out my arguments for the formal condition in Section 2.4 (regarding transcendental self-affection), and for the material condition in Section 2.5 (regarding empirical self-affection). Here, I offer only a basic account of self-affection, first regarding *empirical consciousness* in general and then specifically regarding the perception of moving objects in space.

In Chapter 1, I have suggested that inner sense plays a fundamental role in the constitution of empirical consciousness because it defines the sensible form of consciousness, that is, time. We are now in a position to understand this

---

[49] Self-affection is mainly discussed in the B-Edition (especially B68–9 and B152–6), as well as in *Lectures on Anthropology* (e.g., *Anth* 7:133, 140–1, 161) and in *Reflections* (e.g., *Refl* 5661, 18:319, *Refl* 6311, 18:611, *Refl* 6349, 18:672–4, also *Progress* 20:270). The *Opus Postumum* also contains a few rather puzzling remarks on self-affection, which are not considered here (e.g., *OP* 22:358, 405, 456, 461).

constitutive role in greater detail. Recall that inner sense is introduced as the faculty for "intuiting one's inner state" (A22/B37), which concerns all "modifications of the mind" at a particular time (A99, see also A197/B242). Inner sense is also associated with "empirical apperception", yielding the "consciousness of oneself in accordance with the determinations of our state" (A107, also *Anth* 7:134n, 142). It thus mediates a basic kind of empirical self-consciousness, which in contemporary terminology one may call *state-consciousness*.[50]

The constitutive role of inner sense for empirical consciousness involves a material and a formal aspect. Materially viewed, by immediately relating to one's inner state, inner sense yields an immediate empirical awareness of the representations that constitute this state, which can be understood as *inner sensations* of one's representations. Formally viewed, inner sense contributes the "limiting condition" of time; that is, the mind's synthetic activity of "combination [is] intuitable only in accordance with temporal relations" (B159). In consequence, empirical consciousness is fundamentally *temporal*: it is constituted by inner states following one after the other in time. The main idea of my account is that empirical consciousness arises only through the *interaction* of synthetic activity and self-affection. The latter yields an immediate awareness that accompanies the synthesized representations and that gives the resulting states of consciousness a primitive temporal ordering of *one-after-the-other*.

But what exactly affects inner sense? Strictly speaking, it is not my states of consciousness that affect me, since these only arise through self-affection. Rather, I myself – qua my mental activities – affect my inner sense, as Kant explicitly states in some passages, including the model passage:

> the form of [inner] intuition [is . . .] the way in which the mind is affected by its own activity   (B67-8)

> The understanding therefore does not *find* some sort of combination of the manifold already in inner sense, but *produces* it, by *affecting* inner sense.   (B155)

The idea that the activities of mental faculties affect inner sense can be understood within a broader theory of mental faculties as causal powers that was popular among German rationalists, such as Wolff (1720/1997). Kant indeed acknowledges that mental faculties can be "inner causes" (A99). On a causal-power account of Kant's mental faculties, self-affection can be understood as the effect that a productive mental faculty has on inner sense. This effect results in *inner sensations* of something *mind-internally real* (as opposed to outer sensations of something mind-externally real, which are effected by the causal powers of external objects). A causal-power account is thus suitable to explain

---

[50] See *Prol* 4:300. Indregard (2018) argues that inner sense yields "state consciousness", and Wolff (2006) calls inner sense a "state sense" (*Zustandssinn*).

the empirical-material side of self-affection; however, as will become clear in Section 2.4, it is not sufficient to fully explain its transcendental aspects.[51]

The result of self-affection is primarily *inner sensation*. While it is true that Kant rarely mentions specifically *inner* sensation in connection with consciousness, we find a few hints, in the *Anthropology* and further Reflections, that becoming conscious of one's representations involves the "arousing" or "calling out" of a new sort of sensation:

> [For] the subject [to] order experience in itself[, it] must not merely perceive sensations in itself, but it must arouse them and connect them synthetically, hence affect itself.   (*Refl* 6349, 18:673–4)

> empirical apperception (of sensibility) . . ., when the subject attends to himself, is also at the same time affected and so calls out sensations in him, that is, brings representations to consciousness.   (*Anth* 7:141, Note H)[52]

Self-affection results, more fully viewed, in inner intuitions of oneself in which inner sensations are ordered in accordance with the form of inner sense, that is, time. Yet, to be sure, through inner sense we intuit ourselves, not as "self-active" subjects, but "only as we are internally affected by our selves" and hence "only as appearance" (B156).[53]

These considerations suggest the following picture: (1) by being affected through the mind's synthesizing activity, inner sense receives *inner sensations*, as an immediate accompanying awareness, of the synthesized representations; (2) by intuiting these synthesizing activities in accordance with the form of time, inner sense yields an *intuition of one's inner state*; (3) this inner state is an appearance of the subject's act of synthesis, that is, an *inner appearance*. In consequence, the resulting empirical consciousness is "materially" constituted by inner appearances, which are "formally" ordered according to the form of time. If this picture is correct, it follows that there could not be an empirical consciousness consisting of states, unless the mental contents of these states were accompanied by an immediate

---

[51] Causal interpretations of mental faculties can be found in, for example, Frierson (2014) and Wuerth (2014). Heßbrüggen-Walter (2004:236–8) and Indregard (2017) use causal-power accounts to explain self-affection. Yet for a causal interpretation of self-affection the same word of caution applies as for outer affection; see fn. 29. Heßbrüggen-Walter helpfully cites the passages from the *Lectures on Metaphysics*, in which the "*actio immanens*" is introduced as an "inner cause" (e.g., *L-MP/Volckmann* 28:433, *L-MP/Mrongovius* 29:823, *L-MP/Schön* 28:513, *L-MP/L₂* 28:565), yet Heßbrüggen-Walter does not consider the resulting self-affection as inner sensation. Some commentators detect severe discrepancies in the two kinds of affection such that it would not be justified to construe self-affection on analogy with outer affection, for example, the lack of sensible matter in self-affection (e.g., Allison 2004:283, Paton 1936 I:328–47). Yet these worries seem mitigated by carefully distinguishing empirical and transcendental aspects of self-affection.
[52] "Inner sensations" are explicitly mentioned at *Anth* 7:142.
[53] See also, for example, *Anth* 7:134n; *Refl* 6311, 18:611; *Refl* 6349, 18:673–4.

awareness through the self-affection of inner sense, which also gives these states their primitive temporal ordering. By this, I mean the temporal ordering of *one-after-the-other*, or what I call *sheer successiveness*, in analogy with sheer adjacency through the form of space.[54] In conclusion, all empirical consciousness necessarily involves self-affection and hence an immediate consciousness of one's inner state through inner sense.[55]

Applying this general conclusion to the perception of *moving outer objects*, we can now see that such *outer* perception – as the empirical consciousness of one's outer intuitions – necessarily involves self-affection. We can become aware of a set of outer intuitions only through the activity of apprehending, and this activity then affects inner sense. As a result, inner sense yields intuitions of these outer intuitions, that is, an immediate awareness of them. In turn, the outer intuitions that are apprehended appear in empirical consciousness under the form of time and hence are turned into inner appearances that are primitively temporally ordered as *one-after-the-other*.

This may be reminiscent of sense-data theories, according to which the primary objects of consciousness are the data, or mental images, received through the senses. Perception would then consist in a higher-order consciousness of given sense data. By contrast, on Kant's view, the awareness yielded by self-affection should be viewed as a *first-order* awareness that immediately accompanies the very synthesis of outer intuitions into the representation of a moving object. The fact that, for Kant, perception requires turning outer intuitions into inner appearances does not mean that the content of the resulting perception is *about* inner appearances in the first place. Rather, outer perception is *about* outer spatiotemporal objects, despite the fact that it constitutively involves both outer intuitions and the accompanying immediate *first-order* awareness of these intuitions.[56]

---

[54] Like "sheer adjacency", "sheer successiveness" is understood in a minimal way as a manifold of time that is not yet unified by synthesis, but which is also not sufficient for the representation of temporal relations of sensible particulars. I remain neutral on whether "sheer successiveness" has a pre-synthetic unity. Melnick (2009:18) seems to express a similar idea by the phrase "sheer progressive shifting".

[55] The constitutive role of inner sense for empirical consciousness is rarely acknowledged. Yet acknowledging this constitutive role, as the interactive model does, indeed resolves Allison's problem that Kant incoherently "equates this positing [of representations] first with self-affection and then with apprehension" (Allison 2004:282). Exceptions include Melnick (2009:20) and Indregard (2018). Indregard (2018) fully identifies empirical consciousness with *inner sensation*, yet thereby neglects the constitutive role of apprehension and its distinct form of reflexivity.

[56] Kant's view resembles, rather than higher-order theories of consciousness (e.g., Armstrong 1968), self-representational views according to which a conscious mental state involves a representation of itself (e.g., Kriegel 2009). Yet while such self-representational theories may themselves raise regress problems, Kant's view does not, since it only requires the representation of *an aspect* of that state, that is, outer intuitions, and, for Kant, self-affection is *not* meant to explain the specific self-relation, that is, reflexivity, of consciousness (see Chapter 3).

Outer intuitions can have perceptual salience only if they are apprehended into empirical consciousness via inner sense, and hence give us representations of appearances as the potential objects of cognition, as the following passage suggests: "The first thing that is given to us is appearance [in intuition], which, if it is combined with consciousness, is called perception (without the relation to an at least possible consciousness appearance could never become an object of cognition for us, and . . . would be nothing at all)" (A119–20).

Strikingly, Kant even argues that not only does the perception of motion require us to apprehend a series of intuitions of the moving object, but that the perception of static spatial figures also calls for a successive apprehension. Frequently, Kant appeals to the example of representing a line: "I cannot represent to myself any line . . . without drawing it in thought, i.e., successively generating all its parts from one point, and thereby first sketching this intuition" (A162/B203).[57]

For Kant, I consciously represent a line only if I apprehend it segment by segment under the form of time, that is, successively.[58] One may object that we often see things "at once", for instance, that I immediately see a triangle without needing to take time to discern the different segments of the triangle. In his discussion of the extensive and intensive magnitudes, Kant argues that, although we can represent qualities, for example, redness, through an "instantaneous" apprehension all "at once", we have to apply a "successive apprehension" for the representation of extended spaces and times.[59] So, while we may spatially intuit the triangle "at once", through this intuition we do not yet *perceive* the triangle *as* a spatially extended figure.[60] The perception of outer objects, for Kant, constitutively involves, in addition to spatial intuition, the differentiation of spatial segments and motions, and hence involves both apprehension and self-affection.

To complete the interactive model, we can now formulate the final two conditions that follow from self-affection, the third aspect of the model. The third material condition runs as follows:

(P3-M) Perception requires the self-affection of inner sense through the synthesis of apprehension, which yields immediate inner sensations of one's (outer) intuitions.

The third formal condition is then:

---

[57] See also A102, B154.

[58] This may also explain Kant's spatial metaphor of "positing" or "placing" representations in the mind: perceiving spatial objects requires us to represent them in different "places" of the temporal order of consciousness.

[59] See A163/B204 and A167/B209. Extended magnitudes are represented by successively adding a basic measure (or basic unit); see Kraus (2016).

[60] This objection is also discussed under the heading of "perceptual (or sensational) atomism" by Golob (2014:3); see also Beck (1978:41–50) and Van Cleve (1999:86).

(P3–F) Perception requires inner intuition according to the mere form of time as the primitive ordering function of one-after-the-other.

Note, finally, that the mere form of time should not be understood as an a priori temporal array that exists prior to any mental activity and that is successively filled with incoming outer sensations. Kant explicitly excludes this view by a *reductio ad absurdum* argument in a *Reflection* entitled "Answer to the question: Is it an experience that we think?" There he considers the case of perceiving a spatial figure and asks whether we should assume "another time" that exists prior to – and hence grounds – the time *in* which we perceive our own states. He eventually rejects this assumption as "absurd", since it would lead either to an infinite regress of time-constitutions or to the dogmatic assumption of an a priori representation of absolute time, preconfigured and innate in the mind (*Refl* 5661, 18:319). Neither of these results is attractive for Kant; the latter contradicts specifically Kant's claim, in the first *Critique*, that time is transcendentally ideal.

To conclude, in arguing for the constitutive role of self-affection in perception, I have completed my argument for the basic tenets of the interactive model, specifically with a view to the perception of mind-external objects. According to this model, perception is the empirical consciousness of appearances that arises in *a single interaction* of *outer affection, apprehension*, and *self-affection*. In this interaction, outer sensations are intuited in outer intuitions, and these intuitions are apprehended by way of synthesis and accompanied by an immediate awareness through inner sense.[61] These three constitutive aspects each define two necessary conditions of perception, a material one and a formal one, and mediate three types of relations involved in perception: (1) the relation to the object mediated through sensation, (2) the relation to the subject mediated through apprehension (and apperception), and (3) temporal relations mediated through self-affection.

2.4 Transcendental Self-Affection and the Temporal Conditions of Perception

2.4.1 Subjective and Objective Time

So far, the discussion has shown that the temporal relations of consciousness arise from self-affection. I call this time *subjective time*, that is, the time in which a subject's inner states are ordered. Subjective time is distinctively determined in

---

[61] Mohr suggests an interdependence model in which inner sense mediates between outer sense and apperception and has an *enabling* function for apperception (*apperzeptionsmitermöglichend*) (esp. Mohr 1991:157–9). If by "enabling" Mohr means that inner sense determines a "transcendental condition" of apperception, his account would be incompatible with mine. If "enabling" concerns the material condition, such that apperception requires inner sensations, then his account would come close to mine. Yet he does not acknowledge the need for inner sensation.

terms of *earlier–later* relations, as well as *past, present,* and *future.*[62] Yet it is unclear how from this conception of time we could ever perceive outer objects in *objective time,* that is, the time in which the states of outer objects change.

If perception is to give rise to the experience of an object, then it must track the object's movements, rather than the temporal flow of subjective consciousness. Then it does not suffice to order my outer intuitions primitively in terms of one-after-the-other, nor does it suffice to track the subjective time of my subjective apprehension of outer intuitions. Perception must instead represent objects in *objective time* and as involved in objective causal sequences. The problem of objective time calls for additional conditions that must be placed on perception, namely conditions guaranteeing that the temporal relations we perceive can underwrite objectively valid judgements, for example, about causal relations. To guarantee that perception captures objective time-relations, the mere form of inner intuition in terms of sheer successiveness is not sufficient, but the form of time must itself be informed by the conditions of objective thought, that is, the categories. Kant, therefore, introduces *transcendental time-determinations* that result from *transcendental* self-affection, construed as the a priori "synthetic influence of the understanding on inner sense" (B154). The idea, roughly, is that if the very form under which we apprehend a sensible manifold into empirical consciousness is itself determined a priori in accordance with the categories, then any apprehension of a sensible manifold and hence all perception will be in accord with them, too. For instance, the categories of relation, that is, subsistence, causality, and community, bring about the characteristic time-relations of persistence, objective succession, and simultaneity.[63] I now consider, as opposed to the *mere form of inner intuition,* the *a priori temporal conditions of perception,* which follow from Kant's theory of transcendental self-affection.

An account of transcendental self-affection views all faculties involved as *transcendental* faculties, that is, in terms of *their form,* rather than in terms of the empirical content that they produce or receive (see 1.2.3). By abstracting from all material conditions involved in the interaction of inner sense and understanding, transcendental self-affection accounts for how the mere form of time is determined a priori by the logical forms of judgement.

2.4.2 Two Functions of the Understanding

I briefly outline a basic account of the understanding in Kant, before exploring its role in self-affection. Kant offers a variety of definitions of the

---

[62] See *LB-Leningrad* 1.23–4.

[63] In the model passage, Kant already presupposes that time is explicated in terms of the "relations of succession, of simultaneity, and ... (of that which persists)" (B68), which, strictly speaking, are the results of *transcendental* self-affection.

understanding. In the broadest sense, it is defined as "the faculty for bringing forth representations itself, or the spontaneity of cognition" (A51/B75).[64] More specifically, the understanding is "a faculty of thinking, or a faculty of concepts, or also of judgments" (A126), a "faculty of cognitions" (B137), and a "faculty of rules" (A132/B171). A standard reading takes the understanding to be a capacity to judge and hence regards all acts of the understanding as acts of judgement.[65] Judgement for Kant is predication, consisting in the subsumption of predicates. Moreover, judgements are conditioned by a set of logical forms, including, for instance, the forms of universal, particular, and singular judgements, of affirmation, limitation, and negation, and of categorical, hypothetical, and disjunctive judgements.[66]

Yet the variety of definitions indicates that, while the generic "function" of the understanding is judgement, it may accomplish different tasks in different contexts, as Kant argues in the following passage: "The same function that gives unity to the different representations *in a judgment* also gives unity to the mere synthesis of different representations *in an intuition*, which, expressed generally, is called the pure concept of the understanding" (A79/B105). This passage suggests that the understanding generically accomplishes a unifying function according to its pure concepts. This "same function" can then be exercised in different modes to accomplish different purposes, for instance, the purpose of unifying intuitions or that of unifying concepts into a judgement. Although all modes of employment of the understanding depend in some way on the forms of judgement, not all of them yield instances of judgement.[67] This reading is supported by a further definition of the understanding as "the faculty of combining *a priori* and bringing the manifold of given representations under unity of apperception" (B135) and as the "faculty of unity of appearances by means of rules" (A302/B359). This suggests that the

---

[64] In some contexts, Kant subsumes all intellectual faculties under the faculty of spontaneity, including the understanding in the narrow sense as the capacity to judge, the power of judgement as the capacity to subsume under rules (in judgement), reason as the capacity for syllogisms (e.g., A51/B75).

[65] This view finds support in the following passage: "We can, however, trace all actions of the understanding back to judgments, so that the understanding in general can be represented as a faculty for judging" (A69/B94). Proponents of such a view include Bennett (1966), Bird (2006), Carl (1992:26, 101), Guyer (1987), Pippin (1982:26–30, 104–108), Strawson (1966:94), and Van Cleve (1999). For insightful discussions, see Grüne (2009) and Land (2015a), who both offer – to my mind – good reasons for rejecting what Grüne calls *Urteilstheorie* or what Land calls *judgmentalism*.

[66] See the table of judgements at A70/B95.

[67] I follow in particular Longuenesse (1998:17–18, 211–393) and Land (2015a, 2015b). Interpretations that acknowledge that the understanding is involved in intuition and perception, though not necessarily through an act of judgement, are developed by, for example, Sellars (1968:1–31, 1978:231–44), Ginsborg (2008), Grüne (2009), and Haag (2007:159–296).

understanding is actively involved in synthesis, for instance, in the syntheses of
"the manifold of intuition or of several concepts" (B130). The former results in
perception, the latter in judgement.[68]

Béatrice Longuenesse has offered detailed accounts of how the understanding is involved in these two types of synthesis. She distinguishes two different
uses of the understanding, that is, two different uses of concepts. Concepts in
general are representations of unity. In judgements, concepts serve as predicates and are understood as "discursive rules" (and as "rules of subsumption"):
a concept qua predicate represents a unity of distinctive marks, and reflecting
an object under the concept means predicating these marks of the object.
Making the judgement "A is B" consists, then, in stipulating the rule that an
object that can be reflected under the concept <A> can also be reflected under
the concept <B>.[69] In sensible synthesis, concepts serve as the rules by which
a manifold of intuition is combined, that is, as "rule[s] of intuition" (A106).
According to Longuenesse, a concept serves as rule for sensible synthesis
"insofar as it is the consciousness of the unity of an act of sensible synthesis"
(Longuenesse 1998:50). It represents precisely the unity that is to be brought
about through this act of synthesis. My analysis builds on Longuenesse's
distinction between these two uses of concepts, and for current purposes
I focus on the use of concepts as rules of synthesis.[70]

2.4.3   Figurative Synthesis

With his account of the so-called *figurative synthesis* (*synthesis speciosa*) in the
B-Deduction, Kant offers an explanation of how the categories serve as rules of
apprehension and hence for how the temporal conditions of perception are
determined a priori. The main idea runs as follows: if the understanding is
exercised specifically as the "faculty for thinking of objects of *sensible intuition*"
(A51/B75), then it imposes a set of conditions on intuitions such that these
intuitions can be reflected under concepts and hence underwrite cognition.
This view does not necessarily revise a claim that Kant makes in the
Transcendental Aesthetic, namely that "[o]bjects are … *given* to us by
means of sensibility, and it alone affords us *intuitions*" (A19/B33). Rather,
the Transcendental Analytic now shows that the understanding imposes
additional constraints on those intuitions that contribute to possible cognition.
These additional constraints concern how the representational content of an

---

[68] Some interpretations take synthesis to be involved in the formation of intuition (e.g.,
Land 2014). I remain neutral on this issue, since I focus on perception. My reading allows
for the possibility of unsynthesized intuitions, though not for unsynthesized perceptions.
[69] Longuenesse (1998:50, 63).
[70] Commentators who think along similar lines include Wolff (1973:129), Hoppe (1983:195),
Thöle (1991:227), Haag (2007:220–1), Grüne (2009:181–3), and Land (2015a, 2015b).

intuition is represented according to the conditions of thought. To subject intuitions to these additional constraints – Kant goes on to argue – can be understood as the a priori determination of the forms of intuition, space and time themselves, in accordance with the categories. By determining the forms of space and time a priori, the understanding precisely defines the rules by which a manifold of intuition is synthesized.[71] Roughly speaking, under the influence of the understanding, a sensible manifold is intuited, not just in a primitive spatio-temporal ordering, but such ordering itself displays a complex structure such that salient spatial and temporal relations can be picked out and eventually reflected under concepts. For instance, two items are not simply arranged *one-after-the-other*, but can be represented as *earlier–later* (or as *past–present*, or as *present–future*), and eventually reflected under the concept <cause–effect>.

In §24 of the B-Deduction, Kant explores this a priori configuration of time by introducing the *figurative synthesis* (*synthesis speciosa*) as a productive act of the imagination, namely as the "transcendental synthesis of the imagination" (B151).[72] The imagination, which here is defined as the "faculty for represent-ing an object even without its presence in intuition" (B151), has a double nature, which precisely allows it to mediate between the understanding and sensibility. On the one hand, the imagination "belongs to sensibility", insofar as it "give[s]" sensible representations to the understanding, a capacity that is usually ascribed to the senses alone (B151). On the other hand, the imagination counts – like the understanding – as an active faculty that is capable of "an exercise of spontaneity" and hence of "determining the sensibility *a priori*" (B152).[73] In the Section 2.3.2, the imagination's capacity for generating con-scious representations has already been shown to be crucial for the constitu-tion of empirical consciousness: through the synthesis of reproduction, the imagination "reproduces" the manifold of an outer intuition as the "matter" of empirical consciousness. In the figurative synthesis, the imagination is now viewed as a transcendental faculty, that is, in abstraction from any sensory matter. As a transcendental faculty, the imagination does not merely repro-duce, but produces a manifold of *pure* intuition a priori. This pure manifold can then be determined in accordance with the categories.[74] Hence, by

---

[71] See, for example, "to bring this synthesis [of the manifold of intuition] to *concepts* is a function that pertains to the understanding" (A78/B103).

[72] Although the configuration of space is not directly mentioned in §24, it is alluded to in the summary of figurative synthesis given in §26 (see B160n). The figurative synthesis also accounts for the a priori configuration of representing determinate spaces in perception and in geometry (see Tolley 2016). I will not further pursue this issue here, but follow Kant's striking focus on time-determination.

[73] At times, Kant even subsumes the imagination under the understanding in the broad sense (e.g., B152).

[74] See also A78/B104.

appealing to a synthetic act of the transcendental imagination, Kant is able to explain the a priori "effect of the understanding on sensibility" (B152).

In the second part of §24, Kant then explains more specifically the "synthetic influence of the understanding on inner sense", which, from the perspective of receptivity, amounts to a kind of self-affection (B154). He states: "That which determines the inner sense is the understanding and its original faculty of combining the manifold of intuition, i.e., of bringing it under an apperception [... the understanding] therefore excises that action on the *passive* subject, whose *faculty* it is, about which we rightly say that the inner sense is thereby affected" (B153–4).

There is some controversy over whether the kind of *determination* at play here should be understood either as grasping conceptually (i.e., reflecting under concepts) or as affecting (analogously to the way in which outer sense is affected). Both these options seem incompatible with the assumption that the understanding and sensibility are heterogeneous faculties. On this assumption, it is prima facie unclear why the contents received by sensibility can be reflected under concepts in the first place or how the understanding could have a sensory effect on inner sense.[75] The purpose of the figurative synthesis is thus to explain how the understanding and sensibility can "interact", despite their heterogeneous natures. Therefore, I suggest that the relevant notion of determination should be discerned in the context of Kant's general hylomorphic account of mental faculties. I argue that sensibility and the understanding stand to one another in a kind of *matter–form* relation. Accordingly, the determination of inner sense through the understanding can be construed as *informing* a temporal manifold (as a kind of *pure matter*) through "the categories, as the mere forms of thought" (B150).[76]

My idea is, roughly, as follows: primarily, the imagination produces a pure manifold of inner intuition primitively ordered in the form of sheer successiveness. The imagination does so under the guidance of certain forms, which define structurally more sophisticated spatiotemporal orders. Hence, the pure manifold itself, with its primitive temporal order, can be understood as matter to be informed by a higher-order form, which in this case is defined by the categories of the understanding. The figurative synthesis thus results in an "informing" of the mere forms of intuition through the categories of the understanding. This informing should not be understood as a reflection under the categories, that is, as an application of the categories qua predicates

---

[75] Mohr (1991:158), for instance, thinks that "determination" by the understanding is here used in both ways – as affecting inner sense and as grasping its manifold conceptually. If the latter involves the subsumption under concepts, it seems too strong a requirement for figurative synthesis. See also Longuenesse (1998:239–40, 2005:35), Heßbrüggen-Walter (2004:236).

[76] See, for example, "Sensibility, subordinated to understanding, as the object to which the latter applies its function" (A294/B351n, also A306/B363).

in judgements.[77] It does not yet involve conceptual representations of time and space, but such informing is required to make such conceptual representations possible, which can then serve as predicates in judgements, especially in a priori cognitions in mathematics (see B147). Nor should this informing be construed as a kind of affection: in this case there is no sensory matter involved and the relevant determination is pure and a priori, rather than empirical and efficient-causal.[78] Nonetheless, I call this determination *transcendental self-affection* in order to indicate that it describes the transcendental conditions that make any empirical self-affection possible.[79]

My hylomorphic reading of the figurative synthesis finds further support in §26, in which Kant completes his argument for the synthesis of apprehension that makes perception possible. There, Kant argues from the necessity of the figurative synthesis for the representation of unified spaces and times to the conclusion that even any perception "must stand under the categories" and hence that the categories are the conditions of the possibility of experience (B161).[80] Kant now considers space and time themselves as pure intuitions, each containing a distinctive pure, non-empirical manifold.[81] Space and time can be represented *as unities* only if their distinctive manifolds are a priori determined as unities, which precisely requires the figurative synthesis (see B161n). It follows that these a priori determinations of space and time must be presupposed for any representation of particular *determinate* spaces or times. A fortiori, any perception of an object in a particular space or time must presuppose these a priori determinations, and so does any experience. In line with my hylomorphic reading, space and time themselves can be represented *as unities* only if their distinctive manifolds (as a kind of *pure matter*) are

---

[77] Allison (2004:188, 196) speaks of a "proto-conceptual" employment of the categories in the figurative synthesis.

[78] Kant subscribes to the *"Forma-non-Afficit"* theorem; see Pollok (2017:150–6).

[79] Various commentators fail to acknowledge the difference between *transcendental* and *empirical* self-affection. Most commentators focus only on transcendental self-affection and hence on the temporal conditions of empirical consciousness, for example, Valaris (2008) and Schmitz (2015). Allison (2004:283) identifies self-affection fully with an empirical "affection of inner sense", but then has to conclude that Kant illicitly conflates it with the transcendental figurative synthesis. Such a conflation can indeed be found in various interpretations. For instance, Heidemann first argues that self-affection is an act of synthesis that abstracts from any empirical manifold (Heidemann 1998:129), but later identifies self-affection with psychological-empirical self-observation (Heidemann 1998:136, 139). Similarly, Keller (1998:100) endorses a psychological reading. Transcendental and empirical aspects of self-affection are distinguished by Grünewald (2009:208–15) and Indregard (2017, 2018).

[80] For a detailed discussion of §26, see Allison (2004:193–7). That perception must stand under the categories is necessary *if* it is to be perception of *something determinable* (see fn. 94).

[81] In the Aesthetic, Kant already characterizes time and space as "pure intuitions" to stress that they are non-empirical representations, abstracted from any empirical content, which nevertheless contain a manifold in them (e.g., A20/B34).

represented by a *unifying form* – a form that cannot be provided by sensibility itself, but only by a higher-order faculty such as the understanding.[82]

Longuenesse, similarly, develops a reading according to which sensibility provides only "potential forms" or "indeterminate forms", which must be actualized through an act of synthesis to be applicable in intuition. She construes the figurative synthesis as the *"original acquisition"* of space and time (see *Discovery* 8:221–2).[83] This view is controversial insofar as the idea of "acquiring" space and time may deprive sensibility of its fundamental role in "affording" intuitions, as Allison, among others, has objected.[84] For Allison, the understanding operates only on a manifold that is already given through sensibility in the a priori form of intuition and which the understanding then determines, through the figurative synthesis, as a *formal* (or *determinate*) *intuition*, rather than producing its forms themselves.[85]

The hylomorphic reading of the figurative synthesis I have developed can mitigate this interpretive conflict. It can grant to Allison that the *mere forms of intuition* are given a priori by sensibility, which yields the primitive ordering of sheer adjacency and sheer successiveness.[86] It can also grant to Longuenesse that these mere forms are indeterminate insofar as they are not yet unities or do not yet represent unities. The "original acquisition" of the forms of intuition as *determinate forms* can, on my reading, be understood as the acquisition of certain representational skills for representing determinate spaces and times. These skills cannot be derived from experience alone; their acquisition is therefore "original".

2.4.4 The A Priori Temporal Conditions of Perception

Figurative synthesis defines the a priori conditions according to which spatial and temporal manifolds are synthesized into unified determinate intuitions,

---

[82] On space and time as representational unities, see in particular B153 and B161n.

[83] Longuenesse (1998:214–27, esp. 221, 2005:35–6); also Waxman (1991:118–53, esp.122–26).

[84] Allison (2000:75, 2004:191–2).

[85] Longuenesse's and Allison's dispute is centred on the interpretation of the famous footnote in §26, in which Kant argues that "the *form of intuition* merely gives the manifold, the *formal intuition* gives unity of representation" (B160). Particularly confusing is Kant's ambiguous conclusion that this unity "precedes all concepts, though to be sure it presupposes a synthesis" (B160–1). See Longuenesse (1998:223, 2005:34–5), Allison (2000:75, 2004:112–15). Longuenesse (1998:210–42) suggests an intriguing "rereading of the Transcendental Aesthetic" in §26 by arguing that the forms of intuition, if considered as pure intuition and hence as "infinite given magnitudes", depend on the unity of apperception, though not yet on the categories. This does not exclude that sensibility *alone* affords the *mere* forms of intuition, which I have rendered as not-yet-unified *sheer adjacency* and *sheer successiveness*, respectively.

[86] A point that Longuenesse (2005:34, also 47–9) indeed herself accepts.

which represent particular spaces and particular times. A fortiori, these a priori conditions are also the conditions according to which the representations pertaining to the perception of objects in determinate times and spaces must be apprehended. With respect to time, the figurative synthesis thus determines the *a priori temporal conditions of the perception of objects*. These in turn are precisely the conditions under which an appearance can be represented in *objective time*, as Kant states most explicitly in the Second Analogy, which deals with the principle of causation: "Therefore I always make my subjective synthesis (of apprehension) objective with respect to a rule in accordance with which the appearances in their sequence, i.e., as they occur, are determined through the preceding state, and only under this presupposition alone is the experience of something that happens even possible" (A195/B240). The rule that Kant appeals to in this passage is that according to which we turn a "subjective sequence of apprehension" into an "objective sequence of appearances" that represents the states of an object in objective time (A193/B238). The category that corresponds to this specific rule is in this case the category of causation, and the perception of the objective sequence of states can then be experienced as "something that happens", that is, cognized as a causal series of events.

Perceiving a moving spatio-temporal object, such as the cat running after the ball of wool or the ball rolling off and unwinding its red thread, requires us to represent the object as occupying particular spaces and times. By examining Kant's account of the figurative synthesis, we have now seen that it is the categories that define the a priori temporal conditions under which such a perception is possible. The categories thereby function as the rules of the synthesis of apprehension, by which we take up the outer intuitions (of the cat or of the ball) into empirical consciousness. As rules of synthesis, the categories guide us in "picking out" those aspects of a manifold of outer intuition that can be taken to correspond to a spatio-temporal object of possible experience and can then be reflected under concepts. For instance, the categories of quantity and quality guide us in "picking out" the cat's shape and colour; the category of causation guides us in "picking out" a series of intuitions corresponding to a causal series of states, for example, the ball's motion. Hence, the categories provide *rules for directing our apprehension* of a sensible manifold at spatio-temporal objects of possible experience. They do so by defining generic properties of objects of experience in general, such as having extensive and intensive magnitudes, or being causally connected to other objects.

In the Deduction, Kant does not explicate the a priori temporal conditions of perception in detail, nor does he show *how* each category determines the forms of intuitions. Such a detailed explication is the task of the system of the principles of the understanding (A148–235/B187–294) – along with the Schematism (A137–47/B176–87) – in the Analytic of Principles, which follows the Deduction. There, Kant reformulates the issue in terms of the rules of the "*application* of the category to appearances" (A137/B176).[87] That is, the a priori determinations of inner sense through the understanding are now understood as the *application rules* for the categories with respect to sensible intuitions. A "schema" is defined as "a rule for the determination of our intuition in accordance with a certain general concept" (A141/B180). A "transcendental schema" supplies such a rule for a category (or, in some cases, for a group of categories). It is, roughly, a kind of template or blueprint for how any empirical manifold of inner intuition can be unified in accordance with the categories. More precisely, the transcendental schema explicates the pure (i.e., logical) content of the category, which is defined by the corresponding logical form of judgement, in terms of an a priori temporal determination.[88] Kant, therefore, calls the transcendental schemata "transcendental time-determination[s]" (A139/B178).[89]

For instance, the schema that corresponds to the categories of quantity determines a temporal manifold as a successive "time-series", that is, it determines a rule for how sheerly successive *now-points* can be added up into an *extended stretch* of time (A145/B184). The schema of the categories of quality determines the "content of time", that is, it determines an instant of time as being filled with sensible content (i.e., reality) (A145/B184). The schemata of the categories of relation determine the "order of time" (A145/B184). The schema of substance is the "persistence of the real in time"; the schema of causality is "succession" according to a necessary, objective rule; the schema of community (or reciprocal causality) is "simultaneity" (A144/B183).

The schemata of the relational categories – especially persistence and causal succession – will play an important role for the present study of inner experience. As we will see in Chapter 4, these are the schemata that are *not* properly applicable to a manifold of inner intuition, but the corresponding categories require a substitute sensible explication for inner perception. Before exploring these specific problems, I still have to complete my argument for the very possibility of inner perception, to which I now turn.

---

[87] The Schematism explores the "sensible condition under which alone pure concepts of the understanding can be employed" (A136/B175). For similar views, see Longuenesse (1998:211–42) and Melnick (2009:96–108, 116–17), who interprets figurative synthesis as a "schematized rule".

[88] The categories are defined as the "concepts of an object in general, by means of which its intuition is regarded as determined with regard to one of the logical functions for judgments" (B128). In the Metaphysical Deduction, Kant derives the table of the categories (A80/B106) from the table of judgements (A70/B95).

[89] Longuenesse (1998:243–7) argues – to my mind convincingly – that the Schematism and the principles of the understanding explicate the details of the figurative synthesis with regard to each category. I develop a reading of transcendental schemata as sensible presentations (*Darstellungen*) of the categories in 5.5.

2.5   Empirical Self-Affection and Inner Perception

2.5.1   *Inner Perception as Empirical Consciousness of One's Inner State*

The following discussion expands the account of empirical self-affection and shows that the interactive model developed in Section 2.3 can accommodate the possibility of *distinctively inner perceptions*. I still focus on the case of sensory perception and derive an account of inner perception from the simple case in which the mind perceives an outer spatio-temporal object and subsequently attends to its own perceiving. Yet, if my account is combined with the broader notion of inner sense as the faculty of inner receptivity, as suggested in Chapter 1 (see 1.5), it opens up to a rich phenomenology of inner perceptions. Accordingly, inner sense can be affected not only by the activities of the cognitive faculties, but by all kinds of mental activities, including those of the faculty of desire (*Begehrungsvermögen*), as well as by affective responses, such as feelings of pleasure and displeasure.

In the model passage from which I derived the interactive model Kant continues to discuss the case of inner perception and considers specifically "how a subject can internally intuit itself" (B68). The second part of the model passage runs as follows:

> [4] In human beings this consciousness requires *inner perception of the manifold that is antecedently given in the subject*, and the manner in which this is given in the mind without spontaneity must be called sensibility on account of this difference. [5] *If the faculty for becoming conscious of oneself is to seek out (apprehend) that which lies in the mind, it must affect the latter, and it can only produce an intuition of itself in such a way*, whose form, however, which antecedently grounds it in the mind, determines the way in which the manifold is together in the mind in the representation of time; there it then intuits itself not as it would immediately self-actively represent itself, but in accordance with the way in which it is affected from within, consequently *as it appears to itself, not as it is*.
>
> (B68–9, emphasis and numbering added)

The passage deals with the issue of how a subject can intuit *itself* such that the subject has a distinctively *inner perception*, that is, a perception *about* its inner state, rather than about an outer object. Kant suggests that, like in the case of outer perception, an inner perception requires a "manifold being given in the subject" through some affection [4] and the apprehension of this manifold resulting in an "intuition of itself", that is, an intuition of its own inner state (as opposed to intuitions of outer objects) [5]. This intuition represents the subject, not as a "self-active" mind, but only "as it appears to itself".

In my previous analysis of the interactive model, I showed how in the case of outer perception a manifold of inner intuitions (namely intuitions of the act of apprehending outer intuitions) occurs under the condition of time. Yet so far these inner intuitions were considered only insofar as they contribute to outer perception. Their purpose in outer perception is to bring outer intuitions "to consciousness" and to mark their temporal succession by assigning a sort of temporal index. The interactive model shows that in *all* cases of outer perception a temporal manifold is produced *peripherally*. That means, the mind's attention in these cases is focused entirely on the outer object that is perceived, rather than on the mental act of perceiving itself. For an inner perception, we would have to shift the focus of our *attention* and turn our gaze inwards, as it were.

Let me illustrate the distinction between outer and inner perception with the shooting of a film that results in a discrete series of cinematic images. Each of these images taken by itself provides the watcher merely with a static image, whereas when all of them are put together and shown one after the other at a reasonable pace, it gives the watcher the impression of moving objects in the scene, for example, the cat running at some speed or the ball rolling and unwinding its red thread. In most cases, the watcher would not be able to distinguish between the time in which the cinematic images change and the time in which the real objects have actually moved during the shooting; nonetheless, they are not identical. Analogously, the subjective sequence of apprehension, that is, the sequence of outer intuitions taken up in consciousness, is like the sequence of cinematic images; their pace defines the subjective time of consciousness itself. The time of the real objects during the shooting would correspond to the objective time. The camera follows a particular track and shifts its focus onto different parts of the scene, which are clearly pictured, whereas other parts of the scene are rather blurred or entirely missing. Similarly, it seems that our attention is shifting in the course of a perceptual episode. A series of internal "images", namely intuitions, are passively received, while our attention is actively shifted to focus on particular aspects of those intuitions and to unify them under the guidance of certain concepts. In our example from film technology, shifting our attention *inwards* would correspond to shifting our attention towards the cinematic images themselves. While these images themselves may mostly remain unnoticed by us, they become the focus of our attention, for instance, when they contain surrealistic features that we take, not to correspond to an outer reality, but to be the filmmaker's artistic expression. In other cases, we pay attention to the images themselves, because they display some damage, such as red stripes running across the screen, which we recognize as an intrinsic feature of the film.

In Section 2.4.4, I have argued that the categories – used as transcendental schemata – direct the apprehension of a manifold so as to represent a spatio-temporal particular, which can then be cognized as an object of possible experience. Directing an apprehension in accordance with particular conceptual rules, especially the categorial rules that define generic properties of objects of experience, can precisely be understood as shifting our attention towards a spatio-temporal particular. In a similar vein, I now suggest that the attention-shifting towards some internal matter has to be guided by appropriate conceptual rules as well – rules that guide us in "picking out" the salient aspects of a manifold of inner intuition that pertain to a mental state or series of mental states.[90]

Recall our visual scene of the two cats playing with a ball of wool. Assume, for reasons of simplicity, a temporal manifold containing a series of ten outer intuitions of the ball rolling away during the time we attend to it. Our outer perception can be linguistically expressed by the statement "A ball-shaped object undergoes a series of changes of place for ten time-units from t_1 until t_2". Shifting our attention inwards, our inner perception can now be expressed by the statement "*Seeing* a ball-shaped object undergoing a series of changes of place for ten time-units from t_1 until t_2". Here the focus of outer attention is on the mental state or activity, that is, the seeing itself, whereas the outer intuitions and hence the content of our seeing are peripheral. Similarly, we could imagine listening to a melody, such as the beginning of Beethoven's Ninth Symphony. We can perceive the melody as such only through hearing a few notes and apprehending them into a succession of tonal intuitions. People who are more familiar with the piece will probably need a shorter series of intuitions to recognize which symphony it is, because they are more skilled in interpreting the meaning of their tonal intuitions. Again, we can focus our attention either on the melody itself and enjoy an outer, auditory perception, or on our *hearing of*, or *listening to*, the melody and enjoy an inner perception of our own activity.[91]

In the case of an *inner perception*, we perceive our seeing or hearing (rather than the perceived object) by bringing to our attention the same manifold of inner intuition in time that is already involved in the corresponding outer perception. No further sensory matter is added. By turning our attention inwards, we combine this manifold into a *determinate inner intuition of ourselves* (while outer affection still *peripherally* continues, without being attended to). This is precisely what I take Kant to mean when he claims that "the faculty for becoming conscious of oneself is to seek out (apprehend) that which lies in the mind", by which it "produce[s] an intuition of itself" (B68).

In the case of inner perception (i.e., of becoming conscious of oneself), the same manifold of inner intuition yielded peripherally in outer perceptions is now actively focused on and combined in such a way that it yields a *conscious* intuition of oneself, rather than of an outer object. This requires that the

---

[90] Melnick (2009:15) also presents an account of inner and outer perceptions in terms of attention-shifting. Unlike me, he attributes the activity of attention-shifting to sensibility, rather than to a spontaneous faculty.

[91] On the example of listening to music, see *Anth* 7:136, as well as Grüne (2009:177), Kitcher (1990:152), Mohr (1991:178–9n4); also, Husserl (1928:20ff.), though none of these commentators interprets this as an instance of inner perception.

manifold be combined in accordance, not with the rules for representing outer objects, but with those for representing oneself or one's inner state. These rules enable us to be conscious of our inner appearances *as belonging to our own inner state* (or "*state of mind*") and hence to have an *inner perception*, that is, an *empirical consciousness of our own mental states*.[92] Importantly, shifting attention from outer objects towards one's inner state should *not* be understood as moving towards a higher-order introspection, but rather as a different kind of combining, or apprehending, a given sensible manifold, at the same level as outer perception. Inner perception can thus be understood, on the interactive model, as fulfilling the material conditions of apprehension (P2-M) and of self-affection (P3-M), as well as the formal conditions of apperception (P2-F) and of inner intuition (P3-F) (see 2.3). The material condition (P1-M) that relates perception to an "object" either coincides with (P3-M) (in the case of peripheral outer perception) or concerns the inner appearances that arise through self-affection from other mental activities (e.g., desiring). The formal condition of outer intuition (P1-F) is not required for inner perception, as it is specific for outer perception only.

2.5.2   Attention and the Rules of Apprehension

Kant does not provide a full theory of attention, but indicates in a few places that *attention* concerns the way in which a manifold of intuition is combined through the synthesis of apprehension. The *Anthropology* provides the most explicit account of attention in terms of a voluntary consciousness of one's representation. More precisely, "*paying attention to (attentio)*" is defined as the "endeavor to become conscious of one's representation" (*Anth* 7:131). In turn, "turning away from" a representation, if done involuntarily, is *distraction*, or lack of attention. It is precisely a "holding off ... a representation ... from being in connection with other representations in one consciousness" (*Anth* 7:131). But, if the turning-away is done voluntarily, it is properly speaking an *abstraction* from a particular representation (*Anth* 7:131). Kant later associates attention with the *faculty of apprehension*, glossed as "*attentio*", to "produce intuition" (*Anth* 7:138).

Kant also appeals to the notion of attention in his analysis of figurative synthesis (§24) and describes this synthesis as a shift of attention towards the very act of apprehending, for instance, the segments of a line: "we cannot even represent time without, in drawing a straight line ..., attending merely to the action of the synthesis of the manifold through which we successively determine the inner sense, and thereby attending to the succession of this determination in inner sense" (B154–5). If we "attend solely to the action" of synthesizing a manifold in space, then we gain a perception of our apprehending the line,

---

[92] See especially "In the case of inner experience ... I affect myself insofar as I bring the representations of outer sense into an empirical consciousness of my condition" (*LB-Leningrad* 1.9–11; also A37/B53–4; *Refl* 5661, 18:319).

that is, an inner perception pertaining to our own inner state (B155).[93] In this passage, Kant's aim is to illustrate the transcendental figurative synthesis: so if we further "abstract from this manifold in space" altogether, our mental action "first produces the concept of succession at all", which makes possible the perception of successive states, both of outer objects and of oneself (B155). More generally, we produce the pure temporal forms of inner perception as the conditions under which any inner perception must take place. The concept of succession – as the rule of synthesis – precisely directs our attention onto a particular successive sequence within one's *empirical* inner manifold. Only by combining a manifold under the guidance of this schema can we become conscious of a successive sequence of states. Hence, for perception to be the representation *of something determinable*, that is, of a *(spatio-)temporal particular* that can be the object of possible experience, the synthesis of apprehension must proceed *according to at least some categories*. The categories – as rules of synthesis – are a priori conditions of the very possibility of the perception *of something determinable* (i.e., of an outer object or of oneself).[94]

Hence, directing one's attention towards spatio-temporal particulars cannot be effected by sensibility alone, but must be guided by concepts as the rules of the synthesis of apprehension. It requires spontaneous faculties to provide and apply the general rules for identifying objects in perceptual episodes (of inner or outer perception). The rules for identifying objects are supplied by the understanding in terms of the categories. The faculty to apply such rules in particular cases is the power of judgement, that is, the faculty to subsume particulars under universals by comparing and contrasting representations and identifying common marks. Similarly, in inner perception, attention towards mental acts and inner states must be guided by conceptual rules.

---

[93] Attention always requires self-affection, for Kant (see, e.g., B156n).

[94] For insightful discussions of Kant's account of attention in the *Anthropology*, and of the role of attention in synthesis according to the *Critique*, see Merritt and Valaris (2017), Merritt (2018:81–100), and Indregard (2018). These interpretations emphasize a gradual account of consciousness, according to which consciousness has greater or lesser degrees of *clarity* and *distinctness*. Such a reading seems supported by various passages, for example, "the degree of consciousness of the marks [of a concept . . .] correspond[s] to the amount of attention directed to them" (*CJ First Intro* 20:227n; see also A169/B211, B414–15). All these commentators conclude that Kant allows for a graded notion of perception, too, according to which a perception can be more or less unified by a concept; for example, there can be "scattered [*zerstreute*] perceptions [that are] not yet united under the concept of an object" (*Anth* 7:128). My account can grant the idea that a perception is more or less focused and hence more or less unified by concepts. Yet in order for a perception to count as the representation *of something determinable* at all, it must be guided by at least some categories and hence viewed as the representation of *spatio-temporal particulars* that can be objects of possible experience. I remain neutral as to whether there can be *mere perception* without being perception *of something*, as a non-conceptual account of perception would have it.

In sum, this chapter has offered an argument for the very possibility of distinctively inner perception as the empirical consciousness of one's inner states. The argument was based on an analysis of Kant's interactive model of perception in general, which involves the sensory affection (typically) by an object, the synthesis of apprehension, and self-affection of inner sense. My analysis has carefully distinguished between transcendental self-affection, which determines the a priori temporal conditions of perception in general, and empirical self-affection, which generates inner intuitions in time and gives rise to empirical consciousness. Inner perception is made possible by drawing one's attention inwards and combining a manifold of inner intuitions within a perceptual episode into a first-order empirical consciousness of one's inner state.

While this chapter has argued for the possibility of distinctively inner perception, it has not yet shown whether all categories, and hence all a priori temporal conditions (see 2.4), are applicable in inner perception and whether inner perception requires specific rules of synthesis. As already indicated, while the categories of quantity and quality are straightforwardly applicable, there are problems with the categories of relation.[95] Moreover, if inner perception is understood as a representation of the subject itself (as it appears to itself), then it must be subject to the general conditions of self-consciousness. Self-consciousness, Kant argues in the model passage (and in various other places), requires "the simple representation of the I" (B68). This raises the question whether inner perception must be informed not only by the categories but also by the conditions that make possible the use of the term "I". Hence, I turn next to the conceptual conditions of inner experience. I will examine the conditions of self-consciousness in general and the use of the concept "I", respectively, in Chapters 3 and 4. I will take up the issue of the specific rules of apprehension for inner perception in Chapter 5.

---

[95] On the applicability of the categories of quantity and of quality to inner intuition, see Kraus (2016).

PART II

Self-Consciousness and the "I" of the Understanding

3

The Form of Reflexivity and the Expression "I think"

3.1 Introduction

My inner experience is experience *about myself*, namely first and foremost about *my* thoughts, perceptions, imaginations, desires, and other mental states. It consists of judgements about the one who is making the judgements. Hence, the subject who is having the experience figures in some sense as part of the experience's representational content. In the Introduction, I therefore characterized inner experience as a representation of oneself *as object*, or just as a *self-referential* representation. I distinguished *self-reference* from another sense in which an experience relates to the subject, which I called *reflexivity*. In this latter sense, every experience is reflexive in that it "points back" to the subject who has this experience, and hence goes along with what I identify with consciousness of oneself *as subject*. This chapter explores this general kind of reflexivity that is realized in any experience and explicates the notion of subject that it implies. Only in the final section, Section 3.5, will I indicate how this reflexivity gives rise to self-reference. The task of the two subsequent chapters will then be to explicate the kind of self-reference that is characteristic of inner experience: Chapter 4 examines the logical conditions of I-judgements, whereas Chapter 5 explores the temporal conditions of I-judgements based on inner perception.

Chapter 2 has shown that the appearances arising from inner sense are the contents of empirical consciousness in time, such as particular thoughts, perceptions, and desires, which can – upon attention – become the objects of inner perception. While Kant's theory of self-affection (of inner sense) explains how inner appearances enter empirical consciousness, it does not explain *whose* mental states are represented in inner perception and hence *to whom* these states are ascribed in inner experience. The reason is that, for Kant, inner sense alone does not yield self-consciousness. Neither does it yield consciousness of oneself *as object*, as needed for inner experience, nor does it yield consciousness of oneself *as subject*, as implied in experience in general.

Kant famously introduces a new faculty, namely *apperception*, to account for issues of self-consciousness. Apperception, if viewed as a transcendental faculty, produces the characteristic representation "I think" – a representation that "must be able to accompany" any other representation (B131). It has been notoriously difficult to discern the representational status of this *apperceptive* *"I think"*, as I will call it, and its relationship to inner experience. Inner experience consists in *empirical I-judgements*, which can be characteristically expressed by statements of the basic form "I φ" (and derivations thereof). The subject of predication (or logical subject) therein is always denoted by the first-person pronoun "I", and "φ" is a predicate denoting a psychological determination (see *Refl* 5453, 18:186). In this chapter, I argue that the apperceptive "I think" is fundamentally different from all predicative uses of "I" in judgements.

The central thesis of this chapter comes in two parts. Firstly, I argue that transcendental apperception is the *capacity for reflexive consciousness* in general. This general capacity is fundamental for representing objects of any kind, regardless of whether one represents oneself or something else as object. Only those representations that are in a generic sense reflexive can have representational content *for a thinking subject* and consequently be self-ascribed by the subject in I-judgements. Secondly, I argue that the apperceptive "I think" is merely an *expression* of the reflexivity of consciousness, rather than a judgement predicating something of oneself. The apperceptive "I think", if attached to a representation in thought, merely indicates or expresses the presence of a thinking subject, without determining any features – generic or specific – of the thinker. My argument then has a negative and a positive part.

In a negative sense, I first show that the apperceptive "I think" should *not* be understood as a judgement (or any other kind of representation) that is *about* something: neither about an individual (empirical) thinker, nor about a merely logical subject. Attaching "I think" to a representation, therefore, does *not* amount to predicating this representation of an individual thinker or of a logical subject. I develop this negative argument by discussing the shortcomings of two major readings of transcendental apperception – the act-awareness reading and the self-ascriptive reading. The act-awareness reading conceives of transcendental apperception as the capacity for the awareness of one's synthesizing activities. The self-ascriptive reading conceives of transcendental apperception as the capacity for self-ascriptive judgements, that is, judgements by which one predicates a representation of oneself. While each interpretation captures important issues of apperception, they both fall short of giving an appropriate account of the generic reflexivity of experience.

In a positive sense, I develop an alternative view, on which apperception is understood as the *capacity for reflexive consciousness* in general, that is, the capacity of a thinking subject for producing conscious representations. As a transcendental faculty, apperception defines a transcendental form, namely the general form of the reflexive relation that a subject has to its significant representations: that is, those representations that have content *for the subject* and by which the subject *refers to objects* (in a generic sense) (see 1.2). I show that this form should still be understood as a kind of self-consciousness, which I identify as *transcendental self-consciousness.* Yet such self-consciousness is non-representational: it does not represent the subject as content, but is only the form that any determinate self-consciousness must take. In consequence, this form defines the most general transcendental condition of both outer and inner experience. I finally go on to argue that the apperceptive "I think" should be understood as an *expression of this general form of reflexivity.* By attaching the apperceptive "I think" to another representation in thought, we explicitly express the actualization of this form and hence the realization of transcendental self-consciousness. In this limited sense, "I think" indicates the presence of the individual thinker who in fact apperceives a representation and mediates self-reference, yet without determining the inner nature, or any generic or individuating properties of the thinker.

This chapter proceeds as follows. Section 3.2 situates Kant's account of transcendental apperception in the context of the Transcendental Deduction of the Categories (primarily according to the B-Edition) and outlines Kant's argument *for* transcendental apperception. Section 3.3 discusses two common interpretations of transcendental apperception: respectively, the act-awareness reading and the self-ascriptive reading. Section 3.4 develops an alternative interpretation of transcendental apperception as the capacity for reflexive consciousness and shows that it defines a transcendental condition of experience. Section 3.5 argues that the apperceptive "I think", if explicitly attached to a representation, expresses the presence of a thinking subject.

3.2 Transcendental Apperception in the Deduction

The Transcendental Deduction of the Pure Concepts of the Understanding (henceforth "the Deduction") offers crucial resources for understanding Kant's conception of self-consciousness. Yet Kant's primary goal in the Deduction is to establish the pure concepts of the understanding as transcendental conditions of experience. For this purpose, Kant presents a highly complex and often puzzling argument for the possibility of cognition of sensible objects. The core idea of the argument is that, for an intuition to present the mind with a cognizable object, it must itself stand under the conditions that are imposed by the understanding and that are specified by its pure concepts, that is, the categories. If successful, the argument shows that the categories have "objective reality, i.e., application to objects that can be given to us in intuition" (B150-1). In consequence, the categories determine a priori generic features of objects of experience. A central claim of the Deduction is that transcendental apperception grounds the unity of consciousness and that such a unity is required to combine all those representations that together constitute the empirical cognition of objects. Here I focus on Kant's argument for this specific claim, and call it the *Unity Argument*. In this section, I introduce Kant's notion of transcendental apperception and briefly situate it within the Deduction. By focusing narrowly on apperception, I leave aside various interpretative controversies concerning the Deduction in general.

3.2.1   The Notion of Transcendental Apperception

Kant borrows the term *apperception* from Leibniz, and, like Leibniz, Kant introduces the notion to account for a key feature of the human capacity for representation (*Vorstellungsvermögen*), namely the feature that humans can be conscious of their own representations. Yet by adding the qualification "transcendental", Kant crucially diverges from Leibniz and gives the notion a fundamentally different meaning.

For Leibniz, the mental activity of apperception turns otherwise unconscious, minute perceptions (*petites perceptions*, French) into conscious perceptions.[1] The term itself is derived from the Latin term *apperceptio*, which translates as "I perceive in addition to" or "I add to perception". Leibniz's use of the reflexive French verb *s'apercevoir* ("to perceive for oneself") indicates that apperceiving involves a reflexive relation to the subject who perceives. It is a matter of ongoing debate what exactly, for Leibniz, apperception is. Traditionally, apperception has been thought to lead to a higher-order consciousness of one's first-order world-directed perceptions.[2] More recently, apperception has been understood on a first-order model of consciousness, according to which apperception is the activity of integrating a multitude of unconscious perceptions to the point that their aggregation overcomes a threshold and becomes a single unified conscious perception.[3] *Whether* apperception results in a conscious perception depends, then, on the empirically contingent, quantitative and qualitative features of the minute perceptions involved. For instance, the intensity of a loud bang can immediately catch someone's attention, or the high scrutiny with which someone makes an observation yields particularly clear and distinct perceptions. Regardless of

---

[1] Leibniz (1714a/1989 §14:644; 1714b/1989 §4:638; 1765/1996 Preface, II.9.4:104, II.19.4:164). For the history of this notion, see Carl (1992:60–71), Thiel (2001, 2011), and Wunderlich (2005:131–53).

[2] For example, Kulstad (1991) and Gennaro (1999). Higher-order accounts of consciousness are often criticized on the grounds that they may inevitably lead to an infinite regress. To avoid such a regress, Gennaro (1999:356) considers an apperception as a "nonconscious meta-psychological thought", which – only by drawing one's attention inward – can be turned into self-consciousness.

[3] For example, Jorgensen (2011) and Simmons (2011).

which interpretation one prefers, Leibniz's account of apperception entails the following key features: firstly, while apperception for Leibniz explains specifically the consciousness of world-directed perceptions, it is not a necessary condition for having such perceptions at all.[4] Secondly, while Leibniz grants other kinds of self-consciousness, apperception is not a necessary condition of self-consciousness in general.[5] Thirdly, although Leibniz associates apperception, in some places, with the ability "to think what is called *I*", it does not necessarily involve the ability to make I-judgements or amount to a conceptual self-consciousness.[6]

Kant's transcendental account of apperception inverts these three key features, or so I argue. For Kant, transcendental apperception is the most fundamental feature of the human capacity for representation. It is, firstly, a necessary condition of representations of objects in general, including perceptions; it is, secondly, a necessary condition of all kinds of self-consciousness; and, thirdly, it has a necessary connection to the representation "I think".

In the first *Critique* (and other Critical writings), Kant characterizes transcendental apperception in terms of (1) a particular *faculty*, (2) a particular *act of synthesis*, (3) a kind of *consciousness* that results from this act, and (4) a characteristic representation, the "I think". So we find the following characterizations:

(1) The *faculty* for apperception is contrasted with inner sense (e.g., A107, B152–5; *Anth* 7:134n) and considered as a spontaneous faculty (e.g., B68–9, B132, B150, B278).[7]

(2) This faculty exercises a characteristic *act of synthesis* ("*actus* of spontaneity") by which representations are combined into a unity (B132, also B137).[8]

---

[4] Note that for Leibniz *perception* is a generic notion that denotes any state by which a monad can "express" a state of the world, even non-rational monads (see Leibniz 1714a/1989 §14:644).

[5] Leibniz, for instance, assumes that we have innate self-knowledge of our nature as simple substances, viz. monads, of which we become explicitly conscious through apperception (Leibniz 1765/1996 Preface, II.9.4:104).

[6] Leibniz (1714a/1989 §30:646; see also 1714b/1989 §5:638). Neither on the first-order, nor on the higher-order account does apperception necessarily amount to *conceptual reflection* upon oneself (see Genaro 1999, Simmons 2011). Yet, in some places, Leibniz appears to argue that apperception is a precondition of reflection (Leibniz 1765/1996 Preface, II.9.4:104).

[7] Transcendental apperception is also called *pure apperception* (A116, A123, B132, B138) and contrasted with *empirical apperception*, which is the capacity to be conscious of oneself through inner sense (see A107, B132; *Anth* 7:134n, 141, 161).

[8] In the A-Deduction, *transcendental apperception* is not characterized as an independent act of synthesis, but as the "original and transcendental condition" of the synthesis of recognition (A106).

(3) This apperceptive act results in the *"original-synthetic unity* of apperception" (e.g., B133n, B135, B136, B150, B157; *Anth* 7:134n), which is also identified as the "transcendental unity of self-consciousness" (B132) or as the "pure, original, and unchanging consciousness" of oneself (A107, A117n).

(4) Transcendental apperception produces a characteristic representation: the "I think" that "must be able to accompany all my representations" (B131).

The goal of this chapter is to offer a reading of transcendental apperception that, on the one hand, can explain its crucial function within the Deduction and make sense of these four aspects, and that, on the other hand, clarifies its connection to consciousness in general and the kind of self-consciousness to which it gives rise. Before I outline two common, but I believe misleading, interpretations, I first introduce the specific role that transcendental apperception plays within the Deduction.

3.2.2   The Argument for Transcendental Apperception in the Deduction

My exposition of Kant's argument for transcendental apperception mainly follows the B-Deduction, for reasons already discussed in Chapter 2.[9] It is generally agreed that the B-Deduction falls into two parts: a general first part (§§15–21) and a more specific second part (§§22–7).[10] The first part contains an argument for the applicability of the categories to sensible objects in general, abstracting from the particular forms of intuition, whereas the second part considers the specifically human forms of intuition, space and time. I follow those who construe the Deduction argument as a *regressive*, rather than progressive, argument; yet the reconstruction of Kant's argument for apperception does not depend on this interpretive choice. According to the regressive reading, the Deduction starts from the premise that cognition of empirical objects is possible (for us) and concludes – regressively – that the manifold through which an object is given in intuition must necessarily stand under the conditions defined by the categories.[11] The crucial step of the Deduction is then to show that any manifold (be it a manifold of intuition or a multitude of concepts) can be

---

[9] See my discussion of the synthesis of apprehension in 2.3.

[10] For example, Henrich (1969:641–2), but this point was already indicated by earlier commentators, such as Paton (1936 I:501). For a discussion of different readings of these two parts, see Keller (1998:89–94).

[11] For example, Ameriks (1978), Allison (2004). For progressive readings, see Strawson (1966), Bennett (1966), and Schulting (2012). A progressive reading assumes that the Deduction's goal is to rebut *scepticism* regarding the very possibility of any cognition of the world (see Carl 1989:9, 1992:53).

unified into an objective unity – a unity that represents a cognizable object – only if the synthesis that unifies the manifold is carried out in accordance with the universal logical functions of thinking, that is, the logical forms of judgement (see esp. §19). These logical functions are the categories, which guide the synthesis of a given manifold of intuition.

Before Kant carries out this crucial step, he argues for a more fundamental condition, namely that the manifold by which an object is given in intuition must be unified within one and the same consciousness. The idea, roughly, is that, for a multiplicity of representations to pertain to – and hence represent – one and the same object, this multiplicity must be unified in one and the same consciousness and must be assumed to belong – in a sense to be specified – to this common consciousness.[12] For a manifold of intuition to represent a cognizable object, it must thus be subject to the synthesis of apperception and combined into the *original-synthetic unity of apperception* (§16, B131–4). I focus my analysis on this argument for transcendental apperception, that is, the Unity Argument.

The Unity Argument begins with the following famous passage:

> The *I think* must be able to accompany all my representations; for otherwise something would be represented in me that could not be thought at all, which is as much as to say that the representation would either be impossible or else at least would be nothing for me. (B131–2)

This passage (and indeed §16 as a whole) is not narrowly focused on the conditions of cognition and experience, but more broadly concerned with the conditions of representations that are not "nothing for me". In Chapter 1, I introduced the notion of *significant representations*, that is, representations that have some *representational content for me* and represent an object in the generic sense (see 1.2.1). In this chapter, I will finally spell out what this significance amounts to and how it relates to the generic capacity to become conscious of a representation.[13] The passage above specifies a necessary condition of significant representations in terms of the ability to be accompanied by the "I think". A few lines down, Kant argues that this ability is made possible by the synthesis of apperception: "I call it [i.e., the *actus of spontaneity* of apperception] the *pure apperception*, . . ., or also the *original apperception*, since it is that self-consciousness which, because it produces the representation *I think*, which must be able to accompany all others and which in all consciousness is one and the same, cannot be

---

[12] Kant presupposes that any representation of an object is complex, that is, composed of partial representations, such as a manifold of intuition, a multitude of concepts, or a set of basic numerical units (see Allison 2004:164–5).

[13] My notion of *significant representation* is inspired by, though also broader than, Keller's notion of *semantically significant representations* (see Keller 1998:36–44).

accompanied by any further representation" (B132). The resulting unity is then called the *original-synthetic unity of apperception,* or also "*transcendental*" unity of self-consciousness" (B132). The specific self-consciousness of apperception is a *transcendental self-consciousness.*[14]

I take this passage to suggest that the more fundamental *first* ability, the *ability to synthesize* a manifold of representations into the synthetic unity of apperception, makes possible a *second* ability, the *ability to add the "I think"* to the apperceived representations. These two abilities correspond to two distinct kinds of unity of consciousness, as Kant explicates a few lines down:

> Therefore it is only because I can combine a manifold of given representations *in one consciousness* that it is possible for me to represent the *identity of consciousness in these representations* itself, i.e., the *analytical* unity of apperception is possible under the presupposition of some *synthetic* one.
> (B133)

Here the second ability is identified with the ability to "represent the *identity of consciousness in these* [i.e., apperceived] *representations*", which then leads to the "analytical unity of apperception" (B133).

With the notion of *analytical unity,* Kant commonly refers to the unity that results from the reflection of multiple representations under a common concept: this representational unity represents what "is to be thought of as common to *several*" (B133n, also A79/B105).[15] The analytical unity of apperception is what is common to all apperceived representations, namely the identity of the subject.[16] I take this to mean that for the representation of an object (in the generic sense) to be possible, all representational elements pertaining to the object must be synthesized in one and the same consciousness such that this consciousness *can itself* be represented as being unified (i.e., the "consciousness of this [apperceptive] synthesis", B133).[17] Moreover, I take the above passages to suggest that the "I think" is precisely the concept by which we can represent the analytical unity of apperception, as that which is common to all synthesized representations: the fact that they belong to one and the same consciousness or just to the "identical self" (B135).

---

[14] Though occasionally employed in the literature (e.g., Keller 1998), Kant himself does not use this phrase, but he states, "a transcendental consciousness (preceding all particular experience), namely the consciousness of myself, as original apperception" (A117).

[15] For Kant, a *synthetic* unity is the unity of many ("many in one") and an *analytical unity* is the unity of what "is to be thought of as common to *several*" (B133n) ("one in many"); see Allison (2015:258).

[16] Similar considerations can be found in the A-Deduction (e.g., A117n).

[17] It is universally agreed that transcendental apperception defines a transcendental condition, yet there are stronger readings according to which the synthetic unity of aperception can be realized *only* through a synthesis according to the categories (e.g., Strawson 1966:96, Henrich 1994:34, Allison 2004:174–5, 353; see 3.4).

In sum, the Unity Argument for transcendental apperception, in §16, involves two abilities: the ability to synthesize a manifold into a common consciousness, and the ability to represent the identity of the subject throughout an apperceptive act. The first ability yields the synthetic-original unity of apperception, and the second the analytical unity of apperception. An act of apperception requires only the realization the of first ability, but must be such that the realization of the second ability is possible. The actual attachment of "I think" is thus not necessary to represent objects, but must be possible.

Kant introduces two further unities of consciousness in the subsequent sections. For an apperceived intuition to be the representation of an *object of cognition*, its manifold must be synthesized in accordance with the categories into an *objective unity of self-consciousness* (§18, B139) (or the "objective unity of apperception", §19, B141), rather than a merely "subjective unity of consciousness" (B139). The latter is also called the *empirical unity of apperception* and is identified with the *determination of inner sense*, which, prima facie, is assumed to pertain to the empirical subject, rather than an object (B139).

Hence, the full Deduction contains four notable unities:

- the *original-synthetic unity of apperception* (SU);
- the *analytic unity of apperception* (or the identity of the subject) (AU);
- the *objective unity of apperception* (or the unity of the object) (OU); and
- the *empirical unity of apperception* (as the determination of inner sense) (EU).

Needless to say, these unities, and the relations between them, have been interpreted in various ways and there are numerous points of controversy surrounding this argument. In the subsequent sections, I discuss the Unity Argument and address some of these controversies to the extent necessary to develop my reading of transcendental apperception. Given my purpose of understanding the generic *reflexivity* of consciousness, I focus on the notion of the subject that is laid out in this argument.

To foreshadow my own reading: I take the Unity Argument to show that the original-synthetic unity of apperception is the highest condition of our *capacity to represent significant content in consciousness* and hence of both our capacity to represent objects and our capacity to represent ourselves.[18] Moreover, the capacity to represent myself as an empirical self can then be "derived" from the objective unity "under given conditions *in concreto*" (B140). On my view, the resulting unities can be illustrated by the following "triadic structure", whereby from the *top*, which stands in for SU, the highest, most general condition of significant representations in general, both

---

[18] It defines the "original and transcendental condition" (A106) or the "supreme principle" of cognition in general (B136).

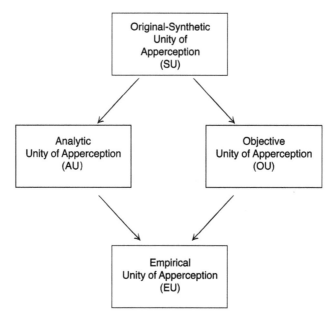

Figure 3.1   Triadic structure of the Unity Argument

AU, a condition of self-representation, und OU, a condition of object-representation, flow (see Figure 3.1).

I now turn to the two standard readings of transcendental apperception in the Deduction.

3.3   The Psychological and the Logical Reading of Transcendental Apperception

3.3.1   Two Standard Readings

The debates about the Deduction in general and transcendental apperception in particular are as complex as they are controversial. My aim here is *not* to give a comprehensive review of the numerous views in these debates, nor to offer a comprehensive critique of particular views. Rather, I present what I take to be two standard readings of or interpretive tendencies concerning transcendental apperception, against which I then develop my own view. The standard interpretations I have in mind are what I call the psychological and the logical reading. In the Sections 3.3.2–3.3.4 I discuss each of the two readings in turn, by drawing on some views from the recent literature. By discussing a view under this or that label, I do *not* mean to imply that the view fully instantiates the reading under which I label it, nor that the author of the view in fact subscribes to the reading. Rather, I merely imply that I take the view to show signs of this or that interpretive tendency and hence to give evidence for the dialectic that I have observed in these debates.

The dividing line between the two standard interpretations concerns the very act of apperceptive synthesis. The psychological reading assumes that the apperceptive act can be realized by acts of synthesis other than judging, whereas the logical reading assumes that such an act can – for all intents and purposes – be realized only by acts of judgement. This difference leads to two different views concerning the self-consciousness that results from this act.

Firstly, in construing transcendental apperception as an act of synthesis other than judging, the psychological reading leads to the conclusion that this act generates – in addition to the synthetic unity of consciousness – the awareness of the synthesizing act itself or of the *subject qua its synthesizing act*. This awareness is not yet conceptual, or at least is not yet a judgement, that is, a combination of concepts, and is therefore assumed to be pre-discursive. It may be assumed to be more similar to an intuitive, immediate grasp of the synthesizing agent, or of the unity that is thereby generated. I call this interpretation a *psychological reading*, since it appeals primarily to a pre-discursive *activity* of unifying mental contents. Calling it "psychological", however, does *not* imply that it is empirically psychological, nor that it is defectively psychologistic.

Secondly, in construing transcendental apperception as an act of judgement, the logical reading implies that the unifying function of apperception consists in reflecting a representational manifold under a common concept, viz. the apperceptive "I think". The resulting self-consciousness then consists in a self-ascriptive judgement of the form "I think R", by which the apperceiving subject ascribes to herself the representation R that results from the synthesis of the manifold. I call this interpretation the *logical reading* since it appeals primarily to the capacity to judge and, more specifically, to the capacity to self-ascribe representations via the "I think", which brings forth a discursive (or conceptual) self-consciousness of the thinking subject. Calling it "logical", however, does not imply that it concerns only concepts and judgements in abstraction from their sensible content, nor that it is defectively logicist.

In discussing these two standard readings, I carve up the interpretive debate according to a particular dimension that may not be suitable for all views that have been proposed. Yet it will serve my purpose of bringing another promising interpretive option to the table, which – I believe – has not received sufficient attention. My reading differs from the former two in that it puts emphasis, not merely on the act or the product of transcendental apperception, but on its status as a *transcendental* faculty and hence on its *transcendental form*. Roughly, my view is that, as the *transcendental faculty for consciousness in general*, transcendental apperception imposes its characteristic form on suitable representational matter in order to produce conscious representations. This matter, I shall argue, can be either sensible or conceptual. Transcendental apperception can thus be realized either by an act of judgement or by an act of synthesis other than judgement, *if* this act is to produce a conscious representation. The transcendental form of apperception is the *form of a unified consciousness* that any representation which can occur in consciousness must display. For rational beings like us, who have the capacity to judge and specifically to self-ascribe representations in judgements, this general form must make such self-ascriptive judgements possible. Therefore, for us, all conscious representation must be *reflexive*, that is, have a suitable relation to the subject. The form of apperception is then the *general form of reflexivity* and can be expressed by the representation "I think". In consequence, though not all acts of apperception are acts of judgement, they all must be – in a sense to be specified – *amenable* to the act of self-ascriptive judgement of the generic form "I think *R*".

Each of the two standard readings captures important aspects of transcendental apperception, but neither of them is able to fully explain the fundamental issue, namely that transcendental apperception defines the general form of reflexive consciousness for rational beings like us. So I follow the psychological reading in allowing transcendental apperception to be realized by acts other than judgement. But, unlike the psychological reading, I do not think that transcendental apperception produces an awareness of the synthesizing act. I also follow the logical reading in accepting that there is an important connection between transcendental apperception and self-ascription. Yet, compared with the logical reading, I argue that transcendental apperception provides the form of reflexivity to a much larger range of mental acts. As a result, my reading can explain our capacity for becoming conscious of a much larger range of mental states, including perceptual states, states of desire, and even – to some extent – emotional states.

In what follows, I develop my own interpretation by carving out the shortcomings of the two standard readings, which can be summarized as follows:

- the *psychological* reading of transcendental apperception as *awareness of the subject qua synthesizing act*;
- the *logical* reading of transcendental apperception as the capacity for *self-ascription*.

My main line of critique is that both readings assume that transcendental apperception adds some *content*, albeit different kinds (non-logical content vs. logical content) to the apperceived representations. By contrast, I argue that transcendental apperception should be understood as exclusively contributing a form according to which the apperceived representations constitute a unified consciousness.

3.3.2 The Psychological Reading: Transcendental Apperception
as Act-Awareness

The *psychological* reading, focusing on the *apperceptive act of synthesis*, is rarely explicitly articulated or openly acknowledged as being *psychological* as opposed to logical. Nonetheless, it is an influential interpretive tendency and, for dialectical purposes, it is instructive to examine its advantages and problems.

The psychological reading emphasizes the act of unifying representational elements into a single consciousness, rather than the relation of these representations to the apperceiving subject. In emphasizing the synthesizing act, the reading allows transcendental apperception to be realized by all acts of synthesis that can bring forward representational unities of a suitable kind. Patricia Kitcher, whose interpretation shows features of the psychological reading, characterizes these unities as the "necessary togetherness" of representations. In order for a representational unity to meet the condition of "necessary togetherness", it must also "be understood as meeting the necessary condition for belonging to a common 'I'" (Kitcher 2011:142). The condition of belonging to a "common 'I'", on the psychological reading, amounts to some sort of pre-discursive awareness of the synthesizing act itself or of the *subject qua its synthesizing act* – an awareness that is not yet conceptual and does not involve a self-ascriptive judgement.[19] Kitcher, for instance, construes this awareness as an "apperceptive act-awareness" that is "produced in the course of cognition" (Kitcher 2011:160) and as the "consciousness of the act of combining" representations into the "necessary togetherness" (Kitcher 2011:145-6).[20]

In order for this apperceptive act-awareness to be some sort of self-consciousness, it must be awareness not only of the synthesizing activity per se, but also of the cognizer or agent of this activity. For Kitcher, this self-consciousness represents the *non-substantial unity* of the "cognizer *per se*", which is "a relation of necessary connection across representations that is understood as such [a non-substantial unity]" (Kitcher 2011:156).[21]

Following these considerations, the psychological interpretation may be articulated by the following three claims:

---

[19] For Kitcher (2011:123–4), the Deduction concerns "not how an individual can attribute a particular mental state to himself" by means of the "I think".

[20] See also Kitcher (2011:139). Kitcher's view has developed over time. In her *Kant's Transcendental Psychology*, Kitcher (1990) rejects the idea of "synthesis-watching" altogether as a non-starter for Kant's argument. Later, Kitcher (1999:348, 368, 373, 377) construes the apperceptive self-consciousness as an "implicit referential self-consciousness", that is, an obscure consciousness of oneself as thinker, without clear grasp of specific mental activities.

[21] In her earlier accounts, Kitcher (e.g., 1984:117, 1990:122, 1999:379) prefers a "sub-personal" or "agent-less" view of the apperceptive synthesis. For critique of this view, see Wunderlich (2005:232–6).

(Psy-1) The apperceptive synthesis is an act of combining representations into a "necessary togetherness", viz. the synthetic unity of apperception, and can be realized by acts of synthesis other than judgements;

(Psy-2) The resulting apperceptive self-consciousness is essentially awareness of the act of apperceptive synthesis, and subsequently the awareness of the apperceiving subject as "non-substantial unity";

(Psy-3) The apperceptive "I think" is the concept that denotes the "belonging to a common 'I'" (viz. the "analytic unity of apperception"), though the concept itself does not have to be present.

There are other accounts of transcendental apperception that emphasize the act of synthesis and appeal to a strong notion of *act-awareness* or *awareness of oneself as agent*, without fully subscribing to the psychological reading as articulated here. Longuenesse, for instance, argues that, in transcendental apperception, "using 'I' in 'I think' expresses the consciousness, by the subject of the activity of thinking, of the unity of the contents of her thoughts, and *thereby* of herself as the agent of that unity" (Longuenesse 2017:81). Yet Longuenesse combines this account with a logical analysis that is more characteristic of the logical reading.[22]

A major advantage of – and the main motivation for – this reading is that it offers a natural explanation for why intuitions are amenable to the conditions of transcendental apperception: the act by which a manifold of intuition is synthesized can carry out an act of apperception if it instantiates the conditions set by transcendental apperception.

The main difficulty of the reading is that it holds that transcendental apperception implies an awareness that is *about* something, namely (1) the synthesizing activity per se, or (2) the agent qua synthesizing activity. This awareness – I argue – is not only difficult to characterize within Kant's classification of representations, but is also difficult to square with Kant's intention in the Deduction (esp. §16).

If apperceptive act-awareness concerns only (1) the synthesizing activity, it is hard to see how transcendental apperception involves self-consciousness and is indeed "a necessary condition for belonging to a common 'I'" (Kitcher 2011:142). If apperceptive act-awareness involves (2) the awareness of the agent qua its synthesizing activity, then it would indeed properly be called *self-consciousness*. This, however, raises the question of how exactly the agent of

---

[22] Longuenesse explains that the consciousness of oneself *as the agent* includes the "assertion of existence" (Longuenesse 2017:94, also 84, 86), which amounts to "the thinker's awareness of being, in virtue of thinking the proposition, the truth-maker of that very proposition" (Longuenesse 2017:82). Similarly, Brook (1994:80) argues that, in apperceptive self-awareness, "I am aware of acts of TA [transcendental apperception] and of myself as their subject." See also Carl (1997).

synthesis is represented in such self-consciousness. One way to spell this out is by appealing to the notion of the *noumenal self* as that which is assumed to underlie all synthetic activity.[23] Kitcher seems reluctant to consider this option, as she sees a proper use for this notion only in the practical realm.[24] But she notices a general difficulty in determining the right kind of representation for apperceptive self-awareness within Kant's taxonomy of representations.[25] Such awareness cannot be a judgement about oneself, since the psychological reading rejects per se that apperception must be an act of judgement. Yet neither can it be an intuition of oneself, since this would involve inner sense. Kitcher grants that apperceptive self-consciousness implies the existence of a thinker only through an intuitive awareness of oneself that is based on inner sense.[26]

In light of this insight, Kitcher comes to the deeply problematic conclusion that transcendental apperception can*not* be the "absolute" transcendental ground of all cognition, but is itself dependent on some sort of empirical self-consciousness and therefore requires empirical apperception via inner sense. While she is puzzled by the fact that Kant never concedes the mutual dependence between transcendental and empirical apperception, she assumes that this might in fact have been Kant's "semiofficial" view.[27] Kitcher's proposal to resolve the problem – appealing to inner sense as another mode of access to oneself or one's mental states – suggests that she feels drawn to construe apperceptive self-awareness as consciousness of the empirical self.

Her reasoning reveals a deeper problem of the psychological reading: by assuming that the transcendental function of apperception depends on an act-awareness that is itself first generated through the apperceptive act, this reasoning runs into a *vicious circle* and undermines the explanatory power of Kant's notion of transcendental apperception. Recall that the transcendental function consists in being a transcendental condition for representing objects, namely in terms of the synthetic unity of all representational elements pertaining to the representation of an object in a single consciousness. On the psychological reading, this synthetic unity is explained by appealing to an awareness of the act by which the dispersed states of empirical consciousness are de facto combined into a unity. This act-awareness is meant to guarantee the "belonging to a common 'I'", but it can only do so by representing the "common 'I'" as *numerically identical* throughout the synthesizing act, that is, as an *analytical* unity. Yet, as Kant unambiguously argues, any analytic unity

---

[23] For example, Wuerth (2014:100ff.).

[24] See Kitcher (2011:178).

[25] See Kitcher (2011:160).

[26] See Kitcher (2011:196). Similarly, Longuenesse (2017:94) grants that apperceptive self-awareness "depends on the *sensation* of thinking", which justifies the "assertion of existence".

[27] See Kitcher (2011:160, also 115).

must presuppose a synthetic one (see B133). Therefore, the awareness *of oneself as being numerically identical* through the act already presupposes an apperceptive synthesis.

This circularity is rooted in the – by and large tacit – assumption that through transcendental apperception a thinker becomes conscious *of herself* and hence features as part of the *content* of the resulting state of consciousness. In Kitcher's specific case, such content is even construed as empirical, namely as concerning the empirical self and based on empirical apperception. The general assumption is in fact shared by the logical interpretation, albeit spelled out in a radically different way. To resolve this problem, I shall argue that the self-consciousness implied in transcendental apperception is *not self-representational*, but a *form* of consciousness.

3.3.3   *The Logical Reading: Transcendental Apperception as Capacity for Self-Ascription*

The logical reading, which primarily appeals to the capacity for self-ascription, prevails in recent literature insofar as most recent accounts focus on the phrase "I think" and draw on some notion of self-ascription.[28] I first articulate a general account of this reading and present some textual evidence from recent literature. I then focus my critique on what I call the logical-subject account. Again, the authors I discuss here may not fully subscribe to the view as I reconstruct it, but show signs of this interpretive tendency.

The logical reading explains the synthesizing function of apperception in terms of the capacity to self-ascribe representations by means of the "I think". The apperceptive synthesis is construed as an *act of judgement* through which the subject recognizes the representations (or representational elements) that are in need of apperception as belonging to itself, the subject. Transcendental apperception brings forth a conceptual consciousness of oneself as thinking subject. This self-consciousness is often understood as a self-ascriptive judgement in which the subject figures as the content of that which is judged about. Depending on exactly what this self-consciousness is taken to be *about*, one can distinguish the following three variants:

- *Noumenal-self account*: Transcendental apperception implies the consciousness of oneself as noumenal self.[29]
- *No-reference account*: Transcendental apperception does not establish reference to anything over and above one's (currently apperceived) representations.[30]

---

[28] For example, Strawson (1966), Brook (1994), Cassam (1997), Carl (1997), Keller (1998), Rosefeldt (2000, 2003), Bird (2006), Howell (2011), Longuenesse (2017).

[29] For example, Wuerth (2014).

[30] For example, Powell (1990), Allison (2004).

- *Logical-subject account*: Transcendental apperception involves consciousness of oneself as the logical subject of predication, also called the "logical I",
that is, whatever is referred to by the "I" of the apperceptive "I think".

The most popular variant is certainly the *logical-subject* account. It centrally
draws on Strawson's notion of a *logical subject*, which he developed in
Individuals (Strawson 1959), independently of his interpretation of Kant.
The logical subject of a judgement (of the generic form "S is P") is that entity
(of whatever kind) to which the subject term ("S") refers and which is then
determined by the predicate ("P"). In his *The Bounds of Sense*, Strawson
construes Kant's transcendental apperception as "criterionless self-
ascription", in contrast to empirical self-ascription (or empirical apperception)
(Strawson 1966:165). By adding "I think" to a representation *p*, I ascribe *p* to
myself as the logical subject of the judgement "I think *p*", without requiring any
criteria for identifying myself. Identification is required for empirical self-
ascription, for which the subject of predication needs to be identified as
a spatio-temporally located and embodied person. Such identification,
Strawson concludes, involves sensibility and requires empirical intuition.

Strawson develops this interpretation in the context of a debate about self-
reference in the analytic philosophy of language, and incorporates an idea that has
later been made popular by Sydney Shoemaker under the name "self-reference
without identification".[31] According to Shoemaker, if a subject is in a certain
psychological state (e.g., of belief, desire, or pain), it enjoys a certain self-
consciousness by which the subject is aware of itself without identifying itself
descriptively via properties. Due to the special character of this self-consciousness
we are unable to err with respect to the person referred to – a phenomenon that
Shoemaker calls "immunity to error through misidentification" (Shoemaker
1968:556–7).

Various Kant commentators cite this debate in their accounts of Kant's
transcendental apperception. Andrew Brook, for instance, explicitly draws on
Shoemaker in arguing that transcendental apperception implies a "nonascriptive reference to oneself as oneself" (Brook 1994:88).[32] For Brook, the
apperceptive "I think" is a "nonascriptive referring expression" that contains
nothing but the "information about the subject ... that it is *me* who is

---

[31] Shoemaker (1968:565). This debate was inspired by Wittgenstein's (1958:66–7) famous
distinction between "two uses of the word 'I'" – the "use as subject" and the "use as object".
While the latter involves the recognition of a particular person and for that matter the
possibility of error (e.g., in the self-ascription of bodily predicates such as "I have a broken
arm"), the former does not raise a question of recognition and therefore leaves no
possibility for going wrong with respect to the person "I" refers to (e.g., in the self-
ascription of mental predicates such as "I feel pain."). Further refinements of this
distinction were suggested by, for example, Castañeda (1967), Lewis (1979), Perry
(1979), Evans (1982), Kaplan (1989).
[32] See Brook (1994:70–94).

representing that object" (of which the apperceived representation is about) (Brook 1994:90). Apperceiving the representation of an object involves this apperceptive awareness of oneself, by which one does not positively identify any (properties of an) entity in the world, except for the property of having the apperceived representation.

Robert Howell draws, in addition to Shoemaker, on Kaplan's theory of the "direct, indexical self-reference via the pronoun 'I'" and on Perry's view of "I" as an "essential indexical".[33] Following Kaplan, Howell argues that Kant's "I think" should be understood as a "mental indexical" that directly designates an entity – without descriptive identification and without "rigid designation".[34] For Howell, Kant's apperceptive "I think" is the mental equivalent of an indexical following the rule that "I" always refers to the thinker, or producer, of the thought in which it occurs.[35] Hence, "the representation 'I' [of transcendental apperception] introduces the self into the content of thought in a direct, propertyless way" (Howell 2001:131), and gives rise to a "genuine first-person self-awareness" (Howell 2001:136).

Although these accounts differ considerably, they share a set of common ideas. Most notably, they all emphasize that transcendental apperception entails *reference* to oneself as the *logical subject*, without identifying this referent or specifying any of its features.[36] The apperceptive "I think" fulfils its transcendental function precisely by adding some positive, albeit *non-empirical and purely logical, content* to the resulting apperceived representations. What this logical content amounts to has been most comprehensively analysed by Tobias Rosefeldt in the context of the Paralogisms.[37] In conceiving of oneself as a logical subject through the representation "I think", Rosefeldt argues, one refers to a *logical something*, that is, an *object of mere thought*, which Rosefeldt aptly calls the "logical I" and the conditions of which are defined by the categories.[38] Applying this to the case of the apperceptive

---

[33] Perry (1979), Kaplan (1989), Howell (1992, 2001).

[34] Howell (2001:126–7). For Kaplan (1989:494, 505), an indexical's referential content is determined by the indexical's *character*, that is, by a semantic rule that accounts for the relation between context and content, and the specific context of its utterance. See 4.3.

[35] Howell (2001:131, 134–6).

[36] That transcendental apperception involves some notion of direct indexical reference also seems important for Carl (1997), Rosefeldt (2000), Bird (2006), and Melnick (2009:35–8, 94f.). Pierre Keller identifies transcendental self-consciousness with an "impersonal (or transpersonal) point of view" that has a "self-referential structure" (Keller 1998:72, 105, 183). For Longuenesse (2012:89–96), Kant's apperceptive "I think" constitutes a referential use of "I" as subject. Yet her account differs from a logical-subject account in arguing that "I think" refers to *the agent of thought*, rather than to a merely logical something (Longuenesse 2017:94, also 82, 86; see 3.4).

[37] Rosefeldt (2000, 2003).

[38] See A290/B346–A292/B348. Rosefeldt draws in particular on Kant's logic lecture, for example, *L-Log/Pölitz* 28:544, and for the "logical I" on *Progress* 20:270. While

"I think", it would mean that by attaching "I think" to a representation, a new representation would result, whose content is expanded by the logical content of the "I think". This logical content would contain at least the content of the concept of "object of mere thought", with an expanded content including the logical predicates of "I". The logical-subject account would clearly reduce the content of the resulting state compared to the psychological reading (which even proposed some sort of empirical content), but nonetheless this minimal logical content is still some representational content that is added to the resulting mental state.

The logical reading of Kant's transcendental apperception may be summarized as follows:

(Log-1) The apperceptive synthesis is construed as an act of judgement by which multiple representational elements are combined in a single consciousness such that the resulting apperceived representation is of an object.

(Log-2) Transcendental self-consciousness is essentially a self-ascription of representations, that is, a judgement of the form "I think *that p*", whereby *p* denotes the apperceived representational content and "I" the logical subject of thought.

(Log-3) The "I" of the apperceptive "I think" refers to the logical subject of the self-ascriptive judgement, that is, whoever is referred to by "I".

3.3.4 Critical Assessment of the Logical-Subject Account

I now argue that the logical-subject account, which appeals to the contemporary debate about self-reference, is insufficient as an interpretation of Kant's transcendental apperception. My main point of critique is that in construing the "I think" as a representation with a *self-referential*, albeit minimal and purely logical content, it is incapable of explaining the transcendental function of apperception and runs counter to the spirit of Kant's Deduction argument.[39]

Kant himself emphasizes that the apperceptive "I think" is empty and lacks content altogether. It is a "simple representation [through which] nothing manifold is given" (B135); it is a "general expression" (B138);[40] it is "wholly empty", that is, without any content, and "purely formal" (A405).[41] It is even

---

Rosefeldt's analysis is greatly instructive for an understanding of the Paralogisms (and will be taken up in 4.3), I argue that it is insufficient for an interpretation of the apperceptive "I think".

[39] I thank Wolfgang Freitag for most helpful discussions of this issue. We jointly developed the general line of critique; see Freitag and Kraus (2020).

[40] See also "the one *I think*" (B140), "the single proposition *I think*" (A342/B400). See also *L-Log/Pölitz* 24:567.

[41] See also "the simple and in content for itself wholly empty representation *I*" (A345–6/B404); "this representation *I* encompasses not the least manifoldness within itself, and . . .

independent of the transcendental conditions of (human) sensibility in general, viz. time and space.[42]

A proponent of the logical-subject account could reply that the requirement of content-emptiness concerns *empirical* content only, to which a purely "logical I" would certainly not contribute. Yet this line of defence will not save the account from its most problematic feature: its assumption of some *self-referential* content contained in the apperceptive "I think", which undermines the transcendental function of apperception in first establishing the very possibility of reference.

The logical-subject account has two basic options to account for the transcendental function of the apperceptive synthesis, that is, for the unification of representational elements into a single thought in a common consciousness, such that this thought represents an object. It can opt either for a higher-order account or for a same-order account. According to the higher-order account, the judgement *I think that p* is understood as a higher-order thought, that is, a thought about the apperceived representation with content *p*. According to the same-order account, through transcendental apperception *I think* is added to the content *p* in a same-order thought such that *I think* is part of any first-order judgement about an object. In either case, transcendentally apperceiving requires the addition of the representational content *I think*. Yet if that is correct, then transcendental apperception is unable to play its transcendental role.

The main thread of my critique is as follows. If transcendental apperception itself exercised its unifying function for the thought *p* by adding the further content *I think* to the thought *p*, then this further content would itself be in need of unification. But this would mean that the augmented thought *I think that p* would itself require an additional synthetic activity that would unify the contents *I think* and *p* into a single whole thought. Depending on whether a higher-order or a same-order account is proposed, either an infinite regress or some sort of circularity is lurking. Let me explain.

If the amplified thought *I think that p* is construed as a higher-order thought, the logical-subject account runs straightforwardly into an infinite regress – under the assumption that the higher-order thought must also be conscious.[43] Then I could only apperceive a thought by apperceiving an infinite series of higher-order thoughts with the contents *I think p*, *I think*

---

is an absolute (though merely logical) unity"; "the simplicity of the representation of the subject"; "the expression 'I', wholly empty of content" (all A355); "consciousness of itself (apperception) is the simple representation of the I" (B68). See also *Anth* 7:134n, 398.

[42] "*I think* is a proposition *a priori*, a mere category of the Subject, intellectual representation without anywhere and anytime, thus not empirical. Whether the category of reality is in it; whether any objective conclusions can be drawn from it" (*Refl* CLX E 48, 23:39, my translation).

[43] A higher-order account may be motivated by Kant's calling the consciousness of pure apperception the consciousness of "reflection" in the *Anthropology* (*Anth* 7:134n, 141).

that I think p, I think that I think that I think that p, etc. Such a construal has been rightly criticized in the history of philosophy, as well as by contemporary theories of self-consciousness, and is deemed to fail.[44] It is hard to see how a finite mind could be capable of exercising an infinite number of mental operations just to become conscious of a single thought. If one allows for the accompanying *I think p* to remain unconscious, then the infinite regress problem would be somewhat mitigated. But to account for the possibility of self-consciousness, one would still have to allow for this thought's becoming conscious and hence for its being apperceived. Both these scenarios would straightforwardly contradict Kant's claim that the apperceptive "I think" is an "original" (i.e., non-derivative) representation that "cannot be accompanied by any further representation" (B132), including by another token of "I think". Otherwise, the first (or for that matter any lower-order) token of "I think" would no longer be original.

If the amplified thought *I think that p* is construed as a same-order thought, then things are more complex. I point out two problems. Firstly, there is a problem for non- or pre-propositional contents. Imagine the case that a thought *p* consists of exactly two elements p_1 and p_2 that need to be unified. Kant's claim that "only because I can comprehend [the] manifold [of an intuition] in a consciousness do I call them all together my representations" (B134) could now be understood literally in the following sense. Apperceiving *p* comes down to a synthetic operation that unifies the two elements of *p* by calling both of them "mine" and by compiling the resulting thoughts *I think that p_1* and *I think that p_2* into the single (same-order) thought *I think that p*.[45] If this construal were correct, then it would require that all representational elements must themselves be able to be part of an "I think *that*"-judgement and hence would already have to be propositional. That is, if transcendental apperception is construed as a series of self-ascriptive judgements regarding the representational elements to be apperceived, then each element must already fulfil the conditions of *discursive* judgement. But then Kant's theory of transcendental apperception could not provide an explanation for why *pre-discursive*, that is, *non-propositional*, elements, such as sensations, can be apperceived in the first place such that they can constitute the matter of empirical judgements. Kant's theory of apperception would be restricted to propositions from the outset. Even if the logical-subject account may find another way of explaining how a manifold of sensation can be unified other

---

[44] For classic critiques of the reflection model of self-consciousness, see Sartre (1943/1948), Henrich (1967, 1976), and Frank (1991, 2012). Moreover, see Shoemaker's (1994) critique of the object-perception model.

[45] If the unified thought is construed as a nested thought of the following form: *I think that [[I think that p_1] and [I think that p_2]]*, then this variant would fall prey to a similar objection as the higher-order account and require the apperception of an infinite series of nested thoughts.

than by a series of *I think*-judgements, there still remains an even worse worry of circularity.

So, secondly, the same-order account appears to offer a circular explanation of the transcendental role of apperception. If the unifying function of transcendental apperception really hinges on the making of a same-order *I think*-judgement, then it follows that the apperceptive synthesis takes place only if such a self-ascriptive judgement is – at least implicitly – actually made. Without the self-ascription of *p* to a logical subject denoted by "I", there would be no unifying synthesis of transcendental apperception and hence no synthetic unity of apperception.[46] Now, self-ascription is itself construed as a judgement that is by definition about some object, albeit only an object of thought, viz. a logical subject. But, again, a self-ascriptive judgement can first have any referential content only if all its components are unified through transcendental apperception in one consciousness. By grounding the transcendental function of apperception in some kind (even if the most minimal kind) of referential content, the same-order account becomes circular. This account appeals to a specific kind of judgement, that is, self-ascription, to explain how transcendental apperception makes judgements in general at all possible, yet without being able to show that such self-ascriptions are in fact possible.

In sum, by construing the apperceptive "I" as a logical subject that features as the object of self-ascriptive thoughts, the logical-subject account turns transcendental self-consciousness into some kind of object-consciousness, rather than proper consciousness of oneself as subject. Transcendental self-consciousness turns out to be consciousness of oneself as the *object* of *I think*-thoughts. Rather than explaining how transcendental apperception grounds the subject–object relation, the logical-subject account applies a notion of self-ascription that already presupposes the well-groundedness of subject–object relations.[47] Some have taken Kant's theory of transcendental apperception to fall prey to this circularity objection.[48] Luckily for Kant, however, the central assumption of the same-order logical-subject account clearly goes against one

---

[46] Brook (1994:90–4) is a notable exception in arguing that the apperceptive synthesis involves only the potentiality for transcendental self-awareness. But by detaching synthesis and self-awareness, he cannot explain how any relation to the self enters into the apperceptive synthesis, if transcendental self-awareness is not realized (on this point, see Keller 1998).

[47] Theories that explain self-consciousness by appeal to a subject-object model have effectively been criticized by, among others, Sartre (1943/1948) and Tugendhat (1979). Tugendhat (1979:50–67) argues that such models illegitimately interweave an identity relation (between that which represents and that which is represented) and an epistemic relation (of the subject to the object). By taking these two relations as mutually grounding one another, subject–object models of self-consciousness lead to circularity.

[48] For example, Tugendhat (1979:50–67). For a defence of Kant against the circularity objection, see Düsing (1997:103–6).

of his central claims, namely that transcendental apperception requires merely that the "*I think* must be *able* to accompany all my representations" (B131, emphasis added), rather than an actual self-ascription. Hence, transcendental apperception must be able to fulfil its transcendental function even in the absence of the "I think" and such function cannot depend on the "I think" being present as a representational content. What exactly "accompanying" means in this connection will become clear in Section 3.5.

3.4   Transcendental Apperception as Form of Reflexive Consciousness

In light of this dialectic between psychological and logical readings, I now develop my own reading of transcendental apperception. My reading consists of three interrelated claims. My *first* claim is that transcendental apperception should be understood as the *transcendental* faculty for consciousness in general: by imposing its characteristic *transcendental form* on suitable representational matter, it produces conscious representations. This form, which can be primarily defined as the *form of consciousness in general*, is the most general necessary condition of any potentially conscious representation. My *second* claim is that for rational beings like us humans, all consciousness is necessarily reflexive, that is, all potentially conscious representations must have a suitable relation to the subject. In a minimal sense, they must be significant representations in that they can mean something *for the subject*. The transcendental form of apperception is, therefore, identified with the *general form of reflexivity*. My *third* claim is that, due to our specific capacity to self-ascribe representations in judgement, the general form of reflexivity must make self-ascriptive judgements possible and hence be – in a sense to be specified – amenable to the forms of such judgements. Hence, transcendental apperception is constitutive of and directed at the capacity for self-ascription, though it is not identical with the latter. In turn, a representation can be significant for a subject only if the subject is *able* to be conscious of it and consequently *able* to self-ascribe it.

The previous discussions of the psychological and the logical reading have shown that transcendental apperception should be reduced neither to a psychological (i.e., non-logical) capacity for self-awareness, nor to a logical capacity for self-ascription. Though neither of these readings is fully adequate, each of them captures an important aspect of transcendental apperception: it can be realized by an act of synthesis other than judgement, as the psychological reading has it, and it is constitutive of our capacity for self-ascription, as the logical reading has it. Transcendental apperception may thus be characterized as a *pre-logical* and *pre-psychological* capacity that is a necessary condition for any mental act leading to a conscious representation, including all logical acts of judgement.

In what follows, I first introduce my reading of transcendental apperception in light of some textual evidence. Then, I show how transcendental apperception grounds the basic *subject–object model* of representation by arguing that its general form of reflexivity is necessary for our capacity to represent objects, regardless of the type of object involved. I defend this reading by a detailed analysis of the argument for apperception in the Deduction, which highlights its significance beyond the context of cognition. Finally, I show why the general form of reflexivity should count as a kind of *self-consciousness*, namely *transcendental self-consciousness*.

3.4.1   Transcendental Apperception as the General Form of Reflexivity

In Chapter 2, I argued that the synthesis of apprehension, which produces empirical consciousness, including perception, is subject to a formal condition. I specified this formal condition simply as the general form of consciousness (see 2.3.2). Now we are in a position to fill out the details of my account.

Firstly, following Kant's claim that transcendental apperception is an original and supreme condition of cognition and "the highest point to which one must affix all use of the understanding" (B134), I argue that transcendental apperception defines the *mere form of consciousness*: the form can be realized by various kinds of mental acts, namely all those acts that lead to conscious representations, including the specific representations that Kant is concerned with in the Deduction, viz. perception and judgement. As original and supreme condition, the form itself can never be subject to determination through a yet higher form of representation.

Kant applies the *form–matter* distinction mainly with respect to mental faculties and their resulting representations. Most notably, he distinguishes the a priori forms of sensibility, that is, space and time, from the matter of intuition, sensation; and the a priori forms of judgement, which give rise to the categories, from the matter of judgements, which is commonly made up of empirical concepts and ultimately of intuitions. Only in a few places does Kant refer to "form" in connection with transcendental apperception (or with the apperceptive "I think"); these are key passages for my interpretation.

In the Paralogisms (A and B), Kant describes the unity of apperception as the "formula of our consciousness" (A354), and, more specifically, as the "formal condition of my thoughts" (A363, also A398) and the "mere form of cognition" (B427). The apperceptive "I think" is, accordingly, considered as representing a "formal proposition of apperception" or just the "form of apperception" (A354). In a notoriously difficult passage introducing the Paralogisms, Kant states that the "I" of "I think" is "a mere consciousness that accompanies every concept" (A346/B404) and that such "consciousness in itself is not even a representation distinguishing a particular object, but rather *a form of representation in general*" (A346/B404, emphasis added).

At the end of the A-Paralogisms, Kant, most explicitly, notes that the "I" is the "mere form of consciousness": "Yet this *I* [which is presupposed in all thinking in general] is no more an intuition than it is a concept of any object; rather, it is *the mere form of consciousness (bloße Form des Bewußtseins)* which accompanies both sorts of representations" (A382, emphasis added). This passage suggests that transcendental apperception defines a form that is applicable to both intuition and concept and, therefore, is more fundamental than either of their genuine forms, that is, space and time, and the categories. It is indeed applicable to any representation of an object, as the *mere form* of consciousness itself.[49]

Secondly, I argue that for thinking beings capable of self-consciousness, such as humans, the mere form of consciousness takes the more specific form of reflexive consciousness or just the *form of reflexivity*. For us, all conscious representation of content must be accessible to self-conscious thoughts and, therefore, must display a suitable relation to the subject who entertains these representations. Without this relation to the subject, a representation "would be nothing for me" and consequently I could neither become conscious of it, nor become conscious of myself having it (B132). To borrow a notion from contemporary phenomenology, the representation would lack *for-me-ness*.[50] Hence, for a representation to have some representational content (of whatever kind), it must fulfil the conditions of reflexive consciousness.

On Kant's hylomorphic account of mental faculties, this reflexive relation can be understood in terms of a general form that is imprinted on all representational contents upon their apprehension into consciousness. This general form of reflexivity is what gives an original-synthetic unity to all apprehended manifolds. By being apprehended according to this general form, the resulting representations have a reflexive relation to the original-synthetic unity to which they belong. Belonging to one and the same consciousness then guarantees the identity of the subject throughout the act of apprehension.

To pre-empt certain terminological confusions, let me clarify my notion of *reflexivity*. My proposal undeniably has similarities with theories of so-called *pre-reflective self-consciousness* (also called *pre-reflexive self-consciousness*).[51] Those theories criticize so-called *reflection models* of self-consciousness according to which self-consciousness is construed as a (conceptual) reflection on a numerically distinct mental state and instead propose that there must be

---

[49] In the *Metaphysical Foundations*, Kant identifies apperception directly with the "faculty of consciousness" (*MFNS* 4:542).

[50] See, for example, Zahavi (2005). The main difference between Kant's account and the phenomenological accounts of *for-me-ness* is that the latter typically take self-consciousness to be minimally *self-representational* (e.g., Kriegel 2009); moreover, they do not draw a necessary link to the capacity for self-ascription, as Kant does.

[51] Most notably, Sartre (1943) and the representatives of the *Heidelberger Schule,* such as Henrich (1967, 1976), Frank (1991, 2011), and more recently phenomenologists, such as Zahavi (2005). On a comparison between Kant's "I think" and Sartre's pre-reflective self-consciousness, see Longuenesse (2017:92–3).

some sort of self-consciousness prior to any reflection. Such self-consciousness – whether construed egologically as consciousness about one-self or non-egologically as "self-less" or impersonal self-consciousness – is, to use common terminology, referred to as *pre-reflective* or *pre-reflexive*, in the sense of *prior to reflection*.[52] I find this terminology potentially misleading and therefore prefer to distinguish clearly between the notions of the *reflexive* (concerning *reflexivity*) and the *reflective* (concerning *reflection*) in the following way. Something is *reflexive* if it has a relation (of a certain kind) to itself. Here in particular I call a representation reflexive if it has a suitable relation to the original-synthetic unity of consciousness to which it belongs and through which it first gains representational significance. A consciousness that is composed of such reflexive representations is then conveniently called a *reflexive consciousness*.[53] By contrast, something is *reflective* if it results from, or consists in, an act of reflection on something *else* that is in some important respect distinct from itself. Accordingly, a reflective representation is a representation of another representation (or representational state) that has resulted from a distinct representational act. In this connection, reflection is commonly understood as conceptual. For instance, my cognizing a cup in front of me can be understood as resulting from a reflection on my perceptual state by means of suitable empirical concepts, resulting in the judgement "This cup is empty." Importantly, the act of perceiving is distinct from the act of judging, or cognizing, and the resulting cognition is a higher-order representation than the perception.

With this distinction in place, I argue, thirdly, that the form of reflexivity can be understood as self-consciousness in a minimal sense. Such self-consciousness is *non-representational*, since – as a mere form – it does not have any representational content concerning the subject (neither with regard to an individual thinker, nor to a generic thinking subject).[54] Rather, it requires an act of reflection upon the original-synthetic unity of apperception to

---

[52] While the notion *pre-reflexive* is often used in the German-speaking debate (e.g., Frank 1991), the Anglophone debate largely prefers the notion of *pre-reflective* self-consciousness (e.g., Jacob 2019). On the distinction between egological and non-egological self-consciousness, see Düsing (1997).

[53] Note that I construe *reflexivity* primarily as a self-relation at the level of representations, and secondarily as a relation to the subject. Similarly, Kant moves from a representation's "belong[ing] to a self-consciousness" to its "belong[ing] to me" as the subject or producer of the representation (B132).

[54] My interpretation shares similarities with Henrich's (1967) account of "*präreflexivem Selbstbewusstsein*", which he famously attributes to Fichte (and later also to Kant). Yet my interpretation differs in crucial respects. My hylomorphic reading of transcendental apperception as a mere *form* of reflexivity leads me to conclude that transcendental self-consciousness is *non-representational*, rather than minimally representational, as is Henrich's "pre-reflexive self-consciousness", which even includes the consciousness of one's diachronic identity.

generate representational kinds of self-consciousness. Most basically, such a reflection consists in reflecting on the "common mark" of all apperceived representations within an original-synthetic unity. This common mark just is their belonging to one and the same unity of consciousness. The concept that captures precisely this common mark is the "I think". Attaching the "I think" to an apperceived representation can now be understood as the additional act of conceiving of the original-synthetic unity *as a unity*, namely as what Kant calls the *analytic unity of apperception*. When Kant speaks, in §16, of calling my representations "mine" or of becoming conscious of my representations as "my own" (B134–5), I take him to refer precisely to this additional act of reflection, which is derivative of the fundamental act of apperception. In consequence, the general form of reflexivity is also a necessary condition of all kinds of *reflective* or *determinate self-consciousness*, and eventually also mediates a *self-referential* relation to the subject of apperception.

Hence, in yielding the general form of reflexive consciousness, transcendental apperception grounds the basic *subject–object model of representation*, as I introduced it in Chapter 1 (see 1.2). This form defines the formal relations that a representation has to the representing subject, on the one hand, and to the object represented, on the other. It thus makes possible both representations of the subject (in reflective self-consciousness) and representations of objects. With his conception of transcendental apperception, Kant draws a necessary link between his theory of self-consciousness and his theory of referentiality (to objects). As a mere form, transcendental apperception can only be actualized upon being presented with some suitable representational matter.

My interpretation of Kant's transcendental apperception as the form of reflexivity (Reflex-) can then be summarized as follows:

(Reflex-1) The apperceptive synthesis is realized in any mental act that results in a conscious representation of an object in the generic sense (including perceptions and judgements). It does so by unifying the involved representational matter according to the *general form of reflexivity*.

(Reflex-2) Transcendental self-consciousness is essentially this *general form of reflexivity*, that is, the form according to which all mental contents have to relate to the subject to be significant *for the subject* and hence potentially conscious.

(Reflex-3) The apperceptive "I think" *merely conceptually expresses* transcendental self-consciousness, without determining the subject as the content of a representation.

In what follows, I explicate and defend (Reflex-1) and (Reflex-2). In Section 3.5, I will then focus on (Reflex-3) and show how my interpretation accounts for specific characteristics of the "I think".

3.4.2   *Transcendental Apperception as the Origin of Referentiality*

Let us now turn to my central claim (Reflex-1) that the apperceptive synthesis is realized in any mental act that results in the conscious representation of an object in the generic sense. Recall, from Chapter 1, that I called such a representation *significant* for a subject and its relation to an object in general *reference*. (Reflex-1) can be more pointedly expressed as the thesis that *reflexivity is a necessary condition of referentiality*. For any representation to have an object in general, it must meet the condition of reflexivity and gain representational content *for a subject*.

My argument for this claim consists in developing a "broad reading" of the argument *for* apperception, viz. the Unity Argument in §16 of the B-Deduction, considering a broad range of representations that fall under the conditions articulated in this argument. I do not dispute that the aim of the full Deduction is to reveal the transcendental conditions of the *cognition* of objects given in intuition. Nonetheless, I submit that the Unity Argument is applicable not only narrowly to cognition and cognitively significant representations, but also more broadly to all kinds of significant representations, including pre- and non-cognitive states such as perceptions and desires. This argument thus reveals the most general condition of the possibility of *significant* representations *überhaupt* and hence of referentiality. Yet, to be sure, this reading is controversial and requires further support, which I now provide.

The central task for me is to show that, while the Deduction argument as a whole is specifically concerned with the transcendental conditions of *objectively valid* representations of sensible objects, that is, cognitions, the Unity Argument reveals more general conditions of significant representations, including both objectively and *merely subjectively valid* representations. Recall from Chapter 1 that for a representation to have an object at all, it does not have to be objectively valid (see 1.2). Rather, its representational content can be influenced by the specific conditions under which the representation itself is produced or had by a particular representer, for instance, by the spectator's specific visual perspective or by some sensory impairment, such as a hearing deficit. In these cases, the representation is (to some extent) merely subjective, representing features that are due to the condition of the subject, rather than due to the object alone. It is widely acknowledged that the Deduction argument is meant to reveal the transcendental conditions of how we come to represent objects in an objectively valid way and hence gain empirical cognition of it. It shows how my subjective intuition of the desk in front of me can contribute objectively valid content to an empirical cognition of the desk, for instance with regard to its spatio-temporal location or other objective features. My task is to show that the Unity Argument applies also to those representations that are significant for the subject, though they are not theoretical cognitions of objects. Here I have in mind *non-theoretical* representations, such as practical judgements concerning one's actions, and aesthetic judgements, as well as merely subjective representations, such as perceptions, imaginings, desires, and feelings. All these representations refer to objects in a generic sense, such as objects of the senses, fictional objects, objects of desire, or – in the case of feeling – the subject's relation to some representational content. In order for those representations to be at all significant for the subject, they have to be subject to transcendental apperception.[55]

What makes my interpretation controversial is that most commentators consider transcendental apperception as necessarily and sufficiently linked with categorial determination, whereas my interpretation suggests only a necessary link. Many commentators conceive of the synthesis of apperception as *necessarily* – and for that matter *exclusively* – realized through the categorial syntheses. Allison, for instance, calls this relation the *reciprocity* between apperception and the categories.[56] These commentators base their reading on passages such as the following from §17 (B-Deduction):

> Consequently the unity of consciousness is that *which alone constitutes the relation of representations to an object*, thus [*mithin*; consequently] their *objective validity*, and consequently is that which makes them into cognitions and on which even the possibility of the understanding rests.
>
> (B137, emphasis added)

This passage is often taken to imply that the original-synthetic unity of apperception is the necessary and sufficient condition ("alone") of cognition of objects and that the Deduction does not allow for other kinds of "relation of representations to an object" that do not have objective validity and that are therefore not (yet) cognition of an object.[57]

Yet this reading is not without alternatives. While I certainly agree that the Deduction argument eventually shows that transcendental apperception is a transcendental condition of cognition, and that cognition is necessarily categorially determined, the argument does not appeal to the demanding

---

[55] Kant suggests that apperception is necessary for practical cognition "in order to subject *a priori* the manifold of desires to the unity of consciousness of a practical reason" (*CpracR* 5:65).

[56] Allison (2004:174–5); see also Kemp Smith (1930:285), Paton (1936 I:502), Strawson (1966:96), Henrich (1994:34), Schulting (2012), Allison (2015:352). By contrast, Keller (1998:78–82, also 114) is one of the few commentators who explicitly distinguish the condition attributed only to transcendental apperception from that attributed to the objectively valid application of the categories. For an insightful discussion, see Wunderlich (2005).

[57] Allison (2004), Schulting (2012). Allison (2015:353) distinguishes between an "object in the 'thick' sense" as an object of possible experience, and an "object in the 'thin' sense" as an object of thought. Yet his "thin" notion of an object is still "thicker" than my generic notion of an object, which also includes objects of representations that are neither judgments, nor in any other way conceptual.

notion of *object of cognition* from the outset. Rather, in §16 (and to some extent §17), I submit, Kant still operates with a more general definition of an object as that which is related to a subject *via any* representation (e.g., mere appearances or objects of intuition), whereas in §§18–19 he specifies the object as that which must be reflected under concepts in judgements (i.e., object as thought *under* concepts). I take it to be a first conclusion of the Deduction argument to specify those objects that are amenable to cognition, rather than to start from the outset with the premise that what can be an object for us must be determined according to the categories.

The passage above can more naturally be read in the following way: the original-synthetic unity is a necessary condition for a unity of representations to become an objective unity and hence to represent an object of cognition. Yet it is *not* a sufficient condition of cognition, from which the objective validity of the original-synthetic unity would analytically follow.[58] That objective validity requires a further condition is indicated by *mithin*, which is better translated as "consequently". On this reading, transcendental apperception does not analytically entail the forms of judgement, although the categorial syntheses of the understanding can be realized only through an original-synthetic unity. That means, the understanding *can* determine an object of intuition only if the corresponding sensory matter upon which it imposes its categorial forms is unified in one consciousness. This second condition of cognition is argued for only in §§18–19. Hence, transcendental apperception is a necessary, but not sufficient, condition for the *possibility* of the understanding as the capacity to judge.

My reading of transcendental apperception as a transcendental condition of representing objects in general, rather than only categorially determined objects, is primarily supported by the fact that §16, in which the Unity Argument is mainly presented, does not make any positive reference to objects at all. This suggests that the argument *for* transcendental apperception does not depend on specifying the kind of relation that a subject maintains to its object.[59] Moreover, Kant's appeal to "intuition" here can be understood in a generic sense as a "representation that can be given prior to all thinking" (B132), which I take to refer to all non-conceptual representations, including feelings, if one allows for a broad conception of inner receptivity (see 1.5). The identity of apperception, Kant explicitly states, "precedes a priori all *my* determinate thinking", which I take to include any determination of intuitions according to the categories (B134).

---

[58] Keller (1998:80) and Longuenesse (1998:185) are among the few to point out that the synthetic unity of apperception is not a sufficient condition for cognition.

[59] In a similar vein, Hoppe reads the apperceptive synthesis as establishing an "intentional object-relation *(intentionale Gegenstandsbeziehung)*" (Hoppe 1983:44, 117ff.). Keller (1998:3, also 66–71) also allows for a broader notion of representational content that has cognitive relevance, without being necessarily objectively valid.

Only in §17 does Kant consider, more narrowly, the principle of the synthetic unity of apperception for "all use of the understanding", which is then understood as the capacity to cognize sensible objects (B136). This principle concerns, more specifically, the manifold of intuition that stands "under the formal conditions of space and time" (B136). The task of §17 is to narrow down the formerly unspecified relation to the object as a "determinate relation", which, as Kant makes clear in the next sentence, should be understood as conceptually determined: "An *object*, however, is that in the concept of which the manifold of a given intuition is *united*" (B137).[60] To relate to an object as conceptually determined has the same requirements, as Kant goes on to argue, as any other kind of relation to an object, namely "unification of representations" and hence "unity of consciousness in the synthesis of them" (B137). Then the passage cited above follows. Considering this subtle distinction between a *relation to an object in general* and a *conceptually determined relation to an object*, we can now understand this passage as follows. The original-synthetic unity of apperception establishes a relation to an object of any kind. Applied to the understanding, it establishes specifically a conceptually determined relation to an object, which can be said to be *objectively valid*.

The definition of an object as "that in the concept of which the manifold of a given intuition is united" (B137) is still ambiguous as to the exact use of the term *concept*. To use Longuenesse's terminology, a concept can be used as (1) the "'consciousness of the unity of the act' of grasping together a sensible manifold", that is, a rule that governs the synthesis of a manifold of intuition; or as (2) the "reflection of this 'unity of act'" in judgement, that is, a predicate that is instantiated by the object.[61] The former use (1) would concern objects of intuition, which result from the concept-guided synthesis of a sensible manifold; the latter use (2) would concern objects of judgement that result from reflection *under* a concept. Kant's aim in the Deduction, of course, is to eventually show that these two kinds of objects – objects of intuition and objects of judgement – can be one and the same, namely an object of empirical cognition (or of possible experience). So he goes on to argue:

> The synthetic unity of consciousness is therefore an *objective condition* of all cognition, not merely something I myself need in order to cognize an object but rather something under which every intuition must stand in order *to become an object for me*, since in any other way, and without this synthesis [of apperception], the manifold would *not* be united in one consciousness. (B138, emphasis added)[62]

---

[60] See Kant's definitions of "objective validity" (in the A-Deduction, also "objective reality") as the *relation of a cogniser to an object* (see A109, B138, B141).

[61] Longuenesse (1998:69); see also Longuenesse (1998:50). See 2.4.2.

[62] See A-Deduction: "without that sort of unity [of apperception], ... the manifold perceptions ... would then belong to no experience, and would consequently be without

Again, I read this passage as stating that a synthetic unity of apperception is a necessary condition for something to "become an object for me" in general, regardless of whether it is an object of intuition or an object of judgement.[63] The purpose of apperception is unification in one consciousness, not determination according to the categories. Only if every intuition is subject to the same general condition of apperception as every judgement, can intuition at all provide suitable representational content for a categorial determination.

The next step in the Deduction of the Categories is then to show that intuitions are unified through a sensible synthesis in such a way that they are amenable to an objectively valid determination, that is, to reflection under a concept in a judgement. This step finally proceeds in §19. Here Kant argues that the only way to determine the relation of one's representations to the object in an "objectively valid" way is via "*judgment*, i.e., a relation that is *objectively valid*" (B142). In a judgement, I combine representations, say the concepts of <rose> and <red>, in such a way that they represent a connection in the object, for instance in the red rose I see in front of me. If I can do so "regardless of any difference in the condition of the subject" (B142), then the resulting judgement is indeed objectively valid.[64]

If the unity of apperception is to lead to cognition, which must be objectively valid, then it must be realized in accordance with the universally valid, logical forms of judgement. Hence, "a judgment is nothing but the manner of bringing given cognitions to the *objective* unity of apperception" (B141). A judgement is thus a particular way of realizing the original-synthetic unity of apperception in accordance with the logical forms of judgement and hence as an objectively valid unity. Those forms are a further transcendental condition of cognition – a condition that is indeed necessary *and* sufficient for cognition to be objectively valid. In consequence, intuitions can be cognitively significant (as providing the content for cognition), only if their manifolds can be unified in accordance with the logical forms of judgement as to present a cognizable object.

---

object, and would be nothing but a blind play of representations, i.e., less than a dream" (A112).

[63] In some places, Kant alludes to a generic notion of *object* that is not yet determined by judgement, for example, "one can, to be sure, call everything, and even every representation, insofar as one is conscious of it, an object" (A189/B234). That is, for something to count as an object it must fulfil only the general condition of consciousness. Cramer (1985:324) calls this notion a "reduced meaning of object".

[64] The fact that a judgement is objectively valid does not mean that it is in fact true of an object. It is controversial whether Kant can allow for *merely subjective* judgements, for instance what he calls "judgments of perception" (*Prol* 4:298). In §19, Kant himself contrasts a subjective judgement ("I feel the pressure of weight") with an objective judgement ("The body is heavy"). My reading suggests that Kant's argument just requires that a judgement is the *only* representation that *can* be objectively valid, but it may not be so in all cases. On subjectively valid representations, see 3.4.3.

Now, the categories are precisely the "concepts of an object in general, by means of which its intuition is regarded as *determined* with regard to one of the *logical functions* for judgment" (B128). Kant concludes in §20 that "the manifold of given intuition is determined with regard to them [the categories]" (B143). For instance, my perception of the red rose must be such that it gives me the right kind of sensible content to make an objectively valid judgement about it. I must be able to *see something* in accordance with the category of substance and hence as endowed with certain accidents such as <being a rose> and <being red> in order to judge *that this object (of my current perception) is a red rose.*

The Deduction finally shows that the understanding – in its real use – unifies sensibly given content through the categories. At this point, it is still unclear how exactly the categories are supposed to guide this unification; that is, how the categories serve as the rule of sensible synthesis of a sensible manifold. This is explained only in the second part of the Deduction, especially §§24 and 26 (which I have already discussed in 2.4) and in the Schematism (which I will discuss in 5.5).

Here my aim was only to show that the Unity Argument should be understood as an argument *for* transcendental apperception as the general condition of representing objects in a generic sense, which does not yet involve categorial determination. It shows that any representational content of which a subject can be conscious, including desires, aesthetic judgements, and arguably even feelings, must be subject to the general form of reflexivity. This form is, therefore, a necessary condition of referentiality *überhaupt.* As a general form it can be realized by different kinds of synthesis resulting in representations of different kinds of objects. The function of the Unity Argument for the Deduction of the Categories hinges specifically on the insight that this form can be realized both by objectively valid judgements and by sensible intuitions. If applied to spatio-temporal sensible matter in particular, the general form of reflexivity turns into a condition of possibility of cognition and is then, properly speaking, a *transcendental form.*

My discussion so far has concerned only the "objective side" of the Unity Argument, arguing for transcendental apperception as a necessary condition of the capacity to represent objects. Yet there is also a "subjective side" to it that draws a necessary link from transcendental apperception to the consciousness of the identity of the subject and eventually to our capacity for self-ascription. The full Unity Argument thus shows that transcendental apperception grounds both object-consciousness and self-consciousness. I now turn to this subjective side and explore transcendental apperception as a condition of self-consciousness.

3.4.3   From Reflexive Consciousness to Reflective Self-Consciousness

Let us now explore my claim (Reflex-2) that the general form of reflexivity is a *transcendental self-consciousness.* In §16, Kant draws an inference from the synthesis of apperception to the capacity to call representations *"my* representations" or to be conscious of them as "belong[ing] *to me*" (B132–5). This suggests that, for Kant, transcendental apperception must be directed at the capacity for self-consciousness and eventually for self-ascription, though it is itself not identical with the latter. For beings capable of self-consciousness, any conscious representation must be such that the subject is able to be conscious of itself as having this representation and hence to self-ascribe the representation in judgement. If the general form of reflexivity were not directed at self-ascription, then it could not guarantee that any conscious representation is accessible through reflection. Rather, there could in principle be conscious representations, and even representations that are significant for me, even though I would not be able at all to call them *mine*. This clearly runs counter to Kant's intentions in §16. Self-ascription, I suggest, is an act of reflection upon my own state by which I turn a representation of mine, *R*, itself into the object of my consciousness and thereby produce the higher-order judgement about this representation, namely the judgement *I think R*. I thus thematize my own state, rather than an external object.

Although self-consciousness is not the main theme of the Deduction, we find further evidence for Kant's theory of self-consciousness in the two sections specifically devoted to this issue, namely §18 and §25. These sections explicate the kind of self-consciousness that Kant takes to be implied by transcendental apperception and distinguish it from other kinds of self-consciousness. Here I focus on §18, but I say more about §25 in Section 3.5.

In §18, Kant famously distinguishes the "objective unity of self-consciousness" from a mere "subjective unity of consciousness" (B139) and writes:

> The transcendental unity of apperception is that unity through which all of the manifold given in an intuition is united in a concept of the object. It is called *objective* on that account, and must be distinguished from the *subjective unity* of consciousness, which is a *determination of inner sense*, through which that manifold of intuition is empirically given for such a combination.   (B139)

This distinction raises the issue of *subjective validity*. This passage is commonly read as suggesting that the "transcendental unity of apperception" is necessarily identical with the "objective unity of self-consciousness" and for that reason opposed to the "subjective unity of consciousness".[65] The latter is empirical and merely subjectively valid for a particular subject, because it is based on the "association of representations", rather than the universally valid laws of logic (B140). Given what I have argued so far, I suggest a different

---

[65] Commentators who explicitly identify the transcendental with the objective unity of consciousness (and contrast it with subjective unity) include Kemp Smith (1930:285), Paton (1936 I:502), Strawson (1966:97ff.), Allison(2004:87–9, 173–8, 182–5), and more recently, Schulting (2012). Exceptions are Cramer (1985:325) and Hoppe (1983:119ff., 210ff.). Again, Hoppe's reading comes closest to my interpretation.

reading of this passage: the synthetic-original unity is called "objective" here only "on that account" that considers specifically cognition. Yet for any representation to have some representational content for me (even if merely subjective content) it must be subject to transcendental apperception. Only through apperception can it become part of *my own* subjective unity of consciousness.

I find my reading indicated by the derivation claim that Kant states with regard to the "empirical unity of apperception" a few lines below:

> That unity [of transcendental apperception] alone is objectivity valid; the empirical unity of apperception, which we are not assessing here, and which is also derived only from the former, under given conditions *in concreto*, has merely subjective validity (B140).

The empirical unity of apperception I take to be the unity of representations of which I am *de facto* empirically conscious of as *my own*. Kant claims that such unity, while merely subjective and based on a "determination of inner sense", is "derived only from" the original-synthetic unity of apperception. Admittedly, this derivation claim is not of any major importance for Kant's present task, in the Deduction, of justifying the applicability of the categories to intuitions. To understand this derivation claim requires us to consider Kant's broader theory of *empirical consciousness*.

Empirical consciousness includes all the representations of which I am conscious through inner sense (e.g., perception). These representations are the candidates for what I can call *mine*. To be sure, empirical consciousness as such does not have to fulfil the standards of objective validity, defined by the logical forms of judgement.[66] For instance, I can be empirically conscious of my dream upon awakening and think about its meaning, although the dream is produced through a merely associative synthesis of the imagination.[67] In the *Prolegomena*, Kant infamously introduces "judgments of perception", which he claims to be merely subjectively valid (*Prol* 4:298), such as the claim that *the room is warm for me*. While there is a controversy as to whether these should be counted as judgements in the proper sense and whether (and if so, in which sense) they depend on the logical forms of judgement, it seems eminently plausible that we can be conscious of such judgements and that they can be part of my empirical consciousness.[68] As judgements about the "modifications

---

[66] See, for example, the distinction between two kinds of representations with consciousness (*perceptio*), namely subjective *sensatio* and objective *cognitio* in the *Stufenleiter* passage (A320/B377).

[67] Kant's claim that without transcendental apperception a representation would be "less than a dream" (A112) suggests that he grants some representational significance to dreams, while acknowledging that they are not objectively valid.

[68] Beck (1978:50) and Guyer (1987:100), for instance, hold that judgements of perception are not based on the application of the categories and therefore do not comply with the definition of judgement in the *Critique*. By contrast, Longuenesse (1998:167–97) argues that the categories are involved in judgements of perception, but only in their logical use:

of the subject's state" (A320/B376), they will later be considered as self-ascriptions of the subject's state, for example, the feeling of warmth.

On various occasions, Kant distinguishes between transcendental and empirical consciousness.[69] According to my general hylomorphic account of mental faculties, we can understand transcendental consciousness as the formal aspect of consciousness. It concerns the forms in which any representational matter must be apprehended to generate conscious representations. The matter stems from the factual "modifications of the mind [that] belong to inner sense" (A99). In the *Anthropology*, Kant considers the distinction between "having a representation" and "being conscious of a representation" (*Anth* 7:135). For instance, I can have various sensations of a person's face from a distance, without having a conscious representation of this face. The former means the mere presence of a representation "in" inner sense, whereas the latter additionally involves its *apprehension* into the subject's empirical consciousness and hence its salience to inner perception (see *Anth* 7:134n).[70] For empirical consciousness in general, there is, firstly, the *material* condition of some existing representational *matter*, for example, sensation, that is to be synthesized into a conscious representation, and, secondly, the *formal* condition of apprehending such matter into consciousness. With my interpretation of transcendental apperception, we can now see that the formal condition just is the form of reflexive consciousness. Any act of apprehension must be in accordance with the general form of reflexivity, and a representation can be part of empirical consciousness, only if it instantiates this form. This reading is explicitly supported in the following passage of the A-Deduction: "all empirical consciousness ... has a necessary relation to a transcendental consciousness (preceding all particular experience), namely the consciousness of myself as original apperception" (A117n). Here, Kant explicates transcendental consciousness as both a necessary condition of *all* empirical consciousness and as a kind of self-consciousness, namely "the consciousness of myself as original apperception", which I identify as *transcendental self-consciousness*.

How exactly does transcendental self-consciousness give rise to the capacity to call representations *mine* and eventually to the capacity to ascribe them to myself in judgement? In §16, Kant gives a hint that this requires us first to "represent *the identity of consciousness in these representations* itself", that is the "thoroughgoing identity of apperception", which Kant renders just as the

---

their formal structure corresponds to the logical forms of judgement, but their representational content is not (yet) determined by the categories. Furthermore, see Hoppe (1983:29–44), Allison (2004:179–80), and Lee (2012:235, 268–70).

[69] For example, A107, *Anth* 7:135, 141.

[70] See also "representation with consciousness (*perceptio*)" (A320/B376); "to represent something with consciousness, or to perceive (*percipere*)" (*L-Log/Jäsche* 9:64); A197/B242. On synthesis of apprehension, see 2.3.2.

"identity of the subject" (B133). Thus, in addition to the act of apperception, we must generate a representation of that which is common to all our apperceived representations. This common mark is, according to my analysis, the general form of reflexivity and – if applied *in concreto* – the fact of belonging to one and the same synthetic unity of consciousness. This common mark is precisely represented by the "I think", which is identical with the "analytical unity of apperception" (B133).[71] This is in line with Kant's claims that the analytic unity always presupposes a synthetic one, and that, while its possibility follows analytically from the original-synthetic unity of apperception, the analytic unity itself is not necessarily represented in each act of apperception.[72] In many cases, we consciously represent an object, say the train arriving at the platform, yet we rarely consciously represent the identical subject as the common reference point of our series of train-intuitions. Even more seldom do we carry out a full reflection upon our current state and make a higher-order self-ascriptive judgement. The analytic unity of apperception is merely a conceptual expression, but not yet a judgement. But if it is viewed as a judgement and analysed according to the categories, one can derive the logical conditions of self-ascription, as I will argue in Chapter 4.

With regard to the derivation claim, we can now see that the empirical unity of apperception – the unity of all representations of which I am de facto conscious as *my own* – requires not only an original-synthetic unity into which all these representations are combined to be conscious at all, but also the analytic unity as the representation of their common subject, *myself.* Hence, the empirical unity of apperception is "derived only from" the transcendental unity of apperception, as Kant claims in §18.

This leaves us, finally, with the question of what we are conscious of in transcendental self-consciousness – the kind of self-consciousness implied in transcendental apperception. My analysis suggests that transcendental self-consciousness just is the general form of reflexivity. It should, therefore, *not* be understood as the perspectival, first-personal consciousness *of* an individual thinker. Rather, it is the non-perspectival, non-individual form of self-consciousness, which becomes a perspectival self-consciousness of an individual only through its instantiation in an act of significant representation by a being capable of self-conscious thought.[73]

---

[71] For Kant, an analytical unity is commonly identified with the unity that is brought about through a concept that represents "that which is common to *several*" (that is, as a "*conceptus communis*", B133-4n, also A79/B105). Allison (2015:258) renders the analytical unity as "one in many", as opposed to the synthetic unity that is "many in one".

[72] Kant calls the principle of apperception an "analytical proposition" (B135, also B138).

[73] Keller (1998) similarly argues that transcendental apperception marks an impersonal, global, numerically identical point of view, rather than an individual perspective; see also Henrich (1994).

How then do individuation and the consciousness of one's individual self enter Kant's theory of apperception? I finally turn to the apperceptive "I think" as expression of individual self-presence.

3.5   The Expression "I Think" and Self-Reference

3.5.1   The Apperceptive "I Think" as an Expression

We are now finally in the position to understand the third aspect of my view that concerns the phrase "I think". On the view proposed here, the apperceptive "I think" is an *expression* of transcendental self-consciousness, without determining the subject as the content of a representation (see Reflex-3 in 3.4.1). Such an explicit expression of transcendental self-consciousness *can* be attached to an apperceptive act, but it does not have to be. My view is, roughly, that the apperceptive "I think", if attached to an apperceived representation, expresses the representation's relation to its original-synthetic unity of apperception and hence to the apperceiving subject. Yet it does *not* express the thought *that* a thinking subject or a particular thinker apperceives it. My view is inspired by a position in contemporary philosophy of language called *expressivism*, as I explain in more detail below.[74]

My central task here is to explicate the sense in which "I think" is an *expression*, as opposed to a *representation* of something determinate (or at least determinable). A mere expression, I submit, does not determine any representational content – neither logical nor empirical – though it may signify something in an indeterminate way. It is *expressive of* some aspect of a subject's state of mind that cannot be fully grasped by a determinate representation. In what follows, I first give some textual evidence for an expressivist reading of the "I think" and introduce Kant's own use of the notion *expression*. I then briefly outline a contemporary theory of expressivism and apply it to Kant's "I think".

An expressivist reading is suggested by Kant's own phrasing in passages such as the following:

the general expression *I think*   (B138)

I think expresses the act (*Actus*) of determining my existence   (B157n)

the proposition that expresses self-consciousness: *I think*   (A398–9)

[the subject] is designated merely through the expression "I", wholly empty of content.   (A354–5)

---

[74] This interpretation was inspired by and has resulted from joint work with Wolfgang Freitag; for a more detailed account of this expressivist interpretation of Kant's "I think", see Freitag and Kraus (2020).

Moreover, Kant concludes the A-Paralogisms with the remark that the representation "I am", which is derived from the "I think", "expresses (indeterminately) what is purely formal in all my experience" (A405). Furthermore, Kant explicitly denies that the apperceptive "I think" is "a concept of a thinking being in general" (A354). That means that it does not serve as a concept by which something is determined and that can be used for predication, such as the empirical concept <apple> or the pure concept <substance>. Considering the apperceptive "I think" as a concept of *something*, Kant argues, inevitably leads to paralogisms, as I will discuss in Chapter 4. Instead, Kant suggests, "I think" is only a "vehicle of all concepts whatsoever", which "serves only to introduce all thinking as belonging to consciousness" (A341/B399-400).[75]

Kant employs the notions of *expression* (*Ausdruck*) and *to express* (*ausdrücken*) in a variety of ways. For instance, an empirical concept expresses a rule of subsumption, and a pure concept of the understanding "expresses [a] formal and objective condition of experience" (A96, see also A142). In another sense, a word is commonly a linguistic "expression designating a determinate concept" (*CJ* 5:316, also 5:351-2). In the *Critique of the Power of Judgment*, Kant uses "expression", more specifically, as opposed to a "determinate representation". For instance, he states that "sensation" "expresses the merely subjective aspect of our representations, [... i.e.,] the material (the real) in them" (*CJ* 5:189). The feelings of gratitude, pleasure, or esteem are expressions that designate, respectively, "[t]he agreeable, the beautiful, and the good" (*CJ* 5:209). Moreover, Kant considers artistic expressions, such as painting and poetry, as expressions of aesthetic or moral ideas that transcend our cognitive capacities (*CJ* 5:321-30). The core meaning of these uses of "expression" is that, if we do not have available a determinate concept, we may use an *expression*, such as sensible symbols, artwork, or metaphorically used words, to present something to the mind in an *indeterminate* way.[76] In this way, we can give an expression to something that we cannot fully put into determinate language and still make ourselves understood by others. We aim "to express what is unnameable in the mental state ... and to make it universally communicable" (*CJ* 5:317). In such cases, words can be used as

[75] See also "The *I*, the general correlate of apperception, ... designates ... a thing of undetermined meaning" (*MFNS* 4:542); "the *I* is not a concept" (*Prol* 4:334), adding in a footnote: "If the representation of apperception, the *I*, were a concept through which anything might be thought, it could then be used as a predicate for other things, or contain such predicates in itself" (*Prol* 4:334).

[76] I take these uses of "expression" to fit the general distinction between presentation (or exhibition, *Darstellung*) and representation (*Vorstellung*) (see, e.g., *CJ* 5:351-4). In expressing some content, the subject presents, or exhibits, that content immediately and actually to the mind. In various cases, Kant invokes the idea that *presenting* certain contents to the mind is a necessary condition for *representing something* through these contents that may not (or cannot) be presently available to the mind (see also 5.5).

"indirect presentations" (or "symbols") to express and indeed designate something without determining it (*CJ* 5:351–2).[77] In a similar vein, I suggest that the
"I think" is an expression of the subject's state of mind, rather than
a determinate representation. It is expressive of a representation's "belonging
to consciousness" (A341/B399–400) and hence "designate[s]" the subject "only
transcendentally" and "wholly empty of content" (A355).

To explain my expressivist reading of the "I think", I introduce
a contemporary theory of expressivism.[78] According to *expressivism*, the
utterance of a sentence expresses a mental state.[79] For instance, the utterance
"The rose is red" can be used to express the belief *that the rose is red*; and the
utterance "Pass me some ice-cream, please" to express a desire *to have some
ice-cream*. In these cases, the semantic content of the uttered sentence coincides with the content of the mental state expressed. Utterances such as "I think
p", "I believe *p*", or "I wish *p*" are special in this respect, since they can express
either the thought, belief, or wish – with content *p* – or the self-ascription of
such thought, belief, or wish. Commonly such utterances are used to express
just the representational content *p*, and the phrases "I think", "I believe", or "I
wish" merely indicate the kind of relation the subject has to the uttered
representational content. This relation is often called the *propositional attitude*.
Note the crucial distinction between the *semantic content* of the uttered
sentence, which includes the content of "I think", etc., and the *representational
content* of the state expressed, that is, the state of thought, belief, or wish. In this
common use, the phrases such as "I think", etc., function only as what one
might call a "mental-force indicator", indicating the *force* of the mental state
expressed.[80]

---

[77] For discussion, see Makkreel (1990:122–8). I will say more about the "symbolic presentation" of ideas of reason in 5.5.
[78] I follow Wolfgang Freitag's (2018) version of psychological expressivism. Expressivism is
inspired by Austin's (1962) view of performative utterances (or just *performatives*) used to
perform an action. If the statement "I promise that I'll come to your party" is used to make
a promise, then the phrase "I promise that" makes explicit what the use of the statement is
without changing the action thereby performed, that is, the promise. It can be called an
explicit performative. Had this phrase "I promise that" been left unsaid, it would not have
changed the performance. For expressivist accounts of I-statements, see also Finkelstein
(2003) and Bar-On (2004).
[79] Note that "express" describes a non-factive relation between a subject and a mental state:
a speaker can express a mental state without being in it (see Austin 1962:12–24 and Searle
1969:62). The expression of thought might be an exception in that the thought-act itself is
typically viewed as a constitutive condition for the linguistic act.
[80] I borrow the notion of a *mental force* from Wolfgang Freitag; see Freitag and Kraus
(2020). It is inspired by what Searle (1969:30ff.), in his speech-act theory, called "illocutionary force", which refers to a speaker's intention *in* making the utterance and hence to
the type of "illocutionary act" thereby performed. Phrases such as "I believe" are *force-
indicating devices*. Mental force, roughly, corresponds to what in contemporary

Consider the following case: If in reply to a question about a flower I want to express my belief *that the rose is red*, I could just say, "The rose is red" or make the state itself explicit and say, "I believe that the rose is red." If we leave aside for now the issue that in ordinary language "I believe" (and "I think") may often be used as a stylistic tool to indicate the speaker's slight uncertainty about a proposition, then it is obvious that in this context both utterances are used to express exactly the same representational content, namely my belief about the rose. "I believe that the rose is red" does *not* express the self-ascriptive proposition *that I – the speaker – have the belief*, although the believer/speaker is semantically present (and in this sense referred to) in the utterance.

In a similar vein, the apperceptive "I think", if attached, should *not* be viewed as expressing the thought *that I – the subject – think the content p*, and should not be identified as a self-ascriptive judgement that is asserted in attaching the "I think". Rather, "I think" explicitly expresses the subject realizing the original-synthetic unity that is necessarily required for a significant representation, without determining anything about the subject. The phrase "I think", if present in a mental or linguistic episode, can be said to "semantically" signify (or designate) the thinker who is producing the episode, without representing the thinker as a representational content itself. Hence, "I think" can be viewed as the mental-force-indicating device for the act of apperception, and in this sense the "vehicle" of all thinking and judging, and indeed of all empirical consciousness.[81]

The expressivist reading offers a plausible account of Kant's repeated claim that the "I think" is an expression "wholly empty of content". As an expression, it only indeterminately manifests the belonging of the apperceived representation to the unity of consciousness and hence indicates its relation to the apperceiving subject. Yet, for apperception to occur, it is not necessary that this belonging to consciousness be explicitly expressed. Moreover, "I think" does not indicate the specific type of representation that is apperceived, but is neutral as to whether the subject is conscious of a cognition or of some other type of representation. Rather, it expresses transcendental self-consciousness, which is entirely non-representational.

The expressivist reading of "I think" can also be squared with Kant's distinction between transcendental and empirical consciousness. Kant himself distinguishes two ways in which the "I think" can be used: as the "formal proposition [*Satz*] of apperception" (A354) or as the "empirical proposition

---

philosophy of mind is called the *attitude* that the subject has towards some representational content (see, e.g., Coliva 2016:31–37).

[81] For a detailed explication of the view, see Freitag and Kraus (2020). That Kant's "I think" does not *describe* one's thinking has also been argued in Henning (2010). Moreover, Longuenesse indicates the expressive nature of the "I think" in various places without offering a systematic account of it, for example, Longuenesse (2017:48, 67, 86, 96n14, 105, 133n9, 134n14, 136n14, 160).

[*Satz*]" "*I exist* thinking" (B420, B422n). The former is used to make explicit the form of apperception, that is, the reflexivity of all consciousness, and abstracts from the concrete realization of this form. The latter does not abstract from such concrete realization and therefore expresses in addition the existence of the thinker to which all conscious representations relate, albeit only "indeterminately" (see B422n).[82]

I now turn to the empirical proposition "I think". I develop an expressivist reading that not only resolves some of the most puzzling passages in §25 (of the B-Deduction) and the B-Paralogisms, but also illuminates the relation between transcendental apperception and *self-reference*.

3.5.2   The Empirical Proposition "I Think" and Self-Reference

In the Deduction as well as in the Paralogisms, Kant makes a few surprising remarks concerning the relation between "I think" and the thinker's existence. In §25, Kant claims that "in the synthetic original unity of apperception, I am conscious of myself not as I appear to myself, nor *as* I am in myself, but only *that* I am" (B157). Primarily, this claim states precisely what my interpretation has been able to explain, namely that transcendental apperception – as the general form of reflexivity – does not amount to a determinate thought about myself as a particular empirical thinker (i.e., as an appearance), nor about myself as a thing-in-itself. Kant, however, makes the additional claim that transcendental apperception amounts to the thought *that I am* (or *that I exist*). But would this not contradict my reading according to which transcendental apperception does not have any representational content at all? I shall argue that the expressivist reading can plausibly account for this claim, if one acknowledges that through transcendental apperception existence is not propositionally asserted, but merely expressed. Let me explain.

In §25, which comes after the discussion of the sensible synthesis, Kant shifts the discussion from transcendental self-consciousness to empirical self-consciousness, since he is concerned that his readers will wrongly take transcendental apperception as some sort of empirical self-consciousness or even as empirical cognition of oneself. In order to pre-empt this confusion, Kant argues that for "cognition of ourselves" we require in addition to transcendental apperception "a determinate sort of intuition, through which [a] manifold is given" (B157). He carries out the argument showing that we can only have cognition of ourselves as appearances by a comparison between outer and

---

[82] Note that, in the Paralogisms, Kant considers a third use of "I think", namely as a problematic judgement, or as "problematically taken" (A348/B406). Such use is determinative and hence no longer an indeterminate expression. As a problematic judgement, "I think" itself is turned into the object of philosophical analysis to derive logical features of thinking subjects (see Chapter 4).

inner experience – an argument that will occupy us in Chapter 4 (see 4.3). The statement above should be understood in this context. In a footnote, Kant then clarifies that the "I think" should still not be understood as the determinate assertion *that I am*, but rather: "*I think* expresses the *act (Actus)* of determining my existence" (B157n). The footnote states two additional requirements for the determination, or cognition, of myself, namely (1) an "existence" that "is thereby already given" and (2) "self-intuition" in the a priori form of inner sense, that is, time (B157n).

On the expressivist reading, the claims in §25 can now be understood as follows: if "I think" is actualized in an act of apperception in a mental episode leading to an occurrence in empirical consciousness, then "I think" expresses not only the form of reflexivity, but also *the fact* that this form is actualized by some existing individual thinker. Importantly, "I think" attached to an empirically conscious representation (in thought or speech) expresses the thinker's existence without determining anything about the thinker. Instead, "I think" is an *expression* that "semantically", though *indeterminately*, designates the individual thinker and hence manifests – as one may say – an *indeterminate self-reference*. Yet it does not determine any representational content and certainly does not amount to the predication (or even the assertion) *that the thinker exists*. Kant explicitly denies that "I think" is a determinative predication, when he writes in that same footnote that "I *cannot determine* my existence as that of a self-active being, rather I *merely represent* the spontaneity of my thought, i.e., of the determining, and my existence remains only sensibly determinable, i.e., determinable as the existence of an appearance" (B157n, emphasis added). Again, "I think" does *not* amount to the determinative claim (or assertion) *that I am*, but "merely represents" existence, which according to my terminology would just mean "*expressing*" existence.[83]

The expressivist reading is confirmed by a passage in the B-Paralogisms, which discusses the "I think" as an "empirical proposition [that] contains within itself the proposition 'I exist'" (B422n). In this footnote, Kant makes the following important claims: the "I think"

(1) "expresses an indeterminate empirical intuition, i.e., a perception (hence it proves that sensation, which consequently belongs to sensibility, grounds this existential proposition)";
(2) "signifies only something real (*etwas Reales*), which was given, and indeed only to thinking in general, thus not as appearance, and also not as a thing in itself (a noumenon), but rather as something that in fact exists (*Etwas,*

---

[83] Some interpreters, by contrast, take the apperceptive "I think" to amount to an assertion of existence (e.g., Henrich 1994:34, Carl 1997). Both Longuenesse (2017:82, 87–91, 93–4) and Allison (2004:353) acknowledge that such assertion cannot involve the categories, and argue that the assertion of existence follows directly (or analytically) from the conception of apperception.

das in der Tat existiert) and is indicated as an existing thing in the proposition 'I think'". (B422–3n)

In this footnote, again, the distinction between an expression that merely "signifies" something and a representation that determines something is salient. What Kant adds here is that the empirical "I think" must be combined with an "indeterminate empirical intuition, i.e., perception" in order to signify "something real". As in §25, "something real" here does not refer to an "appearance" of myself, nor to myself as a "thing-in-itself". Kant adds an explanation of the way in which existence is expressed by "I think". "Existence (*Existenz*)" in this context is "not yet a category", that is, the modal category of existence (*Dasein*) as actuality (*Wirklichkeit*), that refers to an "indeterminately given object" (B422n).[84] Hence, "I think" cannot amount to the predicative determination of existence with regard to a given intuition, but indeed "precedes the experience that is to determine the object of perception through the category in regard to time" (B422n). Nonetheless, we have a concept ("I think") of which we want to know whether or not anything is "posited outside this concept" (B422n). To find some "proof" of the reality of this concept, we need to seek out what is given to sensibility, and that is the mere occurrence of the mental episode of "I think" in inner sense. This occurrence gives us an "indeterminate empirical intuition" or "indeterminate perception" that manifests the existence of the act of apperception and hence the existence of the individual thinker. An intuition is *indeterminate* in that it presents us with "something" that is not in the least determined according to some form, but in principle sensibly determinable. Hence, the "indeterminate perception" associated with the "I think" presents to empirical consciousness, "not the *determining self*, but only … the *determinable self*" (as appearance of inner sense), though still without the least determination (B407). In the *Prolegomena*, Kant refers to this peculiar representation as the "feeling of an existence" (*Prol* 4:334n), since a feeling is by definition a non-determinative representation.

According to my broad reading of inner sense as inner receptivity, one could understand this representation as an *indeterminate inner intuition* that results from an act of apperception and is brought to empirical consciousness. Unlike a determinate inner intuition, it does not represent a particular mental state that obtains at a certain time, but it presents the mind with the *mere fact of an empirical*

---

[84] Kant refers to this non-categorial notion of existence (*Dasein*) in several places, for example, B72, B110, A92/B125, B199, B274; also *Refl* 5755, *Refl* 5772, *Prol* 4:295, and distinguishes it sharply from the modal category of existence (*Wirklichkeit*) (A218/B265). In general, Kant holds the view that finite, receptive beings, like humans, cannot anticipate *existence* (*Dasein*) analytically through mere thinking, but require *sensation* to prove that something in fact exists. Hence, only sensation "grounds this existential proposition" "I think" (B422n).

consciousness that is produced by this act and that contains the conscious representations that were apperceived through this act. Hence, the empirical "I think" is the manifestation of transcendental self-consciousness in an empirical consciousness. In Chapter 4, I will show, more specifically, why there cannot be a determinable inner intuition of the thinking subject as such. Rather, there can only be inner intuitions of particular mental states, which can then be determined through the categories, as I explicate in Chapter 5.

To be sure, "I think" can fulfil this expressive function only if triggered by some "material for thinking" (B423n). Only if there is some representational matter to be apperceived into a conscious representation, can the empirical "I think" occur. In the footnote, Kant therefore concludes that "the empirical" is the "condition of the application" of the "I think" in its transcendental function (B423n). That is, some representational matter provided by the senses is required for the transcendental (or formal) "I think" to be realized *in concreto* in an individual thinker. The concrete realization of apperception in an empirical consciousness can thus be understood as the origin of the individuation of a particular thinker.[85]

The upshot of this discussion is that by supplementing his transcendental conception of apperception with his considerations regarding the empirical "I think", Kant offers the starting point for a theory of individuation and self-reference. My expressivist reading has shown that the empirical "I think", or "I exist thinking", is not an assertion of existence, neither noumenal nor phenomenal existence: it does not assert that something exists *as* a specific kind of object, viz. as a thing-in-itself (i.e., noumenon) or as appearance (i.e., object of the senses). Rather, it is an indeterminate expression that manifests the real occurrence of an act of apperception in empirical consciousness and hence designates the subject of apperception, though without determining it as the content of a representation.

The empirical "I think" can only occur and manifest a thinker's existence if the thinker in fact performs an apperceptive synthesis; otherwise a *performative contradiction* would occur, which for the apperceptive "I

---

[85] Longuenesse (2007:24, also 18) argues that the "empirical 'I think'" is an assertion that "is made true by the individual act of asserting it, and known to be true by the agent of the act referred to by 'I'"; and, more recently, that "the thinker of the thought 'I think the proof is valid' is asserting of herself, ... that she is conscious of being accountable for the proof" (Longuenesse 2017:28). These phrases suggest a *predicative* thought with *I think* as part of its content. Yet in personal conversation she explained that, for her, "I think" is a "*positio absoluta*" that contains within itself the proposition "I exist" (see Longuenesse 1998:352–3). While I agree with her that the empirical "I think" expresses an individual act of apperception, I do not think that this expression amounts to an assertion of an *existential proposition*, nor that it implies *knowledge* of the truth of the expressed judgement. Nonetheless, Longuenesse shows an openness to an expressivist reading (see fn. 81 in this chapter).

think" is impossible.[86] To employ another notion from contemporary philosophy of mind, one could say that the apperceptive "I think" is *immune to error through misidentification*.[87] My expressivist reading explains this immunity by showing that the apperceptive "I think" can explicitly occur in empirical consciousness, only if it expresses the apperceptive synthesis without which there could not be an empirical consciousness at all. The "I think", therefore, necessarily designates the thinker who realizes such synthesis and thereby makes herself actual as the referent of such designation.

It is in this sense that I suggest that individuation should be understood as originating from the concrete realization of transcendental apperception, which manifests itself in empirical consciousness. In this sense, the "I think" mediates an indeterminate self-reference to the individual thinker who realizes apperception and hence realizes herself through apperception. This self-reference is fully indeterminate in that it does not contain any representational content about the thinker. I take this to be the starting point for developing Kant's theory of inner experience by which a subject relates to herself in an object-analogous sense and determines herself as an empirical thinker qua her psychological features. Yet my subsequent analysis of inner experience is for the most part independent of this expressivist reading of the "I think".

3.6   Conclusion

This chapter has developed an interpretation of transcendental apperception as the general form of reflexivity and has defended this interpretation against two alternatives, namely the psychological reading in terms of an act-awareness and the logical reading in terms of self-ascription. I have argued, firstly, that transcendental self-consciousness is essentially the *mere form of consciousness* that applies to all kinds of significant representation of which a subject can become conscious. As the source of the subject–object model of representation, it defines the way in which such representations must relate to the subject who has them in accordance with the original-synthetic unity of apperception. Secondly, I have shown that apperceptive synthesis is realized by any mental act that results in a significant representation, including the formation of perceptions and acts of

---

[86] I take the phrase "performative contradiction" from Austin (1962), according to whom an utterance not only has a truth-value of the sentence uttered, but also performs an action establishing a matter of fact. Carl (1997:157–8) indicates a performative character of the "I think", but then believes that such an interpretation can be extended to all self-ascription of belief and judgement, which – as we will see in Chapter 6 (6.4.3) – is not the case. Rosefeldt (2000:229–34) observes that the making the judgement "I do not exist" is a performative contradiction, but then understands the judgement "I exist" as an assertion of the existence of a "logical I".

[87] See Shoemaker (1968:556–7), Longuenesse's (2017) application to Kant's theory of apperception, and 6.4.

judgement, which must implement this general form of reflexivity. Thirdly, I have argued that the apperceptive "I think" is an *expression* of transcendental self-consciousness *without* determining the subject as the content of a representation. If the "I think" is realized in an apperceptive act and occurs in empirical consciousness, it additionally expresses the existence of the individual thinker and mediates an indeterminate self-reference.

Moreover, I have argued that the capacity for conscious representation, for humans, is essentially self-conscious and centrally implies the capacity to become conscious of one's representation as one's own. Therefore, all empirical consciousness is eventually directed at the capacity for self-ascription. This capacity for self-ascription fundamentally transforms the way in which beings like us represent objects. Finally, this chapter has led to a taxonomy of types of self-consciousness, which I briefly summarize here:

- *Transcendental self-consciousness* is the consciousness of the general form of reflexivity; it is a transcendental condition of any cognitively significant representation, which is itself non-representational (that is, without representational content), non-perspectival, and non-individual.
- *Analytic self-consciousness* is the consciousness of the identity of the subject throughout a mental act that leads to a significant representation. It represents that which is common to all representations involved in this act and can be expressed by the phrase "I think".
- *Existential self-consciousness* is the consciousness of one's existence as thinker without determining any logical or empirical features of oneself. It results from an act of apperception that is made explicit by the empirical proposition "I think" (or "I exist thinking") that is attached to a representation in empirical consciousness and hence appears as an indeterminate inner intuition.

I will discuss the following two types of consciousness in the subsequent chapters:

- *Logical self-consciousness* is the consciousness of oneself as the subject of predication or as the *logical subject*; as such, the subject is turned into an object, albeit merely an object of thought. A philosophical analysis of the "I think" (taken as a problematic judgement) can derive rules for the predicative use of "I" in I-judgements (see Chapter 4).
- *Empirical self-consciousness* is the consciousness of oneself as empirical self through the intuition of inner appearances. It is the basis of inner experience and will be shown to amount to cognition of oneself qua one's psychological features (see Chapters 4 and 5).

In sum, transcendental apperception has turned out to be the first and most general kind of self-realization and to provide the anchor for all kinds of self-determination.

4

The Conditions of Self-Reference

4.1 Introduction

My inner experience consists, basically, in empirical judgements *about myself*, in which I ascribe to myself certain psychological features. Such self-ascriptions primarily concern my occurrent mental states – such as, for instance, my thoughts about how to organize my teaching later today, my current desire for some freshly brewed coffee, or my excitement about finishing up a long-lasting project. Upon further reflection, I may also ascribe to myself past states and long-term features, such as values and commitments, tastes and moods, as well as character traits. All of this requires that I turn myself into the *object* of my own consciousness. It requires, moreover, that I understand myself as continuing to exist throughout all changes of my mental states and even throughout changes of long-lasting properties. In this chapter, I examine how I can determine myself as an object at all and whether I can be a genuine object of my inner experience that is – in a relevant sense – identical through time.

In the Introduction, I have distinguished three different kinds of objects, each of which is defined by the specific way the subject relates to the object: *objects of empirical intuition*, to which one relates via sensation; *objects of thought*, to which one relates via judgements, and *objects of experience*, to which one relates via empirical cognition. Chapter 2 has shown that the mental contents appearing in inner sense can become the objects of distinctively inner intuitions and – by my actively attending to them – the objects of my inner perception. Yet it became clear that inner sense cannot convey the notion of a self that is unified across different representations or even across different times. Chapter 3 has then shown that the self-consciousness arising from transcendental apperception accounts for consciousness being *unified* across all partial representations belonging to one and the same mental act. Yet such self-consciousness does not determine any object-relation at all, but rather defines the general form of reflexivity that is a necessary condition of any object-representation.

In this chapter, I finally turn to *self-reference*. I examine specifically the conditions under which I can relate to myself in judgement, and ask how

I can represent myself, firstly, as an *object of thought* and, secondly, as an *object of inner experience*. Following Kant's terminology in the *Progress Essay*, I consider this distinction in terms of two uses of the term "I": I speak of the *logical "I"*, if the term denotes merely an object of thought, and of the *psychological "I"*, if it denotes an object of inner experience.[1]

A *locus classicus* of Kant's discussion of various problems that may arise from attempts to determine oneself is his set of chapters on the so-called paralogisms. There, Kant primarily aims to critique the eighteenth-century discipline of rational psychology, which defends a "traditional" (broadly Cartesian) metaphysics of the soul, according to which the soul is understood as a simple thinking substance underlying all consciousness. Kant's Paralogisms, therefore, have often been understood as a straightforward attack on metaphysical accounts of the self and certainly as a deconstruction of the traditional metaphysics of the soul. By contrast, in the present chapter, I focus on the positive contributions of the Paralogisms and use a detailed discussion of them to illuminate the distinction between the logical "I" and the psychological "I". This discussion will show that both are legitimate ways of representing oneself and have to be distinguished from illegitimate modes of self-representation, such as those employed by the rational psychologists. In doing so, I pursue two goals in this chapter.

Firstly, I show that the positive contribution of the Paralogisms is to specify a set of *logical conditions* of judgements about oneself. That is, they define rules for using the term "I" in judgements in accordance with the logical forms of the understanding. These logical conditions can then be understood as the predicates of the logical "I".

Secondly, I explicate a crucial disparity between inner and outer experience. I argue that the set of logical conditions that define the logical "I" does not straightforwardly correspond to a set of real conditions that would define the psychological "I" as the object of inner experience. By contrast, for the case of spatio-material objects of outer experience, the Schematism and the principles of the understanding explicate a set of real conditions for intuitions to be subsumable under the logical forms of judgements. In consequence, the categories of the understanding define a set of generic real predicates under which all objects of outer experience must fall. For the case of inner experience, however, the categories of relation, which are needed to trace objects through time, are not straightforwardly applicable to inner intuitions. Most importantly, the First Analogy, which explicates the category of substance as persistence through time, cannot be applied so as to find something persistent in inner intuitions. I shall therefore argue that in order for us to regard ourselves as being – in some sense – identical through time, there is a need for a different kind of sensible explication of substance in inner experience than that of material persistence in

---

[1] See *Progress* 20:270 and *Anth* 7:134.

outer experience. The Paralogisms leave some conceptual room for this need to be filled by reason, rather than by the understanding. Hence, this chapter first articulates the problem that arises from the disparity between inner and outer experience and paves the way to a solution that I will then develop in Chapter 5.

In accordance with these two goals, the chapter divides into two parts. After introducing, in Section 4.2, the distinction between the logical "I" and the psychological "I", I first examine, in Section 4.3, the logical "I" and specify the logical rules for representing oneself in I-judgements, focusing on the First Paralogism of Substantiality. In Section 4.4, I elaborate on the psychological "I" and explore a disparity between inner and outer experience, focusing specifically on the category of substance and the Third Paralogism of Personality.

4.2   The Logical "I" and the Psychological "I"

The distinction between the logical "I" and the psychological "I" is most explicitly drawn in the essay *What real progress has metaphysics made since the time of Leibniz and Wolff?* (1793), but also appears in Kant's lectures on metaphysics and anthropology and is occasionally alluded to in the three *Critiques* and other Critical works. Let us first turn to the passage in the *Progress* essay:

> That I am conscious of myself is a thought that already contains a twofold I [*Ich*], the *I [Ich] as subject* and the *I [Ich] as object*. ... We are not, however, referring thereby to a dual personality; only the *I [Ich] that thinks and intuits* is the person [*Person*], whereas the I [*Ich*] of the *object that is intuited by me* is, like other objects outside me, the thing [*Sache*].
>
> Of the I [*Ich*] in the first sense (the subject of apperception), the *logical I [logische Ich]* as *a priori* representation, it is absolutely impossible to know anything further as to what sort of being it is, or what its natural constitution may be ....
>
> But the I [*Ich*] in the second sense (as subject of perception), the *psychological I [psychologische Ich]* as empirical consciousness, is capable of being known in many ways ...
>
> (*Progress* 20:270, emphasis added and translation amended)

This passage may be on first sight rather puzzling because Kant here seems to conflate a conceptual and a metaphysical distinction in an unhelpful way: on the one hand, the distinction between two representations of "I" (or perhaps better two uses of the term "I") and, on the other hand, the distinction between two kinds of entities, the one who thinks (the *person*) and the one who is perceived (the *object* or thing).[2]

---

[2] Kant here uses the German first-personal pronoun *ich* as a substantive noun (*das Ich*). Rosefeldt (2000:78) explicitly notes this potential conflation and then develops an account primarily of the "logical I".

This puzzlement can be resolved in light of a footnote in the *Anthropology*, in which Kant explicates this distinction in the following way:

> In psychology we investigate ourselves according to our ideas of inner sense; in logic, according to what intellectual consciousness suggests. Now here the "I" appears to us to be double (which would be contradictory): 1) the *"I" as subject of thinking* (in logic), which means pure apperception (the merely reflecting "I"), and of which there is nothing more to say except that it is a very simple idea; 2) the *"I" as object of perception*, therefore of inner sense, which contains a manifold of determination that make an inner experience possible. ... The human "I" is indeed twofold according to form (manner of representation), but not according to matter (content). (Anth 7:134n, emphasis added)[3]

Here it becomes evident that with the distinction between "the 'I' as *subject* of thinking" and "the 'I' as *object* of perception", Kant refers to two uses of "I" or two "manner[s] of representation", one in logic and one in psychology. In logic, I consider myself *as the subject of thinking*, which consists only in having "a very simple idea" without determining any empirical or individual features. By contrast, in psychology, I consider myself *as the object of inner perceptions*. I can then determine my empirical characteristics insofar as they appear in inner sense and can be known through inner experience. So I propose that Kant is here concerned with two different kinds of representations of oneself by means of the "I" in judgement, both of which refer to "one and the same *subject*", although they represent the subject in different ways, or manners (*Anth* 7:134n).

Moreover, I submit that these two ways of representing oneself map onto two different uses of the understanding – the *logical* and the *real use*.[4] The logical use consists in the subordination of concepts to one another, that is, in mere thinking in abstraction from the concept's real content and relation to possibly existing objects. The logical use results in the determination of an object of thought, without making a claim as to whether these logical determinations can be instantiated by a possibly existing object. By contrast, the real use of the understanding, if based on corresponding sensible intuitions, leads to the determination of an object of experience. Hence, I submit that through the *logical* "I", I represent myself as an *object of mere thought*, that is, as the subject of predication of I-judgements; whereas through the *psychological* "I", I represent myself as an *object of possible inner experience*. Let me explain.

---

[3] In his practical writings, we find numerous passages that distinguish two ways of viewing a person: "a person [must be viewed] as belonging to the sensible world [and ...] also belongs to the intelligible world" (*CpracR* 5:87); see also *Groundwork* 4:428, 433, 438, and B155.

[4] Kant draws the distinction between a logical and a real use for both the understanding and reason, but gives explicit definitions only for the latter at A299/B355.

The distinction between the logical and the real use of the understanding hinges on two different uses of concepts in judgement, namely as *logical* and as *real predicates*.[5] A logical predicate can be any concept that can be used as a predicate in a judgement that is in accordance with the logical forms of judgement, indeed "anything one wishes can serve as a logical predicate, even the subject [term] can be predicated of itself" (A598/B626).[6] Whether the resulting judgement is true depends merely on the logical relation between the subject term and the predicate. For instance, in the judgement of the basic form "*S* is *P*", the predicate term *P* is subordinated to the subject term *S*. This judgement is true, if and only if whatever is posited to be *S* can also be posited to be *P*. Take, for instance, the judgement "A unicorn is a horse-like creature with a long horn on its forehead". Such logical determination disregards whether the concepts involved have any relation to something real.[7]

In its real use, the understanding "gives" (*gibt*) or "creates" (*schafft*) concepts, which are then employed as real predicates.[8] This use involves the application of concepts to something real and, if legitimate, must be based on corresponding sensible intuitions. In Chapter 2, I introduced this use with respect to the pure concepts of the understanding, viz. the categories, which thereby serve as the rules of sensible synthesis. A category is applied to a sensible object precisely by synthesizing the sensible manifold through which this object is "given" to the mind in accordance with the category. The resulting "intuition of an object is regarded as *determined* with regard to one of the logical functions of judgment" (B128). In turn, the categories gain sensible content in terms of the generic (spatio-)temporal properties of objects they define. For instance, the categories of relation define generic temporal relations that can be found within and between objects. The category of substance can be understood as giving a rule for synthesizing changing states, or accidents, in relation to that which persists throughout all change, that is, the substratum. In consequence, employing the categories as rules of synthesis then results in real determinations (*reale*

---

[5] Kant discusses this distinction in the context of the ontological proof of God, in which he claims that "existence" is a logical, but not a real, predicate (see A598–9/B626–7). See Rosefeldt (2003).

[6] See *Dissertation* 2:393–4; A52–5/B76–9, B128.

[7] In most places, Kant reserves the notion of *determination* for the "determination of a thing" (A598/B626), that is, of something real. However, at times he also uses Baumgarten's technical definition, according to which "what is either posited to be A, or posited not to be A, is *determined*" (Baumgarten 1739/2011:§34); see Kant's *Reflection* 3520, 17:33. For discussions, see Kannisto (2016) and Stang (2016:37).

[8] See *Dissertation* 2:393; A643/B671. Note that Kant distinguishes two real uses of the understanding, a *transcendental* and an *empirical* use (see A296/B352). Only the empirical use, which must be exercised in light of sensible intuition, is legitimate (see B128). There are obviously intricate questions regarding non-empirical types of cognition, such as a priori philosophical cognition and mathematical cognition. Here I am primarily concerned with empirical cognition.

Bestimmungen) of objects of experience. The real use determines real properties that are judged to be instantiated in objects so determined.

Similarly, the application of an empirical concept as a real predicate to an object given in intuition consists in synthesizing the corresponding sensible manifold in accordance with the empirical concept and, if successful, results in recognizing that the object indeed instantiates this concept. For instance, by reflecting the object of my current perception under the concept <*ball*>, I examine whether the object instantiates the marks that are contained in this concept, such as the marks that are expressed by the partial concepts <*spherical*> and <*able to bounce*>. In general, we can distinguish, for an empirical concept, between what is contained *in* it, that is, its representational marks, and what falls *under* it, that is, the objects that instantiate it.[9]

With this distinction between logical and real predicates in place, we are in a position to better understand the distinction between *objects of (mere) thought* and *objects of possible experience* (which can also be called *objects of empirical cognition*). Through logical predication, we determine an object of thought, which Kant also calls a "logical something" (*L-MP/L₂* 28:544) and an *ens rationis* (A292/ B348). Through real predication based on corresponding empirical intuitions, we determine an object of empirical cognition as something (empirically) real. Kant notices a crucial implication of this distinction in the introduction to the B-Edition:

> To cognize an object, it is required that I be able to prove its [real] possibility (whether by the testimony of experience from its actuality or *a priori* through reason). But I can think whatever I like, as long as I do not contradict myself, i.e., as long as my concept is a [merely logically] possible thought. (Bxxvi(n))

So the determination of an object of thought requires only *logical possibility*, in terms of a judgement that is conceivable without contradiction, but it does not require that the possibility of its real instantiation be proven. A judgement about a unicorn could be a perfectly fine determination of a "logical some-thing" (or *ens rationis*), though it has no real instantiation, whereas a judgement about a round square would, arguably, not even be about a "logical something", but rather a "logical nothing" (or *nihil negativum*), because it is logically impossible to even conceive of a round square.[10] By viewing a judgement only logically, the judgement is taken only

---

[9] This distinction corresponds, roughly, to the present-day distinction between intension and extension of a concept (see *L-Log/Jäsche* 9:95). Kant uses the notion of *content* (*Inhalt*) for the former (e.g., A51/B75, A58/B83, A62/B87, A71/B97) and the notions of *domain* (*Umfang*) (e.g., A71/B96) and *sphere* (*Sphäre*) (e.g., A654/B682) for the latter. For discussion, see Kannisto (2016).

[10] See A290–2/B346–9. For accounts of logical possibility, see Chignell (2014) and Stang (2016:166–71).

"problematically", leaving it "undecided whether it is something [real] or nothing" (A290/B346).[11] We will later see that such a "problematic", non-assertive use of judgements, especially of the "I think", can nonetheless have crucial philosophical value with respect to cognition.

By contrast, the empirical cognition of an object requires an "assurance [that . . .] there is a corresponding object somewhere within the sum total of all possibilities" (Bxxvi(n)).[12] That is, empirical cognition requires *real possibility*: it must be possible that something *real* instantiates the concepts by which we cognize. It is controversial what exactly real possibility entails.[13] With respect to empirical cognition, it seems safe to say that it requires, in addition to logical possibility, a formal and a material condition. It requires *formal possibility* in the sense that the concept (or cognition) "agrees with the formal conditions of experience" (A218/B265). These formal conditions are explicated by the principles of the understanding and depend on both the logical forms of judgement and the forms of sensibility. More precisely, formal possibility can be understood as an agreement with those principles of the understanding that contribute to the *content* of the concept <object of empirical cognition> and that define a priori determinations of such objects. These are the principles that concern the categories of quantity (i.e., Axioms of Intuition), the categories of quality (i.e., Anticipations of Perception), and the categories of relation (i.e., Analogies of Experience).[14] In most places in which Kant speaks of the "determination" (*Bestimmung*) of an object or of a "determinable" (*bestimmbares*) object, he refers to the real determination of objects of cognition, which presuppose determinability in accordance with these principles.[15]

Regarding the material condition, it is a further question whether or not an object of empirical cognition really *exists*, that is, whether it is empirically actual. An object of (actual) experience is an object whose *existence* has been directly confirmed by sensation or which is suitably (i.e., causally) connected with actual objects of sensation such that its existence can be derived. The cognition then fulfils the "material condition of experience (of sensation)" and can be truthfully asserted of an existing object (A218/B266). For instance, I am justified in asserting the existence of the ball I see in front of me, but I am also justified in

---

[11] It is clear in the context of this quotation that Kant here means "something real", rather than a merely logical something (or *ens rationis*), that is, an empty concept without real object.

[12] See also *Progress* 20:105; *L-Log/Jäsche* 9:106.

[13] For discussions of real possibility, see Chignell (2014) and Stang (2016:197–227).

[14] The Postulates of Empirical Thinking concern the categories of modality, that is, possibility, actuality, and necessity, and "do not augment the concept" of an object, but determine "how . . . the object itself [is . . .] related to the understanding" (A219/B266).

[15] For example, A598/B626. As a second condition, a cognition requires *empirical possibility* in that its object must be compatible with the empirical laws of nature and the causal history of the world (see Chignell 2014).

asserting the existence of a distant star, if I have adequate empirical evidence, for example through telescopic observation, and given the laws of astronomy.[16]

A crucial point of Kant's Critical theory of cognition is that real possibility can be meaningfully shown only for those concepts (and judgements) that can be related to possible experience. That is, any legitimate real use of the understanding must be confined to that which can be given in experience.[17] Objects of possible experience are the only ones that are determinable (in the real sense) for us and that we are justified to determine as existing. But, of course, this may not mean that these are the only things that are metaphysically possible or that in fact exist. Kant famously denies that we can cognize things-in-themselves, but his own transcendental philosophy seems to presuppose their existence.[18]

Now, the Paralogisms centrally draw on the distinction between legitimate and illegitimate uses of the understanding and discern errors that occur if one does not carefully distinguish between them. Kant's central goal is to dismantle the arguments of traditional rationalist metaphysics by showing that they are based on an illicit conflation of legitimate empirical, and illegitimate transcendental uses of the categories. A transcendental use ignores the restrictions by the conditions of possible experience and extends to "objects in themselves (without any restriction to our sensibility)" (A139/B178).[19] However, if a category is transcendentally used, then it has "no determinate or even, as far as its form is concerned, determinable object" (A248/B304) and hence results in a "misuse" of the categories (A296/B351). In the Paralogisms, Kant uncovers the dialectical errors that occur if one attempts to determine the subject by means of the categories. The Paralogisms are commonly understood as showing that the logical "I" is the only legitimate representation of oneself, while rejecting any real determination of the subject.[20] My task will be to show

---

[16] Note that "existence", though it is a category with objective validity, can be used only as a logical predicate and cannot contribute to the content of the concept of an object. Whether or not an object exists cannot be anticipated through conceptual analysis, but requires confirmation in light of some sensation (see B72, B110, A92/B125, B199, B274; also *Refl* 5755, 18:345; *Refl* 5772, 18:349–50; *Prol* 4:295).

[17] See A247/B304. Note that mathematical cognition is a legitimate use of the understanding, which depends on the constructability of concepts in a priori intuitions. Since it is, therefore, conditioned by the forms of experience, it is at least formally possible, even though various mathematical objects may not be empirically possible in accordance with the laws of nature and certainly lack material existence. Warren (2001:18n26) forges a helpful distinction between "mathematical possibility" and "physical possibility".

[18] For a discussion of whether we can know the existence of things-in-themselves, see Chignell (2014) and Watkins (2005).

[19] See also A238/B298, A247/B304.

[20] The most detailed account of the "logical I" is offered by Rosefeldt (2000, 2003, 2017) and Carl (1997:157–61, 1998:114); moreover, Keller (1998:169) discusses the "grammatical object of consciousness", Henning (2010) the "logical function of the 'I think'", and Longuenesse (2017:130–1) the "logical subject". My own account largely accords with

that the Paralogisms also leave some conceptual space for a notion of the psychological "I" by which we refer to ourselves as determinable in inner experience. Nonetheless, I will grant that the applicability of the categories to inner intuitions is not as straightforward as in the case of outer experience.

In Section 4.3, I develop a reading of the logical "I" as defining a set of semantic rules for representing oneself as the subject of predication in I-judgements. My reading is inspired by the contemporary notion of a Kaplanian character, which explains the context-dependency of the content of "I".[21] In Section 4.4, I argue that the predicates of the logical "I" do not straightforwardly correspond with some real predicates of the psychological "I". This fact constitutes a major disparity between inner and outer experience. Yet I shall conclude that the Paralogisms show a need for a different – analogical – kind of sensible explication of the category of substance (and other categories of relation), and leave conceptual room for this need to be filled by an employment of reason, rather than of the understanding.

4.3   The Logical "I" as an Object of Thought

4.3.1   "I Think" in the Paralogisms

Kant's Paralogisms are often read exclusively as a critique of rational psychology and hence as a deconstruction of the traditional metaphysics of the soul, rather than as a positive contribution to his own theory of the mind.[22] Yet most commentators overlook the fact that there Kant provides a constructive "logical exposition" of the "I think" (B409, also A341/B399), which follows "the guide of the categories" (A344/B402).[23] Since I aim to draw lessons for Kant's account of self-reference, I focus narrowly on this logical exposition and leave

Rosefeldt's analysis, though I shall depart from it on a key issue: I do not identify the object of inner experience as a *merely logical something*, but make room for a conception of the psychological "I" as that which is determined in inner experience.

[21] See Kaplan (1989).

[22] Strawson's (1966:162–74) interpretation of the Paralogisms as a lasting attack on the traditional metaphysics of the soul has proven influential. Horstmann (1993) and Bird (2000) argue explicitly against the retrieval of any constructive notion of the "I" from the Paralogisms. Exceptions include Ameriks (2000), Rosefeldt (2000), Kitcher (2011), Dyck (2014), and Longuenesse (2017), who offer positive evaluations of the Paralogisms, though in rather disparate ways. Rosefeldt (2000, 2003, 2017) offers an important analysis of the "logical content" of the "I" in the Paralogisms, yet he does not develop an account of self-reference for inner experience. Longuenesse (2017) retrieves important insights for self-reference from the Paralogisms.

[23] Most recent literature on the Paralogisms focuses on analysing the kind of error that Kant diagnoses in the syllogisms of rational psychology (e.g., Grier 2001, Allison 2004:333–56, Wuerth 2010, Rosefeldt 2017). There is a long-standing debate about whether and how the Paralogisms substantiate Kant's transcendental idealism and which ontological status they may attribute to the self (e.g., Ameriks 2000, Melnick 2009, Marshall 2010, Wuerth

aside various other controversies. This logical exposition, I shall argue, defines the logical "I" and explicates the *logical* conditions of self-reference in I-judgements, which in a further step can be understood as the *semantic* rules of the use of the term "I" in empirical I-judgements.

Note that despite my emphasis on the positive role of the Paralogisms, I do not follow those interpreters who see Kant as building up a new pure rational psychology that is in an important sense continuous with the rationalist tradition. Although I do not deny that such interpretations may offer a plausible account of Kant's broader views of the mind, my reading remains neutral on any ontological claims regarding a noumenal self that as a thing-in-itself may underlie any referential use of "I".[24]

One may wonder why the Paralogisms – in which Kant critiques the eighteenth-century discipline of *rational psychology*, which purported to produce a priori (non-empirical) knowledge about the nature of the soul in general – are in any way relevant for an account of *inner experience*. The defenders of rational psychology, such as Christian Wolff and Alexander Baumgarten, claimed to have proven various substantive metaphysical claims concerning the soul's existence as a metaphysical being with properties such as substantiality, simplicity, incorruptibility, and immortality.[25] None of these properties seems to be straightforwardly endorsed by Kant's account of inner experience. Yet the Paralogisms offer the most detailed analysis of the phrase "I think", with a particular focus on the representation "I". In fact, in the A-Edition the Paralogisms are the first and only chapter in which Kant discusses this phrase, whereas "I think" already plays a major role in the B-Edition's Deduction, though not with a particular view to the "I" itself. So by revealing the inappropriate understanding of "I think" that was advocated by rational psychologists, the Paralogisms teach us a lot about the adequate uses of "I", too. Kant's own positive logical exposition of the "I think" can thus be properly understood only in contrast to the specific errors made by the rationalists. The questions Kant deals with in the Paralogisms, I submit, concern the referential use of "I", not the nature of thought itself (as in the Deduction).

Despite various interpretive divergences, there is considerable consensus among commentators with regard to the general thread of Kant's criticism of *rational psychology*. Rational psychology, as traditionally understood by

2014). Moreover, there has been much interest in situating the Paralogisms in the historical context of eighteenth-century philosophy (e.g., Ameriks 2000, Dyck 2014).

[24] Ameriks' (2000) important reconstruction of the Paralogisms makes a good case for Kant's still admitting the rationalist assumption of the existence of the soul as a noumenon, while at the same time acknowledging that Kant offers compelling arguments against the soul being determinable in accordance with the conditions of experience. As my aim here is to give an account of inner experience, I do not pursue this line of argument for a rationalist strand in Kant. For interpretations of the Paralogisms as being continuous with the rationalist tradition, see also Wuerth (2014) and Dyck (2014).

[25] See Wolff (1720/1997) and Baumgarten (1739/2011).

Christian Wolff and Alexander Baumgarten, starts from the premise "I think", the "sole text of rational psychology" (A343/B402), and deduces substantive metaphysical claims about the referent of "I", the thinking being, on the basis of purely rational syllogisms.[26] Now, it is generally acknowledged that Kant's criticism is based on the fundamental insight that by way of deductive inferences from the judgement "I think" we cannot derive the metaphysical features of a real being. The error of the rational psychologists lies, roughly, in a conflation of different uses of certain concepts in the judgments that are taken to follow from the "I think", such as the concept <subject>, without sufficient underpinning through sensibility. What is more controversial is the exact relation between the Deduction and the Paralogisms.

In the Paralogisms, Kant certainly presupposes his own account of the apperceptive "I think" from the Deduction. Recall that – on my view – the apperceptive "I think" is an *expression* of transcendental self-consciousness, rather than a predicative (or determining) judgement. It primarily involves reflexivity, that is, a relation to the subject, rather than determinate self-reference, that is, a determining relation to oneself as object (see 3.5). In continuity with the Deduction, Kant assumes that we cannot have "the least concept" of the "transcendental subject of thought" without encountering "a constant circle" in definition, since "we must always already avail ourselves of the representation of it at all times in order to judge anything" (A346/B404). Yet, in my view, Kant now moves beyond the Deduction by examining the "I think" as a "judgment" or "proposition" (A341–2/B399–400), through which the activity of thinking or a thought-state is predicated of what is referred to by "I". More specifically, Kant considers the "proposition 'I think' . . . taken here only problematically" (A347/B405).[27] In considering "I think" as a *problematic* judgement, one does not yet take a stance with regard to the existence of a thinker, of some activity of thinking, or of some thought-state. Rather, one asserts only the logical possibility of the judgement "I think" being true of someone and, therefore, as will become clear, considers the referent of "I" only as an object of mere thought.[28] This problematic use of "I think" contrasts with

---

[26] There is some disagreement among the rational psychologists at the time as to whether the premise "I think" is gained from inner experience or from pure reflection. Dyck (2014:71–81) points out that Wolff (1720/1997), Baumgarten (1739/2011), and Kant in his pre-Critical writings (especially *L-MP/L₁*) took the "I" to have its origin in reflection upon one's inner appearances and therefore to be a "concept of experience". In the Paralogisms, Kant construes a purified version of rational psychology, taking "I think" to be a non-empirical pure representation. See also Dyck (2009:269–75).

[27] That the "'I think' (problematically taken)" is in line with the apperceptive "I think" is important for the internal consistency of Kant's theory, but it does not mean that Kant merely "reiterates" or "confirms" the results of the Deduction in the Paralogisms, as some commentators think; for example, Grier (1993:277) and Allison (2004:336).

[28] For Kant, "[p]roblematic judgments are those in which one regards the assertion or denial as merely *possible* (arbitrary)" (A74/B100). In other words, in making the problematic

another predicative use, the *assertoric* use of "I think" by which one asserts that someone is in fact thinking or is in a particular thought-state.[29] So Kant first concedes in the Paralogisms that there are possible predicative uses of "I think", but also sees such uses as strictly limited. By reviewing "all the predications of the pure doctrine of the soul with a critical eye" (A348/B406), Kant seeks to distinguish legitimate from illegitimate uses. So I argue that Kant's logical exposition in the Paralogisms defines the logical conditions that are necessary for any referential use of "I" in I-judgements, but which are not yet sufficient for explaining the possibility of the use of "I" in assertoric judgements and hence in inner experience.[30]

Kant introduces the problematic use of "I think", which I shall also call the *problematic* "I think" (as opposed to the *apperceptive* "I think"), as follows:

> The proposition 'I think' is, however, taken here only problematically; not insofar as it may contain a perception of an existence (the Cartesian *cogito, ergo sum*), but only in its mere possibility, in order to see which properties might flow from so simple a proposition as this for its subject (whether or not such a thing might now exist).   (A347/B405)

Insofar as "I think" is taken as a problematic judgement, it does not assert that the predicate <*think*> is true of some being. In this passage, Kant makes it clear which aspect of the "I think" is taken problematically: it is questionable "whether or not such a thing [that thinks] might now exist", that is, whether or not there is a real being who instantiates the judgement. Even though he rejects the substantive claims regarding the subject that the rational psychologists draw, he regards it as an important task to examine "which properties might flow . . . for its subject" from the *problematic* judgement "I think". Since the problematic "I think" is viewed independently of a corresponding "perception of an existence", Kant cannot expect to make an assertion of existence, or to discover any generic spatio-temporal properties or even empirical properties of a thinker. By apprehending the judgement problematically, one entertains only the logical possibility of thinking beings and from this possibility infers certain logical determinations of such beings in accordance with the "mere [logical] functions" of thinking, viz. the pure concepts of the understanding (B407).[31] As long as it is

---

judgement *that p* one entertains the *logical possibility* of *p*'s being true, without asserting or denying that *p* is in fact true of something.

[29] Recall that, in Chapter 3, I argued that the empirical proposition "'I exist thinking'" (B420, B422n), based on an indeterminate perception, should be viewed as an empirical *expression* of the thinker's existence, rather than as an assertoric judgement (see 3.5.2).

[30] Only a few interpretations sufficiently consider the distinction between the problematic and the assertoric use of "I think" (e.g., Henning 2010 and Rosefeldt 2017). Some interpreters explicitly argue that the "I think" of apperception consists in an *assertive* use of "I" in the predication of "thinking" (e.g., Carl 1997:157–8).

[31] In a later footnote, it becomes clear that the problematic use of "I think" does not yet involve the *existence* (or even just the *real possibility*) of a thinking being, since that would

not proven that these logical determinations are instantiated by a real being, the term "I" must be assumed to denote only an object of mere thought, that is, a mere thought-entity (*ens rationis*, that is, an "empty concept without [real] object", A292/B348).[32]

In sum, viewing the "I think" as a problematic judgement, as in the Paralogisms, is in line with the apperceptive "I think" of the Deduction, insofar as the subject is not thereby determined through a *real use* of the understanding, and a fortiori not determined as an object of inner experience. Yet the Paralogisms go beyond the Deduction, in that they imply logical determinations of the subject, insofar as *the subject is now considered as an object of thought*. These logical determinations, taken together, constitute the general representation of a thinking subject *in thought*, more precisely, they define *how* any thinking being represents itself as the subject of predication in "I think"-judgements.[33] Given the results of the Deduction, according to which transcendental apperception defines the general form of reflexivity, we can now understand the problematic "I think" as an original judgement *about* this reflexive relation between the subject and its representations *in first-personal thought*. Hence, with the problematic "I think", we gain a primordial kind of *reflective self-consciousness*.

In the B-Paralogisms, Kant aptly states that the problematic "I think" specifies "all *modi* of self-consciousness in thinking" (B406), which are informed by the logical forms of judgement, but not yet by the forms of sensibility. These *modi* of self-consciousness, I shall argue, are precisely the logical predicates of the "I" that Kant derives through his logical exposition of the problematic judgement "I think". These predicates specify necessary conditions of how a thinking subject must represent itself – *through first-personal thought* – as the object of its own thoughts. The first-person pronoun is precisely the linguistic tool to express a first-personal thought about oneself. These conditions can, therefore, be understood, I shall argue, as semantic rules for how to use the reflexive first-person pronoun "I" in assertoric I-judgements in which real *mental predicates* are self-ascribed. In defining semantic rules for

---

already require "indeterminate empirical intuition", as expressed in the empirical proposition "I think" (B422n).

[32] Kant also calls it "a thing of thought" (A337/B394). That "I" denotes *exclusively* an object of mere thought represented via the "logical I" is a central claim of Rosefeldt's interpretation (2000:72, 77n129, 82; 2003:146–9, 152, 2017). Note that Kant distinguishes two kinds of thought-entities: on the one hand, those thought-entities that have "*conceptus ratiocinati* (correctly inferred concepts)" (A311/B368) and are, therefore, "being[s] of reason (*ens rationis ratiocinatae*)" (A681/B709) (or "object[s] in the [transcendental] idea", A670/B698) that have some good purpose for cognition; and on the other hand, those thought-entities that are merely based on "*conceptus ratiocinantes* (sophistical concepts)" (A311/B368), which necessarily lead to dialectical fallacies. In Chapter 5, I will argue that the logical "I" leads us to a concept of the former, not the latter, kind, namely to the idea of the soul.

[33] Similarly, Longuenesse (2017:83) characterizes the problematic "I think" as a "*type*" of thought "universally shared by all thinkers".

I-judgements, the logical predicates of "I" also determine a set of transcendental conditions specifically of inner experience. In what follows, I will explore these semantic rules of self-reference, focusing specifically on the First Paralogism of Substantiality.

4.3.2 From a Logical Point of View: Logical Predicates as the Semantic Rules of I-Judgements

Kant's logical exposition of "I think" follows "the guide of the categories" (A344/B402). By pinning down the rationalists' error in detailed analyses of their syllogisms, Kant derives a set of logical predicates, that is, predicates that have only "logical significance" (A350), but "no objective significance" (A348), in the sense that they are not (yet) proven to be instantiated by real objects. These logical predicates are derived from the pure (unschematized) categories, that is, the "functions of a judgment without [real] content" (A349). More specifically, it turns out that the minor premise of each Paralogism defines a logical predicate of "I" with respect to one or more particular "functions" of thinking. Accordingly, the "I" is specified as the "constant logical subject of thinking" (A350) (according to the category of substance), as the "logically simple subject" (B407, cf. A351–61) (according to the categories of quality), as having "logical identity" (A363) (according to the categories of quantity and causality), and as a logically possible "non-corporeal" being (according to the category of interaction).[34] All these claims employ the categories only in their logical use and therefore determine the "I" only as a "substance in concept, simple in concept, etc." (A400). In the B-Paralogisms, Kant calls these conceptual (i.e., logical) determinations the "*modi* of self-consciousness" and lists them in the same order as in the A-Edition (B406ff.). Such *modi* are "merely logical functions", which do not provide thought with cognizable objects, not even "my self as an object" (B406–7). Rather, I shall argue, they are merely the logical rules by which we have to conceive of ourselves in I-judgements.

Let me illustrate the derivation of the logical predicates with the example of the Paralogism of Substantiality. This Paralogism is based on the logical function correlated with the category of substance. The traditional rationalist syllogism that is supposed to establish the soul's substantiality runs – according to the B-Edition – as follows:[35]

---

[34] On these predicates, see Rosefeldt (2000:82, 2017); on the minor premises, see Longuenesse (2017:11, 128–9). The order of the categories is reversed in comparison to the table of categories in the Analytic. For the rational psychologists, the leading category is "substance", from which they derive other properties of the soul, such as immateriality, incorruptibility, personality, and immortality (see Dyck 2014).

[35] This syllogistic structure corresponds to the First A-Paralogism, which however uses the unfortunate notion of "absolute subject" and presents the syllogism from the first-person perspective (see A348; also *Prol* §46 4:330–4).

(Major premise) What cannot be *thought* otherwise than as *subject* does not *exist* otherwise than as *subject*, and is therefore *substance*.

(Minor premise) Now a *thinking being, considered* merely as such, cannot be *thought* otherwise than as *subject*.

(Conclusion) Therefore *it* also *exists* only as such a thing, that is, as *substance*.
(B410–11, emphasis added)

Kant's analysis of this syllogism shows that the major and the minor premise apply the middle term of the syllogism, "subject", in different ways and thereby commit a fallacy of equivocation (a *sophisma figurae dictionis*, A402/B411) that renders the conclusion defective. Even though the logical form of the syllogism is valid and the two premises may even be correct, as Kant himself concedes, the conclusion does not hold. The syllogism can be reconstructed as follows:

(Major premise) If x must be *thought of* as SUBJECT, then x *exists* as SUBJECT, and, therefore, as SUBSTANCE.

(Minor premise) A THINKING BEING must be *thought of* as SUBJECT.

(Conclusion) A THINKING BEING *exists* as SUBSTANCE.

Since this syllogism is formally valid, the fallacy is not an error in formal logic, but in transcendental logic, that is, in the way in which concepts are applied to objects.[36] The fallacy is based on a confusion of the different ways of applying the understanding – the *real* use that concerns real determinations of objects and the *logical* use that abstracts from all objects and concerns only relations among concepts. The real use of the understanding is either *transcendental*, that is, regardless of whether the object can be intuited, or *empirical*, that is, limited to those objects that can be given in intuition.

The paralogistic inference is then based on a conflation of two uses of the term *subject* or, more precisely, on a conflation of two different meanings of the phrase "to be *thought of* as subject".[37] The antecedent of the major premise invokes the general *transcendental use* of "thought of in every respect", which implies the real determination of objects that "might be given in intuition" (B411). By contrast, the minor premise uses only a merely logical notion of "thinking" that "abstracts from all objects" and only concerns conceptual combination "in relation to self-consciousness" (B411n). This premise does not assert the existence of an object (or thing) over and above self-consciousness, but represents the subject "relative

---

[36] For the distinction between two kinds of formal errors – in formal logic and in transcendental logic – see A341/B399; see also Grier (1993:275).

[37] Note Kant's emphasis on the ambiguous ways that the middle term "subject" is "thought" (*gedacht*) (B410), "used" (*gebraucht*) (A348), or "regarded" (*angesehen, betrachtet*) (A351). See also Rosefeldt (2017:224, 228–31). On the error in the First Paralogism, see Grier (1993) and Longuenesse (2017:112–25).

only to thinking and to the unity of consciousness" (B411). I understand Kant as saying that the minor premise states only how a thinking being must be *conceived* by means of the concept *<subject>* in a logical sense, which Kant later identifies with the pure category of substance.[38] Yet without relating this concept to a corresponding intuition, it cannot be used for a real determination and hence cannot imply the assertion of the existence of a thinking substance, as is done in the consequent of the syllogism. The consequent precisely asserts the "existence" of a *thinking substance*, that is, of something real in which accidents inhere. Hence, the conflation of a transcendental use of *<subject>* in the major premise and a logical use in the minor premise leads precisely to a paralogistic fallacy in the consequent. The rational psychologist thus deduces from a logical notion of subject the assertion that the subject exists as a determinable substance.

Now, for Kant, the only legitimate real use of the concept *<substance>* is the "empirically usable" one (A349). This is a use of the category of substance as applied to intuition, resulting in the determination of empirical substances as persistent in time, as stated in the First Analogy. Without this limitation to intuition, a transcendentally real use of the concept would reach out to objects beyond the bounds of sense and would thus have "no use at all" (A247/B304, B403), since there would be no possible evidence that such objects existed and in fact had the properties defined by the concept. This unlimited use of the major premise turns into an illegitimate use in the consequent, because the minor premise is not supplied with corresponding intuitions that would confirm the thinker's existence as an object of experience, nor can the thinker's noumenal existence be derived solely on the basis of conceptual analysis. Hence, as Kant puts it in the A-Paralogism, the error of the rationalists lies in the fact that the syllogism "passes off the constant logical subject of thinking as the cognition of a real subject of inherence" (A350). The rationalists apply a real notion of substance as "subject of inherence" without the required empirical underpinning and hence commit a fallacy.

But what exactly is the "constant *logical* subject of thinking"? More generally, what do the predications that are stated in the minor premises of the paralogistic syllogisms – premises that Kant himself endorses – mean? In which sense must we think of ourselves as "*logical* substances", "*logically* simple", and so on?

The fact that I must represent myself via the logical "I" (with logical determinations only) in thought does not imply – as some argue – that all I am is just a *logical something*, an object of mere thought without existence above and beyond thought.[39] This reading would block an account of inner experience, which

---

[38] In the A-Paralogism and in the corresponding passages in the *Prolegomena*, Kant explicitly invokes the traditional Aristotelian definition of *substance* as that of which something is predicated, but which cannot be predicated of something else (see explicitly A348, *Prol* 4:334). Yet this definition is ambiguous as to whether it concerns logical or real predication.

[39] This implication seems entailed in some accounts of the logical "I". Rosefeldt (2000:228–30, also 77) acknowledges that we also "self-ascribe" mental predicates on the basis of "factual

must explain the self-ascription of *real* psychological predicates to something *real*. Others argue that the "logical subject" should be straightforwardly identified with the subject that really performs acts of thought and is conscious of its performing these acts through transcendental apperception.[40] Some even allow those logical determinations to indicate claims about the noumenal self as a thing-in-itself.[41] Yet all these readings collapse into reinterpreting the logical predicates as real determinations of a *real thinking agent*.

By contrast, I propose that the logical predicates of "I" define nothing but conceptual rules by means of which any thinking being refers to itself *in thought*, that is, from a *logical point of view*. In applying these rules to oneself, one turns oneself into an object of *one's own* thought. The conceptual rules of self-reference follow analytically from the capacity for self-consciousness and the reflexive structure of consciousness. Commonly, we use the indexical first-person pronoun "I" to refer to ourselves in thought or speech. If the term "I" is indeed used to express this reflexive self-conception, then it must be used in accordance with these logical predicates. Hence, the logical predicates specify precisely the rules for using "I" to refer to oneself in judgement.

To reiterate the crucial point of my interpretation: the logical predications stated in the minor premises of the paralogistic syllogisms define the way *any* thinking being must conceive of itself in thought, that is, from a *logical point of view*.[42] These logical predications are derived through an explication of the general form of reflexivity, viz. the form of apperception, according to the logical forms of judgement. Any use of the first-person pronoun "I" in judgement must comply with the conditions that these logical predications entail. Interpreted as conceptual rules, the logical predications specify the application rules of the pronoun "I" to oneself as thinking being, rather than any "features" of such a being.

The First Paralogism is particularly important to capture the reflexivity of consciousness. It states, basically, that the term "I" is taken to refer to the subject

---

determinations of inner sense", but he carefully concedes that such self-ascriptions are only problematic and cannot be assertoric, and therefore cannot amount to cognition. Yet his interpretation cannot account for inner experience, nor does he intend to give such an account.

[40] For example, Sturma (1985:68), Carl (1997:158–9), Keller (1998), Allison (2004:333–56), Melnick (2009), Longuenesse (2017:86–7, 94).

[41] Wuerth (2014:183) argues that one must conceive of oneself as "a *substance* in the *most basic ontological sense*".

[42] Longuenesse (2017:130–1), too, develops a reading of the "logical use of the concept *I*", which she identifies with a *universal*, that is, not relative to a particular subject, *first-person standpoint*, and contrasts this standpoint with an objective (or third-person) standpoint towards oneself. My position differs from hers in that I argue that a *first-person standpoint* requires not only a universal logical point of view, as defined by the logical predications, but also – as we will see – a *psychological point of view* under which these logical predications are explicated in *concreto*. Both together make it possible for me to cognize myself in an *objective, albeit first-personal*, way. The logical standpoint by itself still lacks individuation, that is, reference to an individual *in concreto*.

of thinking in such a way that "I" cannot be used as a predicate of something else.[43] Using a notion from contemporary philosophy of language, we could say that "I" has a *direct reference* to oneself – the one who thinks the I-judgement – without specifying any descriptive predicates of oneself. In this sense, Kant's logical "I" accounts for what David Kaplan calls the *character* of the indexical "I".[44] According to Kaplan, an indexical refers directly to a certain object, without descriptive identification and without rigid designation. While an indexical's specific referential content, viz. the object actually referred to, depends on the context of its utterance, one can describe this context-dependency by the indexical's *character*, that is, by a semantic rule that accounts for the dependence of the content on the context. Concerning the indexical "I", Kaplan suggests that this context-dependency can be captured by the so-called *I-rule*:

> (*I-Rule*) 'I' refers to the speaker or writer ... of the relevant occurrence of the word 'I', that is, the agent of the context   (Kaplan, 1989:505).[45]

A context, for Kaplan, is determined by three parameters: time, space, and the agent. Inspired by Kaplan, I now explicate the logical predicates of "I" as *semantic rules of self-reference*, that is, as rules that explain how the term "I" latches onto something *real* and *in concreto*. The following explication of the logical predicates of "I" as semantic rules of self-reference should thus be understood in a Kaplanian sense.[46]

Let me first state the four logical predicates (LP), each corresponding to a minor premise stated in one of the Paralogisms, with reference to Kant's text:

(LP1) I think of myself as "the constant logical subject of thinking" (A350) (i.e., "I, who I think [*Ich, der ich denke*], can in thinking [*im Denken*] always be considered as *subject* [*als Subjekt ... betrachtet werden kann*], and as something that does not merely append [*anhänge*] as a predicate to thought"; B407, translation amended);

(LP2) I think of myself as an "absolute (though merely logical) unity" (A355) (i.e., "logically simple subject"; B407);

(LP3) I think of myself as having "logical identity" (A363) (i.e., "the identity of myself in everything manifold of which I am conscious"; B408);

(LP4) "I think of [*other* things] as *distinguished* from me" (B409).

---

[43] See Kant's appeal to this Aristotelian definition of *substance*, for example, at A348, B407, and *Prol* 4:334.

[44] Kaplan (1989).

[45] See also Kaplan (1989:494).

[46] Similarly, Howell (2001:136) argues that Kant's "I think" should be understood as a "mental indexical", whose reference can be explained by Kaplan's theory of "direct, indexical self-reference". I maintain that, with this claim, Howell gives an adequate account of the problematic "I think" in the Paralogisms, but not, as he claims, of the apperceptive "I think" in the Deduction, for reasons I have spelled out in 3.3.

According to my reconstruction, these logical predications follow analytically from a "logical exposition" of the problematic judgement "I think": they are "analytic proposition[s]" deduced from the "I think" by employing the categories in their pure, that is, merely logical, use (B408–9).[47] The logical "I" denotes a thinking being merely in virtue of the logical characteristics of *thinking*, in full abstraction from any real (e.g., sensible) features such a being might have and without asserting the existence of a referent of "I". As long as there is no proof for the existence of such a being, the predications can be taken only problematically as representations of a *logically possible* being.

The logical "I" is, nonetheless, relevant for inner experience, in which we represent ourselves as psychological beings in time. If these logical predicates define conditions of how one must think of oneself, then they also define conditions of how one must cognize oneself, since cognition presupposes thought. In consequence, if inner experience is possible as cognition of oneself, then these logical predicates also define rules for the use of the pronoun "I" in empirical contexts and hence in assertoric judgements based on inner intuitions. The logical predicates, I argue, then imply four *semantic rules (SR) of self-reference in experience*, that is, rules for the use of the *mental equivalent of "I"* in empirical judgements of the basic form "I φ", whereby <φ> is a mental predicate.[48] These semantic rules could be reconstructed as follows:

(SR1) The mental equivalent of "I" refers to the one who thinks the I-judgement in a given *mental episode* and who ascribes to itself the mental predicate <φ>.

I take this first semantic rule to correspond to Kaplan's *I-rule*, as stated above, and to capture the fundamental reflexivity of consciousness in self-referential judgements. I here replace Kaplan's notion of context with the notion of a *mental episode*. I take a mental episode to be individuated by a single act of transcendental apperception, which binds together all relevant representations into a synthetic unity. If a mental episode occurs in inner sense, it constitutes a temporal episode in empirical consciousness. Such an episode could, for instance, be a perceptual episode in which a manifold of intuition is synthesized into a perception, or the making of an inference through combining a set of logically dependent thoughts. The following semantic rules can then be seen as specifications of this fundamental *I-rule*:

---

[47] Note that the minor premises stated in the Third and Fourth A-Paralogism still involve temporal and spatial determinations, such as numerical identity through time and existence in space. Yet the B-Paralogisms give clear evidence that Kant is willing to accept the minor premises only if they follow "analytically" from "I think" and therefore contain merely logical predicates.

[48] I take <φ> to stand not only for predicates subsumable under <*think*>, such as <*cognize*>, but also for predicates pertaining to other mental faculties, such as <*will*> and <*feel*>. A full account is provided only in 6.3.

(SR2) The mental equivalent of "I" refers to a single referent who cannot be divided into self-standing parts.

This means that "I"-parts, viz. mental states, cannot be referred to independently of the unity of consciousness to which they belong, that is, independently of the referent of "I" (unlike the parts of a material body, which can be referred to independently and as detached from the main bulk of matter). For instance, I cannot refer to *my current joy* independently of, or as detached from, myself, the person whose joy it is.

(SR3) Different occurrences of the mental equivalent of "I" within one and the same mental episode refer to one and the same referent.

"I" can, of course, be used to refer to *different* people in *different* contexts, even in the same conversational episode. Yet within a mental episode, which is defined by an act of apperception, the mental indexical "I" can refer only to one and the same referent, namely the thinker of the episode. Note, however, that the semantic rule is not valid beyond its mental episode and cannot be used to determine a subject as unified across different acts of apperception.

(SR4) The referent of the mental equivalent of "I" is considered to be logically distinct from all things that are not referred to by (or subsumed under) "I" in the given mental episode.

This may include the logical distinction from non-thinking things, from other thinking beings, and, arguably, from one's own body, to which – strictly speaking – mental states cannot be ascribed.[49]

Since so far all my considerations are based on the *problematic* "I think", the semantic rules derived from it must themselves be understood only problematically: they spell out how the term "I" can be used to refer to a thinker only *on the condition that* something real can instantiate the term. In other words, *if* there exists an x such that x is referred to by "I", *then* the semantic rules (SR1–4) must apply for any empirical I-judgement.[50]

What my explication of the logical predicates as semantic rules of self-reference has not yet shown is whether these rules can indeed be instantiated and hence are justified in light of what is given in inner intuition. Moreover, can these rules be extended beyond single apperceptive acts such that they can

---

[49] The fourth is the most controversial of the Paralogisms, especially since the versions from the A- and B-Edition differ substantially. My reconstruction draws mainly on the B-Edition. By "logically distinct", I mean the property of falling under distinct concepts, that is, concepts that differ in at least one mark. For example, two pieces of fruit are logically distinct, if only one of them falls under the concept <apple>.

[50] Note that the semantic rules (SR2–4) also entail conditions of how to refer to *other* thinking beings (via the personal pronouns *you*, *he/she*, or *they*), since it requires "the transference of this consciousness of mine to other things, which can be represented as thinking beings only in this way" (A347).

give rise to the experience of oneself across time? To answer these questions of justification, a logical exposition of "I think" is not sufficient. Rather, the answer requires a kind of transcendental deduction of what one might call the *categories of self-reference*, like the transcendental deduction of the categories of object-reference. Such a deduction would show *that* the predicates of the logical "I" are in fact applicable to that which is given in inner intuition. It would, moreover, require a schematism and principles of inner experience to show *how* a sensible explication of the logical "I" is feasible.

In the General Remark concluding the B-Paralogisms, we find Kant vaguely gesturing towards this problem of justification. He claims that the determination of my existence in time requires "the thinking of myself *applied to* the empirical intuition of the very same subject" (B430, emphasis added). As I understand this passage, Kant here indicates the need for *applying* the logical "I" to inner intuition to make *cognition* of myself possible. This application can be understood as a sensible explication of the logical predicates of "I" in terms of temporal determinations, in analogy with the Schematism that provides a sensible explication of the categories of object-reference. The Schematism precisely explicates the pure, logical content of the categories in terms of "transcendental time-determinations" (A139/B178), which then lead to the principles of the understanding.[51] Only if the logical "I" can be explicated in terms of temporal contents can it be shown to be compatible with the sensible characteristics of mental phenomena. Only then can it serve to denote an object of inner experience.

The application of the logical "I" to inner intuition will turn out to be even more difficult than the application of the categories to outer intuition. The crux of inner experience is that – unlike in the case of outer experience – we *cannot intuit* ourselves in accordance with the logical predicates of "I", but only *think* ourselves in this way. This is in fact the negative result of the Paralogisms. In the remainder of this chapter, I explore the major disparity between inner and outer experience specifically with respect to (SR3) and the Third Paralogism of Personality, and finally argue for the necessity of a different – analogical – kind of sensible explication of the categories of relation in inner experience.

4.4   The Psychological "I" as the Object of Inner Experience

4.4.1   The Paradox of the Determinable Self

What are the conditions under which I can *cognize* myself and determine my inner appearances in time? Do I thereby determine myself as a genuine object of inner experience? Kant seems fairly optimistic with regard to the general possibility of cognizing myself through inner appearances, though he remains

---

[51] On the Schematism, see 2.4 and 5.5.

frustratingly vague throughout the first *Critique* and other Critical works as to what the exact conditions of such a possibility are. Yet he is far more cautious as to whether there is a genuine object of inner experience. Kant is worried that the determinability of oneself in cognition in fact raises a paradox – the "paradox of inner sense", as he calls it in the Transcendental Deduction (§24, B154). Let me first explore what Kant's general worry is, before I then analyse the problem for the case of personal identity across time.

That I cognize myself only if I appear to myself in intuition is a claim that Kant often repeats throughout (and beyond) the first *Critique*. Textual evidence for this determinability claim can be found in numerous places, such as the following:

> we must also concede that … as far as inner intuition is concerned we cognize our own subject only as appearance but not in accordance with what it is in itself. (B156)

> I therefore have no cognition of myself as I am, but only as I appear to myself. (B158)

> Thus I cognize myself not by being conscious of myself as thinking, but only if I am conscious to myself of the intuition of myself as determined in regard to the function of thought. (B406)[52]

At first sight, these passages seem to suggest a parallel treatment of inner and outer experience and hence seem to support what I have called the *parity view* of inner experience (see i.2). According to the parity view, inner experience is considered as empirical cognition of the same kind as outer experience. Starting from the apparent parity between inner and outer sense, proponents of this view argue that both outer and inner experience are constituted by the same two kinds of representation, namely *intuitions* of outer, or respectively, inner appearances, given through the senses, and *concepts* through which an object is thought.[53] A crucial assumption is that inner intuitions can be synthesized in accordance with the categories, including the category of substance, in the same way that outer intuition can be synthesized. Hence, there is a basic parity between the way that the categories are applicable to inner and outer intuitions, respectively, and how they then determine an object of inner or outer experience, respectively.[54]

Yet there is a set of texts in which Kant acknowledges that inner experience involves a paradox, which gives rise to a major disparity between inner and outer experience and eventually poses a fatal problem to the parity view. The set of texts I have in mind are primarily passages that Kant added to the

---

[52] See also B68–9; *Anth* 7:141. On the notion of *determining my existence in time*, see Bxl, B157n, B275–9, B429–31.
[53] For example, Vogel (1993), Chignell (2017).
[54] For a detailed discussion of the parity view, see Kraus (2019a).

B-Edition to discourage an overly idealistic interpretation of his Critical Philosophy. In these passages, Kant emphasizes not only the difficulty of cognizing oneself, but also the significance of outer sense for cognition in general. As examples, I consider two central passages – one from the B-Deduction (§24) and another from the B-Paralogisms.

In the B-Deduction, embedded in his discussion of the figurative synthesis (§24), Kant explicitly diagnoses the paradox of inner sense. The paradox stems from the fact that in inner experience I must represent myself in two apparently conflicting (or even "contradictory", B153) ways, namely, as the subject of thinking and as the object that is intuited. Kant himself is puzzled over this problem:

> But how *the I who I think [das Ich, der ich denke]* is to *differ from the I that intuits itself [das Ich, das sich selbst anschauet]* (for I can represent other kinds of intuition as at least possible) and *yet be identical with the latter as the same subject [dasselbe Subjekt]*, how therefore I can say that *I* as intelligence and *thinking* subject cognize my self as an object that is *thought*, insofar as I am also given to myself in intuition, only, like other phenomena, not as I am for the understanding but rather as I appear to myself, this is no more and no less difficult than how I can be an object for myself in general and indeed one of intuition and inner perceptions.
>
> (B155–6, emphasis added and translation amended)

As I understand this passage, Kant here distinguishes two different ways of representing oneself, both of which can be expressed by using the term "I": the "I that I think" and the "I that intuits itself". Again, I take this to be a conceptual, rather than an ontological, distinction – in line with my reading of the logical "I" and the psychological "I" in the *Progress* essay and in the *Anthropology* (see 4.2). The paradox arises from the fact that these two representations "differ" with respect to their disparate representational contents: what is represented as the subject is commonly considered to be opposed to the object that is intuited and subsequently cognized by the subject. And yet the two "I"-representations must be assumed to be "identical" regarding their referent: the self-same subject.[55]

This problem of self-reference receives a more forceful formulation in the B-Paralogisms. There, Kant distinguishes the "consciousness of the *determining* [or *thinking*] self (*Bewußtsein des Bestimmenden*)" from "that of the *determinable* self (*des bestimmbaren Selbst*)" (B407) and then shows for each Paralogism that from the problematic "I think", we can infer only conceptual rules to think of the *determining* self, but no real determinations of the

---

[55] See specifically "The human 'I' is indeed twofold according to form (manner of representation), but not according to matter (content)" (*Anth* 7:134n) and "It is true that I as thinking being am one and the same subject with myself as sensing being" (*Anth* 7:142). See also B429–30; *Progress* 20:270; and *Anth* 7:134n.

determinable self. This leads him to reinforce his worry about a paradox in his final remark:

> The proposition "I think," or "I exist thinking," is an empirical proposition. But such a proposition is grounded on empirical intuition, consequently also on the *object thought, as an appearance*; and thus it seems as if, according to our theory, the whole, even in thinking, is *completely transformed into appearance*, and in such a way our consciousness itself, as mere illusion, would in fact come down to nothing.
>
> (B428, emphasis added)

Again, Kant detects a conceptual problem for "our theory" of transcendental philosophy: inner experience is supposed to determine an "object thought as an appearance". Yet as soon as "our consciousness itself" is determined and "completely transformed into an appearance", it becomes a "mere illusion", rather than a properly determined object of experience. As soon as I try to turn my own self into a genuine object of my experience, the very object itself becomes an illusion and I destroy the very possibility of cognizing myself altogether. Why is this the case?

Recall that according to Kant's transcendental philosophy, the determining self – qua its mental faculties – is viewed as the source of any representational relationship to an object (see 3.4). By trying to prove that the determining self is identical with the determinable self, we try to determine (i.e., to cognize) this source itself, which, however, is the necessary condition of the very possibility of cognition. To escape this vicious circle, there seem to be two options. Either we dogmatically postulate that the determining self just is identical with the determinable self and hence commit the rationalist fallacy. Or, we accept that the self is elusive and defies cognition altogether and hence choose the path of scepticism. Neither of these options is an acceptable solution for Kant. But how can he avoid these disastrous consequences of his transcendental philosophy? The solution that I eventually propose turns on the idea that we should *not* "completely transform[]" ourselves into *mere* appearances, but instead merely *consider* ourselves as such in an *analogical* way. Now, I show that the Paralogisms leave some conceptual space for the middle path I envision, and I do so in particular for the case of personal identity.

4.4.2 The Crux of Inner Experience: No Persistent Object, but Personal Identity in Time

We undoubtedly regard ourselves as enjoying a continuous mental life, at least under normal psychological conditions. We recall past joys and sorrows, we regret past deeds and remain proud of others; we may enjoy the present moment, knowing that it may be over too soon, or just wait desperately for it to lapse; we feel unsettled in view of developments that we fear will happen to us in the future or a burst of excitement in light of an event expected to take place soon. All these kinds of inner experience require us to consider ourselves as in the relevant sense *identical throughout time*. Kant follows traditional metaphysics, in particular the German rationalists Wolff and Baumgarten, in defining *personal identity* in terms of the capacity to be "conscious of [one's] numerical identity . . . in different times" (A361). But how can Kant's own theory account for this capacity?

The issue of personal identity reveals especially clearly the chasm between viewing oneself as a *mere* appearance and thinking of oneself via the logical "I". Consider the following two basic options in accounting for personal identity, both of which are deeply problematic. On the one hand, following the parity interpretation, the consciousness required for personal identity could be rendered as a kind of cognition, namely as the cognition of one's *persistence* in time according to the category of substance. Yet Kant repeatedly claims that, unlike the physical matter perceivable in outer sense, there is "no standing or abiding self" that could be intuited in inner sense and determined as that which persists through all changes of state (A107, also A364). So, prima facie, it is unclear what else could give rise to the cognition of one's persistence other than the physical matter of one's *human body*. I call this the *persistence view* of personal identity.[56]

On the other hand, acknowledging the lack of something persistent that is intuitable in inner sense, one could propose that the consciousness required for personal identity flows from the *logical identity* that a unified consciousness must have. On this disparity view, the consciousness of one's numerical identity *in time* then comes down to a logical presupposition that is implied by transcendental apperception and is thus part of one's logical self-representation, viz. the logical "I". Then, however, it is prima facie hard to see how the purely logical "I" could contain a temporal predicate and, moreover, how exactly it could give rise to the cognition of inner appearances as mental states of something enduring in time.[57] I call this the *apperceptive view* of personal identity.[58]

How do these views fare in explaining the possibility of inner experience based on their account of personal identity? I argue that neither of them fares well. My discussion comes in two parts. Firstly, with regard to the persistence view, I show, in the current section, that Kant's theory does not allow for the cognition of a mental substance, nor would it be adequate to explain personal identity on the

---

[56] Proponents of the parity view, as I defined it above, commonly defend the existence of some kind of mental persistent substance, for example, Vogel (1993), Chignell (2017). Interpreters such as Strawson (1966:164–9), Rosefeldt (2000:119–27), and Longuenesse (2007, 2017:140–69, esp. 151), by contrast, appeal to the persistence of the human body, as a second criterion for personal identity – in addition to the logical identity implied in transcendental apperception.

[57] Recall that in 4.2, I identified the semantic rule (SR3) without appealing to any temporal determinations.

[58] For example, Henrich (1994), Mariña (2011), Wuerth (2014).

basis of cognition of one's persistent body. I base my argument on passages from the Refutation of Idealism, the Refutation of Mendelssohn's Proof of the Permanence of the Soul, and the *Metaphysical Foundations*. Secondly, with regard to the apperceptive view, I argue, in the next section, that the Third Paralogism (in line with the Transcendental Deduction) rejects any reduction of personal identity to logical identity, but instead opens some conceptual space for a middle path between the persistence and the apperceptive view.

The persistence view suggests that the capacity to be conscious of one's numerical identity in time is based on applying the category of substance to determine something persistent. This view must show that the category of substance can be applied in such a way that it gives rise to the determination of oneself as persistent substance. There are two basic options: either the category is applied directly to inner intuitions and hence gives rise to the cognition of a *persistent mental substance*, or it is applied to outer intuitions that are sufficiently related to inner appearances, such as the intuitions of one's body, and hence gives rise to the cognition of one's *persistent body*.

The first option of cognizing a *persistent mental substance* seems explicitly ruled out by Kant's repeated claim that there is "no standing or abiding self" in inner sense (e.g., A107, also A364). Yet there is an interesting lesson to be learned from understanding Kant's reason for ruling this out. Basically, Kant's argument runs as follows: the manifold of inner appearances are given only through inner sense in the form of time; a merely temporal manifold, however, cannot provide the material appropriate to instantiate the category of substance as something persistent in time, which would be required for the cognition of a persistent mental substance (e.g., A22–3/B37, A107, A350, B412–13). Arguments to this effect can be found in the Mechanics chapter of the *Foundations* and in the Refutation of Mendelssohn's Proof in the first *Critique*. A brief discussion of these arguments reveals the difficulty that Kant detects in finding an adequate *sensible* explication of the category of substance for inner intuition.[59]

In the *Foundations*, Kant presents an explicit argument for the inapplicability of the category of substance as persistence to inner intuition.[60] For outer experience, the category of substance is applied through the "schema of substance",

---

[59] In response, adherents of the parity view offer a deflationary account of substance in outer experience (e.g., Vogel 1993:881, Chignell 2017). They argue that even in outer experience, we have only a "bundle" of intuitions of changing states, which are taken to inhere in a substance only by way of the unifying function of the category of substance. So the evanescence of inner and outer states may differ in degree, but not in kind: both are alterable and can change rapidly; and the applicability of substance does not depend on what is *given* in intuition (e.g., physical matter in space). I do not think that Kant holds such a deflationary account for reasons I spell out in this section.

[60] See Remark to the Proof of the First Law of Mechanics, regarding the conservation of the quantity of matter (*MFNS* 4:541–2). Note that Kant's comparison between outer and inner experience in this Remark should be viewed in the context of his general scepticism, in the *Foundations*, regarding the possibility of psychology as a proper science alongside

which is "the persistence of the real in time, that is, the representation of the real as a substratum of empirical time-determination" (A144/B183). The real is that which is received in sensation and apprehended as the quality of some property, for example, heat or colour. As such, it has only intensive magnitude, that is, a degree, as the Anticipations of Perception show. In outer intuition, there is "something standing and abiding . . . which supplies a substratum grounding the transitory determinations" (A381). Outer sense supplies such a substratum because it represents an aggregate of material *"parts external to one another"* (*MFNS* 4:540). A possible object of outer intuition does not merely have an intensive magnitude (regarding its sensory qualities), but is also spatially extended, that is, has extensive magnitude. Only an extensive distribution of reality can function as a substratum that can be compared at different times and then determined as "the persistent of the real in time". This spatially extended distribution is precisely the distribution of *physical matter in space*.[61]

By contrast, an analogous sensible explication of substance cannot be found for that which is exclusively given to inner sense, as Kant goes on to argue: "By contrast, that which is considered as object of inner sense can have a magnitude, as substance, which *does not consist of parts external to one another*; and its parts, therefore, are not substances" (*MFNS* 4:542). Here "parts" are understood as the "representations in my soul", that is, my inner appearances (*MFNS* 4:542). These parts cannot be determined as separable extensive magnitudes; rather, as parts of one and the same consciousness, they have only intensive magnitudes, and augment or diminish by degrees. A distribution of a purely intensive reality (independent of spatial extension), however, cannot satisfy the condition of a substratum that persists in time. From this, Kant concludes that the "very substance of the soul" and its "parts" cannot be shown to be persistent in time, because they could gradually perish and therefore violate the conservation of quantity of substance (*MFNS* 4:542).[62] To this conclusion one may object that mental states are *temporally* extended and therefore supply an extensive distribution of reality. However, mental states, if viewed as a *temporally extensive* distribution of reality, precisely cannot function as a substratum of time-determination, because such temporal distribution already presupposes a substratum according to which they first are represented as temporally extended.[63]

---

physics (see *MFNS* 4:471). Yet this scepticism should not be understood as a general rejection of the possibility of inner experience.

[61] See also B278. A compelling discussion can be found in Friedman (2013:316–24).

[62] See also my note on (SR2) in 4.3. In the Refutation of Mendelssohn's Proof, Kant argues that the persistence of the soul is "indemonstrable" (B413–18). Similarly, Kant claims that "mathematics is not applicable to the phenomena of inner sense" since the "law of continuity" cannot be applied (*MFNS* 4:471). Although mental phenomena are intensive magnitudes, they lack objective *persistence*.

[63] Similarly, Kant excludes this option in the Third A-Paralogism, arguing that I can consider myself "as *in time*" only as "an object of [someone's] outer intuition" (A362).

In conclusion, a manifold of inner sense does not display the appropriate formal structure to correspond to something persistent according to the category of substance. Inner sense does not supply "a distribution of reality" that can function as the "substratum of ... all time-determination", as required by the First Analogy, the Principle of the Persistence of Substance (A183/B226).[64] Hence, Kant offers a strong argument that we cannot determine (and thus cognize) a persistent mental substance by applying the category of substance to inner intuition. We thus lack an *empirical concept of a persistent mind* that can be determined a priori according to the categories, like the empirical concept of physical matter.[65]

To be sure, this argument does not entail that *no use* at all can be made of the category of substance for inner experience, as interpreters have often concluded.[66] In line with his exposition of the logical "I" in the Paralogisms, Kant here also grants the applicability of the pure, unschematized category of substance to the "I, the general correlate of apperception" that designates "the subject of all predicates" (*MFNS* 4:452).

Since Kant has good reason to rule out the cognition of a persistent *mental* substance, a viable option to save the persistence view of personal identity seems to be to appeal to one's embodiment. According to this second option, a person can recognize herself as numerically identical over time in virtue of cognizing her *persistent body*, since her body is the only relevant material object of outer sense that allows for the determination as persistent substance.[67] Inner intuitions can then be determined as accidents of something persistent, if they are correlated with outer intuitions of one's body in space. Personal identity is then derivative of the person's bodily identity through time.

This option seems to find support in the Refutation of Idealism and the Refutation of Mendelssohn's Proof, both added to the B-Edition. The Refutation of Idealism aims to refute Cartesian problematic idealism, according to which the existence of external objects is "doubtful and *indemonstrable*", while the existence of oneself can be proven through inner experience (B274). By contrast, Kant maintains that "inner experience itself is ... possible only

---

[64] I borrow the term *distribution of reality* from Friedman (2013:323ff.).

[65] Kant entertains the possibility of an "empirical concept of ... a thinking being" (*MFNS* 4:470), but rejects that it entails persistence (e.g., A682/B710; *CpracR* 5:43; *MFNS* 4:542–3).

[66] See Friedman (2013:6–7, 322), Förster (1987:543). Various commentators more or less explicitly subscribe to the claim that for an object to instantiate the categories it must have spatial dimensions and outstrip consciousness (e.g., Nayak and Sotnak 1995, Longuenesse 1998:345n, Pollok 2001, Westphal 2004:134–7, 232–3, Bird 2006:413–16, Emundts 2010).

[67] Strawson (1966:164–9), Rosefeldt (2000:119–27), Longuenesse (2007:157, 2017:140–69). These interpreters acknowledge that personal identity requires a second criterion, namely a logical or formal identity that follows from the "I think" of apperception.

through outer experience" (B277).[68] Kant, basically, argues that, for the deter-mination of oneself in time to be possible, something persistent must be presupposed that is independent of the mind's changing representations and hence actually exists outside the mind. In conclusion, the determination of my existence in time is traced back to the actual existence of a persistent correlate of time, "as, say, impenetrability in matter" (B278).[69]

The Refutation of Mendelssohn's Proof of the Permanence of the Soul rejects, in line with the Paralogisms, Mendelssohn's rationalist argument for the "soul's necessary continuing duration" (B413). There, Kant concludes that the persistence of the soul as such cannot be proven, but allows that it can be assumed in virtue of being tied to the persistence of the human body – at least in life: "the persistence of the soul, merely as an object of inner sense, remains unproved and unprovable, although its persistence in life, where the thinking being (as a human being) is at the same time an object of outer sense, is clear of itself" (B415). The argument that Kant develops here is similar to the *Foundations* argument discussed above: what is given in inner sense can only be an intensive distribution of reality determinable by intensive magnitudes, rather than a subsisting extensive distribution; therefore, the soul by itself cannot be shown to have subsistence through time.

Both passages clearly support the conclusion from the *Foundations* that the category of substance as persistence is not applicable to inner experience. So I agree with the proponents of this second option that the determination of a persistent substance always requires physical matter and cognizing one's persistence thus requires one's embodiment. Yet I do not think that we should identify the notion of personal identity in question with such a strong sense of *persistence*. Textually, none of the discussed passages explicitly excludes the in-principle applicability of the category of substance to inner intuition; rather, the passages leave open the option of applying the concept of substance in a less demanding sense than substantial persistence.

Philosophically, tying the notion of *personal identity* to the consciousness of one's embodiment is troublesome. If Kant really tied personal identity to the consciousness of a persistent material body, then I could cognize the temporal relations of my mental states only if I cognize an actual physical-material object (preferably my own body) as a substratum correlated to these states. On a strong reading, this may require that for each temporal series of mental

---

[68] See corresponding footnote in the B-Preface Bxl.

[69] I will not pursue the controversial issue regarding the role of transcendental idealism in this argument, that is, as to whether the conclusion concerns the existence of external objects in space or of things-in-themselves (see Guyer 1987:303–15, Allison 2004:300, Keller 1998:210). Kant acknowledges that the notion of matter is "presupposed *a priori*" (B278). This might imply that what is required for time-determination is the presupposi-tion of the *empirical concept of matter*, rather than the actual givenness of physico-material objects. For further discussion, see Kraus (2019a) and 5.6.

states to be cognized, I must be immediately conscious of a directly correlated bodily substratum (or a directly corresponding series of bodily states). If inner experience were indeed derivative of the consciousness of an actual substratum, then a malfunctioning body-consciousness or just its temporary failure would severely impede my ability to have a consciousness of my personal identity at all. Not being conscious of my own body might also make it impossible for me to experience and later reflect upon a series of dream states. Alternatively, on a weaker reading, it may only require me to be conscious of a corresponding physical-material framework that serves as the backdrop against which the change of my mental states can be cognized. A direct correlation would be needed only for an objective time-measurement of my mental states by which I determine the exact timing of my mental states in objective time.[70]

Both variants suggest a reductionist view according to which inner experience is derivative of the outer experience of one's body. In consequence, mental states are cognized – alongside bodily states – as the accidents of my body, since no persistent substance other than my body can be identified to which mental states could be ascribed. Hence, only the body could appear to me as the causal ground of my mental states and my mental powers would sensibly appear to me as the causal powers of a material substance, rather than of a thinking being.[71] Textually, this reductionist view is difficult to square with passages in which Kant explicitly distinguishes two irreducible kinds of appearances, such as his emphasis on the need for "representing all *appearances* in space as entirely distinct from the *actions of thinking*" as inner appearances (A683/B711). Most severely, in deriving personal identity from the consciousness of physical-material persistence, the persistence view loses grip on the *self*-relatedness of personal identity. Personal identity requires me to identify, not only *some* persistent object, but myself with this persistent object, that is, to be conscious of my persistent body *as mine*. It still needs to be shown how the sensible conditions of bodily persistence relate to the logical conditions of self-reference.

---

[70] Both readings have been suggested as interpretations of the Refutation of Idealism. For the "substratum" reading see Emundts (2010:168–89); for the "backdrop" reading see Allison (2004:297). For the correlation claim, see also Guyer (1987:315), Keller (1998:204), and Longuenesse (2017:91). For a detailed discussion of the Refutation and a defence of the parity view, see Chignell (2017). For a discussion of objective time-measurement of mental states, see Kraus (2016) and 5.6.

[71] Not all commentators agree that – on this view – mental states could be ascribed as accidents only to bodies, instead suggesting that they can be ascribed to "the current thinker, myself" (Longuenesse 2007:157) or to the "logical I" (Rosefeldt 2000:124–5). But this then leaves open the exact relationship between the thinker as the logically identical "bearer" of mental states and the human body as the supposed "persistent substratum" of a temporal series of such states.

To resolve this issue commentators appeal to Kant's distinction between the notions of "I in the strict sense (*in sensu stricto*)" and of the "self in the broader sense (*in sensu latiori*)" (*L-MP/L₁* 28:265) in his lectures on metaphysics. The latter is taken to refer to the whole human being, including the human body, and hence to account for the "full-fledged consciousness of the individual biography of the empirical human being" (Longuenesse 2017:162).[72] This concept is understood to follow from both the conditions of self-reference, as implied by the logical "I", and the conditions of object-reference, including persistence. Yet these lecture notes date from before the Critical period and still show a pre-Critical understanding of inner sense and the soul. In fact, Kant never justifies the concept of the "self in the broader sense" in his Critical writings, nor is it clear how it could be systematically justified in his Critical Philosophy.

Undoubtedly, the reference to *oneself* in thought must be presupposed for the capacity to be "conscious of the numerical identity of *its Self*" (A361), as Kant's very definition of personal identity mandates. Kant emphasizes the requirement of *self*-reference in his account of personal identity in the Paralogisms: "the identity of the person ... would be understood [as] the consciousness of the identity of *its own* substance as a *thinking* being in all changes of state" (B408, emphasis added). This definition of personal identity suggests that Kant cannot be satisfied with appealing to the persistence of one's material body. Rather, personal identity requires consciousness of oneself as the self-same *thinking being* throughout time. This definition is, furthermore, in line with his account of personal identity in his pre-Critical lectures on metaphysics, where he defines psychological personality as follows:

> Personality can be taken ... *psychologically, if it is conscious of itself and of the identity*. The consciousness of itself and the identity of the person rests on inner sense. But because the body is not a principle of life, inner sense still remains even without the body, thus likewise the personality.
> (*L-MP/L₁* 28:296, emphasis added)

Even though these lectures broadly share the rationalist conception of personhood, I submit that Kant's Critical conception of personal identity still rests on a body-*independent* criterion of psychological endurance. That Kant's Critical concept of a person, while having sensible conditions, is primarily tied to one's intellectual aspects is most evident in the *Critique of Practical Reason*: "a person [who is viewed] as belonging to the sensible world is subject to his own personality insofar as he also belongs to the intelligible world" (*CpracR* 5:87). Regarding myself as a person thus consists in regarding myself as a thinking being that is subject to the sensible conditions under which such being appears in inner intuition.

In sum, there is ample evidence that Kant maintains a psychological account of personhood. This account must crucially make sense of the application of

---

[72] See similarly Rosefeldt (2000 and, esp., 2003:152).

the logical conditions of self-reference to inner intuition and hence must give an explanation for the sensible explicability of the logical "I". This sensible explication is not possible through the conditions of persistence: neither in terms of the persistence of a mental substance, nor in terms of the persistence of the body that is correlated with one's mental states.

4.4.3   The Psychological Point of View in the Third Paralogism

In this final section, I show that a specifically *psychological* concept of a person is also evident in the Third Paralogisms and examine in detail how it is to be distinguished from the logical "I" (with the predicate of logical identity). This also leads me to discard the second account of personal identity sketched above, namely the apperceptive view (see 4.4.1).

The Third Paralogism of Personality concerns rationalist arguments for the soul's personal identity through time. Kant states the rationalist syllogism as follows in the A-Edition:

(*Major Premise*) What is conscious of the numerical identity of its Self in different times, is to that extent a person.

(*Minor Premise*) Now the soul is etc.

(*Conclusion*) Thus it is a person. (A361)

There is considerable consensus that with the major premise Kant restates the definition of a person that – inspired by Locke – is widely shared among eighteenth-century German rationalists.[73] It is far more controversial what the minor premise would be, especially since Kant does not spell it out. Some suggest a third-personal reconstruction, stating that "the soul is conscious of the numerical identity of its self at different times" (Keller 1995:126); others a first-personal reconstruction stating that "I, as thinking, am conscious of the numerical identity of myself in different times" (Longuenesse 2017:141). While either version of the minor premise could certainly be historically adequate with respect to some rationalist thinkers, they would be incompatible with my earlier line of interpretation according to which the minor premise is one that Kant could endorse, and explicates a logical predicate of "I". A reconstruction that would only entail a logical predication could be: "I, as thinking, am conscious of my *logical* identity

---

[73] For example, Ameriks (2000:130), Kitcher (2011:185), Longuenesse (2017:141). This definition is accepted, for example, by Wolff (1720/1997:§924, 1734:§741) and Baumgarten (1739/2011). The German rationalists took decisive clues from Locke's definition of the person (see Locke 1690/1975 II:27.9:335) and, like Locke, relate it to questions of punishment and reward, as well as of incorruptibility and immortality. By contrast, the Third Paralogism focuses on personal identity over time, without considering issues of morality, incorruptibility, and immortality. For discussion, see Dyck (2014:141–59).

at *any* time."[74] This reconstruction makes it immediately clear that the rationalists conflate two notions of identity: *numerical identity [of something complex] in different times* and *logical identity [of something simple] at any time*. Now, I argue that it is crucial for an understanding of the Third Paralogism to distinguish between three, rather than merely two, distinct points of view:[75]

(1) the *logical* point of view, from which one thinks of oneself by way of the logical "I";

and two distinct senses of numerical identity in time:

(2) the *physical* point of view, from which one cognizes material substances as persistent through time; and
(3) the *psychological* point of view, from which one views oneself as personally identical through time.

The concept of personal identity is justified only from the psychological point of view and should *not* be reduced to objective persistence, as argued above, or to logical identity, as I now argue. Let me first offer some textual basis for this threefold distinction, before I refute the apperceptive view.

First, Kant begins his discussion of the Paralogism by considering the phenomenon of "self-consciousness in time" (A362), which – as I will argue – corresponds to the *psychological* point of view: "I am an object of inner sense and all time is merely the form of inner sense. Consequently, I relate each and every one of my successive determinations to the numerically identical Self in all time, i.e., in the form of the inner intuition of my self" (A362). From this standpoint, the "personality of the soul" is not inferred from empirical intuition, but is presupposed as an a priori "proposition of self-consciousness in time" (A362).[76]

Secondly, Kant introduces the *physical* point of view of outer experience by considering "the standpoint of another" (A362). An external observer can consider me only "as an object of his outer intuition", but will *not* be able to thereby "infer the objective persistence of my Self" (A362–3). Rather, through

---

[74] See (LP3) and (SP3) in 4.3.
[75] Note that the Third Paralogism is often viewed in light of the distinction between the noumenal and the phenomenal self. Some readings take Kant to endorse the possibility of a noumenal point of view with regard to personal identity. Ameriks (2000) argues that Kant grants the possibility of a noumenal substantial self that may give rise to a phenomenal self that is continuous over time, although the noumenal self could not have temporal determinations and therefore – strictly speaking – could not fulfil the criterion of personal identity. I think that my reading complements, rather than conflicts with, Ameriks' account in that I show how Kant can restore the concept of a psychological person without appealing to a noumenal substance as the ground of its appearing.
[76] Frequently, commentators argue that this passage describes the perspective of the "I think", for example Longuenesse (2007:152–7, 2017, 144–5), Rosefeldt (2000: 99), Mariña (2011). An exception is Keller (1995), who distinguishes the perspective of "inner experience" from the "I think".

outer sense someone, including myself, is able to cognize my body as a persistent substance. But, as shown above, this standpoint cannot explain how I come to realize that the object I am cognizing as persistent is in fact *my own* body and hence that I *myself* persist in time.

Finally, with the notions of "complete identity" and "the logical identity of the I" Kant appeals to the logical point of view, that is, the standpoint of mere thinking (A363). Contrary to several commentators, I do not think that this logical identity can involve "numerical identity".[77] I take the notion of "*numerical* identity" to imply the identity of something that is *amenable to numeration*, that is, something complex consisting of distinguishable parts, or that can at least be considered at numerically distinguishable times. In this sense, numerical identity presupposes some numerical determination. The logical "I" is the identical, self-same representation that can be employed to think about oneself at any time. As the Second Paralogism has shown, it does not represent something complex with numerically distinguishable parts. The Third Paralogism adds that the logical "I" cannot trace the identity of "I" in numerically distinguishable times. The distinction between (1) the *logical identity* (of something simple) at any time and (3) the *numerical identity* (of something complex) in different times becomes evident in the following passage:

> The *identity of the consciousness of Myself in different times* [1] is therefore only a formal condition of my thoughts and their connection, but it does not prove at all the *numerical identity of my subject* [3], in which – despite the *logical identity of the I* [1] – a change can go on that does not allow it to keep its *identity* [3]; and this even though all the while the *identical-sounding "I"* [1] is assigned to it, which in every other state, even in the replacement of the subject, still keeps in view the thought of the previous subject, and thus could also pass it along to the following one.
>
> (A363, emphasis and numbering added)

Here Kant is cautious not to talk about "numerical identity" with respect to the logical "I", which represents the conditions of a unified consciousness.[78] The simple representation "I" contains the exactly same predicates for all rational beings capable of self-consciousness. All occurrences of this "identical-sounding" "I" within a thought that is unified through apperception will refer to one and the same referent.[79] Yet this "I" is insufficient to establish

---

[77] Cf. Keller (1998:25–32, 174–81).

[78] In the A-Deduction, Kant occasionally uses the notion of *numerical identity* with respect to apperception (A107, 113), but the A-Deduction often runs together temporal-procedural with logical aspects, whereas only the A-Paralogisms separates a distinctively logical from a psychological account of the "I".

[79] Recall my account of the corresponding semantic rule (SR3): "Different occurrences of the mental equivalent of 'I' within one and the same mental episode refer to one and the same referent."

the identity of a thinking being with mental states varying *in time* and hence personal identity, as I now argue.

The *apperceptive view* of personal identity acknowledges that the identity implied by transcendental apperception does not guarantee that there is an *empirical substance* underlying all mental states and that it does not give rise to *cognition* of oneself in time. Nonetheless, the apperceptive view suggests that transcendental apperception should be understood as involving the numerical identity of the self-same thinking being to which different representations can be ascribed at different times.[80] It assumes that the subject whose consciousness is unified through transcendental apperception can be attended to as a *numerically* identical subject at different times. For example, it may take a few minutes or perhaps even hours to understand a mathematical proof by going through it step by step. According to Kant's theory of transcendental apperception, one can properly arrive at the conclusion only if one thinks and affirms all initial and intermediary premises as well as the conclusion in a unified consciousness. The apperceptive view suggests that understanding a mathematical proof in thought requires a consciousness of one's numerical identity throughout the temporal procedure of going through the proof, and concludes that transcendental apperception entails consciousness of oneself in time.[81]

Yet this view conflates the "formal condition of my thoughts and their connection" with the temporal conditions under which my thoughts appear to myself (A363). At *any* time we must think of ourselves as the logical subjects of thought. We do so by referring to ourselves by the "identical-sounding 'I'", which we use under the same set of semantic rules (SR1–4) (see 4.3.2). Yet to guarantee a sense in which I myself am "numerically identical in different times", for instance, when going through a mathematical proof in time, I must show that I am the self-same subject of earlier and later states appearing in inner sense. It requires me to recognize a series of inner appearances as belonging to me, even if my apperceptive act gets interrupted by a daydream, or by a brief nap during my maths class. It requires the ability

---

[80] Mariña (2011:20–2), Henrich (1994), Wuerth (2014). The claim that transcendental apperception involves the self-ascription of mental states to a numerically identical thinking subject within a "train of thoughts" is also supported by Longuenesse (2007:157, 2017:142–6), Rosefeldt (2000:119–27, 2017) and Keller (1998:66–74), but none of these interpreters derives a notion of personal identity *in time* from this claim.

[81] Most explicitly, Mariña (2011:20–2). Some have taken the "logical identity of I" to indicate the numerical identity of an underlying noumenal self as the bearer of mental faculties, for example, Powell (1990:165–73) and Wuerth (2014). Ameriks (2000:129) also considers the numerical identity of the noumenal self to be at stake in the Third Paralogism, but is clear that Kant does not allow for its temporal determination. Given that Kant's definition of person explicitly appeals to time, it would be surprising if Kant here were to allow, or even to consider, the attribution of temporal features to the noumenal self.

to attend to my inner appearances as the temporally distinct states of one and the same underlying mental unity. Transcendental apperception guarantees only the *logically identical form* of my unified consciousness at *any* time, but not the *numerical identity* of a mental unity with varying mental states at *different* times.[82]

Kant struggles with this subtle distinction in a Reflection, in which he famously asks whether it is an experience that we think. Considering the example of a geometrical figure, he concludes:

> the consciousness of having such a thought [of a geometrical figure] is not an experience ... Nevertheless, *this thought brings forth an object of experience or a determination of the mind that can be observed, insofar, namely, as it is affected through the faculty of thinking;* I can thus say that I have experienced what belongs to grasping a figure with four equal sides and right angles in thought in such a way that I can demonstrate its properties. This is *the empirical consciousness of the determination of my condition in time through thought.*   (*Refl* 5661, 18:319 emphasis added)

Kant here distinguishes between the conditions under which the thought of a figure is possible and the conditions under which an inner appearance of that thought can occur in inner sense. The latter do not in the least "affect" the properties of the thought, but are also not analytically derivable from the conditions of thought.

In a similar way, Kant distinguishes in the Third Paralogisms the conditions under which "I can become conscious [of myself] in every representation" in thought *at any time* from the conditions under which I can become conscious of "the identity of the person . . . in all changes of state" *at all times* (B408). That is, he distinguishes the logical proposition expressed by "I think" from the inner experience of one's thinking, which is also expressible through "I think". The latter requires me to become conscious of myself under the condition of time and, therefore, to explicate the concept of identity in temporal terms.[83]

The apperceptive view fails to provide a valid criterion for personal identity, even if personal identity is understood to be valid only first-personally. This view introduces the notion of a *continuing subject* without appealing to a sensible manifold that is synthesized in accordance

---

[82] Rosefeldt (2000:128–35) and Longuenesse (2017:146–8), among others, come to a similar conclusion with regard to the identity of the logical subject, yet they do not see a need for acknowledging a *mental unity across time* that we determine from a specifically psychological point of view.

[83] See also "for the cognition of myself . . . I exist as an intelligence that . . . is subject to a limiting condition that it calls inner sense" (B15). In a series of Reflections on the Refutation of Idealism, Kant struggles with the problem that, in inner experience, we need to bridge the gap between "between transcendental and empirical consciousness" of oneself (*Refl* 6311, 18:610; see also *Refl* 6311–6316, 18:607–623), or between the nonsensible "I" and "the I [as . . .] *substratum* of all empirical judgements" (*Refl* 5453, 18:186).

with the category of substance.[84] But this move is hugely troublesome, because it runs counter to the line of attack pursued in the Paralogisms. There, Kant argues that any inference of a notion of continuity from the judgement "I think" without appeal to sensibility falls prey to a transcendental illusion. Hence, the negative result of the Third Paralogisms is that the problematic "I think", which is derived from the conditions of thought alone, cannot guarantee the numerical identity of something complex with variable states throughout different (or even all) times. It defines only the logical form of self-reference in terms of the logical "I", which is identical for all thinkers and at any time, but which cannot underwrite personal identity.

As a positive result, my considerations suggest that the Third Paralogism establishes a distinction between three distinct ways of applying the concept of substance to oneself:

(1) by applying the *pure* category of substance to oneself as a logical something, one determines the "logical identity of I" as a conceptual rule of self-reference (A363);

(2) by applying the *schematized* category of substance to the outer appearances of one's body, one determines the "objective persistence of my Self" in life (A363); and

(3) by applying the category *in yet another way*, one becomes "conscious of the numerical identity of [one's] Self in different times", that is, personal identity (A361).

This third notion is often not explicitly distinguished from the other two, but rather is subsumed under one of them.[85] Nonetheless, it seems crucial for Kant's account of psychological personhood.

In sum, the Third Paralogism does not offer a full-fledged account of personal identity. But it leaves us with the firm belief that "the identity of person is . . . inevitably to be encountered in my own consciousness" (A362).

---

[84] Henrich (1994) argues that transcendental apperception entails numerical identity in time, but has received – to my mind correctly – much criticism for his interpretation (e.g., Ameriks 2000:140–1, Keller 1998:27–8). Powell (1990:165–73) takes the transcendental unity of apperception to involve a "continuing" mental unity. Mariña (2011) argues that the consciousness of one's numerical identity in time is a condition of "generating" the "I think" of apperception.

[85] Notion (3) is sometimes taken to fall under notion (2) (e.g., Wuerth 2014:181, Longuenesse 2007, 2017:146–52). Others take it to fall under notion (1), either insofar as (1) is understood as a "continuing" mental unity (e.g., Powell 1990:165–73, Kitcher 2011:185–7), or insofar as (3) is taken to be reducible to a merely logical identity (e.g., Rosefeldt 2000:96–108 and – to some extent – Dyck 2014:165–72). Exceptions include Keller (1995), who understands (3) in a broadly Lockean empiricist way, and Ameriks (2000:158), who himself distinguishes three kinds of identity: (i) noumenal, (ii) phenomenal from the third-person perspective, and (iii) as appearance from the first-person perspective; the last (iii) comes closest to my notion (3).

The next step will be to understand how we can explicate the concept of a psychological person – and hence the psychological "I" – such that it considers both the logical conditions of self-reference and the temporal conditions of inner appearances. This chapter has shown that the capacity to be conscious of one's own identity in time can be reduced neither to the capacity for apperception, nor to the capacity for determining a persistent substance. In the next chapter, we will finally turn to reason as the guideline of inner experience through which we can consider inner appearances as belonging to a mental unity across time. In Chapter 7, I will consider Kant's broader notion of personal identity that also includes the qualitative aspects of one's personal character.

PART III

The Human Person and the Demands of Reason

5

The Guiding Thread of Inner Experience

5.1 Introduction

This chapter finally turns to the role that human reason plays with respect to inner experience. I will argue that an idea of reason – the idea of the soul – is required in order for inner experience to be *intelligible* as the determination of a person's inner appearances. The idea of the soul is precisely what enables me to *conceive of myself as a psychological person* who is embedded in the spatio-temporal and causally efficient structure of the world, yet without reducing myself to a *mere appearance*. And only if I conceive of myself as such, can I make sense of *all* my inner appearances – including my perceptions and memories, my desires and volitions, my hopes and fears – as belonging to one and the same person, namely myself. Only by presupposing the idea in a sense to be specified can I comprehend my inner experience as the *empirical cognition* of my inner appearances, alongside other *kinds of experience*, such as the experience of physical objects, of living beings, and of other persons.

My interpretation is centrally based on a claim that Kant puts forward in the first *Critique*'s Appendix to the Dialectic. There, after having deconstructed the misuse of reason common to many rationalist philosophies, Kant proposes a positive use of reason in terms of regulative principles and transcendental ideas. The transcendental idea of the soul, he argues, serves a special purpose as the "guiding thread (*Leitfaden*) of inner experience" according to which we "connect all appearances, actions, and receptivity of our mind (*Gemüth*) . . . *as if* the mind (*Gemüth*) were a simple substance" (A672/B700).

As with any interpretation of Kant's ideas of reason, my interpretation faces a major challenge: while Kant denies – for good reason – that these ideas amount to constitutive principles of experience that describe properties of real objects, he nonetheless holds that these ideas are "transcendental" and have an "indispensably necessary regulative use, namely that of directing the understanding to a certain goal" (A644/B672). This chapter offers a reading of these two key features: the idea of the soul

(1) is *transcendental* in that is "indispensably necessary" for directing the understanding in acquiring a certain kind of experience, namely inner experience;
(2) has a *regulative use* in that it presents or exhibits (*darstellen*) the unity of all inner appearances and thereby provides procedural rules for determining inner appearances, without determining a mental unity as such.

Ultimately, I will argue that these features are grounded in *normative demands* of reason through which the idea has a *prescriptive force* for certain practices, namely for the acquisition of self-knowledge (Chapter 6) and for the practical conduct of a person's mental life, which I will call self-formation (Chapter 7).

In developing an interpretation of the idea's central role for inner experience, I try to avoid two common but, I believe, misleading interpretive paths and instead defend an alternative. Firstly, my interpretation avoids understanding the idea – broadly in line with the traditional rationalist metaphysics of the soul – as a concept that can be known to refer to a thing-in-itself or *noumenon* – an entity that exists over and above the representational activities as their real ground, although we cannot have sensation-based cognition of the entity as such.[1] I call this the *noumenal view*. Secondly, my interpretation avoids understanding the idea of the soul as a *fiction* that is heuristically useful to foster cognition of one's psychological features, although it may not correspond to anything real, but be merely fictitious. I call this the *fictional view*. Both views have difficulties explaining the "indispensably necessary regulative" character of the idea: the noumenal view due to giving too metaphysical a reading of its necessity, and the fictional view due to giving too weak a reading of its regulative nature. By contrast, my interpretation altogether rejects that the idea of the soul – in its regulative use – functions as a *representation* (*Vorstellung*) that describes a given, underlying reality – regardless of whether it does so veridically, as the noumenal view has it, or merely hypothetically (and potentially falsely), as the fictional view has it.

On my view, presupposing the idea of the soul amounts, *not* to making theoretical claims about what reality is like, but to generating a *context of intelligibility*.[2] An idea of reason, I shall argue, must be presupposed to set a stage, as it were, within which a certain *kind of cognition* is first intelligible and the constitutive principles of the understanding can first be operative in determining the corresponding kind of appearance. An idea of reason provides a *presentation* (or *exhibition*, *Darstellung*, rather than a *representation*, *Vorstellung*) of the whole domain within which a certain kind of cognition can be meaningful. For instance, the idea of the world-whole outlines the

---

[1] In Chapter 4, I have already excluded the option that the idea of the soul can be known to refer to an empirical object, since no object is given to inner sense that could be cognized as a persistent substance.
[2] I thank Fred Rush for coming up with this helpful term.

domain within which we can cognize physical objects, and the idea of purposiveness outlines the whole within which we can cognize the parts that together constitute an organism. It is in this sense that an idea of reason outlines the *context of intelligibility* for a particular kind of cognitive practice. And, indeed, I will ultimately argue that transcendental ideas should be understood as *normative demands* that *prescribe* guidelines for certain practices (with either theoretical or practical goals). I call my view the *context-of-intelligibility* view.

The goal of this chapter is to explain the regulative use of the idea of the soul with respect to inner experience. Chapter 4 has shown that a mental whole within which *all* inner appearances may inhere can itself never be intuited, but lies, as it were, at the limits of our experiential grasp (see 4.4). Instead of viewing the idea of the soul as a representation of a given reality (for instance, of my noumenal self), I argue that the idea is used to generate the *presentation (Darstellung) of a mental whole* in relation to which we can determine inner appearances. This idea precisely outlines the domain within which the understanding can be operative in determining inner appearances and hence within which inner experience can have meaning as empirical cognition of these appearances.

Crucial evidence for my view comes from Kant's repeated claim that a transcendental idea of reason serves as the "analogue of a [sensible] schema" (A655/B693). By exploring this parallel between schemata and ideas, I will establish two general claims: firstly, that the regulative use of an idea should be understood as the presentation (*Darstellung*) of a domain of cognition, and, secondly, that from this presentation procedural rules for the *systematization* of cognitions within this domain can be derived by analogy with the schematic rules for synthesizing sensible manifolds. According to the first claim, the regulative use of the idea of the soul should then be understood as the presentation of a mental whole outlining the domain of inner experience. Regarding the second claim, I argue, more specifically, that the procedural rules derived from the idea of the soul do not only serve the purpose of systematization within the inner domain. Rather, more fundamentally, the procedural rules substitute for those sensible schemata that cannot be applied to inner intuitions, such as the schema of substance as persistence (see 4.4.2 and also 2.4). The idea ultimately provides us with the presentation of a whole – the *unity of a person* – that cannot be sensibly given, but which is indispensably necessary for a person to cognize its inner appearances. Hence, employing the idea in a regulative way sets the stage within which inner experience is intelligible: that is, the domain within which I can first cognize inner appearances *as my own* mental states, *as parts* of my mental whole.

In what follows, Section 5.2 outlines Kant's conception of reason in relation to human experience, and Section 5.3 introduces his account of the idea of the soul in the Appendix to the Dialectic. Section 5.4 analyses and eventually rejects the two alternative interpretations, the noumenal and the fictional view. Section 5.5 develops my *context-of-intelligibility view*, and Section 5.6 explicates this interpretation for the idea of the soul and with respect to inner experience.

5.2   Reason and Human Experience

5.2.1   *Reason as the Faculty for Inferring*

One of the first sentences of the Dialectic of Pure Reason runs as follows: "All our cognition starts from the senses, goes from there to the understanding, and ends with reason" (A298/B355); one of its last sentences reads, "Thus all human cognition begins with intuitions, goes from there to concepts, and ends with ideas" (A702/B730). With this Kant indicates that his account of cognition – based on a Critical analysis of sensibility in the Aesthetic and of the understanding in the Analytic – is not complete. Rather, reason and its pure ideas play a fundamental role for empirical cognition. Reason does so, not just negatively by constraining cognition to the bounds of sense, as a first reading of the Dialectic may suggest, but also positively by demarcating domains or contexts of intelligibility for human experience, or so I argue.[3] While a positive role is more easily granted to reason with respect to practical cognition, it is far less widely accepted in theoretical respects.[4] Yet Kant acknowledges an "immanent" use of ideas of reason with respect to empirical (theoretical) cognition in the Appendix to the Dialectic (A643/B671).[5] Here I motivate my interpretation of reason's positive role for inner experience by situating it within Kant's general account of theoretical reason.

Drawing broadly on the Aristotelian-Scholastic tradition and more immediately on Wolffian rationalism, Kant defines reason primarily as the faculty of inferring (*Schließen*).[6] That is, reason's main task is to combine judgements into a higher unity, viz. an inference (*Schluss*). In this function, reason builds on the workings of the understanding – in its function to combine concepts

---

[3]   In the *Prolegomena*, Kant concludes that the task of any future metaphysics is not only to limit the understanding, but to "determin[e] the boundary of pure reason" also in its empirical use (*Prol* 4:350).

[4]   It is widely acknowledged that reason has a positive function in prescribing moral laws in the form of categorical imperatives. For practical purposes, Kant accepts three *practical postulates* that involve three ideas of reason – the ideas of God, freedom, and the soul (see *CpracR* 5:122–34). Yet reason's positive role in theoretical respects is commonly downplayed and severely underexplored. Exceptions include Mudd (2017) and Willaschek (2018).

[5]   In the third *Critique*, Kant develops an account of ideas of reason, for instance with regard to the theoretical cognition of organisms, in terms of the power of *reflective* judgement. While I will draw on some aspects of this account, a detailed discussion of how it relates to the account in the first *Critique* goes beyond the scope of this book.

[6]   Note that at times Kant employs the notion of "reason in general" (e.g., A760/B788) to refer to all higher intellectual faculties, including the understanding and the power of judgement. I use "reason" to denote the faculty in the narrow sense.

(and ultimately intuitions) into judgements – and of sensibility – in its function to combine sensations into intuitions. As we have seen earlier, the functions of the understanding and of sensibility are thoroughly intertwined, as is the function of reason with both of them, or so I shall argue.

The most common employment of reason is in drawing syllogistic inferences. These are inferences of a particular form that connect two judgements (a major premise and a conclusion) through the mediation of a third one (the minor premise).[7] The aim of a syllogism is to derive a *particular* cognition, viz. the conclusion, from a *general* condition, viz. the major, by means of a mediating cognition, viz. the minor. For drawing an inference, reason depends on the understanding for supplying general cognitions that can be used as major premises, and on the power of judgement for subsuming a further cognition under a general one in the minor premise.[8] Different types of syllogisms can be distinguished in accordance with different forms the major premise can take. According to the three forms of judgements of relation, Kant then distinguishes between *categorical, hypothetical,* and *disjunctive* syllogisms: for a cognition that contains the concept A, the major is, respectively, a categorical judgement ("A is B"), a hypothetical judgement ("If A is B, then C is D"), or a disjunctive ("Either A is B or A is C") (whereby A, B, C, and D are concepts that may or may not relate to an intuition).[9]

If these syllogisms are taken merely formally, that is, in abstraction from the content of cognition and without considering possible relations of the involved judgements to real objects, then reason is employed in its *logical use,* analogous to the logical use of the understanding (see A299/B355 and 4.2). In this case, reason is concerned only with the logical entailment relations among judgements. Nonetheless, reason can expand cognition through its logical use, namely through *cognition from principles* (A300/B357): if a general cognition has been established through the understanding (and sensibility), it can then be *used* as a principle, that is, as the major premise in a syllogism, from which further more specific cognitions can be derived. Reason then accomplishes cognition inferentially (or derivationally) by "cogniz[ing] the particular in the universal through concepts" (A300/B357). For instance, assuming that the major premise *that all animals are mortal* is empirically well founded, I can

---

[7] See A330/B386. Syllogisms – as *mediate inferences* – contrast with *immediate inferences.* The latter immediately follow from the rules of the understanding (e.g., from "*all* women are mortal" it immediately follows that "*some* women are mortal"), whereas the former require a mediating cognition that contains a mediating concept (*Mittelbegriff*) (see A299/B355), such as "man" in the following syllogism: (Major) "All men are mortal"; (Minor) "Socrates is a man"; (Conclusion) "Socrates is mortal". For discussion, see Pollok (2017:171–7).

[8] See A304/B360–1.

[9] See *L-Log/Jäsche* 9:121–2.

derive the particular cognition *that all cats are mortal* by using the minor premise *that all cats are animals.* While reason's use itself is merely logical, the derived cognition may of course have a relation to objects of experience.[10]

Yet reason can also have a *real use,* which is far more controversial. Like the understanding, reason – in its real use – is concerned with, or aims for, objects or, more generally, things (from the Latin *res*). Depending on whether these objects lie within or beyond the bounds of experience, Kant distinguishes an *immanent* and a *transcendent* use of reason. Recall that, for the understanding, any legitimate use must be immanent in that it must be limited to possible experience. Such immanent use of the understanding is thus always *empirical,* yielding empirical cognition. If the categories are taken in a transcendent use as the determinations of real things, reaching beyond the bounds of experience, we engage in a "misuse" (A296/B352).[11] With respect to reason, there is also a transcendent and hence illegitimate use if its ideas are taken to be true representations of "real things" that lie beyond possible experience (see A643/B671). Such use underlies the syllogistic inferences of the rationalists and leads into the transcendental illusions that Kant discusses at length in the Dialectic (see 4.3.1). Now, Kant also acknowledges that reason "too will presumably have a good and consequently immanent use" (A643/B671). Yet it is far less clear what such immanent use consists in and whether it should be understood as a real use with respect to some object or rather as a merely logical use. To get a clearer sense of reason's immanent use, we have to turn to reason's own transcendental ideas.

5.2.2   Pure Reason and Transcendental Ideas

In characterizing reason as a faculty that advances the insights of the understanding through inferential reasoning, reason appears to be "merely subordinate" to the understanding (A305/B362): it discovers logical relations among the cognitions of the understanding and thereby promotes the aims of the understanding (A305/B362). Yet in fact Kant conceives of reason as the highest of the intellectual faculties, the "supreme faculty of cognition" (A299/B355) – a faculty that in fact gives rules to the understanding (see A302/B359). As such,

---

[10] Insofar as reason is concerned with "principles" (or "universal rules", *L-Log/Jäsche* 9:120), that is, judgements that are used as major premises, reason is also called the *faculty of principles* (by contrast with the understanding as the *faculty of rules* for generating judgements; see A299/B356).

[11] On the distinction between immanent and transcendent use for the understanding, see also A308/B365, A636/B664, A638/B666. Note that the notion of "transcendental use" is at times used in a more general sense as *use with respect to objects (in general)* (or "objective use"), leaving it open whether these are objects of experience or things-in-themselves (e.g., A296/B352); in other places it is identified with "transcendent use" and hence illegitimate (e.g., A327/B383).

reason can be considered in itself as *pure reason*, that is, in its *pure use* independently from the senses and the understanding (A306/B363). *Pure reason*, considered merely in itself, is "a genuine source of concepts and judgments" (A305/B362, see also A299/B355), namely of *ideas of reason*. Among the ideas, there is a distinct set of so-called *transcendental ideas* (A311/B368), which includes the ideas of the soul, the world-whole, and God. These are "necessary concept[s] of reason" that can be derived from reason's own logical procedures (A327/B383). Unlike empirical concepts or even the pure concepts of the understanding, "no congruent object can be given [to them] in the senses" and hence they cannot be shown to be determinations of empirical objects (A327/B383). But what positive use may these ideas then have, and in what sense could they possibly be said to be *transcendental* with respect to cognition?[12]

To understand their transcendental role, one has to consider how these ideas arise from reason's own procedure. Reason has a tendency to search for *completeness*. This tendency is already implied in its basic logical use. The central step of the logical use is to subsume the condition of a given cognition (minor) under a universal rule (major) and thereby reveal a more general condition of that cognition. In my example in 5.2.1, the syllogism reveals that *cats* are not only subject to the condition of *animality*, but also to the more general condition of *mortality*. Reason thus has an intrinsic propensity to search for further, more and more general, conditions that can then serve as universal rules. It eventually strives towards the most *thoroughgoing determination* (*durchgängige Bestimmung*) of a conditioned cognition (see A571/B579). A thoroughgoing determination of cats would then include all conditions that apply to our experience of cats and taken together, these conditions would fully account for what a cat – as an object of our experience – is. A repeated employment of reason then results in a regress that can only be stopped once the *totality of conditions* is reached and with it something *unconditioned*. These considerations lead Kant to define the *logical maxim* of reason as follows: "to find the unconditioned for conditioned cognitions of the understanding, with which its unity will be completed" (A307/B364).

This maxim is logical in that it uncovers logical entailment relations among judgements, without considering their relations to objects. But what if we consider that those judgements may in fact be related to sensible objects in a truthful way? Wouldn't the logical maxim then amount to a *transcendental principle*? Wouldn't we have to "assume that when the conditioned is given, then so is the whole series of conditions subordinated one to the other, which is itself unconditioned, also given" (A307–8/B364)?[13]

---

[12] Kant also speaks of these ideas as "transcendental presupposition[s]" (A651/B679, A678/B706) and "transcendental principle[s]" (A650/B678, A663/B691).

[13] Note Kant's ambivalence regarding the exact relation of the totality of conditions and the unconditioned, for example, "Now since the *unconditioned* alone makes possible the

This passage raises the concern that reason's logical use may only be properly possible under the assumption that something unconditioned, for example, things-in-themselves, must exist as the ultimate condition of the whole series of appearances. A proper functioning of the logical procedure with regard to cognitions might only be possible if certain transcendental presuppositions regarding given, unconditioned things are in place. Searching for the totality of conditions and ultimately for the unconditioned seems to be reasonable only if we assumed that these do actually exist.[14]

Hence, it seems as if the logical use of reason – in its striving for completeness – would uncover, not only formal relations, but *real conditioning relations*. Corresponding to the three types of logical syllogism – categorical, hypothetical, and disjunctive syllogism – one can construe three types of conditioning relations between the minor and the major, that is, three ways in which a cognition can be conditioned by another condition. These are, according to the categories of relation, *subsistence*, *dependence* (or causality), and *community* (or reciprocity).

The transcendental ideas of reason result from this search for completeness and from ascending to more and more general conditions until one reaches their totality and hence something unconditioned. They arise from the infinite iteration of a logical syllogism and from taking the resulting totality of conditions as something unconditioned that is the real condition of an appearance. Hence, following reason's iterative procedure, one may be inclined to assume that the cognition of an appearance must be grounded in the existence of an *unconditioned* subsistent thing, follows from *unconditioned* causal powers, or is conditioned by an *unconditioned* mutual interaction between real things. The ideas that thereby arise are precisely the concepts of what is taken to be unconditioned. The idea of the soul, for instance, is gained through the categorical syllogism, which is then taken to reveal a real conditioning relation of *subsistence*. Here the iterative procedure results in the concept of the "unconditioned ... for the categorical synthesis in a subject" (A323/B379) and is then understood as the concept of a "simple thinking substance" (viz. *soul*) that is *assumed* as the subsistent ground in which all one's representations inhere (A673/B701).

These considerations seemingly reveal an intrinsic conflict of reason. The conflict of reason lies in the propensity of reason to make up concepts of the unconditioned, such as those of the soul, the world-whole, and God, yet *without* being able to prove that these concepts refer to real things and imply

---

totality of conditions, and conversely the totality of conditions is always itself unconditioned" (A322/B379). This ambivalence may indicate a paradox similar to Russell's paradox regarding the set that contains all sets. For discussion, see Willaschek (2018:94–5), Heßbrüggen-Walter (2004:252–9).

[14] Arguments to this effect can be found, for example, in Watkins (2019).

true descriptions of such things. Even worse, Kant argues that we are led astray as soon as we "take[]" these concepts "for concepts of real things" (see A643/B671). Nonetheless, reason's own "demands" (e.g., A656/B684, A699/B727) and "interests" (e.g., A666–8/B694–6, A686/B714, A704/B732) lead us to strive towards theorizing about these things.[15]

5.2.3 The Regulative Use of Reason and the Difficulty of an Interpretation

In the Appendix to the Dialectic, Kant goes on to argue that this conflict can be avoided by recognizing that transcendental ideas have an "indispensably necessary regulative use, namely that of directing the understanding to a certain goal" (A644/B672). This regulative use is primarily defined negatively, in contrast with constitutive principles. Unlike the latter, a regulative use does *not* give "the concepts of certain objects" (A644/B672); that is, it does *not* amount to true description of something real or to determinate claims about objects, including things-in-themselves.[16] In a positive sense, Kant defines the goal towards which the regulative use of ideas should lead as "the greatest unity alongside the greatest extension" of our cognitions (A644/B672). So reason's positive role consists in directing the understanding towards what he has earlier called the "unity of reason (*Vernunfteinheit*) in appearances" (A326/B383), which is a higher kind of unity than that which is provided by the understanding. Kant now explicates this unity as the "systematic unity ... of the manifold of the understanding's cognition" (A648/B676, also A647/B675).

Reason's regulative function is to foster *systematicity* among cognitions. In this connection, ideas of reason are employed for the generation of hypotheses, which can then be used to derive further cognitions and expand our cognition of nature, or to test consistency among given cognitions. Kant, therefore, calls such use of ideas the "hypothetical use of reason" (A647/B675). As examples, Kant discusses pure ideas from natural science – the ideas of *"pure earth, pure water, pure air"* – which can be used as hypotheses to "question nature" (A646–7/B674–5).[17] These examples have led many commentators to argue that the regulative use of *transcendental* ideas should be considered as a merely hypothetical use for the purpose of "higher" intellectual endeavours, such as *science*. These ideas give rise to hypothetical assumptions concerning the soul, the world-whole, and God from which we – through the merely logical use of

---

[15] Willaschek (2018) argues that this propensity of reason is the subjective source of all metaphysical speculation (i.e., Rational Sources Account of Metaphysics).

[16] See in particular A647/B675. I will discuss the distinction between regulative and constitutive use, and that between hypothetical and assertive (or apodictic) use, in detail in 5.5.

[17] Note that these ideas do not have a general transcendental status, but are specific for scientific purposes; see McNulty (2015).

reason – derive further cognitions and which are then conducive to expand our cognition. Such a procedure, it is often argued, is necessary only for the purpose of those "higher" rational endeavours for which it would not be sufficient to have "merely a contingent aggregate", but which require "a system interconnected in accordance with necessary laws" (A645/B673).[18]

Indeed, systematic unity is primarily introduced as a subjective "demand" (e.g., A656/B684, A699/B727) or "interest" of reason itself (e.g., A666–8/B694–6, A686/B714, A704/B732). Kant repeatedly stresses that our transcendental ideas are suited "to our needs" (A707/B735), the needs of discursive and receptive rational cognizers. Since systematic comprehension is primarily a subjective interest of reason, being regulative is often identified with being "merely heuristic" for us in pursing specific ends, such as science (e.g., A616/B644, A663/B691, A671/B699, A771/B799).

Yet here a similar problem arises as did with regard to the general logical maxim of reason, which seemingly required the transition to a transcendental principle concerning something unconditioned. Kant, again, suggests that the principle of systematic unity cannot be viewed as a *merely* "logical principle", suitable to our needs only, but must presuppose a "transcendental principle" (A648/B676), and argues, "it cannot even be seen how there could be a logical principle of rational unity among rules unless a *transcendental principle is presupposed*, through which such a systematic unity, as pertaining to the object itself, is assumed *a priori* as necessary" (A650-1/B678-9, emphasis added).[19] According to this passage, a transcendental principle does not only subjectively demand the systematic unity of cognitions, without considering whether any systematic connections actually obtain among the objects to which those cognitions purport to refer. Rather, it also ensures that such systematic unity in some sense "pertain[s] to the object itself" (A651/B679). Put somewhat loosely, for our systematizing activities to be successful or at least by and large appropriate, we should be warranted in expecting that the systematic unity of our cognitions corresponds to a systematic unity of objects, and hence that nature itself in fact displays systematic connections among its objects.

The most delicate issue for any interpretation of the transcendental ideas concerns the difficulty of understanding the *transcendental, yet regulative status* of the principles of systematic unity to which they give rise.[20] Prima

---

[18] For such a reading, see Willaschek (2018:168). On the role of ideas of reason in science, see especially Buchdahl 1969 and Zuckert 2017.

[19] Kant elaborates on three specific logical principles, each of which contributes to the general task of systematizing cognition. These are principles of homogeneity, specification, and continuity (see A652–68/B680–96; *CJ* 5:185–6; also *L-Log/Jäsche* 9:96–7). I will elaborate on them in 6.3.

[20] In addition to "transcendental principle" (A650/B678, A663/B691), Kant – more cautiously – uses the notions of "transcendental presupposition" (A651/B679, A678/B706) and "transcendental presumption" (A671/B699).

facie, the notions of *transcendental* and *regulative* seem difficult to reconcile because they seem to divorce the notion of a *transcendental principle* of experience from the notion of being *constitutive* of experience (and thus a priori valid for the objects of experience) in a way so far unknown in the first *Critique*. Up to this point in the *Critique*, the notion of a transcendental principle – as the notion of a necessary condition for the possibility of experience – seems coextensive with that of a constitutive principle. The principles of the understanding are transcendental precisely because they are constitutive of experience and hence determine a priori properties of empirical objects.[21] A regulative principle, by definition, is *not constitutive* of experience and hence does not produce true descriptions of objects. Nonetheless, Kant argues that the regulative principles based on transcendental ideas are in some sense necessary for cognition. So he grants them the status of "synthetic propositions *a priori* [that] have objective but indeterminate validity" (A663/ B691). He later explicates this status as "unavoidably necessary for approximating to the highest possible degree of empirical unity" (A677/B705) and as the status of a "necessary *maxim* of reason" (A671/B699, see also A680/B708). That means, an idea "shows not how an object is constituted but how, under the guidance of that concept [viz. the idea], we *ought to seek* after the constitution (*Beschaffenheit*) and connection (*Verknüpfung*) of objects of experience in general" (A671/B699, emphasis added). These locutions shed light on the crux of Kant's account of regulative principles. Regulative principles are in a strong sense *demanded* for the use of the understanding, rather than merely optional, though without being constitutive of experience and hence without determining properties of objects of experience.

There are two main strands of interpretation: a methodological and a noumenal view. On the *methodological view*, reason's regulative use is *merely logical* in derivational inferences. Transcendental ideas serve for the generation of hypotheses that can never be proven, but which are useful to derive further cognitions and hence achieve, or at least approximate, a higher unity among cognitions. Such a unity of reason is relevant only for particular "higher" reflective intellectual endeavours, such as science. This view leaves open the possibility that these hypotheses may turn out to be untrue fictions, even though the threat of fictionalism seems to undermine their legitimacy as transcendental principles.[22] On the *noumenal view*, reason's regulative use consists in a *real* use with regard to thing-in-themselves. In order for our principles of systematicity to be well founded, we have to presuppose that the

---

[21] Note, even though the dynamical principles of the understanding are only regulative with respect to single intuitions, they are clearly constitutive with respect to experience (A179/ B222, also A664/B692).

[22] For example, Grier (2001), Allison (2004), Willaschek (2018:34, 168).

corresponding transcendental ideas truly describe an underlying noumenal reality, even though we cannot prove their truth. Such a noumenal reality has to be presupposed as the real ground of the unity of reason and hence of the system of cognition that we come to discover, even though this assumption may consist in a hypostatization of our ideas. In Section 5.4, I will discuss these two interpretive strands with regard to the idea of the soul.

My own view will diverge from both these interpretations. I will argue that reason's regulative use is a *real* use, though not with regard to things-in-themselves, which I consider to be illegitimate. Rather, reason's real use concerns the specific *object of reason*, namely the understanding (A664/B692). In several places, reason is defined as the "faculty of the unity of the rules of understanding under principles" (A302/B359).[23] Accordingly, reason's real, regulative use consists not in determining objects of experience (which is the real use of the understanding) but, rather, in *determining the limits of experience:* reason determines the domain (or scope) within which the acts of the understanding can be operative in making out objects of experience.[24]

In accordance with my hylomorphic account of mental faculties introduced in Chapter 1, I will interpret reason as a faculty that is characterized by an a priori form – a form that is imprinted on some suitable matter and defines a characteristic unity (see 1.2.3). The a priori forms of reason are the transcendental ideas, which – as normative demands –inform the acts of the understanding. Presupposing the content of such an idea, then, consists in defining and exhibiting (*darstellen*) a systematic unity within which the understanding can operate and which the understanding *ought to* approximate through its acts. Unlike the methodological view, I will argue that such presuppositions are not just add-ons, as it were, that are nice to have for specific ends of reason. Rather, the presuppositions of reason are *expressions of normative demands* that are binding for *any* act of the understanding. Normative demands of reason may de facto not be realized by each and every act of the understanding and hence they are not constitutive of the very possibility of such acts. But they must be realized for acts of the understanding to be *intelligible* within a certain *context of intelligibility.*[25]

---

[23] See also A305/B362ff., A333/B390.

[24] According to the *Prolegomena*, transcendental ideas serve us to "show us the way to determine [the] boundaries" of pure reason (*Prol* 4:353) and they do so "even with respect to its empirical use" (*Prol* 4:351). On the productive nature of reason, see also Ferrarin (2015).

[25] Some commentators apply the notion of *normativity* also with regard to the understanding, for example, Pollok (2017). If by normative principles in general, we mean principles that have some *prescriptive force* with regard to some act, then we could see the constitutive principles of the understanding as being prescriptive with regard to the *acts of synthesis* by which we first acquire experience. De facto, not all acts of synthesis realize the

In the current chapter, I will focus on giving an account of reason's regulative use as an a priori *act of presupposing* (i.e., *exhibiting*) a systematic whole in accordance with its transcendental ideas. In the next section, I will introduce the idea of the soul more specifically. After reviewing the two standard views concerning this idea in Section 5.4, I outline my account for transcendental ideas in general in Section 5.5, and then specify further details for the idea of the soul in Section 5.6. My argument for why these presuppositions are normatively binding will only be completed in Chapter 6 regarding the acquisition of self-knowledge and in Chapter 7 regarding self-formation.

5.3 The Idea of the Soul in the Transcendental Dialectic

An account of the idea of the soul can be found in the Dialectic of the *Critique of Pure Reason*. In the Appendix to the Dialectic, Kant identifies this idea (which he also calls the *psychological idea*) – in its regulative use – as the "guiding thread of inner experience" (A672/B700). The central claim can be found in the following passage:[26]

> Following the ideas named above as principles, we will first (in psychology) connect all appearances, actions, and receptivity of our mind (*Gemüth*) to the guiding thread of inner experience as if (*als ob*) the mind (*Gemüth*) were a simple substance that, with personal identity, persistently exists (*beharrlich existiert*) (at least in life), while its states – to which the states of the body belong only as external conditions – are continuously changing. (A672/B700, translation amended)

Any attempt to rephrase this claim in simpler terms would already presuppose central interpretive choices. So let me first point out what I take to be the central notions that require careful analysis in this *guiding-thread passage*.

---

constitutive principles of experience, but those that lead to experience must realize them. In this sense, Pollok's usage of the term *normative* aligns with mine.

[26] As far as I am aware, this passage and the central role of the idea of the soul for inner experience are rarely acknowledged (and, if mentioned at all, often marginalized) in the relevant studies, such as Keller (1998), Ameriks (2000), Melnick (2009), Sturm (2009:254–5n87), Kitcher (2011), and Frierson (2014). There are exceptions, such as Klemme (1996:229–34), who claims, however, that the "as-if" model of the soul has been replaced in the B-Edition. Heßbrüggen-Walter (2004) considers the role of reason with respect to self-consciousness, but argues that Kant ultimately fails in offering a coherent account. Serck-Hanssen (2011:69) suggests that the idea should serve to define a "mark of the mental", but thinks that this is not the account that Kant in fact offers. Wuerth (2014) tries to restore an ontological interpretation of the soul in continuity with Kant's rationalist predecessors. Dyck (2014:199–225) acknowledges a methodological role for investigating inner appearances.

First, the notion of a *guiding thread* (*Leitfaden*) indicates a certain regulative, rather than constitutive or determining, status.[27] If one reads the German text carefully, the phrase *Leitfaden der inneren Erfahrung* suggests two possible readings, both of which are grammatically correct. The phrase *der inneren Erfahrung* is taken either as subjective genitive (*genetivus subjectivus*) or as objective genitive (*genetivus adjectivus/objectivus*). In the former case, it denotes something that is in need of a guiding thread – and this need is then served by the idea of the soul. In the latter case, inner experience is itself the guiding thread for something else, such as the activity of "connect[ing] all appearances, actions, and receptivity of our mind (*Gemüth*)" into a higher-order unity. I shall argue that experience alone can never act as a guiding thread if it is not warranted by reason to give guidance in some sense. Given Kant's other uses of the guiding-thread metaphor, it seems most plausible that a guiding thread always requires some involvement of reason, specifically of an idea of reason, and that its proper use must be understood in relation to experience.[28] Hence, I submit that the more natural reading of this phrase is that the idea of the soul serves as the guiding thread to make inner experience intelligible, even though inner experience itself may be possible without it. We may be able to have inner experience of a single mental episode, such as the perception of something red, an indeterminate feeling of fear, or a vivid dream-image. But we are not able to properly make sense of such episodes unless we connect them in accordance with the guiding thread of the soul.

The guiding-thread claim is then spelled out by appeal to Kant's famous "as if" (*als ob*). The phrase "as if" commonly introduces a conditional rather than indicative or assertive claim. The antecedent of the conditional here is that "the mind (*Gemüth*) were a simple substance" etc. It ascribes properties to the mind that are traditionally contained in the concept of a soul, yet it does so only conditionally, or as Kant puts it, "problematically" (in line with the "hypothetical" use of reason; A646–7/B675).[29] This conditional status indicates that the idea of the soul plays its role of a principle of inner experience only through a *regulative* use, rather than a constitutive use by which we would straightforwardly assert these properties.[30] To interpret this passage, it will be of central

---

[27] Kant uses the phrase "guiding thread" in several contexts to indicate that something serves as a "clue" to extend our cognition of nature, although the clue itself lies beyond the bounds of sense; see A623/B651, A691/B719.

[28] This reading of a "guiding thread" is also supported by Kant's texts on the history of humankind: for example, "a guiding thread attached by reason onto experience" (*Conjectural Beginning* 8:110) and "guiding thread a priori" (*Idea* 8:30).

[29] For the traditional view of rational psychology, see Wolff (1734/1994) and Baumgarten (1739/1779).

[30] Kant commonly uses the phrase "*as if*" in his account of the power of judgement, one activity of which is to "judge *as if*" (*CJ First Intro* 20:200) or "consider *as if*" (*CJ First Intro*

importance to ascertain what kind of mental activity is defined by a guiding thread, and how such a guiding thread contributes to experience, as I will clarify in Sections 5.5 and 5.6.

For now, I will just sketch how the idea of the soul arises from reason's own logical procedure. As mentioned above, transcendental ideas are gained through reason's iterative procedure of uncovering the totality of conditions of a given appearance. Here the relevant syllogism is the *categorical syllogism*, which is applied to inner appearances, that is, to representations in empirical consciousness. If we accept the major premise that any representation is held by some subject S (regardless of whatever and whoever the subject in fact is), then for a single representation R_i, we can conclude by means of a categorical syllogism that R_i is held by some subject S_i (whatever and whoever S_i in fact is). The categorical syllogism could run as follows:

For all i from $i = 1$ to $i = n$, it is the case that

(Major) Every representation R is held by a subject S;

(Minor) R_i is a representation;

(Conclusion) R_i is held by a subject S_i.

In the course of our mental lives, we commonly undergo a temporally distributed series of given representations R_i, including perceptions, volitions, and cognitions. Each representation R_i may correspond to a single inner experience IE_i. A repeated employment of the categorical syllogism with respect to the series of given representations R_i now raises the question of whether *all* these representations, and hence *all* inner experiences IE_i, are held by one and the same subject, S.

Recall that the argument for the unity of self-consciousness, based on Kant's account of transcendental apperception, gives us only the unity of those representations that are combined in a single mental act and together constitute a representational state; for example, combined through an act of judgement, they constitute a single experience. On the basis of apperception alone, we are *not* justified, by repeatedly employing the categorical syllogism for *each* single representation R_i, in concluding that *all* given representations R_i are based in one and the same subject S. Moreover, we have no empirical

20:232). In this *merely reflecting use*, the power of judgement seeks to find a universal for a given particular to be subsumed under, as opposed to its determining use by which it subsumes a particular under a given universal. Some take Kant's theory of reflective judgement in the third *Critique* to replace his account of transcendental ideas in the first *Critique* (e.g., Guyer 1990); others argue that transcendental ideas define principles that are required for the merely reflective use (e.g., Allison 2004). In 5.5, I will indicate a possible relation between these accounts. For an insightful discussion, see Makkreel 2001.

basis for claiming that all S_i across different experiences IE_i are in fact one and the same.

Nonetheless, this iterative procedure of reason, if taken to a totality of conditions and hence to an unconditioned, leads to the derivation of the concept of such an underlying subject. Accordingly, the content of the idea of the soul is defined as the "*unconditioned* ... for the *categorical* synthesis in a subject" (A323/B379).[31] With this iterative procedure, we finally reach the idea of the soul as the concept of "the absolute (unconditioned) unity of the thinking subject" (A334/B391).[32] To be unconditioned, for a thinking subject, is to be the ultimate condition *with respect to* all one's conditioned representations.[33]

Recall that the categorical syllogism corresponds to the category of substance and primarily concerns the conditioning relation of *subsistence*. In accordance with this category, the idea can then be further explicated, primarily as the concept of a "simple thinking substance" (A673/B701, see also A345/B403, A689/B717, A784/B812). If we carefully reread the guiding-thread passage, we find the following predicates to be contained in the idea of the soul:

(1) "a simple [thinking] substance that ... persistently exists (at least in life)";

(2) with "its [mental] states [that] are continuously changing";

(3) "to which the states of the body belong only as external conditions"; and

(4) "with personal identity".

I have intentionally arranged the predicates in this order to indicate that they map onto the three categories of relation and their schematized forms according to the Analogies of Experience, namely onto

---

[31] Kant indicates this derivation procedure at A331/B388ff. Note that this basic syllogism makes possible further reconstructions, revealing further predicates of the idea. For instance, a series of ascending conditions $C_1, C_2, C_3, \ldots$ for a conditioned representation R could be construed in the form of a hypothetical conditioning relation: (Major) "If C_i, then C_{i+1}"; (Minor) "C_i is a condition of R"; (Conclusion) "C_{i+1} is a condition of R" (see A410/B438, *Prol* 4:334). For instance, construed as a series of causally related mental states, a representation R_1 (e.g., *seeing a wild animal*) at time t_1 could be understood as the condition of a representation R_2 (e.g., *feeling fear*) at a later time t_2, whereby all representations are eventually conditioned by the ultimate condition of originating in the fundamental mental power of one and the same subject (see predicate (2) below).

[32] Further phrases Kant uses, in the Paralogisms, include the concept of the "absolute subject (*absolute Subjekt*)" (A348, also *Prol* 4:334), the "absolute unity of a thinking being" (A353), and the "unconditioned unity of the *subjective* conditions of all representations in general (of the subject or soul)" (A406/B432). See also, "the idea of the complete subject (the substantial) (*Idee des vollständigen Subjekts (Substantiale)*)" (*Prol* 4:330).

[33] Note that, though the idea of the soul represents the unconditioned *with respect to* representation, such unconditioned may itself be conditioned *in other respects*, for instance in that its existence depends on the existence of other subjects, or things.

(1) <substance as persistence>;

(2) <causality as the law of a temporal sequence of *mental* states>;

(3) <community, as the simultaneity with the external states of the body>.

We get an additional predicate that is more difficult to interpret, but which has already occurred in the Third Paralogism (see 4.4.2 and 4.4.3):

(4) <personal identity>.

I will postpone a full treatment of personal identity until Chapter 7. There I will explicate it not only as numerical identity through time, as previously discussed, but as some sort of *qualitative identity* of a personal character through time. This predicate can then be understood as a second kind of causality, namely purposiveness, which is specifically required for making sense of living beings. Personal identity, thus, concerns the specific purposiveness of *persons*, who characteristically aim to develop a personal character.

Note that there is a disanalogy with the predicates of the logical "I" that I have identified in the Paralogisms in Chapter 4; these were <substance>, <simplicity>, <identity>, and <distinction> (see 4.3.2). This disanalogy, I believe, comes from the fact that the Paralogisms' goal is to uncover the errors of the rationalists, rather than to offer Kant's own views.[34] Nonetheless, the predicates mentioned in the guiding-thread passage display certain continuities with Kant's rationalist predecessors. Above all, the idea of the soul is precisely the concept of a being that is assumed as the subsistent ground of all one's representations (see First Paralogism, 4.3.2). A successful interpretation has to show that, for Kant, the regulative use of this idea is not tantamount to the assertion of such a subsistent ground, as the rationalist would have it, but to the employment of regulative principles in inner experience. In Section 5.6, I will explicate the regulative principles that arise from the predicates of *substance*, *causality*, and *interaction*, and show how they mark out the domain of inner appearances and hence make inner experience intelligible within this domain.

5.4   The Noumenal and the Fictional View of the Soul

I first turn to two alternative interpretations. In line with the two general strands of interpreting ideas of reason – the noumenal and the methodological view – we can distinguish between a *noumenal* and a *fictional* reading of the idea of the soul. Both views have in common that they take the regulative use of an idea to amount to the generation of descriptive statements about a given reality. The noumenal view takes these statements to be about a really existing

---

[34] The predicate of *simplicity* discussed in the Second Paralogism now seems to be subordinated to the predicate of *substance* (see 5.6).

entity – a *noumenal soul-substance* (or a thinking thing-in-itself) – and asserts them as true, although it denies the cognition of such an entity. The fictional view understands these statements as heuristically useful, perhaps even indispensable, working *hypotheses* that foster some kind of cognition of oneself, but grants that these hypotheses could turn out to be false. If they were indeed false, the soul would be an *untrue fiction* (or *mere illusion*) to which no real entity corresponds, but which motivates certain epistemic enquiries. I discuss both interpretive tendencies in turn and give some evidence from the recent literature.

5.4.1   Less Than a Real Thing: Against the Noumenal Interpretation

The noumenal interpretation is rarely explicitly endorsed in the literature. Scholars who see strong connections between Kant's broadly rationalist pre-Critical period and his Critical views may be inclined to accept an interpretation according to which the idea of the soul is taken to refer to the real, though not cognizable, noumenal ground that is assumed to underlie all mental activities and inner appearances of a person.[35] Most explicitly, Julian Wuerth defends the view that we must conceive of ourselves as "a *substance* in the *most basic ontological sense*" (Wuerth 2014:183). Yet, for Wuerth, Kant's alleged endorsement of substantial souls already results from the account of transcendental apperception, which, as Wuerth concludes, yields "an awareness of ourselves as a *thing in itself*" (Wuerth 2014:183). Wuerth specifies that the basic sense of "subsistence" he has in mind concerns not a person's persistence through time, but "an existence that does not inhere in another substance as accident, nor do our accidents inhere in another substance" (Wuerth 2014:185). While I have already discussed and rejected this view as an interpretation of transcendental apperception in Chapter 3, I reconsider Wuerth's account as a possible interpretation of the idea of the soul (see 3.3).

The *noumenal interpretation* finds support in passages that appeal to ideas of reason as the "concepts of real things" (A643/B671), and to the "objective, but indeterminate validity" of their corresponding principles (A663/B691). Moreover, this interpretation seems to offer a natural explanation for the legitimacy of the regulative principle to seek systematic unity in inner experience: it is backed by a transcendental principle that asserts the existence of a noumenal substantial soul in which all inner states inhere.

Yet the fundamental assertion of the existence of a substantial soul does not seem warranted, given the findings of the Dialectic and of the Appendix. The Paralogisms forbid any real determination of oneself on the basis of the "I think", including determining oneself as a substance of inherence. Similarly, in the Appendix, Kant explicitly states that ideas of reason are "misunderstood" if "taken for concepts of real things" (A643/B671): "they

---

[35] For accounts of noumenal grounds in general, see Stang (2016) and Watkins (2019), and specifically with respect to the subject, see Wuerth (2014) and Watkins (2016).

should not be assumed in themselves, ... they should be grounded (*zum Grunde gelegt*) only as analogues of real things, but not as things in themselves" (A674/B702).[36]

If we employ the idea of the soul in an "objective use" to describe a thing-in-itself (see A357), we effectively do what Kant warns us against in the Dialectic: we "hypostatiz[e]" an idea, that is, "mak[e] thoughts into things" (A395; see also A384, B402, A615/B643), rather than taking the idea to correspond to an "imagined object" (A671/B699) or "analogue[] of [a] real thing[]" (A674/B702). This employment would necessarily be "transcendent" (as opposed to immanent) and hence "deceptive" (see A327/B383, A643/B671), leading to error.

Moreover, Kant denies that we can make existential assertions on the basis of mere thought, as he famously argues in his discussion of the ontological proof of God that "*being* [existence] is obviously not a real predicate" (A598/B626). From merely thinking the idea of the soul, we cannot infer the existence of a corresponding thing. Now one might argue that the fact that inner appearances occur gives us an intuitive warrant to claim the existence of an underlying substance. Yet this only justifies the weaker claim that there is *some* ground, or substantial condition, for *each* single inner appearance. It does not legitimize the stronger claim that there is *one unified* ground, or substance, underlying *all* inner appearances. Hence, we have neither a conceptual, nor a sensible basis for asserting the existence of an underlying pre-existing noumenal reality that grounds the unity of *all* inner experience.[37]

But even if we lack an epistemic warrant for asserting the existence of a substantial thinking thing, one might argue that we have subjectively sufficient grounds for a weaker form of taking to be true (*Fürwahrhalten*), namely in terms of doctrinal belief (*doktrinaler Glaube*) (A822/B850). Believing for Kant does not require that we have objectively valid grounds for taking some claim to be true, but only that there are subjectively sufficient grounds for assuming its truth.[38] In the case of inner experience, the need for a systematic unity of inner appearances seems a subjectively sufficient ground to *believe* that the soul really exists. Yet conceding a mere belief is too weak for the adherents of the noumenal view to get the explanation they desire. For a belief, while subjectively warranted, could still turn out to be objectively false. If they have to grant that the fundamental assertion of a substantial soul could be false, then their explanation for what grounds the unity of inner appearances loses its effectiveness. An interpretation that appeals to belief, instead of knowledge,

---

[36] In a Reflection, Kant states that the object of an idea "is no real object or given thing, but a concept, in relation to which appearances have unity" (*Refl* 5554, 18:230).

[37] Note that the existential claim of the noumenal interpretation is different from the proposition that *I exist thinking*, which for Kant signifies "something real, [... but] not as a thing in itself (a *noumenon*)" (B422-3n).

[38] See A820-31/B848-59. Note, however, that some argue that Kant's notion of doctrinal belief is, rather than an epistemic, a practical attitude (Willaschek 2018:272-4).

therefore is rather an instance of the second interpretive tendency, to which I now turn.

5.4.2 More Than a Heuristic Fiction: Against the Fictional Interpretation

On the fictional view, the regulative use of the idea of the soul amounts to the generation of hypotheses that are heuristically useful, perhaps even indispensable, in fostering some kind of cognition of oneself, although these hypotheses could be false or lack any reference altogether. In this case, the soul would be an *untrue fiction* (or *mere illusion*) to which no real entity corresponds.

A broadly methodological approach to ideas of reason in general has been prevailing in the recent literature, and is often understood on the model of scientific hypotheses. The fictional view appeals in particular to those passages in which Kant invokes notions such as the subjective "interest of reason" (A648/B676), merely "regulative" principle (rather than constitutive), "hypothetical use" (rather than apodictic use), merely "heuristic" (rather than ostensive) principle (A663/B691; A671/B699), and "heuristic fiction" (A771/B799). The view takes seriously the findings of the Dialectic and the Appendix in that it rejects as illusory the claim that the idea of the soul adequately describes, or even only successfully refers to, a real thing. The view offers a positive account of the regulative use of reason: the logical principle to seek systematic unity is understood as a *merely* subjectively valid maxim that facilitates the expansion of cognition of nature, whereas the transcendental principle – taken to state that nature really *is* systematically unified – is considered to be a "self-serving delusion" (Guyer 1979:42), an "inevitable illusion" or "illusory postulation[] of reason" (Grier 2001:263, 276).[39] Grier, for instance, distinguishes between "fallacies (*Täuschungen*)" resulting from an avoidable fallacious misemployment of the idea and "illusions (*Blendwerke*)" resulting from an unavoidable illusory employment of the idea (Grier 2001:263). The former consist in a necessarily erroneous determination of things-in-themselves through the ideas, whereas the latter consist in the "transcendental and illusory postulation that nature . . . is already given as a complete whole" (Grier 2001:275) and hence presented to us as a unified "object[] about which we should seek knowledge" (Grier 2001:279). An idea is thus inevitably "hypostatized" as the "intelligible ground" or "nonsensible ground" of *all* appearances in nature, although a referent of that sort may in fact not exist for the idea (Grier 2001:297, 301; see A384, A395, B402, A615/B643).

---

[39] Versions of this view are defended in Vaihinger (1911); Guyer (1990, 2003); Grier (1997), and specifically with respect to the idea of the soul in Dyck (2014:81–103).

This view is often modelled on hypothesis formation in science. Reason's principles of systematicity are taken to be conducive to our higher-order scientific theorizing, especially for the discovery and articulation of empirical laws of nature.[40] Considering all cognitions as systematically connected aids us in discovering further cognitions that are compatible with the ones we already have and in articulating a system of empirical laws that govern these cognitions (e.g., Kepler's more specific laws of planetary motions can be subsumed under Newton's general laws of motion). The systematic unities posited through transcendental ideas are taken to delineate the domain, or subject matter, of particular scientific disciplines.[41] The idea of the soul, for instance, defines the domain of psychology.[42]

The main problem I see with this view is that it fails to offer a stable explanation for why the ideas – employed as regulative principles – are binding at all. The fictional view is faced with the following situation: on the one hand, reason's ideas facilitate, or appear to ground, the possibility of seeking the systematic cognition of nature; on the other hand, the ideas are illusory postulations that entail the possibility of being blatantly false. Yet I submit that the possibility of falsehood makes any explanation of the principles' bindingness ineffective.[43]

Adherents of the fictional view have the following options to resolve this dilemma: (*Fiction_1*) they bite the bullet and defend that potentially false descriptive assumptions can ground heuristically useful regulative principles or (*Fiction_2*) they argue that the principles' merely subjective validity, based on subjective needs of reason, is sufficient to ground the principles' heuristic use. I briefly discuss both options in turn.

(*Fiction_1*) *Potentially false descriptions ground regulative principles.* In science, a working hypothesis is commonly assumed to be productive as long as it is not yet falsified. Yet one may argue that idealizations in science typically involve inaccurate or even false assumptions, but nonetheless are widely held to be pragmatically useful for the pursuit of scientific knowledge. To give an

---

[40] See Grier (1997:22, 2001:288–92); also Willaschek (2010:185, 2018). For applications of the methodological approach in Kant's philosophy of science, see, for example, Buchdahl (1969, 1971), Ph. Kitcher (1986), and Sturm (2009: 127–82).

[41] See Sturm (2009:127–82). See also Grier (2001:298–300) and Zuckert (2017).

[42] See Grier (2001:297), Dyck (2014:217–25), and Kraus (2018). For Dyck (2014:210), the idea is a useful device for "organizing our knowledge and directing the understanding to the discovery of new cognition".

[43] Some proponents of the fictional view explicitly assign a prescriptive function to reason, prescribing goals or ends to theoretical enquiries (Grier 2001:276, also Zuckert 2017). While the general assumption of a "legislative reason" is certainly justified (see A695/B723, A819/B847), the problem is that the view bases the prescriptive force of reason in an unwarranted theoretical claim. My discussion shows similarities with the debate on how lawfulness, or lawlikeness, can be bestowed on empirical laws in Kant – a relation that I cannot explore here in detail.

example from today's physics, the assumption that the motion of a material object can be described by Newton's laws is – in light of Einstein's theory of relativity – strictly speaking false, but still gives us a useful approximation to reality that is adequate for many goals, such as for the science-internal theoretical goal of simplifying physical equations for small velocities or for the science-external practical goal of engineering a car. Similarly, transcendental ideas could be understood as pragmatically useful, though theoretically false idealizations. There is, however, an important difference: scientific idealizations unproblematically refer to objects of possible experience, but they assign ideal properties to them that are only slightly inaccurate, but close enough to a true description of the given object. By contrast, by employing an idea, we postulate the existence of a noumenal thing that may not exist at all and, therefore, cannot possibly be said to be close enough to a true description of *a given thing*, if the very kind of thing is taken to be illusory altogether. There may be other ways to defend this situation.[44] But these seem to come at the risk of proposing an intrinsically incoherent position, which seems inappropriate for an account of Kant's rational principles of systematicity. Moreover, such a position could be easily attacked by those who find Kant's account of reason in the Appendix inconsistent, if not contradictory, and therefore propose that reason's function can be only negative.[45]

(*Fiction_2*) *Subjectively valid descriptions ground regulative principles*: In defence of the fictional interpretation, its proponents could appeal to the distinctively subjective nature of regulative principles in serving reason's subjective interests and needs. Their regulative force is only "subjectively necessary", that is necessary only relative to or "*for us*, as rational, discursive knowers" (Grier 2001:286) and relevant for an end set by reason itself.[46] Yet this still raises the question as to why these subjectively valid principles should be adequate for promoting objectively valid cognition of nature. Kant himself asks, in the third *Critique*, whether nature could remain "a raw chaotic aggregate" for us (*CJ First Intro* 20:209) or display an "infinite multiplicity of empirical laws" (*CJ* 5:184).

The problem of fictionalism resurfaces. Although our empirical cognitions may appear to us as systematically ordered, the system itself may be only contingent or even a subjective artefact of our intellectual activities. The question whether our system of cognitions really reflects systematic relations in nature remains a question for an infinite future empirical enquiry. This enquiry could, in the best case, lead to an inductive corroboration of our system; in a worse case, to irreconcilable inconsistencies among cognitions, and in the worst case, to a result that is completely misguided in light of what

---

[44] For such attempts, see, for example, Vaihinger (1911) and, recently, Appiah (2017).
[45] For example Strawson (1966:229), Horstmann (1989:259n10).
[46] Similarly, Guyer (2003:287–8).

nature really is. Since the view cannot exclude these bad cases, it loses an effective justification for why the regulative principles *are* useful heuristics. It only offers subjective grounds for believing, or hoping, that the best case will emerge from our empirical enquiries.[47]

Moreover, if the need for systematic connections is only a subjective interest of reason, then the understanding may be free to "opt out" and not subscribe to reason's specific need, but rather pursue a different operational mode, perhaps according to the maxim of maximal chaos. If reason's regulative function is based on merely subjectively valid assumptions, then a Kantian principle of systematicity seems similar to a Humean principle of subjective association: reason associates – in a Humean fashion – otherwise unrelated cognitions *without rational justification*.[48]

The consequences of this view are perhaps more drastic for the idea of the soul in that it cannot avoid a Humean "bundle" view. If the idea of the soul is a merely subjective and even optional guideline for inner experience, then there is no guard against the assumption that a person's mental life – the psychological reality that is to be grasped in inner experience – is merely a "raw chaotic aggregate", a mere heap of representations, or a contingent bundle of perceptions, without inner coherence and unity. After all, the very idea of having a unified mental life or of being a unified mental subject throughout time could turn out to be false. It would be perfectly conceivable for someone to be a *staccato mind*, that is, to live only in the present mental episode, without memory of past episodes or projections for future episodes to live through.[49]

In sum, both the noumenal and the fictional view take a regulative use of the idea of the soul to amount to truth-apt descriptions of some underlying noumenal reality – descriptions that the noumenal view accepts as true, and the fictional view as merely heuristically useful, though potentially false. Both views fail to justify the normative bindingness of regulative principles based on ideas.

---

[47] See my discussion of *doctrinal belief* above. Similarly, Mudd (2017) argues that, on the merely methodological reading, the regulative principles can be shown to be valid only a posteriori.

[48] Similarly, Geiger (2003:287–91) critiques – rather unattractive – Humean empiricist tendencies in various accounts of systematicity in Kant.

[49] Avery Goldman (2007, 2012) develops yet another version of a methodological reading, arguing that the idea of the soul explains the "boundaries" of Kant's very own method of transcendental critique or "transcendental reflection" in the first *Critique*. While Goldman's view may offer an alternative account of the idea's role within Kant's overall project, it does not explain the idea's regulative function specifically with respect to inner experience.

5.5   Ideas of Reason and Contexts of Intelligibility

To resolve this deadlock between the two standard interpretations, I now develop my view of transcendental ideas as generating contexts of intelligibility, rather than describing a given reality. On this view, the function of these ideas is to mark out contexts of intelligibility within which the understanding can first meaningfully operate. More specifically, reason's regulative use is understood as an a priori act of outlining to the mind a systematic whole, defined by an idea, within which a certain kind of experience first becomes intelligible. This act of presenting the mind with the sketch of a whole is precisely what I take to be invoked in Kant's claim that transcendental ideas serve as *"analogue[s]" of sensible schemata* (A665/B693).

My view shows some similarities with the methodological reading, according to which ideas give rise to heuristically useful hypotheses. Yet it substantially differs in that I do not understand these hypotheses as truth-apt descriptions of an underlying noumenal reality from which logical inferences can be drawn, though they may turn out to be untrue fictions. Rather, on my view, the regulative employment of transcendental ideas is a *real use* through which reason first generates rules for the understanding, namely rules for attaining systematic unity among cognitions. Reason does so in analogy with the real use of the understanding – that is, the use through which the understanding, by means of transcendental schemata, generates the rules of synthesis for sensible intuitions. The central point of this analogy is that both – the schematization according to a category and the systematization according to an idea – involve an a priori act of *presenting* (or *exhibiting*; *darstellen*) a conceptually defined unity in such a way that it can be "filled in" by suitable sensible (or experiential) content. In what follows, I offer a detailed reconstruction of this analogy between schemata and ideas, which also requires me to take a stance on transcendental schemata. I first introduce a general outline of this analogy, then present a reading of transcendental schemata as a priori acts of presentation, use this reading to illuminate the regulative use of ideas, and finally explicate the analogy between schemata and principles of systematicity.

5.5.1   *Transcendental Ideas as Analogues of Transcendental Schemata*

To explore the analogy between the *systematizing function* of reason and the *synthesizing function* of the understanding, we need to have a better grasp of how reason relates to the understanding. Reason assists the understanding not only in logically deriving more specific cognitions from an already established general cognition, but also in first finding general cognitions under which particulars can be subsumed. It is this latter task – the ascent from particular appearances to universals – that is at stake in the analogy. Reason in its regulative use – Kant explains – furthers the empirical use of the understanding "by opening up new paths into the infinite (the undetermined)" (A680/B708).

The understanding necessarily faces limitations in that some of its empirical syntheses cannot be completed within experience. Commonly, a synthesis by which a sensible manifold is unified in accordance with the categories takes place within (or through) well-defined spatio-temporal units. In perceiving a spatial object, say the cup of coffee sitting on my desk, I synthesize a spatial manifold into a determinate geometrical figure contained within a well-defined space, say my room; in perceiving a causal series of events, say a train passing me, I synthesize the spatial locations of the train's coaches within a well-defined period of time. Yet not all sensible syntheses can be completed or fully executed within experience: for instance, when we approach the temporal beginning of the world or its uttermost spatial boundaries or when we seek to determine the smallest parts of a composite substance – examples Kant discusses in the Antinomies (A405–567/B432–595). Another example of an empirical synthesis that remains incomplete from the perspective of experience, I submit, is the synthesis of inner intuitions according to the category of substance. As we have seen in Chapter 4, the temporal manifold that inner sense provides cannot be synthesized in accordance with this category. Such a synthesis can be carried out only in the case of outer experience, in which a spatially distributed manifold can be determined as the "substratum" that persists through change. I, therefore, concluded that the *schema of persistence* cannot be applied in the case of inner experience (see 4.4.2).

In the case of an incomplete empirical synthesis, Kant goes on to argue in the Antinomies, reason can "free a concept of the understanding from the unavoidable limitation of a possible experience". By "making the category into a transcendental idea", reason can give "absolute completeness to the empirical synthesis through its progress towards the unconditioned" (A409/B436). A transcendental idea is precisely the concept of the unity that would be attained, if the empirical synthesis for a given appearance were to be completed and yielded the totality of the appearance's conditions.[50] Yet its regulative use in the completion of an empirical synthesis should not be misunderstood as the determination of an object. Rather, it enables the understanding to approach this unity "asymptotically, as it were, i.e., merely by approximation" (A663/B691).[51]

---

[50] Recall that an idea of reason is the concept of "the totality of conditions to a given conditioned thing", which "contains a ground of synthesis for what is conditioned" (A322/B379). In the *Prolegomena*, ideas represent the "progression from the conditioned to its condition" (*Prol* 3:354).

[51] For the notion of *approximation*, see also A479/B507, A647/B675, A677/B705, A692/B721.

In the Appendix, Kant then explicates the "completeness" that we approximate by means of an idea as the *systematic unity* of the manifold in cognition. Reason's regulative use consists in "mak[ing] systematic the unity of all possible empirical actions of the understanding", or what I will just call *systematization* (A664/B692). For the activity of systematization, reason requires a transcendental idea as an "analogue of a schema of sensibility", which Kant also calls a "schema of reason" (A665/B693). In other words, Kant argues that an idea – in its regulative use – does for reason's task of systematization what a schema does for the understanding's task of synthesis. In a first approximation, this can be understood as follows: a sensible schema gives "a rule for the determination of [the unity of] our intuition in accordance with a certain general concept" (A141/B180). Similarly, a "schema of reason" gives "a rule or principle of the systematic unity of all use of the understanding" (A665/B693). The crucial point is that both – a schema and an idea – define procedural rules to attain some unity. The schema of sensibility defines a rule to attain the *unity of a manifold of intuition* in accordance with a category and within an empirically accessible, well-defined spatio-temporal unit. In a similar vein, an idea – in its regulative employment – defines a rule to attain the *systematic unity of manifold cognitions* in accordance with the idea's conceptual content – a unity that, however, can only be approximated in experience.

These preliminary considerations suggest a twofold relation between schemata and ideas. Firstly, reason supplements the understanding with ideas, where schemata fail to be effective and hence cannot provide rules for applying the categories to appearances. Ideas substitute for the function of schemata for those empirical syntheses that cannot be completed within experience, but approach the limits thereof. Secondly, ideas serve as analogues of sensible schemata for the systematization of empirical cognitions. Ideas share with schemata the notion of a rule by which a manifold (of intuition or cognition) is unified in accordance with a concept.

5.5.2 Transcendental Schemata as Sensible Presentations (Darstellungen) of the Categories

The Schematism is a notoriously difficult and obscure part of Kant's transcendental philosophy. Here I present a reading of Kant's notion of *transcendental schema* that I take to prove helpful in illuminating the regulative use of ideas.

The Schematism of the categories is supposed to show "how the *subsumption* of the [intuition] under the [categories]" is possible and hence how "the *application* of the category to appearances" is possible (A137/B176). So its task is to mediate between the purely conceptual categories and appearances, given through a purely sensible manifold of intuition. This task is carried out by means of a "mediating representation", a so-called *transcendental schema*

(A138/B177; later called *schema of sensibility*, A665/B693).[52] In Chapter 2, I have construed the categories as the rules according to which such a sensible manifold is to be unified in order to match our forms of judgement (see 2.4). Schemata can now be understood as explicating the *application conditions* for these conceptual rules. That is, schemata explicate the *sensible* conditions that a sensible manifold must display to be suitable for the subsumption under a category. They determine how a sensible manifold must be like such that the corresponding synthesis can be operated on it. Robert Pippin suggests an intriguing interpretation of a schema as a "*method for using [the categories]*", that is, "a method projected by the imagination for specifying the conditions under which the rule can be used" (Pippin 1976:162). In consequence, the schemata give "sensible meaning" to the categories.[53] In support of this reading, we find Kant arguing that the schema of number is the "representation of a general procedure" or "of a method for representing a multitude" (A140/ B179, also *CJ* 5:253). Hence, schemata define *procedural rules* for carrying out the acts of synthesis.

The imagination plays a key role in the generation of these procedural rules, which are also introduced as the "transcendental product of the imagination" (A142/B181), that is, I submit, as the a priori product of the figurative synthesis. In Chapter 2, I have suggested a hylomorphic reading of the figurative synthesis, according to which the imagination generates a pure sensible manifold that is "informed" by the categories and hence displays sensible patterns that correspond to the unities defined by the categories. For instance, if a sensible manifold can be synthesized such that it displays a spatial distribution of parts that is stable throughout a series of intuitions, then this distribution can be recognized as instantiating the unity of a substance that persists through time. The schema can now be understood as a general procedural rule for "imprinting" a categorial form onto a sensible manifold. The schema produced by the imagination should, however, *not* be understood as an *image in concreto*. Rather, it only "expresses (*ausdrücken*)" a categorial form in a suitable way (A142/B179), namely as a temporal expression, or "pattern" displayed by temporal manifolds.[54] The imagination produces this schematic expression by projecting a priori what the completed synthesis according to

---

[52] Note that, while my exposition of the Schematism (A137–47/B176–87) focuses on *transcendental schemata*, that is, the schemata of the categories, Kant considers other kinds of schema, for example, the schema of empirical concepts and mathematical schemata. For discussion, see Allison (2004:204–13).

[53] See *MFNS* 4:478. See also Pendlebury (1995), Allison (2004:213, 219).

[54] There has been a controversy as to whether schemata should be understood as pure intuitions determined according to a priori rules (e.g., Guyer 1987) or as concepts with temporal determinations (e.g., Allison 2004) or as another "third thing" (A138/B177). Pippin's and Pendlebury's readings of schemata as methods or synthesizing dispositions seem to avoid this conflict.

this category would look like. In effect, the imagination provides us with a "monogram (*Monogramm*)" (A142/B181), or "the outline (*Umriß*) (*monogramma*) ... of the whole" (A833/B861). This sketch of a *sensible whole*, or a *Gestalt*, may not fully appear in empirical intuition, but must logically precede the synthesis of any sensible manifold given in intuition.[55] Think, for instance, of the back side of a visual object, like my cup, which may not show up in my current empirical manifold, but which I nonetheless cognize as part of the whole.

In the *Critique of the Power of Judgment*, Kant expands his account of schemata by explicating the notion of a "presentation" (*Darstellung*), "*as making something sensible*" (*Versinnlichung*): the schema is *a presentation that makes a concept sensible* (*CJ* 5:351). Kant uses also the Latin notion *exhibitionis*, the Greek notion *hypotyposis*, and the Latin phrase *subjectio sub adspectum* (which translates as "throwing under the eye"). These notions indicate the meaning of a "model", "sketch", "outline", or "pattern".[56] So the basic idea seems to be that a concept is supplemented by a sensible model that can be exhibited in intuition and that sufficiently corresponds to the concept. The schema of a category is the a priori sensible presentation (*Darstellungen*) of the unity defined by the category, and presents us with the model of a sensible whole to be realized by any corresponding empirical synthesis.[57] This a priori model delivers the procedural rule for applying the category to appearances. The principles of the understanding are the a priori cognitions that result from applying the categories to appearances and that describe a priori properties of objects of experience. For instance, the schema of substance is "the persistence of the real in time" (A144/B183) and the corresponding principle, viz. the First Analogy, states that "[i]n all ... appearances substance persists" (B224).

In sum, Kant's account of transcendental schema focuses on two key features: firstly, transcendental schemata determine the *application conditions* under which a sensible manifold can be synthesized in accordance with the categories, and hence define *procedural rules* for installing the categories as the rules of synthesis for intuitions. Secondly, as the products of an a priori synthesis of the *imagination*, they are the *sensible presentations* of the unities

---

[55] On the notion of *Gestalt*, see Pippin (1976:168). How the imagination proceeds in outlining the whole depends on the category. For instance, the schema of magnitude follows from "the successive addition of one (homogenous) unit to another" (A142/B182).

[56] Helfer (1996:23). On the genealogy of the notion of *Darstellung*, see Helfer (1996:9–50).

[57] This prescriptive formulation indicates that schemata are *normative* for the sensible synthesis of intuition, although they are *constitutive* for experience itself (see Allison 2004:205, Pollok 2017). Note that the "schema of magnitude" explicates all three quantitative categories, and the schema of "being (in time)" or "filling (time)" explicates all three qualitative categories (A142–3/B182).

that are defined by the categories and that are to be attained through the corresponding empirical synthesis in intuition.

5.5.3   The Regulative Use of Ideas as an Act of Presentation (Darstellung)

In accordance with these defining features of schemata, I will argue that ideas of reason – in their regulative use – similarly display two key features: firstly, a regulative use of a transcendental idea determines the *application conditions* under which manifold cognitions can be systematized in accordance with the idea, and hence defines *methods* for installing the ideas as rules of the understanding. Secondly, a regulative use of ideas also involves the *imagination*, through which the *presentation* of the unity that is defined by the idea is produced. However, such a whole can never be instantiated through sensible synthesis of intuitions. Rather, the presentation can only be *symbolic* in outlining, or sketching, the systematic whole defined by an idea.

In the Appendix, Kant explains the analogy, as well as the difference, between sensible schemata and ideas as follows:

> Thus the idea of reason is an *analogue of a schema of sensibility*, but with this difference, that the application of concepts of the understanding to the schema of reason is not likewise a cognition of the object itself (as in the application of the categories to their sensible schemata), but *only a rule or principle of the systematic unity of all use of the understanding*. (A665/B693, emphasis added)

As with sensible schemata, the use of ideas generates rules for attaining some unity. Like schemata, ideas prescribe rules to a type of mental act, though not to the acts of sensible synthesis, but to the acts of cognition. While schemata generate rules for synthesizing sensible manifolds in accordance with categorial unities (in order to ultimately cognize objects), ideas generate rules for combining multiple cognitions into a *systematic unity*, yet without thereby cognizing an object to which all these cognitions pertain.

Note that, in both cases, the unity to be attained is ultimately derived from "an application of the concepts of the understanding (*Verstandesbegriffe*)". The difference is, however, that in applying the categories to a sensible manifold, the logical unity of judgement must be instantiated in experience and is therefore constitutive of experience. By contrast, for "the schema of reason", a systematic unity is derived from the categories and supposed to give order to the logical unities of judgement *within it*. Kant later adds that the schema that is needed for ideas is not only "the outline (*Umriß*) (*monogramma*)", but also "the division (*Einteilung*) of the whole into members" and the "order (*Ordnung*) of the parts" (A833/B861). So the task of ideas is not only to outline the scope, or domain, within which acts of the understanding take place, but also to give some a priori structure or order to a domain of experience.

These considerations suggest – in line with the reading of schemata as application conditions for the understanding – that ideas are also application conditions for the understanding – not locally with respect to a single experience, but globally with respect to the whole (or a domain) of experience. Indeed, Kant argues that the principles that an idea establishes "indicate the procedure in accordance with which the empirical and determinate use of the understanding in experience can be brought into thoroughgoing agreement with itself" (A665/B693–4).

But how exactly does an idea generate procedural rules, or methods, for the understanding? In various passages, Kant associates the regulative use of ideas with the "presupposition (*Voraussetzung*) " of a transcendental principle that pertains to the object itself, or with the presupposition of an "object in the idea (*Gegenstand in der Idee*)" (A670/B698) (or what Kant also calls a "transcendental thing (*transzendentales Ding*)", A682/B710). Such an "object in the idea" is precisely *not* an "object absolutely": neither an object of experience, nor a real thing (A670/B698). Rather, by merely presupposing the "analogues of real things" (A674/B702), reason generates rules for completing the unity of cognitions. Kant, then, specifies his account of a schema of reason: "this transcendental thing is merely the schema of that regulative principle through which reason, as far as it can, extends systematic unity over all experience" (A682/B710).

Now, I argue that the act of *presupposing* the object described by an idea should be understood as *an a priori* act of *presentation (Darstellung)*. In presenting, or exhibiting such an object to the mind, reason produces procedural rules for how to seek systematic unity with respect to given empirical cognitions. An object in the idea, Kant writes, is "only a schema for which no object is given, not even hypothetically, but which serves only to represent other objects [of cognition] to us, in accordance with their systematic unity, by means of the relation to this idea, hence to represent these objects indirectly" (A670/B698). According to this passage, the "object in the idea" is "not even hypothetically" given. I understand this passage to be implying that we should not even hypothetically assume that there is a real thing that the idea describes. Rather, in presupposing a "transcendental thing", we entertain the content of the idea and exhibit this content as an intentional object to the mind. Such a presentation I take *not* to amount to the assertion of a truth-apt claim about some given object, not even a hypothetical claim, since this would inevitably and illegitimately amount to the hypostatization of the idea.[58]

Nonetheless, the mere act of *presupposing* the object in the idea should not be understood as merely fictitious either, in the sense of having no objective purport regarding the empirical reality we cognize. Rather, an idea gains its

---

[58] See, for example, A674/B702.

objective purport by offering procedural rules for the understanding to attain systematic unity among its cognitions. In Chapter 6, I will explicate how these procedural rules can be understood as normative principles that, for instance, guide the formation of empirical concepts. Yet here also lies an important difference with sensible schemata. Schemata define procedural rules that a sensible synthesis needs to follow to yield the cognition of an object at all.[59] Schemata are, therefore, constitutive of experience and give rise to true descriptions of objects of possible experience. By contrast, failing to realize the rules generated by an idea does not likewise result in failing to cognize an object per se. An idea provides only regulative principles for putting one's cognitions into an intelligible order. So I will argue below that a failure to recognize an idea results in a failure to make an experience *intelligible*.

To illustrate how the presupposition of an "object in the idea" can be understood as an act of sensible presentation, a comparison with mathematical cases is instructive. Mathematical cognition is a crucial example of how our own imagination exhibits an intentional object, without such an object being given to our senses and having a proven physical existence. For Kant, mathematical cognition requires us "to construct a concept" and that is "to exhibit *a priori* the intuition corresponding to it" (A713/B741). Here the imagination productively *constructs* a sensible intuition in accordance with a mathematical concept and thereby provides the mind with an intentional object, such as a geometrical figure, that "never exist[s] anywhere except in thought" (A141/B180, also A713/B741). The point of a geometrical proof is that in exhibiting a mathematical concept in intuition, we come to see further properties of the mathematical object that is thereby produced.[60] Similarly, I maintain that an *object in the idea* should be viewed as the product of an a priori act of presentation in accordance with an idea of reason. This act presents to the mind a *systematic unity* as an *intentional something* to be attained. Yet this act of exhibition does not consist in postulating a real thing's existence beyond the mind's own activity of systematization.[61]

Now, it is true that in the Appendix Kant does not elaborate on such an a priori act of presentation through the imagination. Nonetheless, we find hints that suggest an involvement of the imagination, most explicitly in the statement that an idea defines a *focus imaginarius* – a point that we only imagine as the "focus" to which all cognitions systematically relate (A644/B672). Moreover, we find passages that indicate a productive activity. For

---

[59] Although it is in general not required for a schema to be applicable that a real object is *actually* given to the senses, the schemata of relation and modality require "the *existence* of appearance in general" (see A160/B199).

[60] On the role of the imagination in geometrical construction, see Shabel (2007), and in symbolic construction in arithmetic and algebra, see Young (1982) and Shabel (1998).

[61] In Chapter 7, I will argue that, even though no object is given to us that corresponds to the idea, we can gradually realize such an object in the course of our mental activities.

instance, the notions of "posit[ing] (*setzen*) a thing corresponding to the idea" (A674/B702) and of "realiz[ing] (*realisieren*) an idea" in the following passage could be understood in this way: "I am not only warranted but even compelled to realize this idea, i.e., to posit for it an actual object" (A677/B705).

The act of presupposing an object in the idea displays a fundamental difference with the acts of construction or of exhibiting a category in intuition a priori. An idea cannot be presented "*in concreto* at all" (A683/B711), that is, it cannot be sensibly instantiated by a corresponding intuition. The content of an idea exceeds, by definition, that which is presentable (*darstellbar*) in sensible intuition. For this reason, Kant introduces, in the *Critique of the Power of Judgment*, a second kind of presentation, which he calls *symbolic* (see *CJ* 5:351–4). In this case the synthetic function of the imagination operates only *indirectly*, by means of symbols that stand in for the idea and that are "expression[s]" of these ideas (*CJ* 5:352). Yet symbols are not randomly chosen; rather, their symbolic force derives from an analogy with schematic presentations. Kant thus offers an account of the presentation of an idea in terms of an analogy with the procedure of schematization. In symbolic cognition "the power of judgment proceeds in a way merely analogous to that which it observes in schematization; i.e., it is merely the rule of this procedure, not of the intuition itself, and thus merely the form of reflection, not the content, which corresponds to the concept" (*CJ* 5:351). Kant here suggests that the *procedural rule* for schematizing a concept is *analogous* with the *procedural rule* for symbolizing an idea of reason. While a full exploration of this account – and of the role of the power of judgement in it – goes beyond the scope of this book, I now elaborate on the specific analogy that I take to be at play between transcendental schemata and ideas.

5.5.4   The Analogy between Schemata and Principles of Systematicity

The analogy that Kant seems to have in mind may be described as follows: the *procedural rules* (viz. sensible schemata) for synthesizing a unified intuition according to a category are *analogous* with the *procedural rules* (viz. schemata of reason) for bringing cognitions into a system according to an idea of reason. In virtue of this analogy, we can derive the rules for systematization from those for schematization.

The notion of analogy in philosophy can be understood on the model of a *mathematical analogy*, namely in terms of quantitative proportion between four variables ($a : b = c : d$). In the mathematical case, if three variables are known and one is unknown, we can infer cognition of the fourth by drawing an inference from one pair of variables to the other. In the philosophical case, we deal with the "identity of … two *qualitative* relations" (A179/B222). Yet, similarly, Kant argues that we can draw inferences from one relation to another and thereby gain cognition of the fourth member.[62] Examples of philosophical analogies are indeed the Analogies of Experience that concern the relations among appearances: they "compare" logical relations, such as <*substance–accidents*> or <*cause–effect*>, to the relations found in intuitions, and hence among appearances. Through this "comparison", the cognition of the unknown fourth element can be inferred. The fourth element is that in appearance which corresponds, for instance, to the logical unity of a substance. As a result, the Analogies of Experience generate a priori cognition of dependence relations among appearances: the First Analogy, cognition of the relation between a substance and its inhering accidents; the Second Analogy, cognition of the relation of a cause to its effect.

The First Analogy may be symbolically represented as follows:

$$\frac{category\ of\ substance}{category\ of\ accidents} :: \frac{intuition\ of\ that\ which\ persists\ in\ all\ appearances}{manifold\ intuitions\ of\ changing\ appearances}$$

The schema of *substance–accident* provides a procedural rule for finding something in appearance that persists and for distinguishing it from its changing states. Here the rule itself consists in drawing an analogy between the logical relation of <substance–accidents> (left-hand side) and the dependence relation of a persistent substance to its changing states (right-hand side). What is detected as sufficiently stable in our perception can be cognized as "something *lasting* and *persisting*" (A182/B225). The schema of persistence hence "gives general expression" to the concept of substance (A183/B226).[63]

In the third *Critique*, Kant considers a broader notion of philosophical analogy – one that does not give rise to a priori cognition, but in which we nonetheless "transfer [the] characteristic of the specific difference from one [case] to the other" (*CJ* 5:465). Instead of inferring cognition of objects, we only *think* something *by analogy* with the logical categories of relation. For instance, on the basis of the "relation between grounds and consequences (causes and effects)" (*CJ* 5:464n), we can *think* of human or animal action as being the ground of an effect, for example, an artefact or the beaver's dam. In these cases, we do not have transcendental schemata available that generate a priori cognition of objects.[64] What we effectively do is to transpose the procedural rule that we gained through a schema and apply it so as to

---

[62] See also *L-Log/Philippi* 24:478. For discussion, see Callanan (2008) and Allison (2004:226).

[63] Note that as the schema gives a temporal expression of substance as persistence, it can operate only on a *spatio*-temporal manifold, as argued in 4.4. The schema of substance gives us a method for determining empirical substances (*phenomena*) that are relatively persistent. The First Analogy may be taken to make a stronger claim about the necessity of an *absolute* substratum as the "constant correlate of all existence of appearances" (A183/B226). See 5.6.

[64] On the two kinds of analogy, see Maly (2011:51–8).

symbolically, or indirectly, present the underlying logical relation in a different case. Such a symbolic presentation can be a linguistic expression or other "sensible signs" (*CJ* 5:352). This *transposition* of "the mere rule of reflection" (*CJ* 5:352), as Kant calls it, makes it possible for us to get a handle on cases that we *cannot fully* cognize, because they exceed our intuitive capacities. There is an open question whether such symbolic presentation still offers rules for gaining cognition of appearances at least to some extent or whether it even allows for a qualitatively different kind of cognition, which one may call *symbolic cognition*. I discuss this question with respect to inner experience in the next section.[65]

This broader notion of a philosophical analogy is precisely what is at play in the case of transcendental ideas. We exhibit the systematic unity of cognition by *thinking of* it by analogy with the categories of relation. For instance, we think the systematic unity *as if* it were a substance in which cognitions inhere as accidents. Any suitable empirical substance can then serve as the symbol of such systematic unity. By thinking this analogy with the schema of *substance-accident*, we can derive a procedural rule – as a regulative schema – for ordering cognitions within this systematic unity. This analogy may be symbolically represented as follows:

$$\frac{intuition \ of \ that \ which \ persists \ in \ all \ experiences}{manifold \ intuitions \ of \ changing \ appearances} \ ::$$

$$\frac{systematic \ unity \ of \ cognitions}{multitude \ of \ cognitions}$$

What is *qualitatively* identical in this analogy are the *relations* that obtain, on the one side, between an intuition of something as persistent and a sensible manifold of intuitions and, on the other side, between a systematic unity and multiple cognitions. Note that the left-hand side lies fully within the bounds of sensibility and can be exhibited a priori in intuition, whereas on the right-hand side, each single cognition is within the bounds of sense, but the systematic unity itself remains beyond our intuitive grasp.

In the Appendix, Kant explicitly suggests an analogical procedure of this kind for the ideas of the soul and of God:

> we think a relation to the sum total of all appearances, which is analogous to the relation that appearances have to one another.   (A674/B702)

> we cannot think except in accordance with the analogy of an actual substance.   (A675/B703)

---

[65] In the third *Critique*, this transposition of a rule of reflection amounts to the making of a *reflective judgement* and is attributed to the power of judgement. On symbolic cognition, see Maly (2011:51–8 and 65–72).

For the sensible exhibition of these ideas, we think "a sum total of all appearances" by analogy with the schema of substance and thereby derive procedural rules for how to order appearances in relation to such a sum total. The relation between empirical substances and their accidents is then analogous to the relation of the sum total and its appearances.[66] There is one fundamental difference between the two ideas: with the idea of God as the *sum total of all possibility*, we seek to find not only the systematic unity of objects in *nature*, but of everything that can exist (A573/B601). Hence, it seems that both "elements" of the right-hand side of the analogy exceed our sensible capacities, and that this analogy does not contribute methods for the cognition of *nature*. By contrast, the idea of the soul concerns the systematic unity of inner appearances, to which we have an intuitive access. What we lack is an intuitive grasp of the whole to which all these inner appearances belong. In the next section, I explicate the analogical procedure for the idea of the soul and derive the specific principles of relation for the *determination* of inner appearances.

Let us take stock. Firstly, transcendental ideas of reason are necessary in cases in which our transcendental schemata are no longer effective, since we have reached the boundaries of our sensible capacities. Similar to schemata, ideas provide *procedural rules* specifically for keeping the empirical use of the understanding within these boundaries and for systematically ordering the understanding's cognitions within this domain. Secondly, like the schematic rules, these rules are gained from an a priori act of exhibiting (*darstellen*) the whole of cognition within that domain. Yet, unlike in the case of schemata, such a whole cannot be instantiated in intuition, but its exhibition must proceed *symbolically*, that is, *by analogy* with a corresponding schema. Through this analogy, a schematic rule for synthesizing intuitions is transposed and applied as a procedural rule for *systematizing* cognitions. The resulting principles of systematicity are, unlike the constitutive principles of the understanding, only *regulative* for attaining a rationally intelligible systematic unity among cognitions, and hence for comprehending a rational order among the corresponding appearances.

Failing to obey these regulative principles does not make experience per se impossible; however, it makes experience *unintelligible* within a particular context of intelligibility. For without "the government of reason", our cognitions could remain a mere "rhapsody" (A832/B860). We have to take the whole in view to recognize the limits of our cognitive efforts and to orientate our particular cognitions – with the aim, not to determine the whole, but to determine parts within a whole. For instance, if we do not subject our experience of outer objects to the regulative idea of the world-whole, we cannot make

---

[66] Note that, in the case of the idea of the world-whole, the analogy with the category of substance already leads to the First Antinomy (A426–33/B454–61) and is therefore not productive for ordering outer appearances.

sense of them as cognitions of physical bodies within a single *physical space* that is systematically connected according to laws of physics. If we do not subject our experience of living beings to the regulative idea of purposiveness, we cannot make sense of them in terms of mechanisms that contribute to a single organic whole. Without these ideas of the whole, our cognition of physical powers or of biological mechanisms would remain blind and rhapsodic.

Hence, the regulative use of a transcendental idea generates a *context of intelligibility* within which we can make sense of our cognitions in a rational order. By reflecting our experience under such an idea, we make sense of it as a certain *kind of cognition* that is available within a particular *domain of nature*.

5.6   The Regulative Principles of Inner Experience

Based on my reading of transcendental ideas, I now argue that the idea of the soul defines that domain of nature that concerns human beings qua their psychological features, or what I just call *inner nature*. Only through a regulative use of this idea can I first make sense of my *inner experience* as the cognition of my own psychological features (though without cognizing myself as a substance). This section presents a close reading of a passage in the Appendix in which Kant elaborates on the regulative use of this idea, the so-called deduction of the idea of the soul (A682–4/B710–12). Then, it explicates the analogies that are at play in inner experience and which give rise to a special set of principles of relation for inner experience.[67]

5.6.1   *The Presupposition of a Mental Whole*

In the second part of the Appendix, Kant presents a deduction of the idea of the soul (A682–4/B710–12).[68] This deduction is supposed to offer an argument for why one requires an idea of "myself, considered merely as thinking nature (*denkende Natur*) (soul, *Seele*)" (A682/B710).[69] "Thinking nature" I take to

---

[67] Some scholars have concluded that Kant's theory of the soul is – at least for the purpose of theoretical self-knowledge – doomed to fail; for example, Heßbrüggen-Walter (2004), Klemme (1996), and Emundts (2017), and to some extent Serck-Hanssen (2011).

[68] I do not offer a final position regarding the relation between the two parts of the Appendix – between the first part (A642–68/B670–96), which deals with principles of systematicity (see Chapter 6), and the second part (A669–704/B697–732), which deals with the three transcendental ideas of soul, the world-whole, and God. On this relation, see McLaughlin (2014).

[69] It is a matter of controversy whether such a deduction is possible and whether Kant succeeds in providing one, especially given his earlier claim that "no *objective deduction*", but only a "subjective derivation" is possible (A336/B393). Horstmann (1989), for instance, thinks that Kant fails in providing a deduction since it is not possible to give one; Ciami (1995) argues that a deduction is necessary and successfully provided by Kant;

concern precisely the psychological nature of a "thinking being (*denkend Wesen*)", that is, of *a mind insofar as it is embedded in a (spatio-)temporal world*.

At the beginning of the deduction passage, Kant restates the specific problem of inner experience: we lack an adequate concept of the *object of inner experience*, that is, a "concept of experience [*Erfahrungsbegriff*] (of that which the soul actually is)" (A682/B710). The context makes it clear that here Kant refers to the issue of "explaining the appearances of the soul" for which we have to "ask experience" (A682/B710), rather than to the soul as a thing-in-itself. Commonly, the concept of an object of outer experience is a priori determined by the categories and sensibly explicated through corresponding schemata.[70] Yet for inner experience, we lack adequate sensible explications for the categories of relation. Recall, from Chapter 4, that, for instance, the schema of substance as persistence is not applicable to inner intuitions, because we are not given anything "standing and abiding" in inner sense (A107, A350).[71] More specifically, since inner sense has available only a temporal manifold, the schema of persistence does not get a hold, as it were, and cannot make out anything persistent in the ever-fleeting states of consciousness. Hence, we cannot complete an empirical synthesis, according to the category of substance, on a manifold of inner intuition and, therefore, cannot cognize a mental substance. In consequence, we lack an empirical concept (*Erfahrungsbegriff*) of a mental object, or mind.

The crucial step of the deduction is now to substitute the unavailable empirical concept of a mind with an idea of reason and to show that the regulative use of this idea substitutes for the schemata that are not applicable to complete the corresponding syntheses in inner experience. Kant describes the procedure of reason as follows:

> reason takes the concept of the empirical unity of all thought, and, by thinking this unity unconditionally and originally, it makes out of it a concept of reason (an idea) of a simple substance, unchangeable in itself (identical in personality), standing in community with other real things outside it – in a word, the concept of a simple self-sufficient intelligence.
>
> (A682/B710)

So reason frees the "concept of the empirical unity of all thought", which it cannot exhibit in intuition, from its sensible conditions and turns it into an idea – the idea of the soul or of "a simple self-sufficient intelligence".[72] This

---

McLaughlin (2014) argues that, even though a deduction is possible and necessary, Kant's attempts to provide one have failed. In my effort to give a detailed reconstruction of the idea's regulative use, I side with those who find the idea justifiable.

[70] In the *Foundations*, Kant offers such an explication specifically for the "empirical concept of matter [*Erfahrungsbegriff der Materie*]" (*MFNS* 4:470). See Friedman (2013:1–34).

[71] See A22–3/B37, A107, A350, B412–13.

[72] Recall the definitions of the idea of the soul at the beginning of the Dialectic: "absolute (unconditioned) unity of the thinking subject" (A334/B391) and "unconditioned unity of

idea contains a set of predicates, as this passage mentions (in agreement with the guiding-thread passage):

(1) "a simple substance" that is

(2) endowed with "one unique fundamental power" (as is added a few lines below);

(3) "standing in community with other real things outside it"; and

(4) "unchangeable in itself (identical in personality)".

If the empirical syntheses of inner intuitions could be completed in accordance with the categories of relation, then we would cognize a mental object that would be characterized by these predicates. Yet, since those syntheses cannot be completed in inner experience, the idea merely gives us a model of the "systematic unity of all the appearances of inner sense" (A682/B710).

In the remainder of the deduction, Kant explicates the predicates of the idea as regulative principles for inner experience to attain this systematic unity, that is, as "principles of the systematic unity in explaining the appearances of the soul" (A682/B710). Kant spells them out in a series of "as if" claims (here indicated by "considering . . . as"):

> by considering [1] all determinations as in one subject, [2] all powers, as far as possible, as derived from one unique fundamental power, [3] all change as belonging to the states of one and the same persisting being, and by representing all *appearances* in space as entirely distinct from the actions of *thinking*. (A682-3/B710-1, numbering added)

In line with my general considerations above, I take these "as if" claims (here numbered in accordance with the predicates above) *not* to be hypothetical descriptive claims about an underlying noumenal reality, since they are "not presupposed *as if* [they] were the real ground of properties of the soul" (A682/B71). Rather, presupposing these propositions amounts to an a priori act of exhibiting the required systematic unity of a mental whole as an intentional object in the idea. Through this act of exhibition, we gain procedural rules for systematizing single inner experiences. These rules are spelled out as principles of relation that are specific for determining inner appearances within a mental whole.

In the final part of the deduction, Kant points out that such a regulative use of the idea is entirely different from its use in rational psychology and that the content of the idea differs from what is traditionally endorsed. The idea does not allow us to draw conclusions from "windy hypotheses about the generation, destruction or palingenesis of souls" (A683/B711). Neither does it allow us to ask questions about what the soul as a thing "of a spiritual nature" is in

the subjective conditions of all representation in general (of the subject or soul)" (A406/B432).

itself, since such questions have "no sense" with respect to experience. These traditional predicates of the soul play no regulative role in approximating the systematic unity of *inner experience*, and hence must be dismissed altogether as meaningless in this context. Kant thus draws a subtle line between those predicates of the idea of the soul that are useful for gaining explanations of inner appearances and those that are beyond any meaningful relation to inner appearances.[73]

5.6.2   *The Principles of Relation for Inner Experience*

After providing the textual evidence for my interpretation from the deduction passage, I now reconstruct the analogies that I take to be at play in the regulative use of the idea of the soul. For each predicate contained in the idea, we can discern a regulative principle by explicating the analogy with the corresponding transcendental schema.

Firstly, we need a concept of substantiality to exhibit the mental whole to which all inner appearances are considered to belong. The predicate of "a simple substance" precisely amounts to the proposition that "all determinations [are considered] as in one subject". This proposition should be understood as a regulative principle that follows from the following analogy:

$$\frac{\textit{intuition of that which persists in all appearances}}{\textit{manifold intuitions of changing appearances}} ::$$

$$\frac{\textit{idea of a [thinking] substance with inhering states}}{\textit{manifold intuitions of changing inner appearances}}$$

Through this analogy, the schema of substance as persistence (left-hand side) is transposed and analogically applied as a procedural rule for systematizing inner experience within a mental whole (right-hand side). The systematization, in a first approximation, here comes down to relating a sequence of inner intuitions to one and the same whole. Presupposing a mental whole a priori is necessary to make sense of those inner intuitions as representing inner appearances of one and the same subject. Only then can I consider those inner appearances as the *parts* of a mental whole, or as the *mental states* of a temporally unified mind. For recall, without the regulative use of the idea, we lack a sufficient empirical concept of the mind and hence cannot represent mental states at all.

In employing the idea, we do *not* gain cognition of the mental whole as such, that is, cognition of a mental substance, since the whole always remains beyond

---

[73] Note that Kant reintroduces a proposition regarding immortality as a Postulate of Pure Practical Reason in his practical philosophy (see *CpracR* 5:122f.). Immortality, for Kant, is required for exhibiting the concept of the highest good and hence for gaining practical cognition concerning one's actions.

our intuitive grasp. Yet, I maintain, by exhibiting the mental whole symbolically (that is, by analogy with persistent substances), we do gain cognition of
inner appearances. Employing an idea on the right-hand side of the analogy
does not mean that all of the right-hand side is beyond a determinate grasp of
experience. We cannot make out anything in intuition that corresponds to
a mental whole, but we can make out states that are considered to relate to such
a whole. Thus, I submit, we can still apply the schematic rules for *determining
accidents* (of a substance) to inner appearances.

Recall that transcendental ideas outline contexts of intelligibility, within
which the constitutive principles are first operative so as to determine appearances. An idea, Kant argues, "shows not how an object is constituted but how,
under the guidance of that concept [viz. the idea], we ought to *seek* after the
constitution (*Beschaffenheit*) and connection (*Verknüpfung*) of objects of
experience in general" (A671/B699).

In the case of inner experience, we do not seek to determine the constitution and connection of *outer objects,* but the constitution and connection of
mental states. While the idea of the world-whole outlines the context of
intelligibility for determining outer appearances as outer objects, the idea
of the soul outlines the context for determining inner appearances as mental
states. Hence, I emphatically conclude that *inner experience is empirical
cognition of inner appearances*, though it does not involve cognizing the
sum total of inner appearances as a mental substance. This determination
of inner appearances can be carried out further in accordance with the other
categories of relation.

Secondly, in accordance with the category of cause, we consider "all powers,
as far as possible, as derived from one unique fundamental power
[*Grundkraft*]". That is, we employ the regulative principle that the mental
whole be considered as the seat of a fundamental causal power of the mind
from which all its mental states, viz. inner appearances, originate. The schema
of causality defines a method for finding cause–effect relations among appearances, such that, whenever the cause is posited, the effect follows (see A144/
B183). More precisely, the schema gives us a rule for deriving, from
a "subjective sequence" of apprehended intuitions, an "objective sequence of
appearances" in accordance with the logical relation of <cause–effect> (A193/
B238). The schema of causality may then be illustrated as follows:

$$\frac{category\ of\ cause}{category\ of\ effect} :: \frac{intuition\ of\ the\ appearance\ of\ a\ cause}{intuition\ of\ the\ appearance\ of\ an\ effect}$$

It is not entirely clear from Kant's elaboration in the Second Analogy what
exactly an *appearing* cause and an *appearing* effect are. On a plausible reading,
the appearing causes in outer experience are, typically, the attractive and
repulsive forces of a material object, and the appearing effect is the alteration

of the state of another object that is thereby set in motion.[74] In general, one may assume that an appearing cause is the "action" or "force" that the causal power of a substance exerts on another object, and the appearing effect is the resulting objective sequence of appearances (A204/B249).

The analogy for the idea of a fundamental power could then run as follows:

$$\frac{intuition\ of\ the\ appearance\ of\ a\ cause}{intuition\ of\ the\ appearance\ of\ an\ effect}\ ::$$

$$\frac{idea\ of\ a\ fundamental\ power\ as\ that\ appears\ as\ cause}{intuition\ of\ an\ objective\ sequence\ of\ inner\ appearances\ as\ effect}$$

Again, through this analogy, the schema of causality is transposed and analogically applied as the procedural rule for systematizing inner experiences by way of temporal ordering. This comes down to considering a sequence of inner appearances as originating from the same fundamental mental power and thus as being objectively ordered in accordance with a necessary rule.

Kant apparently assumes that the empirical effects of each mental faculty can be understood as causal powers on the model of causality explicated by the schema above.[75] What is problematic in the mental case is not only that the schema of causality builds on that of substance and implies that there is a substance in which a causal power inheres – a claim that has already proven difficult for the mind (see A204/B250). What is at stake now is that we seek a *fundamental* power that unifies *all* mental faculties and explains our mental self-efficacy across distinct mental faculties. While we can "not at all ascertain whether there is such a thing" as a fundamental power, we require an idea of it for the "systematic representation of the manifoldness of powers" in the mind (A649/B677). Only then can we consider ourselves as the causal origin of all mental acts and representations, regardless of the kind of mental faculty from which they arise. Only then can we understand our own mental self-efficacy across the three fundamental faculties – the faculty of cognition, the will, and feeling – and hence represent ourselves as a "self-sufficient intelligence".

Again, I deny that, by employing this idea regulatively, we gain cognition of the actions of a fundamental power or assert the existence thereof, even if only hypothetically. Yet I strongly endorse that, by transposing the schematic rule, we do gain cognition of objective sequences of inner appearances. Even though we have no intuitive access to a mental substance with a fundamental power, we are able to represent a mental whole such that we can determine *given* inner

---

[74] See Watkins (2005:209–17), Frierson (2014:53–4). By contrast, Allison (2004:258) reconstructs the Second Analogy in terms of the relation between an occasioning cause-event from which an effect-event follows in time. This event-causality reading is, however, difficult to square with the analogy with fundamental powers that is at stake here.

[75] For accounts, see Wuerth (2014:189–205), Frierson (2014:53–4).

appearances within an objective time-series in accordance with a necessary rule of causality. For instance, we can cognize that our perception of a wild animal is followed, first, by the thought that this animal might be dangerous, then by a feeling of fear, and finally by the intention to run away. Such sequences of mental states are certainly intelligible to us and can be fully explained on the basis of causal psychological laws. The causal order of mental states we thereby cognize is *objective* in the sense that it represents the psychological reality of a person. It does not yet amount to the determination of mental states in objective time, as I discuss below.[76]

Now, one may object that my interpretation of psychological causation based on an idea of reason is not compatible with stronger claims that Kant makes on various occasions. For instance, in the Refutation of Idealism, Kant argues that "inner experience in general is possible only through outer experience in general" (B278-9). In the General Remarks of the B-Edition, Kant claims that we "grasp the inner alteration through the drawing of this line (motion), and thus grasp the successive existence of ourselves in different states through outer intuition" (B292). Here we have to distinguish between two of Kant's concerns, which he himself conflates at times. Neither concern excludes the possibility of psychological causation as I understand it.

Firstly, Kant is concerned about kinds of *idealism* that take the cognition of our mind to be more certain than the cognition of outer objects and that make outer experience in some fundamental sense dependent on inner experience. Secondly, Kant is concerned about the *unity of time*: even if time is a subjective form of apprehension, we experience all appearances as in *one* time – the time that pertains to all material objects or just *objective time*. In the Refutation of Idealism, Kant attempts to guard his own philosophy against the first concern. The Third Analogy of Experience deals specifically with the second concern. I consider both concerns in turn.

Regarding the first concern, Kant attempts, in the Refutation of Idealism, to refute what he calls *material* idealism, in particular Cartesian problematic idealism, according to which we can be certain only of our own mental existence, but not of the existence of external objects. Kant offers a proof that is supposed to show that I cannot be "conscious of my existence as determined in time" without being conscious "of the existence of other things outside me" (B275-6, see also Bxl, 157n, 430-1). Note, first, that here Kant refers to a specific kind of inner experience, which I take to involve the temporal determination of one's mental states in *objective time*. Setting aside various controversies regarding the scope and effectiveness of the proof, Kant

---

[76] Frierson (2014:52–85) offers highly illuminating discussions, and examples, of the parallels between psychological causation and physical causation, even though he does not recognize that psychological causation requires the idea of the soul as endowed with a fundamental power.

offers, in Note 2, an argument concerning the relation of inner and outer experience.[77] There, he argues that for *time-determination* itself and hence for the determination of any change *in objective time*, we must presuppose that something *persistent* can be intuited that is independent of the mind's changing representations and thus exists external to the mind itself. He then identifies that which "persists in space" as the impenetrable "matter" of physical objects (B278), as he did earlier in the First Analogy.[78] He specifies that the persistence of matter "is not drawn from [a specific] outer experience, but rather presupposed *a priori* as the necessary condition of all time-determination" (B278). I take this explanation to imply that what is primarily required for time-determination, and a fortiori for the determination of mental states in time, is the presupposition of the *empirical concept of matter* (and its a priori determinations) and the actual existence of any physical-material objects that instantiate this concept.[79]

Hence, I take the Refutation *not* to show that for inner experience to be possible there must be a physical *substratum* in which mental states inhere; nor that there must be an underlying physical-material framework that serves as a backdrop against which the changing inner states can be measured through direct correlation of each mental state with a physical state of the framework. On my reading, the Refutation's claim about inner experience comes down to the assertion that to determine one's mental states *in objective time*, we need to borrow from outer experience the empirical concept of matter and its transcendental schemata of persistence and causality, for the purpose of the analogies sketched above.[80]

Similarly, in the First Analogy, Kant argues that the determination of change (*Wechsel*) in general must be modelled on the determination of the "alteration (*Veränderung*)" of the states of material substances. This may imply the even stronger claim that there must be an *absolute* substratum as the "constant correlate of *all existence* of appearances" (A183/B226, emphasis added).[81] On my reading, this claim could be understood only as an idea of a material world-whole, or of "*nature* taken substantively (*materialiter*)", which Kant discusses in the Antinomies (A419/B446n). Employed as a regulative idea of reason,

[77] My reading remains neutral on the question whether the Refutation makes the weaker, epistemic claim that we require the existence of outer appearances for the *cognition* of temporal order, or the stronger, metaphysical claim that the temporal order itself is grounded in the existence of "external" things-in-themselves.

[78] See also Bxl, A186/B229–30, A213/B260.

[79] See *MFNS* 4:467. In the General Remarks, Kant concludes that the application of the categories of relation to appearances requires the "intuition in space (of matter)", specifically "in order to exhibit" persistence and alteration (B291).

[80] For more details of my reading, see Kraus (2019a). For the "substratum" reading of the Refutation, see Emundts (2010:168–89); for the "backdrop" reading, see Allison (2004:297). For the correlation claim, see also Guyer (1987:315), Keller (1998:204), Allison (2004:297).

[81] For example, Allison (2004:244–6).

I suggest, it marks out the domain of outer nature within which the schemata of substance and causality can first be operative for the determination of appearances.

Kant considers the second concern – the problem of determining different objects in one and the same time – in the Third Analogy. There, Kant construes a solution with the category of "community [*Gemeinschaft*]" that allows us to determine the "reciprocal influence" (i.e., causal interaction) objects have on one another (A213/B260). The schema of community shows the simultaneity of the determinations of one substance with those of the other substance. Yet to determine such reciprocal influence, we must represent objects as standing "outside one another" and hence as being simultaneous in *one* space (A215/B262).[82] This requirement obviously poses a problem for determining inner appearances in the same time.

Indeed, I do not claim that the principle of psychological causation that I have discerned above allows for the determination of inner appearances *in objective time*. It allows only for the determination of a *qualitative causal order* of mental states. Take the following example: Imagine yourself in a room that is completely shut off from all external sensations and in which you find yourself reciting a poem – verse by verse – in your mind. The idea of a fundamental mental power will allow you to determine the *order* in which your mental states – here the conscious representation of each verse of the poem – appear in your inner sense. But you cannot determine how much time has objectively lapsed between the beginning and the end of your recital. For the latter, we need to consider the correlation with some material states. So I concede that we require outer intuitions to quantitatively measure the temporal relations of mental states in objective time.[83]

Luckily, Kant introduces a third predicate of the soul that makes such a determination possible by analogy with the schema of community. In the deduction passage, Kant mentions the predicate of "standing in community with other real things outside [the soul]" (A682/B710). He then translates this predicate into the regulative principle that "all change [be considered] as belonging to the states of one and the same persisting being, and by representing all *appearances* in space as entirely distinct from the actions of *thinking*" (A682-3/B710-1).

In the deduction passage, Kant is primarily concerned with the problem of keeping the causal laws of inner appearances separate from, and thus irreducible to, the "laws of corporeal appearances" (A683/B711). Yet this third predicate not only fends off psychological materialism, but it also opens a way to define a regulative principle for the *temporal determination* of mental states – on the model of the Third Analogy. In the original guiding-thread

[82] For discussion, see Watkins (2005:215–32).
[83] For a discussion of quantification and measurement in inner experience, see Kraus (2016).

passage, Kant demands, more aptly, that we consider ourselves as a substance "to which the states of the body belong only as external conditions" (A672/B700). My thought here is that by way of correlating inner appearances to "external conditions" (for instance, the states of our own body) we can draw conclusions about the simultaneity of both bodily and mental determinations, as if they were in *one space*, and subsequently determine inner appearances in objective time. The analogy of community may then run as follows:

$$\frac{\textit{intuition of substance A causing an effect in substance B}}{\textit{intuition of substance B causing an effect in substance A}} ::$$

$$\frac{\textit{idea of a mental substance causing an effect in a material body}}{\textit{intuition of a material body causing an effect on inner appearances}}$$

Again, through this analogy, the schema of community (left-hand side) is transposed and analogically applied as the procedural rule for systematically correlating mental and bodily states by way of simultaneity. Employing this procedural rule, we can quantitatively and qualitatively determine ourselves in objective time based on a correlation of our inner appearances with outer appearances, for example, of our own body. Again, this does not mean that we cognize ourselves as persistent substances. Nor does it mean that we thereby reduce the mental whole of inner appearances to a material substance and cognize inner appearances as states that inhere in our body.[84]

Quite the opposite. Only through employing the idea of the soul can we first make sense of inner appearances as mental states and – following the schema of community – determine these mental states in objective time through the correlation with external states. Without presupposing the idea of the soul, we fall prey to an unfounded materialism and reduce the self-standing unity of mental states to the material unity of the body.[85]

5.7 Conclusion

In this chapter, I argued that inner experience is cognition of inner appearances, *without* thereby *cognizing* oneself as (1) a substance that is endowed with (2) a fundamental causal power and (3) stands in interaction with other substances. In order for us to make sense of inner intuitions as representations of our own inner appearances, we must employ these three predicates (1)–(3) of the soul in a regulative way. My argument came in two crucial steps.

---

[84] The Fourth A-Paralogism could be understood as arguing for the simultaneity of both inner and outer appearances insofar as both are equally real in one and the same time (esp. A372–3). See also *Prol* 4:336.

[85] For a reconstruction of Kant's arguments against psychological materialism in the *Prolegomena* based on the idea of the soul, see Kraus (forthcoming).

Firstly, I developed a reading of transcendental ideas of reason in general, according to which their regulative use marks out contexts of intelligibility in which we can make sense of certain kinds of cognition. Such use is based on an analogy with transcendental schemata, from which we borrow the procedural rules for symbolically exhibiting (*darstellen*) the whole of experience within a certain domain. The resulting rules can be understood as regulative principles that direct the acts of the understanding towards attaining a systematic unity of all cognitions within this domain. These principles define how – and within which scope – the constitutive principles of the understanding can be properly and coherently used.

Secondly, I applied this general reading to the idea of the soul and showed that this idea outlines the domain of inner nature within which we can first make sense of inner experience as the cognition of inner appearances. Employing the idea regulatively generates a priori a symbolic presentation of the systematic mental whole of all inner appearances, from which we can derive procedural rules by analogy with the transcendental schemata of relation. I explicated the three analogies that correspond to the three main predicates of the soul and derived a set of principles of relation for inner experience. These principles substitute the schemata of substantiality, causality, and community, which are not applicable. In consequence, the three Analogies of Experience were shown to be operative in inner experience, though in a reduced form. Specifically, the predicate of substantiality is required to recognize all inner appearances as mental states of one and the same trans-temporally unified mind. The predicate of a fundamental power is required to recognize these states as the causal effects of the same self-efficacious mind and to determine their qualitative causal order according to psychological laws. The predicate of community is required to quantitatively measure the temporal relations of mental states in objective time by drawing correlations with the states of outer objects, especially the human body. I postpone a discussion of the fourth predicate of "personal identity" until Chapter 7.

I acknowledge that inner experience has a higher degree of indeterminacy than outer experience, since no persistent substance can be made out. Yet my reconstruction shows that there is no qualitative difference in the way both inner and outer experience rely on the regulative use of ideas. In both cases, the presupposition of a whole – the world-whole or the mental whole – must *logically precede* the determination of its parts – material objects or mental states. The whole itself has reality only in virtue of the empirical reality of its parts.

In subsequent chapters, I will expand this interpretation and show that the idea of the soul expresses normative demands that originate from reason and that normatively guide the acts of the understanding: in Chapter 6, with respect to the theoretical goal of acquiring self-knowledge, and in Chapter 7, with respect to the practical goal of the self-formation of a person.

6

The Demands of Theoretical Reason
and Self-Knowledge

6.1 Introduction

This chapter offers an account of empirical self-knowledge – the theoretical knowledge I have of myself as a psychological person based on my inner experience. While the previous chapter focused on reason's *regulative* role with regard to inner experience, this chapter will highlight reason's *normative* role in coming to know oneself through inner experience. In its normative role, reason concerns not only the conditions under which I can represent myself in experience, but specifically the conditions under which I can have a *true* representation of myself. So the transcendental ideas of reason are now understood as defining, not only the context in which a certain kind of experience is intelligible to beings like us, but a *normative standard* for the good, that is, truth-conducive, use of the understanding.

Following Kant's general theory of knowledge (*Wissen*), I shall argue that self-knowledge requires – in addition to cognition (*Erkenntnis*) of myself – an attitude of *assent* towards this cognition and an *epistemic ground* for holding this cognition to be true, that is, an *epistemic justification*.[1] By laying out different types of epistemic grounds, I shall distinguish corresponding levels of self-knowledge. For Kant, the highest level of knowledge requires – as it does for his rationalist predecessors – complete a priori comprehension through reason. Yet, unlike the rationalists, Kant does not think that such knowledge is ever available, arguably not even in a divine mind. Rather, we can only approximate such knowledge by following reason's demand for systematicity, that is, by seeking knowledge of a system based on an a priori idea of the whole – a demand that is characteristic of science. Therefore, I shall argue that the highest level of self-knowledge is a complete and systematic comprehension of myself as a whole. While this highest level can never be attained, it sets a normative standard for all lower levels of self-knowledge from which criteria

---

[1] I will clarify the relation of knowledge (*Wissen*) and cognition (*Erkenntnis*) in 6.2, following a recent proposal by Watkins and Willaschek (2017a, 2017b).

(i.e., *touchstones*) for assessing the truth of empirical self-cognitions can be derived.

Reason's normative demands, I shall furthermore argue, give normative guidelines to the basic conceptualizing and cognizing activities of psychological phenomena in experience, *if* such experience is to be oriented towards *truth*. Due to reason's demands of systematicity, we are bound to conceptualize all psychological phenomena in accordance with a *system of psychological predicates*. This system must reflect the diversity of mental states that can be found in inner experience, as well as their causal relations and relations to more general psychological properties, such as psychological dispositions and character traits.

The specific demands of reason with regard to self-knowledge are, again, expressed by the idea of the soul. The idea of the soul, I shall argue, serves as the highest genus concept of the system of psychological predicates. The a priori predicates contained in this idea, such as <substance>, <fundamental power>, and <personal identity>, express normative guidelines for the formation of psychological predicates. Moreover, the idea of the soul can be understood as a regulative guideline for approaching one's *complete self-concept*, which, if available, would completely describe an individual person.

Finally, I shall examine the possibility of error in acquiring self-knowledge and in failing to meet reason's normative demands of systematicity. I thereby distinguish *self-blindness*, that is, conceptual blindness with respect to given inner appearances, and *self-deceit*, that is, error in cognizing general psychological properties, such as character traits. This will finally lead me to revaluate the doctrine of *transparency* that is often ascribed to Kant.

This chapter proceeds as follows. Section 6.2 distinguishes levels of self-knowledge in accordance with Kant's general theory of knowledge and introduces reason's demand of systematicity as the highest standard of knowledge. Section 6.3 examines the normative demands of reason in the acquisition of psychological predicates. Section 6.4 explicates these normative demands in the acquisition of empirical self-knowledge, and reassesses the transparency of, and the possibility of error in, one's self-cognition.

6.2   From Inner Experience to Empirical Self-Knowledge

6.2.1   *Knowledge and Epistemic Grounds*

In this subsection, I set out Kant's general theory of knowledge and his notion of an epistemic ground. Knowledge, for Kant, is one of the modes of the attitude of *holding-to-be-true* (*Fürwahrhalten*) (or *assent*), which one can have towards representations such as judgements. The other two modes that Kant distinguishes in the Canon of Pure Reason, as well as in his lectures on logic, are *opinion*

(*Meinung*) and *belief* (*Glaube*).[2] These modes are differentiated based on the kind of *ground* (*Grund*) (or reason) that leads a person to hold something to be true.[3] Such a ground can be either *subjective*, concerning the state of the subject, or *objective*, concerning the conditions of the proposition that is assented to. For an attitude of assent to be knowledge, the person's grounds must be both subjectively and objectively sufficient (see A822/B850). There has been a substantial amount of debate on what Kant may mean by *subjectively* and *objectively sufficient* ground. In what follows, I outline a reading broadly in line with recent accounts given by Andrew Chignell, Eric Watkins, and Marcus Willaschek.[4]

In requiring grounds that are both subjectively and objectively valid, Kant's account of knowledge shows both an internalist and an externalist strand. According to the internalist strand, a person knows *p* only if she has a subjectively sufficient ground. Having a subjectively sufficient ground requires her to have some consciousness of her own ground for holding *p* to be true and to find such ground convincing for herself. Her holding-to-be-true then is a "conviction (for [her]self)" (A822/B850). For Kant, such subjective consciousness can, for instance, consist in an actual experience that one has on the basis of an occurrent perception, in the memory of a past experience, or in the testimony that one receives from someone else. Whether such consciousness of one's ground must be explicit or whether it suffices if it is accessible only upon reflection is a question I leave open here.[5]

According to the externalist strand, a person knows *p* only if her grounds for holding *p* to be true are based on the conditions that make *p* itself true. In this connection, Kant appeals – in line with the traditional *correspondence theory of truth* – to what he calls a "nominal definition of truth" (A58/B82), which underlies his account of experience in general: "*Truth* . . . rests upon agreement with the object" (A820/B848). Whether the representation of an object is veridical depends on whether it is in agreement with the object. The representation may be subject to transcendental conditions due to the kind of mind that produces it. Nonetheless, if the representation is to be true, it must agree

---

[2] See A822/B850ff; also, *L-Log/Jäsche* 9:66ff.

[3] Kant's notion of *Grund* may be more properly translated as "reason" in light of the analytic debates in epistemology. Due to a potential confusion with the faculty of reason (*Vernunft*), I will use the notion *ground*. Following the rationalist tradition, Kant distinguishes between epistemic and explanatory grounds. *Epistemic grounds* (traditionally called *ratio cognoscendi*) are grounds for which someone holds something to be true (see "*consequently* determining ground" or "ground of knowing", *ND* 1:392). *Explanatory grounds* explain why something is the case, has come to exist, or has changed (see "*antecedently* determining grounds" or "the reason *why*, or the ground of being or becoming", *ND* 1:392). They include what is traditionally called *ratio essendi* (*ground of being*) and *ratio fiendi* (*ground of becoming*). On this distinction, see Stang (2016:82–91).

[4] For example, Chignell (2007), Watkins and Willaschek (2017a, 2017b).

[5] For discussion, see Chignell (2007) and Stang (2016).

with the object independently from the contingent quirks of particular minds that would make it merely subjectively valid.

Yet the agreement of a representation with an object is difficult to assess if we have no access to the object "outside" of representation. The nominal definition thus does not give us a "general and certain criterion" for assessing the truth of a cognition (A58/B82), nor a "touchstone (*Prüfstein*) of the correctness" of all the pieces of cognition (A65/B90). In the Canon passage, Kant therefore offers a criterion of truth in terms of *universal assent*: "consequently, the judgments of every understanding must agree" with regard to the object (A820/B848).[6] To be sure, the very possibility of universal assent is based on the fact that "the ground of the agreement of all judgments, regardless of the difference among the subjects, rests on the common ground, namely the object" (A821/B849). Hence, for Kant, truth is essentially agreement with the object. Only as a consequence do all minds with the same mental set-up – if no error occurs due to some subjective failure – come to a universal agreement on how to represent the object veridically.

Shifting his discussion from agreement with the object to universal assent gives Kant a workable account of an *objectively sufficient ground*. An objectively sufficient ground is thus a ground that is "valid for the reason of every human being" (A820/B848). The standards for objective sufficiency are now defined "within" reason itself, rather than by a criterion that is "external" to representation. The "presumption" of universal assent can be a justificatory ground "through which the truth of the judgment [can be] proved" (A821/B849). Intersubjective agreement can then be an indicator for having an objectively sufficient ground that leads to "*certainty* (for everybody)", rather than mere "*conviction* (for myself)" (A822/B850).

There is a controversy as to whether Kant's appeal to *sufficiency* indicates a gradual account of certainty, which should be best understood in terms of a probabilistic account of confidence, as Chignell (2007) suggests. I will not be able to settle this controversy, but instead sketch a position that I take to be plausible in light of central textual evidence and which explains *objective sufficiency* in terms of a normative reading of the regulative principles of systematicity. While I think that Chignell's probabilistic interpretation is hard to square with the rationalist strand in Kant's account of knowledge, I side with Chignell on the point that systematicity should not be included in the constitutive conditions of knowledge. Yet I argue, in the next subsection, that systematicity is constitutive of the highest standard of rational knowledge and, therefore, sets a normative demand for *all* activities that aim towards knowledge.[7]

---

[6] See also "what I *know*, finally, I hold ... to be universally and objectively necessary (holding for all)" (*L-Log/Jäsche* 9:66).

[7] Similar views have been developed by Buchdahl (1967, 1969), Geiger (2003), and Abela (2006). Watkins and Willaschek (2017b) indicate that systematicity may provide criteria for knowledge, though it is not a constitutive condition of knowledge.

6.2.2   Degrees of Certainty and Systematicity

In this subsection, I examine the normative role of reason for knowledge in general. I consider different kinds of knowledge – empirical and rational knowledge – and argue that rational certainty – the highest degree of certainty – sets a normative standard for all lower levels of certainty and hence for all kinds of knowledge. This normative standard is then identified with the "law of reason" to seek systematic unity (A651/B679). Let me first introduce the distinction between empirical and rational certainty and the notion of *rational cognition*.

Knowledge, for Kant, can display different kinds of certainty, which divide broadly into *empirical* and *rational certainty*. The most comprehensive discussion of certainty can be found in the *Jäsche Logic*. There, Kant distinguishes rational certainty from empirical certainty "by the consciousness of necessity" that is attached to the former, but not to the latter (*L-Log/Jäsche* 9:71). That is, I know the proposition *p* only with empirical certainty, if I assert *p* without being conscious of the necessity of *p*'s truth, which I take to mean, without knowing the necessary conditions that make *p* true. In this case, I have only *assertoric certainty* of *p* (*L-Log/Jäsche* 9:71). I typically gain empirical certainty "through experience": either immediately through my own experience of *p* or derivatively through someone else's experience. For instance, I can empirically know that there is an apple tree in the garden if I have seen the tree myself or if someone trustworthy has told me about it.

By contrast, I know *p* with rational certainty if I am conscious of what makes *p* true; then I have *apodeictic certainty* of *p* (*L-Log/Jäsche* 9:72). Examples of apodeictic certainty include knowledge of mathematical propositions, such as the Pythagorean theorem, for which I have an a priori valid demonstration. I gain rational certainty by having "*a priori* insight" into *p* through reason without relying on any experience (*L-Log/Jäsche* 9:71). What *having insight through reason* amounts to, I submit, can be understood as what Kant calls elsewhere *rational cognition*, as opposed to *historical cognition* through experience (A836/B864). Rational cognition is characterized as "cognition from principles", by which a particular is cognized through a universal principle, for instance, by subsuming it under a general rule in a syllogism (A300/B357).[8]

In the *Jäsche Logic*, Kant distinguished seven degrees of cognition. There, he cashes out rational cognition in terms of the two highest degrees of cognition. These highest degrees are "perfections" of the fifth degree, that is, of "cogniz[ing] something *through the understanding by means of concepts*" (*L-Log/Jäsche* 9:64–5), and are defined as follows:

> The *sixth [degree]*: to cognize something through reason, or to *have insight* into it (*perspicere*). . . .

---

[8] On the logical use of reason, see 5.2.

> The *seventh [degree], finally: to comprehend* something (*comprehendere*),
> i.e., to cognize something through reason or *a priori* to the degree that is
> sufficient for our purpose.   (*L-Log/Jäsche* 9:64–5)

The fifth level of *conceptual understanding* is realized by any empirical cognition that takes the form of a judgement and results from reflecting intuitions
under empirical concepts. The sixth level of *rational insight* and the seventh
level of *a priori comprehension* add onto this condition and require an active
involvement of the faculty of reason.

Having insight through reason, for Kant, typically consists in having insight
into why something is the case, has come to exist, or has changed, that is, in
cognizing an *explanatory ground*.[9] Reason – in its capacity for syllogistic
inferences – subsumes particular cognitions under more general principles
and thereby gives us insights into the conditioning relations of that cognition.
Reason, for example, assists us in understanding the planetary motions as
instances of mechanical motions in general, or in recognizing a newly dis-
covered plant as an instance of a plant family.

The highest degree of cognition then consists in the comprehension of all
conditioning relations of a given cognition. Humans can never achieve such
a complete comprehension, rather they achieve comprehension that is "only
relative, i.e., sufficient for a certain purpose" of a particular investigation, for
example in mathematics or in the sciences (*L-Log/Jäsche* 9:65). Elsewhere,
Kant adds that such comprehension requires the a priori idea of a whole that
precedes its parts and from which we can derive all more specific conditioning
relations that obtain with regard to a particular cognition.[10]

This highest degree of cognition is particularly relevant for scientific knowledge, since science aims to understand "the complex of a cognition as
a system", rather than as "a mere aggregate" (*L-Log/Jäsche* 9:72). Since
a "proper science" for Kant requires the highest degree of certainty, that is,
apodeictic certainty, it must be a rational science that pursues the complete
systematic comprehension of its subject matter (whereby completeness is still
relative to the specific subject matter) (*MFNS* 4:468). Such systematic comprehension is based on an a priori idea of the corresponding science, from
which all parts of the system of knowledge can be schematically derived.[11] To
achieve scientific knowledge of the highest kind, empirical cognition has to be
subsumed under universal and necessary laws of nature, which are a priori
known and justified.[12]

---

[9] In his pre-Critical works, Kant describes an explanatory ground as a "ground that
determines antecedently", in the sense that "were [the ground] not posited, that which
was determinate would not occur at all" (*ND* 1:393).
[10] For example, A832/B860. Also *L-Log/Jäsche* 9:71.
[11] See A832/B860; *MFNS* 4:468.
[12] The paradigm examples are, for Kant, Newton's laws of physics (see *MFNS* 4:476–7).

To take stock, whether knowledge is empirically certain or rationally certain depends not only on the source from which it is derived (i.e., through experience or through reason), but also on the objective content of the underlying cognition. Roughly, Kant's idea is as follows: if I cognize an object based on immediate experience (or a testimony thereof), I have an objectively sufficiently reason for *empirically knowing* the object (with respect to the specific content that is immediately present to me in experience). If I cognize in addition what this experiential content entails, that is, its conditioning relations, then the resulting cognition also has rational certainty and gives an objectively sufficient ground for some rational knowledge of the object.[13] In accomplishing rational cognition, reason fulfils not only an explicatory, but also a *justificatory* role for the acquisition of knowledge based on this cognition. By revealing the conditions of a cognition through syllogistic reasoning, ideally in terms of necessary and universal laws of nature, reason provides us with objectively sufficient grounds for taking that cognition to be true. In this case, the explanatory grounds for why the object of cognition exists in such-and-such a way also serve as an epistemic ground (*Erkenntnisgrund, ratio cognoscendi*) for why we hold that cognition to be true. Kant makes it clear that rational certainty, if achievable, is preferable over empirical certainty.[14] Rational certainty is thus the highest standard of knowledge. Kant indeed thinks that all empirical knowledge must be normatively oriented towards this highest standard.

So I submit that we find further evidence that Kant thinks that rational certainty sets a normative standard towards which any knowledge should aspire. In various places, Kant indeed portrays reason as the faculty that gives rules to the understanding and that defines a standard for what a *good use* of our cognitive abilities is: a good use is the use that is conducive to finding truths regarding the objects of cognition.[15] In the Appendix, Kant then explicates such use as the "coherent use of the understanding", through which cognitions are brought into a systematic unity (A651/B679).

Taking another look at the Appendix, we find Kant developing an argument that shows reason to set a normative condition for the understanding in terms of the "law of reason to seek unity". Recall that Kant considers the transition from "a logical principle of rational unity" to the presupposition of a corresponding "transcendental principle" that is assumed to pertain to the object itself (A650/B678).[16] In Chapter 5, I considered this transition with respect to the regulative principles of systematicity that are defined by transcendental ideas. I offered

---

[13] Kant explicitly allows that knowledge can be both empirically and rationally certain at the same time (e.g., *L-Log/Jäsche* 9:71). On conditioning and entailment relations, see 6.3. I do not here consider the possibility of having knowledge without cognition (for discussion, see Watkins and Willaschek 2017b).

[14] For example, *L-Log/Jäsche* 9:71.

[15] For example, A302/B359.

[16] For a discussion of this "transition" from the logical to the transcendental principle of reason, see Willaschek (2018:103–26). See also 5.2.3.

a reading of these principles as determining the application conditions and hence the scope of the understanding (see 5.5). Now, I argue that these regulative principles should be understood as normative conditions that reason imposes on the understanding for the purpose of acquiring knowledge. In consequence, reason's principles of systematicity can be used to derive criteria by which the truth of cognitions can be assessed, namely so-called *touchstones of truth* (see A647/B675). Kant's argument for this epistemic function of reason can be found in the following passage:

> For the law of reason to seek unity is necessary, since without it we would have no reason, and without that, no coherent use of the understanding, and, lacking that, no sufficient mark of empirical truth; thus in regard to the latter we simply have to presuppose the systematic unity of nature as objectively valid and necessary.   (A651/B679)

I reconstruct Kant's argument as a *reductio ad absurdum*:

Thesis: The *law of reason* to seek unity is *necessary* for knowledge based on cognition through the understanding.

Premise 1: Assume for the sake of the argument that reason would not seek unity.

Premise 2: If reason did not seek unity, then there would be no reason, since it is essential for reason to seek unity through employing principles of systematicity.

Premise 3: If no principles of systematicity were employed, then there would be no *coherent use of the understanding*, because it would not be possible to assess whether the resulting cognitions cohere with one another.

Premise 4: If there were no coherent use of the understanding, then it would not be possible to obtain a *sufficient mark of empirical truth*.

Premise 5: (*implicit*) If there were no sufficient mark of empirical truth, it would not be possible to have an *objectively sufficient ground* for taking a cognition to be true and, consequently, to acquire *knowledge*.

Conclusion: Hence, in order for knowledge based on cognition through the understanding to be possible, the understanding must be subject to the law of reason to seek unity.

Note that the law to seek unity is necessary for the understanding *not* in the sense of a constitutive principle. That means, implementing the law of reason is not necessary for an act of cognition to produce a veridical representation of an object. As noted earlier, we can have a single piece of empirical knowledge on the ground of a single immediate experience (or testimony thereof), without actually assessing whether this piece systematically coheres with other knowledge claims we hold. For instance, although – to my regret – I have myself never been to Rome, I can know with empirical certainty that the city of Rome exists based on a friend's reporting her visit to Rome to me. I still have empirical knowledge of the city, even without connecting this piece of knowledge with other pieces of geographical knowledge I have.[17] Yet I am *in principle* able to make further enquiries, gain further cognitions, and assess their systematic coherence such that I can gain rational certainty of the existence of Rome. It is also possible that – upon further research – I find out my friend lied to me or confabulated and hence that I was wrong in assuming I had some empirical knowledge of Rome in the first place. For all empirical knowledge claims, Kant assumes, I must in principle be in a position to discern criteria for distinguishing between those claims that are justified and indeed amount to knowledge, and those claims that are falsely assumed to be knowledge.

So I take the argument above to show *that* for the pursuit of *knowledge in general* to be possible for rational thinkers like us, we must subscribe to the law of reason as being normatively binding for *all* acts of the understanding that are supposed to contribute to knowledge (of any kind). Without subscribing to this law, we would lack the ability to assess whether a particular knowledge claim is indeed true. This implies, I submit, that this law is binding even in cases of single pieces of empirical knowledge based on immediate experience. In these cases, the law, however, is not explicitly applied, but implicitly at the level of conceptualization, as I explain in 6.2.3 and in 6.3.

While my reconstruction of the argument demonstrates *that* the law of systematic unity must be normatively binding to the understanding, it does not show *how* its normative force is enforced on the understanding's activities. In an explicit enforcement of the law, reason itself serves as the arbiter of empirical truth in the acquisition of knowledge: by explicitly "presuppos[ing] the systematic unity of nature as objectively valid", reason generates a working hypothesis against which particular cognitions can be tested as to whether they are "coherently connected" (A647/B675) in a chain of syllogistic reasoning. The criterion of *epistemic coherence*, in the most basic sense, consists then in *logical consistency*: a set of cognitions should not mutually contradict each other. In a more advanced sense, it requires the mutual agreement of all cognitions within a system that captures their *real* conditioning relations, as I discuss in Section 6.4 for the case of self-knowledge. A cognition that does not pass the coherence test within a set of already accepted cognitions has to be rejected as false or at least as rationally unfounded. Hence, the explicit employment of reason's law of unity consists in supplying a so-called *touchstone of truth* for assessing cognitions and hence for finding objectively sufficient grounds for holding them to be true (A647/B675).[18]

Yet Kant's claim that "we simply have to presuppose the systematic unity of nature as objectively valid and necessary" (A651/B679) can also be understood as a transcendental presupposition that implicitly guides the understanding's more basic conceptualizing and cognizing activities. If the lower-level activities of

---

[17] See Kant's example of knowledge based on a "historical belief" in *Orient* 8:141.
[18] See Willaschek (2018:47–56).

empirical cognition are ever to give rise to knowledge, then these activities must already be oriented towards rational certainty as the highest standard of knowledge. To avoid discrepancies and incoherencies among our cognitions as much as possible, we *ought to* proceed with our lower-level cognitive activities in accordance with reason's law of systematicity such that these activities can contribute to a complete systematic description of nature. Hence, to implement the prescriptive force of the law of reason, we simply *presuppose* that the systematic unity of nature is "objectively valid and necessary" for *all* levels of cognitive activities that are supposed to contribute to knowledge.

For instance, the fifth degree of *conceptual understanding*, according to the *Jäsche* passage cited above, should already be guided by the presupposition of systematicity. At this level, the transcendental presupposition of the systematic unity of nature amounts to the presupposition that nature can be described by a *system of concepts*, according to which any possible intuition can be conceptualized into experience. While we have no proof that this is actually the case for nature, we must proceed *as if* nature itself were a systematic unity for *our* purpose of rational comprehension. In Chapter 5, I explicated this transcendental presupposition of systematicity as an a priori act of marking out the context of intelligibility. Now, we are finally in a position to see that this transcendental presupposition is a normative demand that is relative to *our* purpose – the purpose of *human reason* – for acquiring knowledge that aims at the highest standard of rational certainty. After the passage I reconstructed in detail above, Kant indeed goes on, in the Appendix, to argue for three principles of systematicity that are required for the formation of empirical concepts. In Section 6.3, I therefore explicate how this transcendental presupposition plays out at the level of conceptualization with respect to the formation of psychological predicates.

In sum, reason's law of systematicity is not a constitutive condition of knowledge per se, but constitutive of knowledge of the highest level of certainty, which requires complete a priori comprehension. This highest level of epistemic justification that is available to us is set as the standard for the good, that is, truth-conducive, use of the understanding. It, therefore, sets normative requirements that are binding for all acts of cognition that are supposed to contribute to knowledge. Any lower-level cognitive activity must be normatively guided by this standard if it aims towards truth.

6.2.3   Degrees of Self-Cognition and Levels of Self-Knowledge

In this subsection, I apply the insights regarding knowledge in general to the case of self-knowledge. I argue that self-knowledge also comes in different levels of empirical and rational certainty, and that these levels map onto corresponding degrees of *self-cognition*. Before outlining these levels, I ward off a common concern regarding self-knowledge.

Self-knowledge is often thought of as concerning the private items of a person's consciousness and therefore of as not lending itself to the standards of objective knowledge. So one may argue that we cannot meaningfully define what objectively sufficient grounds for self-knowledge are, since such grounds would presuppose that self-knowledge could be "valid for everybody". But, seemingly, self-knowledge is valid for a single person only – the person who has such knowledge and whom this knowledge is about.

In Chapters 2 to 5, I have developed a complex argument showing that inner experience can be understood by analogy with outer experience. As a consequence, I concluded that there is some empirical reality that is cognized in inner experience, even though inner experience – strictly speaking – is not cognition of an object. This empirical reality is constituted by the person's mental life and primarily consists of the person's mental states occurring in time. If there is an empirical reality that can be cognized under the condition of cognition, then the resulting empirical cognitions can be assessed as to whether they represent this reality in a veridical way. Hence, inner experience is a candidate for an empirical cognition to be held true and hence can give rise to *objectively valid* self-knowledge.

The grounds for a person's holding a self-concerning cognition to be true are primarily based on the having of an inner experience, yet not exclusively. As I will argue below, considerations of systematicity should also play a major role. What counts as an objectively sufficient ground can now be understood in a counterfactual way: a ground is objectively sufficient for holding a self-cognition to be true, if everybody presented with this ground in *their own* inner experience would assent to this self-cognition (even though only the person concerned in fact has access to this specific ground). Moreover, an important criterion for an objectively sufficient ground in the Canon is the "possibility of communicating it" (A820/B848). This suggests that, if a person is able to conceptualize and then communicate her grounds for a self-knowledge claim to others, then these grounds can be assessed as to whether others would agree on the basis of the ground they have been presented with in communication.[19] The objective sufficiency of a person's grounds can even in the case of self-knowledge be understood in terms of universal assent. Hence, the objection concerning the alleged privacy of the items of self-knowledge does not refute the possibility of having objectively sufficient grounds for self-knowledge. So there is no obstacle that prevents Kant's account of knowledge from being applied to the case of self-knowledge.

---

[19] A similar criterion of communicability can be found with regard to aesthetic judgements in the third *Critique*. There, "subjective universal communicability" is identified with a "state of mind in the free play of the imagination and the understanding" – that is, a subjective state that "must be valid for everyone and consequently universally communicable (*CJ* 5:217–18).

In line with the results of the earlier chapters regarding inner experience, we can now distinguish the following *degrees of self-cognition*:

(1) *Immediate self-cognition*: Cognition of mental states through inner experience based on immediately given inner appearance(s) within a mental act.

Such immediate self-cognition may include:

- cognition of a *temporal mental state* by reflecting on the corresponding inner appearance that occurs within a mental act under a psychological predicate, resulting in simple I-judgements such as "I *see* a red rose", "I *believe* my friend is in danger", and "I *feel* joy";
- cognition of an objectively ordered *series of mental states* by reflecting on a series of inner appearances that occur within a mental act under a necessary rule in accordance with the principle of causation, resulting in more complex I-judgements such as "I've just seen a dangerous animal, then I've felt fear, and now I just want to run away" and When I noticed my friend's agitated face, I came to believe that she needs my help, and now I am deliberating what I can do for her".

(2) *Mediate self-cognition*: Cognition of (more) *general psychological properties* mediated through inner experience and rational inferences.

Such mediate self-cognition may include:

- cognition of relatively stable properties that obtain across several mental acts by subsuming inner experiences of mental acts occurring at different times under a more general condition, resulting in I-judgements such as "Whenever I fear encountering difficulties, I desire to run away from them" or "Whenever I see someone in need, I am willing to help".

(3) *Comprehensive self-cognition*: Cognition of my *character* through reflecting upon myself as a whole.

Such comprehensive self-cognition may include:

- cognition of *empirical character traits* that are assumed to remain stable throughout most of my mental life by reflecting all self-cognition (concerning a particular subject matter) within a system, resulting in I-judgements such as "I'm timid", "I'm courageous", or "I'm high-minded".[20]

The highest level of self-cognition would be a complete a priori comprehension of myself as a whole in accordance with an a priori idea of myself. In this

[20] In the *Anthropology*, Kant discusses empirical character in terms of a person's "*natural aptitude[s]* or natural predisposition[s]" and "*temperament*" (*Anth* 7:285), which can, for instance, include the habitual disposition for "timidity" (see 7:306; also 7:256–60).

case, I would be able not only to subsume all inner appearances I could ever encounter in my life under this a priori idea of myself, but also to derive each and every one of them from this idea and hence sufficiently explain all my inner appearances. This idea would then reflect my *intelligible character*, that is, my character insofar as it is completely and a priori intelligible through reason. The characteristics of my intelligible character would have to be represented such that they are not only independent from particular experiences, but also from the conditions of sensibility altogether. I can only cognize myself fully and a priori through reason insofar as I abstract from all particular mental states I am having, as well as from my particular spatio-temporal constitution altogether. I think here in particular of virtues that can be defined without reference to some empirical content, such as honesty as seeking the truth or justice as seeking the right.[21]

Kant defines the distinction between a person's *empirical* and *intelligible* character primarily in the context of human agency and morality. The intelligible character is thereby viewed as the explanatory ground of one's empirical character.[22] In the current context, I suggest a literal reading of intelligible character as the character that is fully intelligible and that hence is a *ratio cognoscendi*, a ground for knowing my empirical character, for instance in form of general laws that explain my empirical character. Both knowing myself as empirical character and knowing myself as intelligible character require the comprehension of myself as a whole. Knowing my empirical character can only ever be approximated through the systematization of inner experiences. Knowing myself as intelligible character would require me to comprehend myself completely and a priori, which for humans, Kant thinks, is impossible. Nonetheless, the very idea of having an intelligible character has practical implications for the acquisition of self-knowledge (see 6.4) and for the purpose of self-formation (see 7.3).[23]

If this outline of degrees of self-cognition were adequate, what would be the levels of self-knowledge corresponding with increasing levels of certainty?

---

[21] In the first *Critique*, the intelligible character is defined as "that in an object of sense [viz. the person] which is not itself appearance" (A538/B566). In the *Anthropology*, Kant specifies the intelligible character as the "way of thinking" (*Denkungsart*), by which a person prescribes to herself practical principles (*Anth* 7:291). See also *Religion* 6:47; *Groundwork* 3:393, 451.

[22] Character is understood as the "law of ... causality" that explains human actions (A539/B567). The empirical character is then seen as the sign of the intelligible character in the world of sense, whereas the intelligible character is thought of *as if* it were a "thing in itself" that "would not stand under any conditions of time" (A539/B567). As such, it is often understood as the real ground, or *ratio essendi*, of the appearing empirical character (for discussion, see Willaschek 1992:131–48, esp. 135). On my reading, this *as-if* claim is understood, rather than as the assertion of a real existing ground, as a transcendental presupposition for explanatory purposes (see 5.6) and for the purpose of self-formation (see 7.3).

[23] In a note related to the *Anthropology*, Kant specifies an intelligible character as a "determinate character", that is, a character "from which one can judge in advance everything that can be determined through rules" (*Refl* 1158, 15:512).

I suggest the following taxonomy of self-knowledge as dependent on different kinds of objectively valid grounds and on an increasing involvement of reason:

(1) *Immediate self-knowledge*: Knowledge of my mental states within an occurrent mental episode.

The epistemic ground for such immediate self-knowledge may include:

- my having an inner experience of an immediately given inner appearance;
- my having an inner perception of a series of inner appearances and my conscious reflecting upon these appearances under a necessary rule, which results in the inner experience of an objectively ordered series of inner appearances.

(2) *Mediate self-knowledge*: Knowledge of my (more) general psychological properties.

The epistemic ground for such mediate self-knowledge may include:

- my having insight into the conditions of a particular inner experience through reason, that is, having insight into the explanatory grounds of an inner appearance, such as my current feeling of joy;
- my consciousness of a general inner cause of a mental change, that is, of a psychological disposition that has brought about a series of inner appearances, such as my readiness to help others.

(3) *Comprehensive self-knowledge*: Knowledge of my character as it unfolds within my entire mental life.

The epistemic ground for such comprehensive self-knowledge may include:

- my consciousness of the epistemic coherence of an inner experience within a system of self-cognitions;
- my consciousness of subsuming a series of inner appearance under a general psychological law.

These levels of self-knowledge involve the activities of reason to an increasing extent and thereby gain rational certainty with regard to an increasing number of cognitions. The highest level of self-knowledge would then be a complete a priori knowledge of myself as a whole. This, again, would require me to have an a priori idea of myself and hence would enable me to have a full rational grasp of my *intelligible character*.

Kant is clear in various passages that such full rational self-knowledge is not attainable for humans during their lifetime, and that we often remain ignorant with regard to practical principles that guide our life-conduct.[24] Nonetheless, if my previous analysis of knowledge in general is correct, then it follows that the

---

[24] For example, *Groundwork* 4:420n, 451; *CpracR* 5:86.

lower levels of self-cognition must be normatively guided by the highest epistemic standard of rational certainty in order to be oriented towards truth at all. Cognizing myself through reason in accordance with an a priori idea is the epistemic ideal that all cognitive activities seeking self-knowledge must aspire towards, if they are to generate self-knowledge at all. Pure reason provides us with an a priori idea that normatively guides our self-cognizing activities such that they are oriented towards acquiring self-knowledge: the *idea of the soul*. Hence, I now argue that this idea plays not only a regulative role with regard to inner experience, but also a normative role with regard to the acquisition of self-knowledge. In the next two sections, I examine the idea's role in the formation of psychological predicates (6.3) and in the acquisition of an individual *self-concept* (6.4).

6.3 The Conceptualization of Psychological Phenomena

In this section, I examine how reason's normative demand for systematicity is passed on to the more basic conceptualizing and cognizing activities involved in inner experience. By basic conceptualizing activities, I mean specifically the activity of reflecting given inner appearances under psychological predicates. By basic cognizing activities, I mean specifically the activity of applying those predicates in empirical judgements yielding inner experience. Both these activities require the prior acquisition of psychological predicates. In general, the acquisition of a concept consists in acquiring a set of *conceptual abilities*, including the abilities to reflect given intuitions under the concept, to distinguish objects that fall under it from those that do not, and to use the concept in judgements.[25] In what follows, I focus on the acquisition of *psychological predicates* and examine the normative role of the idea of the soul in this process. For this purpose, I first introduce Kant's theory of concept-formation in general, thereby building on the account recently developed by Lanier R. Anderson.[26] Then, I argue that the idea of the soul serves as the highest genus concept in the system of psychological predicates and defines normative principles for generating further predicates within the system.[27]

6.3.1 Concept-Formation and Systematicity

The theory of concept-formation that Kant lays out in the Appendix of the first *Critique*, as well as in his lectures on logic, presupposes Kant's general taxonomy of representation, according to which concepts are general representations that relate to objects in a "mediate" way "by means of a mark (*Merkmal*), which can

---

[25] Note that the possession of a concept does not guarantee that the corresponding conceptual abilities are always correctly exercised.

[26] Anderson (2014).

[27] For a closer discussion, see Kraus (2019b).

be common to several things" (A320/B377). In forming a concept, we sort together a complex of "marks" that we detect in several objects, all of which are to be denoted by the concept. The marks that constitute the concept give rise to a set of predicates contained *in* the concept.[28] The activity of concept-formation is guided by three regulative principles: the principles of *homogeneity*, *specification*, and *continuity*.[29] The principle of *homogeneity* – as the principle "of the *sameness of kind* in the manifold under higher genera" (A657/B685) – guides us in seeking, for every pair of concepts, a genus concept with a larger "domain" such that both these concepts can be subsumed under it (A654/B682). The principle of *specification* – as the principle "of the *variety* of what is same in kind under lower species" (A657/B685) – guides us in finding for every given concept further sub-concepts (or species concepts) that are richer in "*content* ([i.e.,] determinacy)" (A654/B682). By assuming *continuity* between different concepts – according to the principle "of the *affinity* of all concepts" (A657/B685) – we finally arrive at an interconnected hierarchical system that proceeds, not only vertically from elementary genus concepts to fine-grained species concepts, but also horizontally between neighbouring concepts.[30]

Consider, for instance, the concept <tree>. By finding common marks through an analysis of the concepts <tree> and <shrub>, one may form a genus concept that contains these common marks only (e.g., <plant>) and under which both <tree> and <shrub> can be subsumed. By perceiving a variety of different trees, one may find additional marks and combine them into more specific concepts, such as <oak>, <birch>, and <linden>.[31] Searching for further commonalities between trees and shrubs, one may consider concepts such as <(having a) trunk> and <(having) leaves>, which are, as it were, horizontally connected and each of which is contained *in* <tree> and <shrub> (which is just to say that <tree> and <shrub> can be subsumed *under* them). That means, for instance, that the collection of things that can be classified by the concept <(having a) trunk> includes the collection of things that can be classified by <tree>.

Primarily, the principles of homogeneity, specification, and continuity are introduced as *logical* principles, concerning only *analytic entailment relations* among concepts and abstracting from the concepts' relations to objects. In abstraction from objects, the logical principles primarily serve the subjective

---

[28] In the lectures on logic, a mark is defined as the "ground of cognition ... in the comparison of things" (*L-Log/Vienna* 24:834, also *L-Log/Blomberg* 24:106). I remain neutral on whether a mark itself is merely *sensible* in the intuition of the things to be compared, or whether it is already in some sense *conceptual*. For discussion, see Longuenesse (1998), Ginsborg (2006), and Anderson (2014).

[29] See A652–8/B680–96; *CJ* 5:185–6; *L-Log/Jäsche* 9:96–7; also *L-Log/Blomberg* 24:240–60; *L-Log/Vienna* 24:905–13; *L-Log/Dohna-Wundlacken* 24:755.

[30] For a detailed discussion of Kant's logic lectures, see Watkins (2013).

[31] On the analysis and synthesis of marks, see *L-Log/Blomberg* 24:132.

"interest of reason" in organizing our manifold cognitions in the most efficient and economical way (A648/B676). They are also called "principle[s] of parsimony" or "principle[s] of economy for reason" (A650/B678). Together, the three logical principles explicate reason's demand to seek "a certain systematic unity of all possible empirical concepts" (A652/B680). Hence, for Kant, all conceptualization strives towards a *system of concepts*, and the content of a concept is properly defined only in terms of the concept's entailment relations within the system.

Yet theoretical reason – in its epistemic function – aims at a *true* description of nature. Seeking the systematic unity of concepts is thus reason's means to accomplish an increasingly comprehensive, increasingly determinate, and increasingly dense description of nature. We aim for concepts with increasingly broad empirical content so as to grasp more and more similarities between objects. The higher up a genus concept is in this hierarchy, the greater is its generality, the thinner its content, and the larger its domain, viz. the set of objects that fall under it. Moreover, we look for concepts with increasingly rich empirical content so as to grasp more and more details of a particular object. The lower down a species concept is, the greater is its determinacy, the lower is its generality, and the richer is its content, that is, the set of (more general) concepts contained *in* it. And, finally, we aim for a dense description of nature, covering as many objects and interrelations among them as possible. The more intermediary concepts are found between two concepts, the denser the system of concepts is.

Therefore, Kant argues, each logical principle is applicable to nature only if "a transcendental principle is presupposed, through which such a systematic unity, as pertaining to the object itself, is assumed *a priori* as necessary" (A650–1/B678–9). The three corresponding transcendental principles of homogeneity, specification, and continuity do *not* abstract from the concepts' relations to empirical objects. Rather, they are supposed to guarantee the adequacy of our concepts: the analytic entailment relations among our concepts ought to adequately map onto the real conditioning relations among the objects (or states) in nature thereby described.[32] Together, these three transcendental principles culminate in the *transcendental presupposition* of the systematic unity of nature

---

[32] Similarly, Anderson (2014:369–72) construes Kant's theory in terms of a "qualified form of holism about conceptual content" (Anderson 2014:364). Anderson recognizes both the need to present content by means of analytic containment relations, and the irreducibility of synthetic relations, which result from synthesizing conceptual marks. He makes a compelling case for distinguishing the logical aspects of a system from the irreducibly synthetic aspects of conceptual content, while acknowledging their mutual interdependence. For a stronger holistic reading, see Geiger (2003). Ginsborg (2017, also 2006), by contrast, offers a weaker reading according to which concept-formation is oriented towards functional "adequacy" and based on "natural sorting dispositions" for discovering common marks. For an instructive critique of Ginsborg, see Anderson (2014:342–7).

itself. In Section 6.2, I argued that this transition from a logical to a transcendental principle of systematicity is necessary to enforce the prescription of the ideal of rational certainty for the lower-order cognitive activities. In seeking to know nature as a system, we seek to acquire a system of empirical concepts that allows for a true description of nature, and, for that, we must presuppose that nature itself is in some sense systematic or at least does not defy being systematically described.

In line with my normative reading of reason's law to seek systematic unity (see 6.2), we can now understand these principles of systematicity as *normative demands*. If the formation of each new concept is guided by these normative demands, then it is guaranteed a priori that the *conceptual containment relations* between all concepts can constitute a system. Whether these containment relations adequately correspond to the *real conditioning relations* between the appearances described by these concepts can then be assessed a posteriori by considerations of systematic coherence. That is, reason can offer auxiliary hypotheses as "touchstones" or "mark[s] of empirical truth" for assessing the coherence of judgements in which these concepts are used and hence for assessing the adequacy of concepts in light of ongoing experience (A651/B679).[33]

In sum, the acquisition of empirical concepts can be understood as an ongoing complex activity of systematization according to the principles of generalization, specification, and continuity. In light of ongoing experience, our system of empirical concepts is continuously assessed and refined as to its adequacy by adding (or revising) increasingly comprehensive genus concepts, increasingly determinate species concepts, and further intermediary concepts. In turn, the newly acquired concepts inform the ongoing activity of acquiring empirical cognition and eventually a system of knowledge.

Despite our greatest efforts in finding a complete system of concepts, our conceptual abilities are limited insofar as we can never be in the possession of a lowest species concept, the *infima species* (L-Log/Jäsche 9:97).[34] That is, we can never grasp a unique individual through a complete concept that contains all predicates applicable to the individual; and, arguably, such a concept does not exist. For Kant, the content of any empirical concept can never be rich enough to ensure the full determination of individuals. To pick out an individual, we must rely on intuition through which we immediately relate to objects.[35] By contrast, Kant affirms the existence of a highest genus concept, the *conceptus summus*

---

[33] See also A65/B90, A647/B675.

[34] A655/B683; *L-Log/Wiener* 24:911; *L-Log/Jäsche* 9:97. See Watkins (2013).

[35] Kant rejects Leibniz's thesis of complete conceptual determination, according to which each individual (viz. each monad) is determined from the moment of creation through a complete individual concept, which is fully known only by God (Leibniz 1686/1989:§8).

(*L-Log/Jäsche* 9:97).[36] The highest genus concept of a system of *empirical* concepts is the most general concept of a thing that falls in the domain of nature described by that system. For nature in general, this highest genus concept is the concept <object of experience in general>.[37] The predicates contained in this highest genus concept are determined by the a priori conditions of experience. These conditions include in particular the categories of the understanding (e.g., <substance> and <(seat of) causal powers>) in terms of their (spatio-)temporal explications (e.g., <persistence> and <objective temporal order of cause and effect>). What counts as an object of experience is precisely that which instantiates this highest genus concept.

6.3.2 The Idea of the Soul as the Genus Concept of Inner Nature

The concepts required for inner experience concern only a particular domain of nature, namely the domain of psychological phenomena, that is, humans qua their psychological features. In Chapter 5, I called this domain *inner nature*, or as Kant sometimes puts it, "thinking nature" (A682/B710, *MFNS* 4:467). The corresponding system of concepts is a system of psychological predicates, which primarily describe (aspects of) inner appearances. The idea of the soul seems the natural candidate for the highest genus concept of the system of psychological predicates.[38] It is important to note the distinction between inner nature and an individual's mental life. Inner nature comprises all possible inner appearances that can occur in any human's mental life, that is, the *sum total of all possible inner appearances*. It is the subject matter of general psychological knowledge.[39] By contrast, an individual's mental life is constituted by all those inner appearances that in fact belong to one and the same person and of which only that person can have *inner* experience. This *sum total of an individual's actual inner appearances* is the subject matter of *self-knowledge*.

Both the acquisition of psychological knowledge and the acquisition of self-knowledge rely on a system of psychological predicates, which – as I now show – is unified by the *idea of the soul*. Primarily, the idea of the soul serves – according to the principle of homogeneity – as the highest genus concept that

---

[36] In his lectures, Kant identifies this highest concept as the concept of "something" (*L-Log/ Wiener* 24:911), of "a thing" (*L-Log/Dohna-Wundlacken* 24:755), or of "a possible thing" (*L-Log/Blomberg* 24:259).

[37] See Anderson (2014:368) on the concept of <object in general> (or what he calls the *Ur-concept*).

[38] Note that I will not give a general account of how the three principles of concept-formation relate to ideas of reason.

[39] Recall Kant's definition of "nature as the sum total of all appearances (*natura materialiter spectata*)" (B163, also A257/B312, A419/B447). For a discussion of psychological knowledge, see Kraus (2019b).

first defines the domain of psychological phenomena. In the case of an individual's mental life, I shall furthermore argue in the next section, the idea of the soul serves – according to the principle of specification – as a template for the lowest species concept. Such a species concept, if it were available, would completely and adequately describe the individual person. I thus call it the *complete individual self-concept*.

Prima facie, there is a fundamental difference between the concept <object of experience in general> serving as the highest genus concept of (outer) nature, and the idea of the soul serving as the highest genus concept of inner nature. The former is instantiated by any object of experience falling in the domain of (outer) nature, whereas the latter can never be instantiated by any sensibly given object, but serves only as a regulative guideline for inner experience, as discussed in Chapter 5. The idea of the soul defines inner nature as the class of beings that can be *reflected upon* under the concept <soul>, without thereby determining these beings as a soul or as a mental substance. Such beings are precisely those to whom psychological predicates can be assigned. Due to the regulative character of the idea, the a priori predicates it contains – such as <substance>, <fundamental power>, and <personal iden-tity> – cannot be instantiated by inner appearances either. Rather, as discussed in Chapter 5, by reflecting upon inner appearances in accordance with these predicates (by analogy with the corresponding transcendental schemata), we can determine these appearances in inner experience, without thereby deter-mining an underlying mental substance. These predicates, as will become clear, define *normative principles* for the acquisition of *empirical* psychological predicates, which are needed to describe psychological phenomena.

It is instructive to compare the case of psychological beings with that of living beings. In the *Critique of the Power of Judgment*, Kant argues that we can experience an organism only by reflecting upon a heap of matter under an idea of reason, namely the idea of purposiveness.[40] Angela Breitenbach has recently offered a reading according to which the idea of purposiveness serves not merely as a heuristic guide for the discovery of causal explanations of organ-isms, but as a "necessary condition for representing something as purposively organized" and hence "for making possible a conception of the living world" (Breitenbach 2014:133).[41] By reflecting upon a heap of matter, for example a flower, in accordance with the idea of an organized whole, we view the flower as a whole made up of functionally structured parts, such as the flower's stalk, leaves, and calyx. Together, these parts are understood as striving towards a common purpose: the survival of the organism. This reading aligns well with my current reading of the idea of the soul. Accordingly, we could now under-stand the idea of purposiveness as the highest genus concept of a <purposively

---

[40] See esp. *CJ* 5:359–84.
[41] See also Breitenbach (2009), Geiger (2009), and Nassar (2016).

organized whole>, which defines the domain of living nature and gives rise to a system of biological predicates by which all organisms can be described. By using the concept <purposively organized whole>, we do *not* determine a heap of matter *as an organic whole*, but only presuppose such a whole for the purpose of making something out as a living organism and for then cognizing its parts in relation to one another and to the whole.[42]

Similarly, the idea of the soul defines the domain of inner nature and guides us in recognizing what counts as a psychological being. How do we then acquire a more and more comprehensive system of psychological predicates that reflects the diversity of mental states and psychological dispositions, as well as the dependence relations between them, and that is nonetheless universally applicable to all human persons? For explicating a system in accordance with an a priori idea, the idea must be supplemented by schemata. Such schemata provide "the outline (*monogramma*) and the division of the whole into members in conformity with the idea, i.e., *a priori*" (A834/B862). The a priori predicates contained in the idea of the soul, such as <substance> and <fundamental power>, I submit, serve as such schemata for the execution of the system. They can be understood as *transcendental presuppositions* delineating the various dimensions of the whole system of inner nature. Hence, they precisely give an outline of the systematic structure of inner nature according to which any psychological phenomenon can be classified (see 5.5).

In line with my normative reading of reason's law of systematic unity (see 6.2), we can now understand these a priori predicates as *normative demands*. Each explicates a unity that *ought to* be approximated in experience, if such experience is normatively oriented towards the ideal of systematic rational knowledge. For instance, the predicate <substance> demands that inner appearances ought to be cognized *as if* they were the states of one and the same subject. The predicate <(seat of a) fundamental power> demands that inner appearances ought to be cognized *as if* they were mental states originating from one and the same mental power and thus effects of the person's causal self-efficacy (see 5.6). Only if the basic conceptualizing activities in inner experience are bound by these normative demands can they contribute to the rational ideal of self-knowledge.

From the schematic outline defined by the a priori predicates, a system of psychological predicates can be derived. If the formation of each new predicate is guided by these normative demands, then it is guaranteed a priori that the *conceptual containment relations* between all psychological predicates can

---

[42] In the third *Critique*, Kant counts teleological judgements concerning living organisms under so-called *reflective judgements*. In contrast to a determining judgement, by which a particular is determined by given universal concepts, a reflective judgement seeks to find more general concepts under which a set of given particulars can be reflected (*CJ* 5:351, also 5:386–90). On the relation between the regulative use of ideas of reason and the reflective power of judgement, see Guyer (1990) and Makkreel (1990).

238 THE HUMAN PERSON AND THE DEMANDS OF REASON

constitute a system. Whether these containment relations adequately correspond to the *real conditioning relations* between the psychological phenomena described by these predicates can, again, be assessed a posteriori by considerations of systematicity. In general, the content of a psychological predicate is determined only within the system, yet not only a priori through the analytic relations it has to other concepts, but also a posteriori through the synthetic relations found in experience.[43] If our conceptualization is adequate, then the conceptual containment relations among concepts reflect the real conditioning relations among inner appearances directly found in experience, as well as the conditioning relations between those appearances and more general psychological properties, derived through syllogistic reasoning.

Let me finally sketch how this system of psychological predicates can be fleshed out in light of further results of Kant's transcendental philosophy. Considering Kant's tripartite division of the mind, which he takes to be justified a priori by transcendental definitions of the basic faculties of cognition, desire, and feeling, then the basic system of psychological predicates arising from the idea of the soul could be schematically illustrated by Figure 6.1.[44] This basic system describes primarily short-term mental states passing through the mind.

Furthermore, we can understand Kant's *Anthropology* as an application and refinement of this basic system. There, Kant develops a fine-grained taxonomy of general mental faculties and more specific psychological dispositions. While his taxonomy is not yet fully systematic, he submits that it should be guided by a set of classificatory schemata that "gradually unites [this taxonomy] into a whole through the unity of the plan" (*Anth* 7:122).[45] So Kant's *Anthropology* itself is structured in accordance with the basic system of psychological predicates shown in Figure 6.1. According to the tripartite division of the mind, the first part is divided into three books, each investigating one of the three basic faculties. Kant also takes this systematic approach in deriving a taxonomy of mental disorders and illnesses (see *Anth* 7:214, 2:256–60). Following the internal structure of each cognitive faculty, Kant presents a detailed taxonomy of cognitive disorders, including "deficiencies of imagination" (= "distraction"), "lack of judgment" (= "stupidity" or "silliness"), and "weakness of understanding" (= "simpleton"), and

---

[43] See: "anthropology [... is] supplied by the inner sense with content" (*Anth* 7:398, also 7:143; *L-Anth/Friedländer* 25:473).

[44] On transcendental definitions of faculties, see 1.2. Recall that my reading of the idea as generating the domain of inner nature is stronger than a fictional (or methodological) reading, such as Dyck's (2014:210). Serck-Hanssen (2011:69) acknowledges that the soul defines the "mark of the mental", but rejects this reading as an interpretation of the Appendix.

[45] I argued elsewhere that the idea of the soul can also be understood as the guiding idea of the science of empirical psychology and hence of anthropology, insofar as it is concerned with matters of psychology (Kraus 2018). On the difficulty of defining the guiding idea of Kant's anthropology, see Brandt (1999).

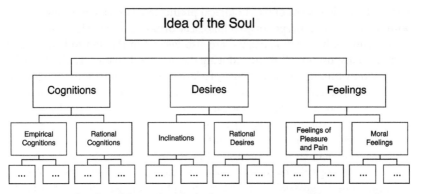

Figure 6.1 The idea of the soul as the highest genus concept of the system of psychological predicates in accordance with the tripartite structure of the basic mental faculties

of "mental illnesses", including "deranged imagination" (= "dementia", *Wahnsinn*), "deranged judgment" (= "insanity", *Wahnwitz*), "deranged understanding" (= "amentia", *Unsinnigkeit*), and "deranged reason" (= "craziness", *Aberwitz*).[46] Interestingly, Kant assumes that not only healthy minds can be categorized according to a system, but also the deviations from the normal can be thus classified.

The second part then develops a complex conception of character that concerns long-term characteristics of persons. Kant starts from the traditional account of the four temperaments – sanguine, melancholic, choleric, and phlegmatic – which he interprets as "dispositions" (*Stimmung*) and "propensities" (*Hang*) to show certain moods and behaviours (e.g., *Anth* 7:287–91). He supplements this account with a notion of moral character (i.e., "way of thinking", *Denkungsart*, *Anth* 7:291f.), which results from prescribing practical principles to oneself. He adds multiple behavioural observations within social settings (e.g., a study of facial expressions and gestures, *Anth* 7:300f.). So the second part of the *Anthropology* is not narrowly focused on matters of psychology, but offers a broader classification of human character traits. These traits can, nonetheless, be understood as rooted in psychological dispositions and hence as corresponding to a person's more general, temporally stable psychological properties. Kant's account of character then gives rise to an important new dimension of higher-order "character" predicates to be included in the system of psychological predicates, such as "perseverance", "cheerfulness", "thoughtlessness", "high-mindedness", "slyness", and "stubbornness" (see *Anth* 7:287–91). Hence, Kant's anthropological considerations

---

[46] For a detailed reconstruction and discussion of Kant's taxonomy of mental deficiencies and illnesses, see Frierson (2009a, 2009b).

enrich the basic system of psychological predicates, as sketched in Figure 6.1, with a variety of concepts of psychological disposition, which – due to the wider scope of his *Anthropology* – are also viewed in relation to behavioural and social dispositions.[47] By introducing the notion of character, which can be grasped only through the experience of a larger set of mental (and behavioural) states, Kant expands the system of basic predicates that describe relatively short-term mental states by a new dimension of higher-order predicates that describe long-term properties of persons.

In sum, this section has shown that the idea of the soul serves as the highest genus concept of inner nature and supplies normative principles for the acquisition of psychological predicates. A person who has acquired a psychological predicate is in the possession of a set of conceptual abilities; she is, for instance, able to reflect her inner appearances under this predicate and to use it in empirical judgements yielding inner experience. Moreover, the person is able to discriminate psychological beings to which this predicate can apply from other *kinds of beings*, and to discriminate specific individuals to whom the predicate in fact applies from those to whom it does not apply. The content of a psychological predicate is defined by the conceptual containment relations that the predicate has to other concepts within a system. The system itself is outlined by the a priori predicates contained in the idea of the soul. They operate as normative demands in our continuous efforts to refine conceptual content and to accomplish an increasingly comprehensive, specific, and dense system of psychological predicates, whose conceptual containment relations reflect the full variety of psychological phenomena to be observed in nature. The most general predicates of the system are the a priori predicates that describe the basic mental faculties. While they must be realized in *all* human minds, the more specific predicates describing particular psychological disposition may be realized only in *some* persons. Both kinds of predicates should be able to be corroborated by empirical observations in a science of empirical psychology, as well as in everyday life. The possession of a psychological predicate, however, does not guarantee that the corresponding conceptual abilities are always exercised correctly or completely. Rather, it is a further step to assess the adequacy of a particular application of a predicate to some individual, and hence to assess the truth of the resulting empirical judgement and to gain empirical self-knowledge.

6.4 Empirical Self-Knowledge and the Possibility of Error

So, I, finally, turn to the acquisition of empirical self-knowledge and discuss the possibility of error in this context. I argue that the acquisition of empirical self-knowledge, like the acquisition of psychological predicates, is also based on considerations of systematicity. The highest epistemic standard for assessing

---

[47] On the relation of empirical psychology and anthropology, see Kraus (2018).

the truth of one's self-concerning cognitions consists precisely in assessing whether these cognitions constitute a system unified under a common idea, namely the idea of myself as a soul. Following the previous considerations regarding the acquisition of psychological predicates, I first show that the normative demands of the idea of the soul are passed on to the basic conceptualizing and cognizing activities involved in inner experience, which result in the formation of a *self-concept*, that is, a concept of oneself as an *individual person*. Then, I examine possible errors in one's self-directed cognitions, such as *self-blindness* and *self-deceit*, and revaluate the doctrine of *transparency* that is often ascribed to Kant.

6.4.1   The Idea of the Soul as Template for a Complete Self-Concept

The principle of specification demands that we search for a more and more determinate concept of ourselves as individual persons. Yet, since Kant denies that we can ever have a lowest species concept, he must also reject the acquisition of a *complete individual self-concept* – a concept that, if it were available, would completely and adequately describe the person. Nor can we ever possess the corresponding concept for any other individual. Nonetheless, the principle of specification – together with the idea of the soul – gives some normative guidance for how to acquire more and more predicates that veridically describe oneself and hence to approximate one's self-concept to an increasing extent. Note that acquiring an empirical self-concept includes two crucial activities: firstly, applying a psychological predicate to oneself yielding a self-directed judgement and, secondly, taking this judgement to be true of oneself on the basis of an objectively sufficient ground. Hence, by successfully extending my self-concept through inner experience, I acquire some empirical self-knowledge.

Like other kinds of knowledge, self-knowledge requires a justification in terms of an objectively sufficient ground. As suggested in Section 6.2, such a ground can be gained on the basis of (1) an immediate inner experience, (2) a mediated cognition of more general psychological properties, or (3) a consciousness of the epistemic coherence of my self-directed cognitions within a system. Depending on the kind of epistemic grounds, we gain different levels of self-knowledge. Importantly, I have argued that all conceptualizing and cognizing activities in inner experience must be guided by the highest epistemic standard of rational knowledge if inner experience is to be oriented towards truth and hence towards self-knowledge at all.

The idea of the soul, again, prescribes specific normative principles for the activities involved in acquiring self-knowledge. Yet in this case, the idea serves, rather than as the highest genus concept, as a "template" for the *lowest species concept*, the complete individual self-concept that would completely and adequately describe the individual. The a priori predicates contained in the idea of the soul, again, can be understood as principles for the execution of this idea in light of ongoing inner experience. A priori predicates, such as <substance>, <fundamental power>, and <personal identity>, explicate the most general dimensions according to which I should first seek for possible psychological predicates that are applicable to me. Hence, these predicates delineate an outline or "sketch" of any such self-concept. I use this "sketch" to progressively "fill in" my self-concept with psychological predicates that I take to be applicable to myself. If all goes well, then I approximate my complete individual self-concept.

Again, the a priori predicates of the idea do not determine generic properties of psychological beings, but define normative demands: they define systematic unities that ought to be approximated in inner experience, such as the transtemporal unity of the subject. As normative principles, they can be used to derive *touchstones* for assessing whether the predicates that one takes to be contained in one's self-concept are in fact adequate for oneself. The psychological predicates we ascribe to ourselves can range from rather specific predicates concerning single mental states, such as a perception, desire, or feeling had at a particular time, to more general predicates concerning long-term psychological properties and even seemingly invariable character traits, such as gratitude, honesty, and wit.

Corresponding to the conceptual containment relations within the general system of psychological predicates, the specific predicates that adequately describe a particular individual can be arranged in a systematic manner as well. Taken together, these predicates constitute a unified system. Within this system, one can ascend from more determinate concepts specifying mental states occurring in particular moments, for example, particular perceptions, desires, or feelings, to more general concepts defining long-term psychological properties, such as character traits like shyness, kindness, and confidence. Here the idea of the soul substitutes for the lack of a complete self-concept, the most determinate concept of the individual that would be located "at the bottom" of the hierarchy. From there, potentially infinitely many less determinate psychological predicates (of different levels of determinacy and generality) branch out. Although a complete concept of an individual can never be fully grasped (and arguably cannot even exist) from an empirical perspective according to Kant, normative principles guide our conceptualizing and cognizing capacities such that we seek to approximate this concept. We seek to approximate such a concept by determining more and more adequate psychological predicates within a systematic unity, which becomes increasingly fine-grained, dense, and general. The concept towards which we thereby converge would potentially contain infinitely many psychological predicates *in it*, but only one individual falls *under it*: the unique individual person.

In sum, we acquire self-knowledge through expanding our individual self-concept in light of ongoing inner experience. We do so by incorporating

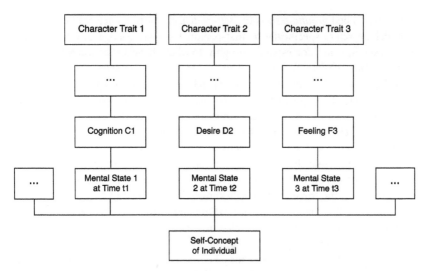

Figure 6.2   The idea of the soul as the template for the lowest species concept, viz. the complete individual self-concept

further and further psychological predicates into the self-concept for which we have sufficiently objective grounds to believe that these predicates adequately describe us. The idea of the soul normatively guides us in assessing the truth of these predicates. With its a priori predicates, the idea defines the most general dimensions of systematic unity and order according to which we ought to assess the adequacy of our self-concept. Hence, the idea serves as an a priori template for the unavailable complete individual self-concept of a person. Figure 6.2 schematically illustrates the function of the idea of the soul as the placeholder for the lowest species concept of an individual person in which *all* psychological predicates ever applicable to this person are contained.

6.4.2   *The Possibility of Self-Blindness and Self-Deceit*

One may now wonder whether the account of self-knowledge I have presented so far implies that self-knowledge for Kant is in some sense *epistemically privileged* over knowledge of external objects. It may, for instance, be less prone to error than ordinary object-knowledge, or may even be infallible. Descartes has often been associated with the thesis that the knowledge we have of our own mind is more certain than knowledge of external objects.[48] In contemporary philosophy of mind, there is a debate as to whether at least a particular kind of self-knowledge has special epistemic features, such as what

---

[48] In the Second Meditation, Descartes takes this thesis to be an implication of his *Cogito* argument (Descartes 1641/1996 7:33).

have been called *groundlessness* (or *self-evidence*), *transparency*, and *authority*.[49] The debate refers specifically to first-personal self-knowledge of one's current mental states, which corresponds, roughly, to what I have, in Section 6.2, classified as *immediate self-knowledge*. Since interpretations of Descartes' account of self-knowledge, as well as the contemporary debate on issues of epistemic privilege, are controversial, my goal here is *not* to assess how Kant's account would fare in comparison to Descartes' or in the contemporary debate. Rather, I aim to explore the kinds of errors to which self-knowledge can succumb according to Kant.[50] I then assess whether there is still a sense in which self-knowledge, for Kant, can be taken to be epistemically privileged over object-knowledge. In doing so, I use the contemporary debate as a point of reference. In what follows, I discuss these issues with respect to the three levels of self-knowledge I defined in Section 6.2.

Regarding the first level of *immediate self-knowledge*, there is no doubt that Kant is hugely critical of self-knowledge immediately based on self-observation. In several places, he points out a range of epistemic difficulties and even practical dangers that may be involved in inner experience immediately and exclusively based on self-observation. For instance, in the *Anthropology*, he warns that in paying too close attention to oneself, one may involuntarily change the course of one's thoughts and feelings, which can lead to "illuminism or even terrorism" (*Anth* 7:133). One may be confused about one's state of mind in light of "supposed higher inspirations and powers" that one only imagines (*Anth* 7:133). One's power of imagination, as the source of many creative ideas, can also be the source of various "fantasies" (*Anth* 7:167f.) and, in the worst case, can lead to "enthusiasm" (*Anth* 7:171). Hence, one has to be careful if one grounds one's inner experience on self-observation. In the *Metaphysical Foundations,* the epistemic difficulties of self-observation give Kant reason to doubt the scientific status of empirical psychology, since "the manifold of inner observation ... cannot be held separate and recombined at will" and therefore does not lend itself to scientific experimentation (*MFNS* 4:471). Rather, self-observation is particularly prone to distortions and self-manipulation, and even entails the risk of madness.

These passages suggest that inner experience that is immediately based on inner perception, like perception-based outer experience, is often subject to error. Recall that according to my interpretation in Chapter 2, inner perception is – with qualifications – understood on a perceptual model, that is, on Kant's account of perception as empirical consciousness of one's intuitions. For outer experience, Kant distinguishes appearance (*Erscheinung*) from mere illusion

---

[49] For accounts of these notions, see Coliva (2016:51–76).

[50] Here I will only outline possible *kinds* of errors, without providing a full explanation of how they arise, since the latter would require a general theory of error in Kant in the first place.

(*bloßer Schein*) (e.g., *Prol* 4:314; A38/B55, B69–70, A293/B350).[51] As the main source of error in judging outer objects, Kant cites "subjective causes, which are falsely regarded as objective" (*Anth* 7:142, also A294/B351). Similarly, we can think of a distinction between *inner appearance* and *inner illusion*.[52] For instance, we can falsely take a hallucination for the perception of a real object; we can falsely take a desire we have for a duty towards ourselves or even for the command that someone else has given us; we can falsely take a state of sadness for a state of anger; a hope for a belief; and so on. Hence, we can apply slightly inadequate or even outright false psychological predicates to our inner appearance and hence incorrectly classify the *type* of mental state we are currently in. Moreover, we may be mistaken about the *content* of our mental state, which adds further complications. Pathological cases often involve severe errors in how we judge about our occurrent mental states.[53]

These considerations show that Kant's account of self-knowledge allows for what one may call *self-blindness* concerning the *kind* of mental state one is in. Self-blindness consists in applying an inadequate psychological predicate to an observed mental state. *Self-blindness* appears to be more common with regard to affective states than to cognitive states that are results of activities of thinking, such as judgements, cognitions, and inferences.[54] The latter states constitutively involve the application of principles of the understanding and are regulatively guided by principles of reason. These principles come with certain conditions of correctness and hence are intrinsically normative in nature. Only if these principles, such as the Analogies of Experience, are correctly applied, can the resulting state really be cognition. Hence, being in a state of cognition involves some sort of consciousness of the correct application of the cognition-constituting principles. Failing to recognize such a state as a cognition would most likely amount to failing to cognize and hence to failing to be in such a state altogether.

Our immediate self-knowledge concerning occurrent conscious mental states, such as beliefs, desires, perceptions, imaginations, and feelings, is grounded in inner perception, which gives us intuitive access to our mental states and – under normal conditions – an objectively sufficient ground for self-knowledge. Yet due to the epistemic shortcomings of self-observation,

---

[51] Kant's examples include the moon illusion (see A297/B354). There Kant draws a distinction between how the world visually seems to us (e.g., the rising moon seems larger than the moon at its highest position) and how the world actually is (e.g., the moon always has the same size), though still as an appearance of outer sense and in accordance with the human conditions of experience.

[52] In the *Prolegomena*, Kant contrasts outer experience with mere "dreams" and inner experience with mere "imagination" (*Einbildung*) about oneself (*Prol* 4:337).

[53] See Frierson (2009a, 2009b).

[54] Merritt (2018:33–46) puts forward an interesting argument showing that affects and passions by their nature involve a blindness that makes them a mode of reflective failure.

Kant is wary of claims to such knowledge. Nonetheless, he acknowledges its importance. To avoid the danger, he then advises us to interpret the appearances of our self-observation only within a more comprehensive theory of human nature in general:

> [K]nowledge of the human being through inner experience, because to a large extent one also judges others according to it, is more important than correct judgment of others, but nevertheless at the same time perhaps more difficult . . . So it is advisable and even necessary to begin with observed *appearances* in oneself, and then to progress above all to the assertion of certain propositions that concern human nature; that is, to *inner experience*. (Anth 7:143)

This passage suggests that, while we have to start from the observation of ourselves, we should supplement these observations with general "propositions that concern human nature", for instance, psychologial and anthropological insights, and then make more general inferences about ourselves.[55] As a result, we gain what I have called mediate self-cognition, which typically involves cognition of one's more general properties and allows for the intermediary level of self-knowledge, which I classified as *mediate self-knowledge*.

Kant does not offer extensive discussions of possible errors regarding *mediate self-knowledge*. In his practical writings, Kant is fairly pessimistic that we can ever know our motives for actions and the underlying principles according to which we act, viz. maxims.[56] It is a rather common phenomenon that we take ourselves to have nobler motives than we actually do and that we misjudge our character to our own advantage, by ignoring problematic traits and overestimating favourable traits. In severe pathological cases, persons live under a serious delusion with regard to their personal character, as I will further discuss in Chapter 7 (see 7.3).

Given how common false inferences are with regard to outer matters, such errors seem equally likely with regard to inner matters. So Kant's account of self-knowledge allows for what one may call *self-deceit*. Self-deceit concerns errors in our mediate self-cognition regarding our more general psychological properties, such as commitments, values, and single character traits. Such errors may simply result from false inferences that we explicitly draw on the memory of multiple self-observations, which can easily be distorted. But, more commonly, self-deceit consists in taking certain background assumptions about oneself for granted without ever assessing their truth or even without being aware of having these assumptions. Such assumptions can involve positive claims such as "I am always honest" as well as negative claims such as "I would never wrong an innocent person". Such assumptions may be

---

[55] For a close discussion of this passage, see Kraus (2019b).
[56] For example, *Groundwork* 4:396.

deeply mistaken and may not line up at all with the behaviour we in fact show. In consequence, being mistaken, for instance about our practical maxims, we rely on distorted explanations, or even lack an explanation altogether, of the specific intentions we have in certain situations. Such general self-cognition is often not explicitly represented in consciousness, but can be made conscious only upon reflection. Given that such reflections involve multiple mental operations, the likelihood for error seems significantly higher than for claims to immediate self-knowledge.[57]

To avoid these multiple sources of error and to eliminate false background assumptions, Kant suggests not only that we reflect for ourselves, but also that we test our self-cognition in light of the testimony of others and of "propositions regarding human nature" in general, that is, by comparison with general psychological and anthropological knowledge (see *Anth* 7:143).[58] After all, universal assent is a mark of truth and, in empirical matters, intersubjective consensus can therefore be an indicator for objectively sufficient grounds for self-knowledge. The highest epistemic standard to which self-cognition can rise is, again, systematic coherence with respect to all cognitions involved – self-cognition, cognition by others, and general scientific cognition.

This brings us, finally, to the highest level of self-knowledge: *comprehensive self-knowledge*, which is typically grounded in the consciousness of epistemic coherence among a set of self-cognitions within a system. The highest level of systematic knowledge with regard to outer nature can be accomplished, for Kant, only through natural science, which requires an a priori foundation from which each empirical cognition can be derived. A full comprehension of some subject matter is gained by humans, if at all, only relative to some purpose and with regard to very few topics.[59] Similarly, we can have comprehension of ourselves only relatively and with respect to few aspects, such as specific character traits. We will, however, never have *complete self-knowledge*, as we can never be in the possession of a complete and fully adequate self-concept. Nonetheless, all efforts to gain a higher degree of self-knowledge are guided by the rational ideal of complete self-knowledge. In turn, errors in our self-cognition, resulting in self-blindness or self-deceit, can also be regarded as a matter of degree: errors can be understood in terms of the extent to which our self-cognition falls short of the ideal of systematic coherence and hence their level of severity corresponds to the *degree of incoherence* in our system of self-cognitions.

In sum, my account of self-knowledge in Kant shows that there is no a priori guarantee of the correctness of our self-cognition, and that several types of

---

[57] For an excellent account of reflection, see Merritt (2018). Merritt (2018:33–48) comes to a similar conclusion with regard to the possibility of self-deceit; see also O'Neill (1989).
[58] See Kant's discussion of the "logical egoist" at *Anth* 7:128.
[59] See *L-Log/Jäsche* 9:65.

errors are possible and indeed very common among humans. We can suffer from *self-blindness*, that is, the lack of an adequate psychological predicate, with regard to occurrent (empirically conscious) mental states of *any kind*. Yet being mistaken with regard to affective or conative states is more likely than with regard to cognitive states, since the latter must be – due to their cognitive nature – in accord with principles of the understanding and therefore are more amenable to rational conditions of coherence. Moreover, we can lapse into *self-deceit*, that is, have erroneous self-cognitions with regard to more general psychological properties, such as commitments and principles of actions. Finally, we can misconstrue global properties, such as identity-defining character traits, which require the comprehension of ourselves as wholes. Would these results still vindicate a sense in which self-knowledge for Kant may be epistemically privileged over object-knowledge?

6.4.3   Is Self-Knowledge Epistemically Privileged for Kant?

In contemporary philosophy of mind, various philosophers argue that first-personal self-knowledge of one's occurrent mental states has special epistemic features, such as what has been called *groundlessness* (or *self-evidence*), *transparency*, and *authority*. This kind of self-knowledge broadly corresponds to what I called *immediate self-knowledge*. Attributing these three features to immediate self-knowledge would, roughly, involve the claims that immediate self-knowledge is:[60]

- *groundless*, if it is true that I do not need to infer such knowledge from other beliefs I hold or observe it through a special sense;
- *transparent*, if it is true that, if I am in a particular mental state, then I am in the position to believe, or know that I am in this state;
- *authoritative*, if it is true that, if I believe that I am in a particular mental state, then I am in that state.

Since the accounts of these features, as well as the question whether they apply to self-knowledge, are controversial in the contemporary debate, my goal here is not to settle whether Kant would subscribe to these claims and whether, on his view, immediate self-knowledge would indeed display these epistemic features. Rather, I use this terminological framework to reassess the extent to which self-knowledge for Kant may be epistemically privileged.

Firstly, since, for Kant, a necessary condition of knowledge in general is having an objectively sufficient ground, it seems hard to square his position with the idea of *groundlessness*. Nonetheless, we find in Kant the related idea that being conscious of a mental state immediately supplies me with an objectively sufficient ground for knowing that I am in this state, without

[60] For accounts and discussion of these notions, see Coliva (2016:51–76).

inference or self-observation. Recall that Kant has – with qualifications – a sense-based model of consciousness: being in a mental state constitutively involves my being – at least to some degree – conscious of that state, that is, it requires my taking up or apprehending its content through inner sense into empirical consciousness. For each conscious mental state, my being conscious of that state always amounts – under normal conditions – to an objectively sufficient reason for immediate self-knowledge about the state.

Secondly, and more controversially, my analysis of self-knowledge raises an obvious objection to *transparency*. Various commentators take Kant to support some variant of the *transparency principle* of self-knowledge, according to which, if one has a mental state, one is in a position to *judge*, *believe*, or *know* that one has it. Patricia Kitcher and Matthew Boyle, for instance, argue that Kant's theory of empirical cognition requires him to accept the transparency principle, at least with respect to judgements, though perhaps not with respect to sensory and affective states.[61] They support their claim by appealing to the principle of transcendental apperception, which they interpret either according to the self-ascriptive reading (as in Boyle's case) or according to the act-awareness reading (as in Kitcher's case). I discussed both readings in Chapter 3 (see 3.3).

On my view, Kant does not subscribe to an a priori transparency principle with regard to *self-knowledge*, since, as I have argued above, self-blindness cannot be a priori excluded even with regard to mental states resulting from the higher intellectual faculties, such as judgement. But the devil is in the details. More precisely, I argue that if I am making a judgement, then I am necessarily (i.e., guaranteed a priori) in a position *to judge* that I am making this judgement. Yet I am *not* necessarily (i.e., guaranteed a priori) in a position *to know* what kind of epistemic attitude I have towards this judgement, for example, whether I believe the judgement to be true on objectively sufficient grounds or merely hope that it may be true on subjectively sufficient grounds. Note that *judging* is a neutral activity for Kant that generates a certain type of cognitive content and that is involved in various epistemic (and other) attitudes I may have towards this content. For instance, when making the judgement *that it rains*, I may know, wish, hope, believe, or desire that it is true.

The first part of my claim, *that I am a priori in a position to judge that I am in that state*, follows from my interpretation of transcendental apperception and self-reference. Recall, in Chapter 3, I argued that every mental act that brings about a potentially conscious representation must fulfil the general condition

---

[61] Kitcher (2011:251–65) argues that, although for Kant all kinds of self-ascription are based on inner sense, her reconstruction of Kant's account of rational cognition would allow for a principle of transparency with respect to judgements, though not with respect to sensation. Boyle (2009), who intends to give not an interpretation of Kant, but rather an account of self-knowledge of a "Kantian provenance", distinguishes between two kinds of self-knowledge: one with regard to active mental states and one with regard to passive states. He argues that the transparency principle holds for the former, but not for the latter.

of reflexive consciousness (according to the principle of transcendental apperception) and therefore constitutively involves the subject's ability to be conscious of itself as having this representation. In exercising this ability, I am primarily conscious of myself as identical throughout the apperceptive act, which I can express by attaching "I think" to the apperceived representation (see 3.5). Yet in contrast to the readings of Boyle and Kitcher, this expression of self-reference should not be considered as a self-ascription of the mental state. The latter, as I argued in Chapter 4, would amount to a self-consciousness of oneself as object, by which I represent myself as the content of a self-ascriptive judgement. In all I-judgements, I directly refer to myself via the first-person pronoun "I". The semantic rules of the "I" are derived from the logical conditions of reflexive consciousness (see 4.3.2). In consequence, I cannot be mistaken about the referent of an empirical I-judgement, namely myself. The reason for this is, as argued in Chapter 4, that any competent use of the first-person pronoun "I" involves a successful application of the semantic rules of the "I". Nonetheless, I can be mistaken about the specific mental predicate that I ascribe to myself (except for the predicates <thinking> and <judging>), as discussed in 6.4.2.[62]

Finally, as to *authority*, I do not think – due to the possibility of error at all levels of self-cognition – that Kant's view lends itself to a simple principle of authority, as I have stated it above. However, we have a certain kind of authority, not over our self-knowledge, but over the "object" that is thereby known, viz. our person: we can "make" ourselves to be in a particular state. Here is why I think there is still a sense in which, for Kant, self-knowledge is, not epistemically, but *practically privileged* over object-knowledge: self-knowledge is practically efficacious in the formation of ourselves as persons, as I will argue in the next chapter.

To conclude, following from Kant's general theory of knowledge, I argue that self-knowledge first arises from assessing the truth of one's self-cognition and that different kinds of self-cognition can give rise to different kinds of objectively sufficient grounds, and hence to different levels of self-knowledge. I discussed three levels: (1) *immediate self-knowledge of conscious mental states*, typically based on inner experience of immediately present inner appearances, (2) *mediate self-knowledge of general psychological properties*, typically based on a set of immediate inner experiences and further rational inferences; (3) *comprehensive self-knowledge of my character as a whole*, typically based on the comprehension of my self-cognitions within a system. Each level lends itself to particular errors and hence there is no a priori guarantee of the truth of any self-cognition.

---

[62] This result shows similarities with the contemporary account of immunity to error through misidentification, for example, Shoemaker (1968). While Shoemaker (1968:565) argues that this immunity holds for a specific class of psychological predicates only, my analysis suggests that it holds for any competent use of the pronoun "I". For discussion, see Longuenesse (2017).

7

The Demands of Practical Reason and Self-Formation

7.1 Introduction

This chapter finally proposes a theory of *psychological personhood* as an account of the kind of entity that we come to know through inner experience. It finally articulates what I called, in the Introduction, the self-formation view and establishes its central thesis that psychological persons first form themselves as such in the course of realizing their mental capacities under the guidance of a unifying idea. Persons are understood as *empirical reality in the making*: they are empirically real in virtue of the mental states by which they are "materially" constituted and yet they are always in need of further realization in accordance with an a priori form – the form of a systematic mental whole, as defined by the idea of the soul. This chapter shows that, with respect to the practical realization of oneself as a person, reason demands that the diverse aspects of one's mental life become unified into a *single integrated mental whole*. This gradual realization of a mental whole in accordance with the idea of the soul is what I call the *self-formation* of an individual person.

Chapter 5 showed the idea of the soul to be *regulative with respect to inner experience*, namely by presenting to the mind the mental whole within which inner experience is first intelligible for us. It argued that the idea defines *transcendental presuppositions* that are necessary, though not constitutive, for cognizing inner appearances as the mental states of a person: *myself*. For inner experience to be intelligible to us, we are bound to view ourselves as (1) *simple substances*, as endowed with (2) a *unique fundamental power*, and as having (3) *personal identity*. In Chapter 6, these presuppositions were, then, shown to be normative demands for the *theoretical purpose of self-knowledge*. This chapter will show that these same presuppositions also are normative demands for the *practical purpose of self-formation*; they serve as *prescriptive principles* that are practically efficacious in bringing about the individual person in the form of a systematic mental whole. Reason demands, I shall argue, that we realize ourselves (1) as *unified* across time (according to the presupposition of sub-stantiality), (2) as the *self-efficacious* common cause of all mental activity (according to the presupposition of a fundamental power), and (3) as *self-*

directing towards a rational personality (according to the presupposition of personal identity, which I will interpret, more broadly, as the call for character formation). These demands are now understood as a set of norms that governs all first-order mental acts through which we realize ourselves as persons.

Self-formation is conceived of as an overarching mental activity carried out throughout a mental life and constituted by the multitude of first-order mental acts, such as perceiving, judging, believing, recalling, deliberating, and willing. The normative demands that guide self-formation require that these first-order mental acts are to be brought into accordance with reason's principles of systematicity. Self-formation is realized by the *whole series of first-order mental acts* and results in a progressive actualization of the systematic mental whole that is assumed to underlie the *whole series of inner appearances* in empirical consciousness. A particular mental state, such as a desire or a cognition occurring at a particular time, is understood not only (1) as "part" of a trans-temporally unified mental whole and (2) as the "effect" of a unified set of mental faculties, but also (3) as contributing to developing one's overall character and as being conducive (or not) to the ends that one has set for oneself. How a mental state shapes *who* we are depends on the role it plays *within the whole* of our mental lives. The extent to which we have in fact realized ourselves as mental wholes varies with time and is never completed.

Let me illustrate the conception of self-formation I am arguing for by the example of six-year-old Sophia, who has recently started playing the piano. While enjoying her first piano lessons, she develops a deep passion for piano music and becomes increasingly aware of her desire to improve her piano skills. Now, there are fundamentally different scenarios for how this desire could play out in her later life. In the case in which Sophia tenaciously acts on this desire such that she becomes a highly distinguished piano player later in life, this passion for music becomes one of the identity-defining features, which are most causally efficacious in her life. Yet in cases in which this desire is overruled, for example by the passion to help others or the desire to have a more stable career path, the passion for music will play only a marginal role in her adult life and it may happen that she pursues the career of a medical doctor instead. In any case, her desire to improve her piano skills will be part of the mental whole that she realizes throughout her life. But what this desire means for her exactly will only unfold within the whole of her mental life. In turn, she will be able to know her own identity, and the role that this desire plays for her identity, only by drawing systematic connections between this desire and other features of her mental life. Of course, whether and how one acts on a desire is not entirely independent from external constraints, such as social expectations or the need for financial security. While the account I am proposing does not rule out such external constraints, it focuses on those features that are to some extent in the person's control and therefore feed into the person's self-formation.

In arguing that both self-formation and the acquisition of self-knowledge are normatively guided by one and the same set of a priori demands of reason, I acknowledge that reason here operates not exclusively in its *theoretical use*, but also in its *practical use* (and I will argue that the two uses do not exclude one another). Reason in its practical use is typically thought of as playing a normative role for acting in the world. Yet here I am not concerned with Kant's account of agency in general, nor do I focus on the specific role that reason plays with respect to moral agency, notably in the deliberation about maxims for action and in the prescription of categorical imperatives. Rather, I give an account of mental agency, which consists in all activities of our mental faculties. In doing so, I will eventually show that Kant offers us material for a self-standing account of a psychological person – an account that is intrinsically normative and can yet be defined independently of the norms of morality.[1]

Section 7.2 introduces my conception of self-formation. It first reviews various levels of self-realization discussed in previous chapters and then shows the idea of the soul to be practically efficacious as the unifying form of mental life. Section 7.3 specifies three prescriptive principles of self-formation, based on the presuppositions of (1) substantiality, (2) a fundamental mental power, and (3) personal identity. Section 7.4 explicates the normativity of personhood as inner systematicity in three interrelated spheres – the epistemic, the practical, and the affective.

7.2 Self-Realization and Self-Formation

7.2.1 Kinds of Self-Realization and Kinds of Self-Related Unities

Our mental lives consist of all the *mental activities* we ever exercise, as well as all inner appearances occurring in empirical consciousness, which result either directly from these activities or from affective responses to these activities. Primarily, I take a mental activity (*Tätigkeit*) to involve at least one active (i.e., spontaneous) faculty, such as the understanding or the will.[2] Throughout this book, we have mainly focused on those activities that contribute to cognition, such as perceiving and judging. But recall, from Chapter 1, that Kant derives a variety of representations from his rich taxonomy of mental faculties, each of which falls under one of the three basic faculties of cognition, desire, and

---

[1] My account shares similarities with *self-constitution* accounts, such as Korsgaard's (2008, 2009). Focusing on practical agency, Korsgaard identifies the principle of becoming a whole as a *constitutive* principle of personhood that follows from the *constitutive* principle of morality, viz. the Categorical Imperative. By contrast, on my view, the principles of self-formation are the normative conditions of personhood per se, which can be defined independently of morality.

[2] Perceiving thus counts as mental activity, since it involves a synthesis of the understanding, whereas intuiting may not be counted as such, if it is taken to involve only passive faculties, that is, the senses; see 2.3.

feeling. Exercising any of these faculties contributes content to our mental lives and hence provides "material" for our self-formation.

Chapters 2 to 5 have discussed a set of mental activities related to inner experience, each of which comes with a corresponding set of formal conditions (or simply forms). In the current context, each of these activities can now be understood as a way of realizing one's mental life, or of what one may call *self-realization*. Their corresponding forms can be understood as principles of unity, each defining the kind of *self-related unity* that corresponds to the level of self-realization. Self-formation can then be understood as an overarching activity, providing unity for all these mental activities: the *unity of the person*, which concerns mental life as a whole.[3] Let us briefly review the different levels of self-realization and their corresponding self-related unities from the previous chapters.

Chapter 2 has offered an account of inner appearances as the basic items of empirical consciousness and discerned the temporal conditions under which these appearances occur in inner sense and hence can become the objects of inner perception. Having a temporal series of mental states in empirical consciousness can now be seen as the most basic kind of self-realization. Sophia's stream of consciousness may include, for instance, the perception of piano sounds, the momentary appetite for practising the piano, and the delight in listening to piano music. This "stream" of mental states in empirical consciousness is the most basic manifestation of a person's mental life. The corresponding principle of unity precisely combines all mental contents into one and the same *primitively temporally ordered consciousness*. Higher-order principles of unity come into play if we become aware of our mental states in inner perception. Perception in general is subject to further temporal conditions according to the categories, yet – as we have seen – not all of these conditions are straightforwardly applicable to the case of inner perception; the principle of substance as persistence is especially problematic. Moreover, I argued, to achieve these temporal unities, perception itself must be subject to transcendental apperception.

Chapter 3 has, therefore, argued that all empirical consciousness must be realized according to the general form of reflexivity, which concerns the relation of representations to the subject. This basic form of reflexivity is due to the faculty of apperception and can be expressed by attaching the apperceptive "I think". It gives unity to, and thus first makes possible, what I now call a *first-order mental act* (*Handlung, actus*). A first-order mental act is a mental

---

[3] I prefer to call this overarching activity *self-formation*, rather than *self-constitution*, since it does not contribute new mental contents that "materially" constitute the self, nor is it determined by constitutive principles. Rather, self-formation is normatively guided by regulative principles that give a *form* to lower-order mental activities. For self-constitution views, see Korsgaard (2009) and Engstrom (2009).

activity that results in a conscious representation of a particular kind. The resulting representation occurs at a particular time or within a particular mental episode in empirical consciousness and can be attended to as an object of inner perception. Examples of such first-order acts include the acts of perceiving an object, of making a judgement, of drawing an inference, or of forming an intention to act. Each first-order act is conditioned by the form of apperception and can in turn be thought of as realizing the transcendental unity of apperception. All the partial representations that constitute the act, such as the manifold of intuition, a set of concepts, or a set of judgements, must be combined in one and the same consciousness and hence are related to the same representing subject. In consequence, each first-order act implies the consciousness of the *identity of the subject throughout the act*, that is, analytic self-consciousness.

Chapter 4 has examined the logical conditions of I-judgements, that is, judgements by which one predicates something of oneself. Such self-predication can now be seen as a higher form of self-realization through which the primitive identity of the subject is further conceptually determined by the logical concept of oneself, viz. the logical "I". The logical "I" introduces, in addition to the mere form of reflexivity, further *conceptual unities under which any referent of I-judgements must be reflected*, yet without determining anything about the referent's empirical nature. Its predicates include that of <logical simplicity> (by which the referent of "I" is determined as a simple unity without self-standing "I"-parts), and that of <logical identity> (by which the referent of "I" is determined as being one and the same in a series of I-judgements within a mental episode).

Chapter 5 has then enquired into the kind of unity that is required for inner experience. Inner experience consists in empirical I-judgements concerning the psychological "I", which result from reflecting inner appearances under the idea of the soul. Sophia, for instance, may make I-judgements such as "I want to play the piano in a concert" or "I enjoy listening to Mozart's piano sonatas". Since *not* all experience-constitutive principles can be applied to inner experience, above all the principle of persistence, inner experience requires regulative principles that define the temporal dimensions of the mental whole that is to be approximated in inner experience. For instance, to ascribe a series of mental states to oneself, one needs to presuppose that these states belong to one and the same *mental whole*, although this whole cannot be intuited and a fortiori not cognized. The mental whole defined by the idea of the soul is now understood as the *unity of the psychological person*, and it corresponds to the highest level of self-realization, that is, the realization of oneself as a *person*.[4]

---

[4] There can be, of course, higher forms of self-realization within or through social communities, resulting in the formation of social identities, such as cultural, national, or religious identities, or of a moral community.

The purpose of the current chapter is to argue that this highest level of self-realization has a practical efficacy in normatively governing all lower-order mental acts. The idea of the soul does not only *present* a sketch of the unity that is approximated through inner experiences, but also *prescribes* how such unity ought to be brought about through the acts that feed into a person's self-realization. The very formation of oneself as a mental whole is then understood as an activity of reason in its practical use, by which the very object of inner experience – the individual person – is brought about. The idea of the soul becomes practically efficacious in self-formation. Kant occasionally identifies this "activity of reason" with the "self-activity (*Selbsttätigkeit*)" that concerns the human being as a whole and the "idea of its vocation (*Bestimmung*)", rather than the spontaneity (*Spontaneität*) of single mental faculties.[5]

The different levels of self-realization are schematically presented in Table 7.1.

7.2.2   The Idea of the Soul as the Form of Mental Life

To understand the practical efficacy of the idea of the soul, a few general remarks on the relationship between theoretical and practical uses of reason are in order. The distinction between theoretical and practical reason is characterized by Kant as follows: while theoretical reason is concerned with theoretical questions about "what is", practical reason is concerned with practical questions about "what ought to be" (e.g., *L-Log/Jäsche* 9:86). Both uses fundamentally rely on rational inferences. In the theoretical case, inferences are employed to derive theoretical conclusions from theoretical principles, as exemplified in the sciences. In the practical case, inferences are employed to derive practical propositions (or precepts for action) from practical principles (though typically in conjunction with theoretical propositions). Such practical inferences are typically exercised in the context of moral agency and therefore practical reason, taken in the narrow sense, has a moral connotation: it specifically concerns the idea of determining one's will in accordance with the moral law. In a more general sense, practical reason is understood as being efficacious with respect to the realization of its objects. The theoretical and the practical use of reason can thus be distinguished in terms of the relation that the mind has to its object in each case, as Kant himself states:

> cognition can relate to its object in either of two ways, either merely *determining* the object and its concept (which must be given from else-where), or else also *making* the object *actual*. The former is *theoretical*, the latter *practical* cognition of reason.   (Bix–x)[6]

---

[5] See *Groundwork* 4:452 and *CJ* 5:292.

[6] "Cognition" is here used, in a broad sense, to refer to representations of reason, rather than of the understanding.

Table 7.1 *Levels of self-realization and corresponding kinds of self-related unities*

Level	Material	Form	Activity	Product	Major faculties involved	Self-related unity
0	Sensations and feelings	Pure forms of space and time	Sensing, feeling	Primitively ordered empirical consciousness	Sensibility, feeling	None
1	Representational elements belonging to a first-order mental act, e.g., intuitions, concepts, inclinations	Pure form of apperception (plus more specific forms corresponding to the kind of act)	**First-order mental acts,** e.g., perceiving, judging, desiring	Conscious representation of an object (in the broad sense), e.g., perception, judgement, desire	Apperception, understanding, will, etc.	**Identity of the thinking subject throughout the mental act**
2	Inner appearances	Forms of inner experience (including the logical forms of I-judgements and the regulative idea of the soul)	Acts of **inner experience** (as acts of judging about or cognizing oneself based on intuition)	Inner experience (as an empirical I-judgement)	Inner sense, understanding	**Presentation of a mental whole (as context of intelligibility for inner experience)**
3	**First-order mental acts**	**Idea of the soul**	**Self-formation (= self-activity of reason)**	**Actualizing oneself as a mental whole**	**Reason**	Unity of a person (as normative principle of self-formation and self-knowledge)

practical reason even has the causality actually to bring forth what its
concept contains.   (A328/B385)

Stephen Engstrom helpfully elaborates on this distinction in terms of what he calls
"the direction of existential dependence" (Engstrom 2009:119). According to
Engstrom, theoretical knowledge is existentially dependent on the actuality of its
objects, whereby the object is "given from elsewhere" – either empirically through
affection of the senses, or transcendentally through a mere concept.[7] Theoretical
knowledge can determine something only if the corresponding object can be
proven to exist. By contrast, practical knowledge determines an object that is to
be realized. The realization of this object is existentially dependent on its practical
cognition being actualized in someone's consciousness. The practical use of reason
thus aims at "making the object actual" and specifically presupposes "an object
(*matter*) of the faculty of desire as the determining ground of the will" (*CpracR*
5:21). The object of practical knowledge is commonly identified with a particular
action or, more precisely, with the good that an action brings about.[8] For instance,
I may cognize that listening to Mozart's piano sonata would give me the kind of
relaxation that I would need to finish this chapter. As a consequence, I turn on
iTunes and play some of Mozart's piano sonata. In doing so, I start bringing about
the desired object, that is, the action of writing this chapter, which, if completed
successfully, also includes the actualization of the end, that is, the completion of
this chapter.[9]

Central for my self-formation view is the notion that the idea of the soul is *in
some sense practical*, rather than purely theoretical. This idea prescribes a principle
that guides the activity of "making actual" the very object that is cognized in inner
experience, rather than describing a reality that is "given from elsewhere". My
interpretation builds on accounts of reason that take it to be a unified faculty in
which originate both the theoretical use of systematizing experience and the
practical use of deriving practical principles. My view also takes up the thesis
that the practical use of reason has primacy over the theoretical. Yet I will not
provide an argument for this general account of reason here.[10] Rather, I confine

[7] While Kant acknowledges that reason can give objects to the understanding, he denies
that we can have proper theoretical cognition of these objects without suitable intuition.
I leave it open whether he allows for theoretical knowledge of them. For discussion, see
Watkins and Willaschek (2017a).
[8] Korsgaard (2009:1–18), for instance, identifies an action with the actualization of
a practical syllogism; see also Engstrom (2009:119).
[9] For an insightful discussion of Kant's account of action, according to which an action is
an "act-for-the-sake-of-an-end", see Korsgaard (2009:8–14). According to my terminology above, an action can be constituted by several *first-order (mental) acts* that are unified
with respect to the end that is to be accomplished by the action.
[10] For accounts of the unity of reason, that is, the idea that theoretical and practical uses of
reason originate in one and the same faculty, see O'Neill (1989), Neiman (1994), and
Mudd (2017).

myself to the case of self-formation, which primarily concerns mental agency. My main thesis is thus that the idea of the soul is practically efficacious in *making myself actual* as a person, that is, as a systematic mental whole. The best way to account for the practical efficacy at work, I believe, is – in accordance with Kant's *hylomorphic* theory of mental faculties – in terms of an a priori *form* that is made actual by the intake of suitable material under this form. Hence, I suggest that the idea of the soul defines the a priori *form of mental life* that ought to be made actual through all mental acts that constitute such a life. By realizing these mental activities according to this form, I fashion myself as a person in the course of my mental life.

We already find some evidence for this hylomorphic understanding of the soul serving as a principle of mental life in Kant's early lectures on anthropology. There, Kant is reported to endorse a conception of the soul that, though still influenced by the prevailing rationalist metaphysics, concerns living beings that have intellectual capacities to represent themselves and the world. More specifically, the soul is identified with the "modes of how [such beings . . .] can be alive" (*L-Anth/Philippi* Bl.4, my translation). Kant then distinguishes "three modes of how we can be alive" (*Arten, wie wir uns lebend verhalten*) (*L-Anth/Philippi* Bl.4, my translation), which correspond to three "perspectives" according to which we can consider ourselves, as the following passage states:

> We observe, however, the soul (*Seele*) from a threefold perspective, namely as *anima* (soul) (*Seele*), *animus* (mind) (*Gemüth*), and *mens* (spirit) (*Geist*). Insofar as the soul is thought of in combination with the body and cannot prevent what *affects* the senses from being communicated to it, it is soul, and there it is merely passive. Yet insofar as the soul reacts (*resigniert*) to sensible impressions and proves itself active, it is *animus*, and to the extent it represents something completely independently of all sensibility it is *mens*.
> (*L-Anth/Parow* 25:247, translation amended; see also *L-Anth/Collins* 25:16)

So Kant distinguishes three aspects of the soul in accordance with three essential aspects of human mental life as follows. As intellectually active producers of representations, who are independent of any sensible constraints, we view ourselves as spirits (*mens*). As passive receivers of sensations, we view ourselves as souls in the narrow sense (*anima*).[11] As jointly intellectually active and constrained by sensible conditions, we view ourselves as minds (*animus*). With this distinction, he breaks with the German rationalist metaphysics of his predecessors, according to which the soul is conceived of as a broadly Cartesian thinking substance (*res cogitans*).[12] Rather, Kant seems to

---

[11] Similarly, in his lectures on metaphysics, Kant associates the soul specifically with the sensible conditions of mental life and defines the soul as the object that affects inner sense (e.g., *L-MP/L₁* 28:222, 28:263ff., 28:275; *L-MP/L₂* 29:876ff.).

[12] Descartes (1641/1996) replaces the Aristotelian hylomorphic conception of the human being, which appealed to the soul as *forma substantialis*, with a dualistic conception of two

incorporate the broadly Aristotelian distinction between *anima*, as the principle of life of an organic body, *animus*, as the specifically human soul, and *mens*
(as a translation of *nous*), as the rational part of the human soul or as the purely
active intellect.[13]

Despite the fact that Kant does not explicitly maintain this threefold distinction concerning the soul (in the broad sense) in his mature Critical works,
I submit that the conception of the soul displayed in these lectures anticipates
the hylomorphic account of the soul as an idea of reason developed in his
Critical Philosophy. Kant's Critical account of the soul as the a priori form of
mental life can be seen within the long-standing tradition of understanding
how the pure intellect manifests itself in human life under the conditions of
time and finitude.

In his Critical writings, Kant defines *life* in general as the "faculty of a being
to act in accordance with its representations" (*MM* 6:211), and hence to make
oneself (or something external to oneself) actual in accordance with an end.
For living beings in general, life consists mainly in the self-preservation of
one's own organism and in the propagation of the species.[14] For human beings,
the faculty for life is additionally specified by their rational capacities, which
enable them to set ends for themselves in accordance with practical reason and
to have a particularly phenomenologically rich *mental life*.[15] This suggests that
to live the life of a human person is simply to live in accordance with the
representations of reason; that is, more precisely, to live in accordance with the
idea of reason that defines the form of human mental life. Hence, on the self-

distinct substances: the soul is a thinking substance which exists in union with an
extended material substance, viz. the human body. The Wolffian rationalists endorse
this dualistic ontology and refine it by a detailed faculty psychology (for a historical
overview, see Wunderlich 2005 and Falduto 2014:1–33). Wolff discards a teleological
account of the soul and models its representational powers on the Newtonian conception
of mechanical forces of matter (see Wolff 1720/1997:§66; see also Blackwell 1961:347–8).

[13] For Aristotle, the soul in general is the vital principle of an organic body (see Aristotle
c.350 BCE/2016, *De Anima* i.4 and ii.1); the human soul – as *forma substantialis* – gives
form and purpose specifically to the human body and unity to all mental faculties (see *De
Anima* ii.1–2). The intellect (*nous*) is "the part of the [human] soul by which it knows and
understands" (*De Anima* iii.4, 429a9–10), or, more specifically, the *active intellect* (*nous
poiêtikos*) that is "separate and unaffected and unmixed" with human sensibility (*De
Anima* iii.5, 430a17–18). This tripartite distinction – between *anima* (= soul in general),
animus (= specifically human soul), and *mens* (= pure intellect) – crucially shapes the
debate throughout the medieval period.

[14] See also *MM* 6:26.

[15] In his practical writings, Kant identifies the human faculty for life primarily with the
faculty of desire (*Begehrungsvermögen*), for example, *CpracR* 5:9n; in the *Anthropology*,
additionally with the feeling of one's life, for example, *Anth* 7:231. In the third *Critique*,
the "mind" as a whole is endowed with a "principle of life" (I 5:278), and according to
some lectures on metaphysics, a person (or "personality") is characterized by a "principle
of life" (e.g., *L-MP/L₁* 28:296).

formation view, *the idea of the soul is practically efficacious as the unifying form of mental life.*

7.3   Psychological Personhood and the A Priori Presuppositions of Self-Formation

7.3.1   *Practical and Psychological Personality, and Two Notions of Character*

While Kant's notion of a person is mainly discussed in the context of his theory of morality, Kant himself draws a distinction between *psychological* and *practical personality* (*Persönlichkeit*), and frequently suggests that the former is a necessary condition of the latter.[16] The self-formation view can be developed as an interpretation of Kant's notion of psychological personhood, which can then be taken to underlie Kant's practical account of personhood. Since my focus remains on the psychological person, I only indicate its relation to practical personhood without carrying out a full argument that the former is a condition of the latter. The self-formation view primarily explains how reason's principles of systematicity play out as a priori presuppositions for realizing oneself as a person in time and for developing an individual character throughout one's mental life. It, secondarily, offers an explanation of how the temporal dimension of personhood is compatible with the idea of the purely intelligible and moral character of a person.

In his lectures on metaphysics, Kant defines the distinction between psychological and practical personality as follows: "Personality can be taken *practically* and *psychologically; practically,* if free actions are ascribed to it; *psychologically,* if it is conscious of itself and of the identity [which . . .] rests on inner sense" (*L-MP/L₁* 28:296, see also *L-MP/Dohna* 28:683 and *L-MP/ Vigilantius* 29:1036). Kant accepts – in line with the rationalist conceptions of personality held, among others, by Wolff and Baumgarten – that what characterizes a psychological person is the capacity to be conscious of one's personal identity based on inner sense, which Kant primarily understands as *numerical identity* throughout time.[17] By contrast, practical personality involves the ascribability or imputability of free action and hence the

---

[16] For example, *MM* 6:224, *L-MP/L₁* 28:296, *L-MP/Dohna* 28:683, and *L-MP/Vigilantius* 29:1036.

[17] See A361 and B408–9. Kant's lectures of metaphysics discuss *personality* with respect to questions concerning the temporal dimensions of souls, especially those concerning immortality and the afterlife. There, personality is typically characterized by the capacity of a being to be "conscious of itself", though without explicitly invoking inner sense; see, for example, *L-MP/L₁* 28:276; *L-MP/Dohna* 28:683; *L-MP/K₂* 28:763; *L-MP/Mrongovius* 29:913; and *L-MP/Vigilantius* 29:1036. See also 4.4.

idea of freedom.[18] Despite emphasizing that a practical personality in general requires freedom and rationality, Kant frequently acknowledges specifically the temporal dimension of *human* personality. For instance, Kant repeatedly claims that a human person must consider herself as "belonging to the sensible world" and hence as being subject to empirical conditions, including the limitations of a temporal existence (*CpracR* 5:87).[19] Indeed, we can be held morally responsible for past deeds and for present and future choices only if we are capable of recognizing our personal identity throughout all these actions.[20] Hence, Kant's account of practical personality for humans builds on, or is even conditioned by, his account of a psychological person in time.

A central notion of Kant's account of practical personality is that of a character. In his anthropological writings, Kant is most explicit about the importance of forming (*ausbilden*) a character for morality.[21] While the distinction between psychological and practical personality is less explicit in his Critical writings, Kant there introduces the distinction between two kinds of character – one concerning empirical-natural aspects and the other concerning rational-moral aspects of character. Although these two distinctions do not exactly map onto one another, developing an interpretation of psychological personhood can illuminate the relation between these two kinds, or aspects, of character.

Firstly, in the *Anthropology*, Kant distinguishes between a natural character that depends on a given nature and an acquired character that depends on "what the human being *makes of himself*" (*Anth* 7:292). The former includes "natural aptitudes" and "predispositions" (*Anth* 7:285), as well as one's temperament, and is summarized as the "way of sensing (*Sinnesart*)" (*Anth* 7:292). The latter is

[18] See *L-MP/L₁* 28:296 and *L-MP/Dohna* 28:683. In Kant's Critical works, a person is typically characterized in moral terms: for example, as the bearer of "moral [or inner] worth" (*Groundwork* 4:394), as being an "end-in-itself" (*Groundwork* 4:428; *CpracR* 5:87–8), as a "lawgiver" (*Groundwork* 4:438), as the proper addressee of "respect", as a "subject of duty" (*MM* 6:418; also 423), and as being motivated by the moral law (*Religion* 6:27–8).

[19] That personality requires *rationality* is explicitly stated, for example, at *CpracR* 5:122; *Religion* 6:25 and 6:28; *L-MP/Dohna* 28:688; and *L-MP/Mrongovius* 29:91. That *human* personality is additionally subject to sensible conditions is mentioned, for example, at *CpracR* 5:99 and *Groundwork* 4:455.

[20] The temporal character of human persons also plays a role in the Practical Postulate of the Immortality of the Soul, which demands the "*existence* and personality of the same rational being continuing *endlessly*", even beyond physical death (*CpracR* 5:122). The self-formation view primarily concerns personhood "in life" and in conjunction with a living body (see B415, A672/B700).

[21] For example, *Anth* 7:291–2, 294–5, 324–5; *L-Anth/Friedländer* 25:630; *L-Anth/Pillau* 25:832; *L-Anth/Mrongovius* 25:1398; and related Reflections, for example, *Refl* 1113, 15:496; *Refl* 1158, 15:512; *Refl* 1179, 15:521. See also *Groundwork* 4:393; *CpracR* 5:98–100, 153; *MM* 6:331, 407, 420.

what Kant calls the "way of thinking (*Denkungsart*)" (or *Charakter schlechthin*) (*Anth* 7:285, 292). Only the latter has a specifically moral connotation. A *character schlechthin* consists precisely in the "firmness and persistence in principle" that guides a person's moral conduct. Yet a human being is not naturally born with such a character, but rather has to acquire (*erwerben*) or form (*ausbilden*) it gradually *in time*. Such formation of a character requires, according to Kant, the "absolute unity of the inner principle of conduct (*Lebenswandel*) as such" (*Anth* 7:295).[22] In a related note, we find such a character described as the "general ruling *principium* in the human being for the use of his talents and qualities" (*Refl* 1113, 15:496). This emphasis on an "absolute unity" and a "governing principle" is reminiscent of Kant's account of ideas of reason. So I will argue that the idea of the soul provides guiding principles for such character-formation.

Secondly, in the first *Critique*, Kant distinguishes between the *empirical* and the *intelligible character* within a discussion of the idea of freedom.[23] There, character in general is defined as a *law of causality*, or a *law of determination*, that describes the workings of an effective cause (A539/B567). The intelligible character is defined specifically as "that in an object of sense [viz. the person] which is not itself appearance" (A538/B566) and is ascribed to "pure reason" (A551/B579). The empirical character is, in turn, understood as the "mere appearance" of the intelligible character in the world of sense.[24] In his complex argument for the idea of freedom, Kant makes the remarkable claim that the empirical character is the *sensible schema* of the intelligible character (A553/B581). While the intelligible character is thought of *as if* it were a "thing in itself" that "would not stand under any conditions of time" (A539/B567), the empirical character is precisely what "exhibits" the intelligible character *in concreto* and hence under the conditions of time.

The relation of intelligible and empirical character has commonly been interpreted – in the context of Kant's transcendental idealism – as the distinction between one's character as a noumenon (or thing-in-itself) and one's character as an appearance (and hence object of possible experience). Accordingly, the intelligible character is often viewed as the real noumenal ground for being, or *ratio essendi*, of the appearing empirical character.[25]

---

[22] On natural and acquired character, see Merritt (2018:131–6).

[23] See Third Antinomy of Pure Reason (A444–51/B472–9).

[24] On the self-knowledge of one's empirical and one's intelligible character, see 6.2.

[25] I will not provide a full discussion of this interpretation. For critical discussions, see Willaschek (1992:131–48, esp. 135), and Frierson (2014:142–6). Willaschek (1992:149) concludes that a "realist" interpretation of the intelligible character as a "thing-in-itself" leads to a failure of Kant's solution of the Third Antinomy and eventually rejects this interpretation, in line with the self-formation view. On the noumenal interpretation of the soul, see also 5.4.

By contrast, the self-formation view offers an alternative interpretation that does not appeal to the controversial assumption that a thing-in-itself must exist as the atemporal real ground of one's observable empirical character. Rather, by appealing to the self-activity of reason in accordance with ideas, the self-formation view offers a framework within which the formation of a person is understood as developing in time and yet as guided by a priori, purely rational principles. Likewise, the formation of a character can now be understood as a dynamic process that arises empirically in a person's life and is normatively guided by rational principles based on ideas of reason. On this view, the intelligible character just is the unified set of rational principles that governs a person's life as a whole, whereas the empirical character is the sensible concretization of such principles in the person's observable actions and conduct of life (*Lebenswandel*). The self-formation view, I submit, can thus capture both the idea of a person's empirical character appearing in time and the idea of an intelligible character as the purely rational characteristics of that person. The view can, moreover, make sense of Kant's complex claim that a person can acquire a character only *in time*, while a character itself – understood as the "absolute unity of the inner principle" – must be considered as *not* being conditioned by time. And, finally, the view takes seriously the claim that the empirical character is the sensible schema through which the intelligible character is concretely exhibited in a person's life.

Based on these general considerations, I now show how the self-formation view explains the temporal dimensions of a person's life, such as trans-temporal endurance, agency in time, and character development, by appeal to demands of reason. I shall explicate three prescriptive principles of self-formation, based on the three major a priori predicates of the idea of the soul: (1) substantiality, (2) being a fundamental mental power, and (3) personal identity. These principles can be understood as three normative demands, namely that we ought to realize ourselves (1) as *unified* across time, (2) as the *self-efficacious* common cause of all mental activity, and (3) as *self-directed* towards a rational personality (which I will now interpret as the call for character formation).[26]

7.3.2   Substantiality and Trans-Temporal Unity

Recall, from Chapter 5, that the a priori predicates of the idea of the soul serve as analogues of schemata for inner experience; they delineate a priori the

---

[26] Note that, in Chapter 5, I introduced the further predicate of "standing in community with other real things", including one's own body (see 5.3 and 5.6.1). This predicate was shown to be crucial for the determination of mental states in objective time (see 5.6.2). It is not relevant for the current purpose of explaining *intrapersonal* self-formation. Yet it may be important for an account of the interpersonal and social dimension of self-formation, which I do not consider here.

universal characteristics of inner nature, which are instantiated by each person. These a priori predicates can now be understood as prescriptive principles of practical reason by which we ought to *make ourselves actual as persons* and hence make actual the very object of our inner experience.

A fundamental aspect of personhood concerns the ability to recognize one's identity across different times and across different mental states. In Chapter 5, I have argued that the predicate of "a simple substance" amounts to the transcendental proposition that "all determinations [are considered] as in one subject". Presupposing a priori a mental whole across time is necessary to make sense of those inner intuitions as representing inner appearances of one and the same subject and hence for determining those inner appearances as psychological accidents of oneself.

The self-formation view considers this regulative principle of substantiality as an *a priori presupposition* that has *practical efficacy* with regard to the "object" that is made actual, namely oneself. This principle now demands that I realize my mental acts under the condition that the appearances of these acts that occur at different times ought to belong to one and the same mental whole across time. Hence, I gradually make myself actual as a mental whole only insofar as (or to the extent that) I combine my inner appearances into a whole in the course of realizing my mental faculties. Combining inner appearances into a mental whole can precisely be understood as generating inner appearances in such a way that I am able to be conscious of them as unified across time. This combination into a whole does not require my actual consciousness of cross-temporal unities in each single case or even of all inner appearances at once. Rather, it requires merely the capacity to be conscious of my inner appearances as unified across time. Complying with this condition is co-dependent with my capacity to recognize my *numerical identity* across time. Note that this condition is normative, rather than constitutive, for personhood – unlike the condition of a unified consciousness based on transcendental apperception, which is constitutive for any mental act. As will become clear, I can fail to meet this condition on single occasions without thereby failing to be a person altogether.

Due to this normative requirement, the self-formation view differs dramatically from a Humean bundle-of-perceptions view. According to the latter, the self denotes whatever it is that results from the merely arbitrary association of representations in a Humean fashion. On the self-formation view, the multitude of mental states appearing in consciousness is not a mere aggregate or chain of events loosely strung together. Rather, in being a person, I commit myself to realizing a certain form. Therefore, for mental states to contribute to the states of my person, they must occur under the condition of implementing the form of a systematic mental whole. Most basically, this just means that they must belong to one and the same mental whole and that they cannot – arbitrarily or at will – be divided into different wholes, that is, into different personalities. Hence, the self-formation view naturally shows the co-dependence of both the capacity to realize oneself as a person in time and the capacity to be conscious of oneself as such across time.

This a priori demand for trans-temporal unity is, furthermore, a necessary condition of the *capacity to deliberate actions*. In deliberations, especially those concerning major life decisions, we aim to make well-informed choices that reflect who we are, including the personal values and core commitments that we (currently) have. To find out about such personal matters, it would not suffice to consider only our momentary mental states, but we also take account of past experiences and memories, as well as of expectations, fears, and hopes with regard to the future. So to decide on an action we must view ourselves as being the one who underwent those past experiences and who will be affected by and responsible for the consequences of this action in the future. Consider Sophia as a teenager, who, soon to finish high school, now faces the choice of college. In reviewing past experiences, she may first encounter her current reluctant feelings due to her boring music classes in high school, but then remember how excited she was when she first began to take piano lessons. She may realize only in hindsight that she had lost her desire to play the piano during her teenage years, as she got newly involved in her time-consuming hobby of climate activism. Only in consciously attributing these diverse experiences to herself can she come to the informed conclusion that she really is passionate about music, and hence decide to apply to colleges with excellent music programmes. The self-formation view naturally shows the demand for trans-temporal unity to be a necessary condition of the human capacity to act in general and hence of *human agency*.

7.3.3   *A Fundamental Mental Power and Self-Efficacy*

A further condition of *human agency* is the a priori presupposition of a fundamental mental power. To be able to act as a person, I must assume a priori that I – as a whole – am the causal origin of my action and of all action-related representations, such as desires and feelings. Only upon this a priori presupposition can I become causally efficacious in bringing about the unified representation of an intended action and hence in realizing this action.

In Chapter 5, I have argued that only by considering "all powers ... as derived from one unique fundamental power [*Grundkraft*]" can we under-stand ourselves as self-efficacious across all mental faculties and represent ourselves as a "self-sufficient intelligence" from which objective sequences of mental states arise (A682/B710). This principle of a fundamental power is now also understood as an *a priori presupposition* that has *practical efficacy* in a person's life and hence makes a person's self-efficacy first possible. Only in recognizing that the diverse representations that belong to the unified repre-sentation of an action – involving cognitions, desires, and feelings – causally originate in one and the same subject can a person commit herself to this action and hence shape her future life by this action. Only in representing her pleasures regarding music, her desire to practise the piano, her belief that she is a talented piano player, and her knowledge about some college's music programmes as originating from herself can Sophia intend a unified action and dedicate herself to pursuing it in the future. She may of course find other passions, commitments, and beliefs within herself that interfere with this decision. But by a priori presupposing a fundamental power, she views all of these dispositions as being "seated" in herself and considers herself as a whole to have the power to actualize any of them at any time (if not impeded by external constraints). She thus takes herself to have *causal self-efficacy* over her own mental life.

The a priori presupposition of a fundamental mental power that is efficacious across different mental faculties and different psychological dispositions is crucial for the kind of *self-determination* that is essential for persons. To represent oneself as having the capacity for such self-determination requires, in addition to the idea of the soul, the *idea of freedom*. That is, persons have to take themselves to be capable of free action, to have free "*self-activity*" (A418/ B446), and to be able to begin "a series of successive ... states *from itself*" (A448/B476). While I acknowledge the central significance of the idea of freedom for practical personhood, it is not my main concern here. A close examination of the idea of freedom in relation to the idea of the soul has to remain for another investigation.[27]

7.3.4 Personal Identity and Character Development

In the guiding-thread passage, Kant explicitly distinguishes – in addition to the predicates of <simple substance> and <fundamental power> – a further a priori predicate of the soul, namely <personal identity> (see A672/B700, A682/B710). While in many commentaries this predicate is often identified with numerical identity across time, the fact that Kant names it separately from the other two predicates may hint at another a priori presupposition that Kant has in mind. In addition to realizing oneself as a trans-temporal unity across time and as a causal unity across one's mental faculties, a person also ought to realize herself as a unity in a *qualitative* sense.[28] That is, the variety of psychological qualities should be subject to a single *inner principle*. Recall that, in the *Anthropology* and related notes, Kant describes the formation of a character as subjecting one's life under the "absolute unity of the inner principle of conduct" (*Anth* 7:295) and as adopting a "general ruling *principium* ... for the use of his talents and qualities"

---

[27] Munzel (1999:92–107) offers a detailed account of how the faculty of desire is guided by the demand for unity.

[28] Brandt (2003) emphasizes that personal identity involves not only quantitative, but also qualitative aspects.

(*Refl* 1113, 15:496). Hence, the a priori presupposition of personal identity can be understood as a necessary condition for the possibility of personal development and character formation.

When deliberating on her college and career choice, Sophia aims to make a well-informed life choice that reflects her character. So she not only reviews and consciously ascribes to herself a set of diverse experiences, but she also assesses these experiences in light of what she takes herself to be at this point of her life. She evaluates these experiences in light of the values and commitments she identifies with, as well as of the character traits and long-standing passions she finds in herself. This does not exclude the possibility of her deciding to break with her previous habits, values, or commitments. Despite her passion for music, she can decide to pursue her commitment for helping others and apply for a premedical programme instead. She can take her life in a new direction, as it were. In any case, the conscious choice to either continue to live in line with particular personal characteristics or to change these characteristics, perhaps even radically, presupposes the consciousness of one's personal qualities. Such choices require Sophia to be able to make judgements about her more general psychological properties, such as character traits and long-standing attitudes, and to gain more comprehensive self-cognition. More importantly, they require her to understand that it will *be herself* who is affected by her decision. Through her decision, she determines her own future states and psychological properties, as well as the *qualitative* role that each of them will play for her life as a whole.

What her identity "materially" consists in – that is, what her particular psychological features are – may very well partly be beyond her control: it depends on her own psychological development and on the world around her, and is therefore time-dependent and may change over a lifetime. Sophia may, for instance, continue to act on her passion for music and pursue the professional career of a piano player until she decides in her late thirties to go to medical school, because she has lost the passion by then, or because it has been overruled by the commitment for helping others, or because of financial considerations and the felt need of a more stable career path.

On the self-formation view, the presupposition of personal identity is now understood to concern the *qualitative identity* that a person aims to acquire in the course of her life by deciding to act upon certain representations and to supress other representations. In doing so, the person actively decides – at least to some extent – which qualitative roles different psychological features play for her life and hence carves out an individual character. With this presupposition, Kant outlines a notion of personhood that is more demanding than many accounts of personhood today that focus on numerical identity only.

Kant even goes a step further in arguing that a person ought to realize herself as a qualitative unity by submitting all conduct of her life to one and the same "inner principle". That is, a person should strive to become a *Charakter schlechthin* that can be described by a single rational principle. This rational ideal of personhood is precisely what Kant, in other passages, identifies with the call for forming a moral character or a "way of thinking (*Denkungsart*)". While this formation – from the standpoint of inner experience – takes place *in time* and involves a diversity of empirical-psychological determinants, the resulting character can, if self-formation is ultimately successful, be described in purely rational terms. Yet, as Kant points out, not everyone ultimately manages to have a *Charakter schlechthin*. Rather, many of us remain subject to an irreconcilable diversity of guiding principles or lack stable principles altogether.[29]

Let me finally clarify a potential *problem of circularity* that one may detect for the self-formation view.[30] On this view, someone is a person – or has personhood – in an empirically real sense, if – and as long as – she engages in self-formation, that is, if – and as long as – she realizes her mental capacities in accordance with the idea of the soul. At the same time, the *person* is construed as the mental whole that is first and only gradually realized through the exercise of self-formation and hence as the result of such self-formation. To resolve this alleged circularity, it is important to acknowledge that the very activity of self-formation presupposes that there is a subject endowed with mental faculties, without presupposing anything about the inner nature of such subject, except of basic functional definitions of its mental faculties, especially the faculty of reason. The self-formation view then gives an account of the conditions under which such a subject is a person. Being a person just consists in living one's mental life according to the corresponding a priori presuppositions such as substantiality, fundamental power, and personal identity.[31] Only under these a priori presuppositions can a subject experience itself as numerically identical through time and as the causal origin of its mental states. The self-formation view does not offer an explanation for how a subject first enters personhood or how a person first comes into being. It assumes that an individual person exists from the moment in which human conscious mental life sets in, such that mental states are generated under the form of a mental whole. The exact moment in which this first occurs might be difficult to discern. Hence, a person is more properly understood as an *empirical reality in the making*: persons are empirically real in virtue of the mental states by which they are "materially" constituted. And yet, in life, they are always in need of further realization in accordance with an a priori form.

---

[29] For example, *Anth* 7:291. On Kant's account of the weakness and lack of character, see Sturm (2009:418–34).
[30] I thank Marcus Willaschek for raising this issue.
[31] This articulation of the self-formation view is inspired by Marya Schechtman's *person life view*, which she characterizes as saying, "that to be a person is to live a person life" (Schechtman 2014:111), although her account of the basic elements of a person life differs fundamentally from my own.

The self-formation view thus offers an account of the process of individuation through which a person develops in time into an individually determined mental whole – the fully realized *individual person*. This process may never be completed, and during life, the person always falls short of being a whole that could be described by a complete individual self-concept.

This distinction between personhood and individuality raises further questions regarding the normative status of these presuppositions and the extent to which they are actually fulfilled by a person. Can we fail to comply with the norms expressed by the idea of the soul? Can we, for instance, fail to recognize our personal identity? Would we in such a case cease to be persons at all? Finally, is this account of psychological personhood too intellectualist in that many people may fail to meet the high normative standards set by an idea of reason, at least on single occasions, and yet we still want to maintain that they are persons in the full sense?

7.4   A Normative Concept of a Person

In this final section, I at last show why for Kant personhood is essentially normative, and I specify the kind of normativity as a *demand for inner systematicity*. At the beginning of this chapter, I set out with the claim that the idea of the soul provides normative principles for both self-formation and self-knowledge. I now revisit this claim and show, first, that Kant's account of epistemic coherence, based on the principles of systematicity in the *Appendix*, provides a model for understanding the normative demand for inner systematicity that guides self-formation. By expanding the model of epistemic coherence so as to include practical coherence and mental harmony, I develop an account of inner systematicity that provides a normative standard for assessing the success of self-formation as a person, that is, for assessing the extent to which one successfully realizes oneself as a systematic mental whole.

7.4.1   The Normativity of Personhood and Cases of Mental Disunity

What does it mean to say that personhood is essentially normative? A normative account of personhood captures the idea that we often fail to recognize the a priori presuppositions of personhood, yet without thereby failing to be persons altogether. These presumptions do not describe generic features of which it can be empirically proven that a person necessarily instantiates them at all times. Rather, they prescribe goals towards which a person is bound to strive, although these goals can never be fully or adequately realized in a person's mental life.

There are numerous ways of failing to realize oneself as a unified, integrated mental whole. Cases of disunity and disintegration of consciousness can be observed, for instance, in connection with *dissociative* phenomena, in which the person detaches herself from certain beliefs, memories, emotions, or physiological experiences. Mild forms of dissociative episodes include common phenomena such as daydreaming or being absorbed in an activity. In pathological cases, dissociative phenomena involve experiences of distinct identities (or "personality states"), of the fragmentation of identity, of depersonalization, and of dissociative amnesia (memory loss and dementia).[32] All these phenomena severely undermine the idea of a unified self and are often symptoms of mental disorder.

Intuitively, one would certainly not deny people with a *dissociative identity disorder* their personhood. A psychotherapeutic treatment of this disorder aims to uncover the patient's alternative identities and to teach the person to again view herself as a single person. This disorder is often caused by traumatic events during childhood from which the person – as part of a coping strategy – has detached herself. A common practice in psychotherapy is to revisit the traumatic events and retrieve the patient's memory of them, such that the patient can learn how they have affected later stages of her life, and have given rise to the dissociation. It seems that the underlying paradigm of this psychotherapeutic treatment is precisely that a person *ought to* realize herself as a unified self.

The self-formation view accounts for the possibility of a dis-unified mental life as a matter of failing to comply with a rational norm. It implies that reason – via the idea of the soul – does not impose an external normativity onto personhood, that is, an external "ought" that prescribes how we *should* (or *ought to*) live as persons. Rather, the idea of the soul gives expression to the specific kind of normativity that is intrinsic to personhood itself. In serving as the highest genus concept of inner nature, the idea of the soul *describes* how we conceive of ourselves as persons, that is, how we conceive of ourselves as someone who instantiates, or corresponds, or conforms to the *concept of a person*. In turn, the idea *prescribes* what it takes to instantiate, or correspond, or conform to the concept of a person and hence what it takes to do it *well*.[33] The idea of the soul defines a normative standard according to which one can assess the extent to which someone realizes her personhood well. The pathological examples of failing to conform to this standard indicate that realizing oneself as a person is a matter of degree: as long as a minimal degree of

---

[32] See definitions of dissociative symptoms according to the *Diagnostic and Statistical Manual of Mental Disorders* (DSM–5) of the American Psychiatric Association.

[33] Korsgaard, similarly, argues that the concept of a person has an intrinsic normativity, according to which "a good person is good at being a person" (Korsgaard 2009:26). I agree with her account on the importance of a unified agent for personhood, but depart from it in that I do not think that the principles of unity are constitutive of personhood per se, at least not in Kant's sense of constitutive in the Appendix (cf. Korsgaard 2009:133–58, esp. 158). In consequence, my account can accommodate the disunity of involuntary, merely passive aspects of mental life, as well as the failure to integrate one's reflected principles.

rationally guided conscious mental life is going on, we can realize ourselves as persons to a higher or lower degree, to a greater or lesser extent, or just *better* or *worse*.

7.4.2   The Normativity of Personhood as Inner Systematicity

Finally, I explicate this intrinsic normativity of personhood in terms of *inner systematicity*. While Kant develops an account of systematicity mainly with respect to theoretical reason, the notion finds more general application with respect to practical matters and – as I shall argue – with respect to mental life as a whole. A *system*, roughly speaking, is a whole in which all parts have their proper place or function and in which all parts are mutually consistent such that the whole can be said to be systematic.[34]

Kant uses the related notions of *consistency, coherence,* and *harmony* for practical matters. In his moral philosophy, considerations of consistency play a major role in discerning whether one's maxim is consistent with the idea of a universal law and thus in accordance with the moral law.[35] Moreover, Kant's conception of *happiness* centrally draws on the notion of being in a harmonious state internally with respect to one's own desires and ends, as well as externally with respect to the states of others and those of nature.[36] With respect to affective matters, Kant argues that *pleasure* results from susceptibility to the internal harmony of one's mental faculties, and hence that the ground of judgements of beauty is the harmony, or what he calls the free harmonious play, of the cognitive faculties in light of the perception of an object.[37]

Hence, I argue that inner systematicity is composed of, firstly, *epistemic coherence*, which includes logical consistency, as well as conceptual and cognitive coherence; secondly, *practical coherence*, which includes subjective volitional consistency and objective universality; and thirdly, *mental harmony*, which concerns the harmony of the internal faculties that gives rise to pleasant affective responses. A systematic mental whole is then understood as being composed of three conceptually distinct, though materially related spheres: the theoretical sphere (= the subsystem of theoretical cognitions), the practical sphere (= the subsystem of practical principles and motives, i.e., maxims and intentions), and the affective sphere. Each of these spheres has its own

---

[34] See, for example, A833/B861; *CJ First Intro* 20:195, 20:208f., *CJ* 5:257, 359.
[35] For "system" of maxims, see *CJ* 5:274. For other notions, see *Groundwork* 4:429–31, 434; *CpracR* 5:110, and moreover, *MM* 6:233; *TP* 8:293.
[36] See "*Happiness* is the state of a rational being in the world in the whole of whose existence *everything goes according to his wish and will*, and rests, therefore, on the harmony of nature with his whole end as well as with the essential determining ground of his will" (*CpracR* 5:124). See also A800/B828.
[37] See, for example, *CJ* 5:218, 241, 292, 321; *L-Anth/Parow* 25:379.

normative standard based on the specific goal(s) each pursues: truth in the theoretical sphere, happiness and ultimately morality in the practical sphere, and pleasure and ultimately beauty in the affective sphere. The success of self-formation can then be assessed as the composite of the respective degrees of systematicity displayed by one's mental states and more general psychological properties in each sphere.

In seeking self-knowledge, we assess our inner experiences as to their coherence within our system of self-related cognitions and thereby may discover potential incoherencies within our mental life as a whole. So, through seeking self-knowledge, certain *incoherencies* in the theoretical sphere of our cognitions and in the practical sphere of our desires and principles of action, as well as with regard to our overall mental harmony, are first revealed to us. Note that, while the system of self-related cognitions is a subsystem of our system of cognitions in general and hence subject to the normative standard of epistemic coherence, it consists of cognitions whose subject matter concerns *any* spheres of our mental life, including the practical and the emotional spheres. Accordingly, the incoherencies that we discover in seeking self-knowledge may concern, not only our theoretical beliefs, but also our principles of actions and desires, as well as emotional states. Yet the overall normative standard of inner systematicity plays out differently in the different spheres (or "subsystems").

Inner systematicity with respect to the practical sphere is primarily understood as the *practical consistency* of our subjective principles of action, that is, maxims. Onora O'Neill offers an insightful discussion of what such practical consistency with regard to our actions consists in.[38] She first considers the corresponding *practical inconsistency* and distinguishes between "conceptual inconsistency" and "volitional inconsistency" (both in the practical sphere) (O'Neill 1989:89). An agent's maxim is conceptually inconsistent if it involves two contradictory elements and is therefore an impossible aspiration. For instance, the maxim to be both popular and reclusive is conceptually inconsistent. Volitional inconsistency is more complex, and can be understood as a violation of one of several requirements. For instance, a requirement of volitional consistency is that, if one wills a certain action, then one must also will the means that are constitutive of this action. Moreover, if one adopts a set of specific intentions, then volitional consistency requires that these intentions be mutually consistent.[39] For example, recall teenage Sophia in the moment of deciding on her college. Upon reflection, she may find out that she has a strong desire to become a professional piano player, as well as a strong desire to help

---

[38] O'Neill (1989:81–104).

[39] O'Neill (1989:91–2) explicitly distinguishes five requirements: (1) to seek means that are both necessary and sufficient for the action; (2) to seek to make means available when they are not; (3) to seek the constitutive components of an action; (4) to seek mutual consistency within a set of specific intentions; and (5) the requirement that the foreseeable consequences of an action be consistent with the underlying intention.

others in a medical profession. Adopting both desires as intentions of her actions does not involve a literal contradiction, but they may not be practically feasible, since the means necessary for becoming a piano player would conflict with those necessary for becoming a medical doctor. It may thus be volitionally inconsistent to pursue both the career of a professional piano player and that of a medical doctor.

The notion of practical inconsistency does not rule out the *psychological fact* that we have certain desires that may conflict with one another. A common phenomenon of life is to suffer from not being able to satisfy two conflicting desires, but having to settle for satisfying only one of them instead. Rather, the notion of practical inconsistency applies to principles of action. Kant often uses the locutions of "making something my maxim" or of "adopting some-thing as my principle of action", which indicates an "actus of will".[40] Making it my maxim to act upon a particular desire consists in the act of determining my will such that the incentive that drives my action is in accordance with this desire. Practical consistency requires, first of all, that all the general principles of action that I have adopted and hence committed myself to act upon are mutually consistent. In concrete situations, the more specific intentions I form on the basis of such general principles may conflict. For instance, Sophia's role as professional piano player and her role as mother of two children can conflict in concrete situations, though they are in principle consistent with one another. The concrete choice to follow one of them, rather than the other, results in the determination of a higher-order principle of action, for example, the principle of valuing family matters over professional matters. All principles of action are part of one's empirical self-concept. Note that this notion of practical consistency primarily concerns the consistency among the subjective principles of volition that are chosen by a particular person, which I just call *subjective volitional consistency*. It does not yet concern the universalizability of one's maxim, which Kant requires for morally worthy actions.[41]

With respect to the affective sphere, I suggest, we can explicate inner systematicity in terms of an *overall mental harmony*. For Kant, feeling is the overall susceptibility to relations within one's mind, that is, between mental faculties and between their resulting mental states. All feelings together feed into, or are an expression of, the subject's "feeling of life [*Lebensgefühl*]" (*CJ* 5:204). Yet not all feelings are equally constructive in enhancing one's life. Pleasure, or "enjoyment", is "the feeling of promotion of life", whereas dis-pleasure (or pain) is the feeling of "a hindrance of life" (*Anth* 7:231–2).

---

[40] For example, *Groundwork* 4:417; *CpracR* 5:27; *Religion* 6:45; *Anth* 7:295.

[41] Peters (2018) develops a holistic account of *Gesinnung*, broadly in line with my idea of self-formation. By contrast, Willaschek (2009) is sceptical that Kant's account allows for the notion of an individual will and hence for individual standards of inner systematicity.

The ground of pleasure is the harmony that one feels between certain mental faculties. Practical pleasure is the feeling of agreeableness that results from the satisfaction of any desire and hence from the harmony that is felt between one's desire and the determination of one's will (and finally the completion of an action in the world).[42] There are also pleasures that are "attached only to the representation by itself", that is, "contemplative pleasure" or "inactive delight", commonly associated with judgments of taste (*MM* 6:212).[43] Aesthetic pleasure, more specifically, is grounded in the free, harmonious play of the cognitive faculties.

In his *Anthropology* and in his practical writings, Kant also offers a rich phenomenology of unpleasant or painful feelings, such as jealousy, boredom, and sorrow. These are feelings that result from an *inharmonious* relation of mental faculties, or of the resulting mental states.[44] Practical displeasure is the disagreeableness of certain actions, which result in a dislike of or aversion to an object; for instance, the feelings of "anxiety, anguish, horror, and terror" are "degrees of aversion to danger" (*Anth* 7:256). In his moral philosophy, Kant examines more complex affects and passions that include evil inclinations, such as envy, which are particularly destructive for one's moral conduct (see *MM* 6:458).

Central for the current purpose is the idea that the kind, intensity, and duration of feelings can be viewed as expressions of the overall mental harmony of a person and hence as indicators for the overall happiness of a person. Feelings of pleasure and displeasure indicate the degree to which there is an inner harmony among the mental faculties and the extent to which mental states harmonize with one another. Happiness is thus a state in which a person feels an overall harmony, not only with respect to her desires, but with respect to all mental spheres, and hence feels an agreement with her final end.[45]

In sum, inner systematicity – as the normative standard for a person – can now be understood as a combination of epistemic coherence in the theoretical sphere, practical coherence (i.e., subjective volitional consistency) in the practical sphere, and mental harmony, expressed through feelings. In all these spheres, there is a possibility of incoherence, inconsistency, or disharmony. Our means to find out about these incoherencies is through seeking self-knowledge. The discovery of incoherencies is an occasion for the practical efficacy of self-knowledge to come into play. Upon discovering inconsistencies in any of these spheres, a person has the rational impulse to overcome these inconsistencies and harmonize their states. For

[42] For example, *MM* 6:212, *CpracR* 5:9, *CJ* 5:203, 206–9.
[43] See also *CJ* 5:222.
[44] See esp. *Anth* 7:230–50.
[45] Kant frequently invokes the notion of the *final end* (*Endzweck*) of human beings, which he eventually determines as "the human being under moral laws" (*CJ* 5:445); see also *CpracR* 5:124, *MM* 6:441 and *Anth* 7:119.

humans, the discovery of *inner incoherence* is accompanied by painful feelings, such as shame or disgust, since any digression from their inner systematicity feels like a "hindrance" to living the fully coherent life of a person. The pain felt upon such violations of inner systematicity is the ultimate "incentive for activity" (*Stachel der Tätigkeit*) (*Anth* 7:231). As rational beings, we cannot conceive of ourselves other than in accordance with the idea of the soul as a coherent mental whole. Hence, we naturally have a desire to resolve all our incoherencies and to revise those psychological features that stand in conflict with one another, with the aim of forming a coherent mental whole. Seeking self-knowledge turns out to be a condition of self-formation.

With this notion of inner systematicity, we can now more fully understand what it means to form oneself in accordance with the idea of a systematic mental whole. It does not mean that we should never encounter inconsistent beliefs, conflicting desires, or painful feelings that indicate a disharmonious inner state. Rather, it means that we keep being moved by the rational desire to resolve such incoherencies and strive to become a coherent mental whole. All these inconsistent beliefs, conflicting desires, and unpleasant feelings, of course, define aspects of our empirical self-concept; they are properties of ours at a certain time in life. In consequence, the empirical self-concept that we come to acquire on the basis of inner experience is itself a complex system of psychological predicates and may involve internal incoherencies. In committing to being a person, we commit to revising those parts of our mental life that are reflected in those incoherencies and strive to live up to a more internally coherent concept of ourselves. The normative standard of inner systematicity results in a set of maxims of reason: for the theoretical sphere, it consists in the maxim to seek and adopt further beliefs and to revise or even reject inconsistent beliefs; for the practical sphere, in the maxim to further determine oneself by adopting further principles of action and to revise or even reject those principles that are practically inconsistent; for the affective sphere, in the maxim to overcome unpleasant feelings. Again, this does not mean that we simply deny having such feelings, but rather that we acknowledge suffering from these feelings and seek ways of overcoming them. Especially with respect to complex affects, involving immoral inclinations, we ought to prevent them from determining our character and from having practical impact on our future lives. The self-formation of a person does not consist in denying that we undergo a multitude of inharmonious states; rather, it consists in following the demand for resolving the mental disharmony of these states and in living up to the idea of a coherent mental whole. In this sense, the self-formation view of a person, as articulated in this chapter, finally establishes the idea of the soul as the unifying form of personal mental life.

EPILOGUE

Individuality and Wholeness

This book set out to explore what, for Kant, makes us unique individual persons and how we come to know ourselves as such. It has done so by examining levels of representational self-determination and by showing how the bits and pieces of a mental life constitute a unified person. Beginning with the lowest levels of self-affection and inner perception (Chapter 2), it moved to the levels of self-consciousness (Chapter 3), logical self-determination (Chapter 4), and inner experience (Chapter 5), and, finally, arrived at the normative demands that govern both the acquisition of self-knowledge (Chapter 6) and the self-formation as a unified person (Chapter 7). These normative demands are based on the idea of the soul, which has been shown to define the *unifying form of a person's mental life.* It is the idea under which we have to conceive of ourselves as persons and the idea that prescribes what it takes to be a person at all.

The normative concept of a person that this book has defended can be articulated in the form of two imperatives, that is, commands that are binding for all those who recognize themselves as persons, namely the *imperative of self-knowledge* and the *imperative of self-formation.* The *imperative of self-formation* can be formulated just as *seek to be a systematic whole.* To be persons at all, we have to subject ourselves to the normative standard of inner systematicity. This does not mean avoiding any mental dissonance, such as inconsistent beliefs, conflicting desires, or unpleasant feelings, as these states are the "raw material" of our mental life. Rather, it involves recognizing what is true of oneself (at least for the time being), identifying oneself with particular states (i.e., committing to them or making them one's own), and revising or even rejecting those states that do not cohere with these. Through these activities of self-formation, we carve out the standard of inner systematicity in genuinely individual ways.

The acquisition of *self-knowledge* plays a key role in this process of self-formation. A person is bound to a second imperative, which can be simply stated as *know thyself.* Without knowing our current mental states and more general psychological properties, including all momentary inconsistencies, we would not be able to respond to these inconsistencies in adequate ways and to strive towards becoming a coherent whole. In the *Metaphysics of Morals*, Kant himself recognizes the command to "*know* (scrutinize, fathom) *yourself*" as a "dut[y] to oneself" (*MM* 6:441), which if followed successfully results "in the harmony of a being's will with its final end" (*MM* 6:441). On the self-formation view, this command is an intrinsic normative condition of being a person at all. The ultimate wisdom gained through self-knowledge aligns with the ultimate harmony of being a whole.

In my presentation of the self-formation view I have not taken into consideration whether the whole that a person seeks to become is *good* in itself. Moreover, I have not examined whether the individual standard of inner systematicity that a person develops through her acts of self-determination must – due to the very nature of rational beings – strive towards a morally good standard, or whether a person can choose to digress, perhaps even radically, from the universal moral law and nonetheless progressively realize herself as a coherent mental whole. These moral questions would need to be answered to expand the current view to an account of practical personhood.

For Kant, the answer to these questions is given by his specific conception of *pure* practical reason. Pure practical reason is conceived of as an autonomous practical will, which is the giver of the objectively valid moral law. The moral law that follows from this objective conception of pure practical reason is the categorical imperative, which can be explicated as a command for universalizability: a moral action requires that the maxim behind the action is universalizable. The soul as a transcendental idea of reason can be understood as an integral part of this conception of pure practical reason. Kant himself explicates moral implications of this idea in the Postulate of the Immortality of the Soul, which go beyond its regulative use in inner experience. There, Kant argues that only "an *endless progress* toward [the] complete conformity" with the moral law can guarantee the realizability of the highest good, and this implies the presupposition of an endless existence of the "personality of the same rational being" (*CpracR* 5:122). According to Kant, the demands of the moral law are binding for all humans qua rational beings, as are the demands of seeking the truth. This suggests that the objective standard of morality sets limits to possible individual standards of inner systematicity. Yet since morality cannot fully determine the specific content of our lives, we are still called to fill out our existences in *genuinely individual* ways, though always within the constraints of objective moral laws.

An account of practical personhood can, then, be expanded by appealing to a refined distinction between a moral, ethical, and pragmatic use of reason, as suggested by Jürgen Habermas.[1] The *moral use* of reason is universally and necessarily binding; the *ethical use* considers the values of historically developed ethical communities, including their cultural practices and traditions, and the *pragmatic use* concerns the standards that are bound to particular life

---

[1] Habermas (1991).

choices and to the adoption of particular social roles. These three uses of practical reason have a hierarchical order, with the moral use being the most general. The pragmatic use is most important for adopting an individual way of life (*Lebensform, Lebensentwurf*) and for acquiring an individual self-understanding (*Selbstverständnis*).

By arguing for the self-formation view, the book has shown that Kant's Critical Philosophy can accommodate the notion of genuine individuality in accordance with his universalistic conception of reason. Being a genuinely individual person involves committing oneself to becoming an individual mental whole. It involves committing oneself to a self-concept by recognizing the normative standards that come with one's choices. As long as a person recognizes a particular commitment, value, or principle of action *as her own*, this commitment, value, or principle will be binding for her, and her success in realizing herself as a person will be measured by her individual standard for being this particular person. A person may of course choose differently at different times. This issue raises exciting questions regarding the possibility of personal change and transformation – questions that will have to remain for a further investigation.

Regardless of all our individual choices, by being a person, we commit ourselves to integrating our conscious mental life into a coherent whole. We commit ourselves to the imperatives of self-formation (*Seek to be a whole*) and of self-knowledge (*Know thyself*). It is in this sense, I believe, that we can acknowledge all our failures and weaknesses, as well as all our successes and accomplishments, the tragedies of our lives and the moments of sheer luck, as well as everything in between, as belonging to our personal lives and as shaping us as individual persons. We do so in the *hope* that all will come together in the end and that each and every part of our lives will eventually find its proper place within the whole – a hope that can and will never be fully realized as long as we live, but which always remains the ideal towards which we as persons must unswervingly strive. The idea of the soul gives expression to this hope – the hope that we will become individual harmonious wholes, rather than fragments loosely strung together. It is this hope that drives our personal lives, because "reason is driven by a propensity of its nature ... to find peace only in the completion of its circle in a self-subsisting systematic whole" (A797/B825).

BIBLIOGRAPHY

Primary Literature

All references are according to *Kants gesammelte Schriften*, edited by the Königlich Preußischen Akademie der Wissenschaften (Ak.), 29 vols. (Berlin: De Gruyter, 1902–).

I usually provide the *Akademie* page number. With respect to the *Critique of Pure Reason*, I employ the standard A/B pagination.

Abbreviations

In citing Kant's text the following abbreviations are used.

Anth	*Anthropology from a Pragmatic Point of View* (1798) (Ak., vol. 7)
CJ	*Critique of the Power of Judgment* (1790) (Ak., vol. 5)
CJ First Intro	First Introduction to the *Critique of the Power of Judgment* (1790) (Ak., vol. 20)
Conjectural Beginning	*Conjectural Beginning of Human History* (1786) (Ak., vol. 8)
CpR	*Critique of Pure Reason* (1781/1787) (Ak., vols. 3–4)
CpracR	*Critique of Practical Reason* (1788) (Ak., vol. 5)
Discovery	*On a Discovery Whereby Any New Critique of Pure Reason Is to Be Made Superfluous by an Older One* (1790) (Ak., vol. 8)
Dissertation	*Inaugural Dissertation* (1770) (Ak., vol. 2)
Dreams	*Dreams of a Spirit Seer (Elucidated by the Dreams of Metaphysics)* (1766) (Ak., vol. 2)
Enlightenment	*An Answer to the Question: What Is Enlightenment?* (1784) (Ak., vol. 8)
Groundwork	*Groundwork of the Metaphysics of Moral* (1785) (Ak., vol. 4)
Idea	*Idea for a Universal History with a Cosmopolitan Purpose* (1784) (Ak., vol. 8)
L-Anth	*Lectures on Anthropology*

L-Anth/Busolt	*Anthropology Busolt* (1788–9) (Ak., vol. 25)
L-Anth/Collins	*Anthropology Collins* (1772–3) (Ak., vol. 25)
L-Anth/Friedländer	*Anthropology Friedländer* (1775–6) (Ak., vol. 25)
L-Anth/Mrongovius	*Anthropology Mrongovius* (1784–5) (Ak., vol. 25)
L-Anth/Parow	*Anthropology Parow* (1772–3) (Ak., vol. 25)
L-Anth/Philippi	*Anthropology Philippi* (1772–3) (not included in the Ak.)
L-Anth/Pillau	*Anthropology Pillau* (1777–8) (Ak., vol. 25)
L-Log	*Lectures on Logic*
L-Log/Blomberg	*Logic Blomberg* (1780s) (Ak., vol. 24)
L-Log/Dohna-Wundlacken	*Logic Dohna-Wundlacken* (1780s) (Ak., vol. 24)
L-Log/Jäsche	*Jäsche Logic* (1800) (Ak., vol. 9)
L-Log/Philippi	*Logic Philippi* (1770s) (Ak., vol. 24)
L-Log/Pölitz	*Logic Pölitz* (1780s) (Ak., vol. 24)
L-Log/Vienna	*Logic Vienna* (1780s) (Ak., vol. 24)
L-MP	*Lectures on Metaphysics*
L-MP/Dohna	*Metaphysics Dohna* (1792–3) (Ak., vol. 28)
L-MP/Herder	*Metaphysics Herder* (1762–4) (Ak., vol. 28)
L-MP/K$_2$	*Metaphysics K$_2$* (early 1790s) (Ak., vol. 28)
L-MP/L$_1$	*Metaphysics L$_1$* (*Metaphysics Pölitz*) (mid-1770s) (Ak., vol. 28)
L-MP/L$_2$	*Metaphysics L$_2$* (1790–1?) (Ak., vol. 28)
L-MP/Mrongovius	*Metaphysics Mrongovius* (1782–3) (Ak., vol. 29)
L-MP/Schön	*Metaphysics von Schön* (late 1780s?) (Ak., vol. 28)
L-MP/ Vigilantius	*Metaphysics Vigilantius* (*K$_3$*) (1794–5) (Ak., vol. 29)
L-MP/Volckmann	*Metaphysics Volckmann* (1784–5) (Ak., vol. 28)
LB-Leningrad	*Loses Blatt Leningrad I* (*Vom inneren Sinn*) (1780–90?) (not included in the Ak.; In Reinhardt Brandt and Werner Stark (eds.) (1987). *Kant-Forschungen* I. Hamburg: Meiner. 18–27.)
MFNS	*Metaphysical Foundations of Natural Science* (1786) (Ak., vol. 4)
MM	*Metaphysics of Morals* (1797) (Ak., vol. 6)
ND	*Nova Dilucidatio* (*New Elucidation of the First Principles of Metaphysical Cognition*) (1755) (Ak., vol. 1)
OP	*Opus Postumum* (1804) (Ak., vol. 21/22)
Orient	*What Does It Mean to Orient Oneself in Thinking?* (1786) (Ak., vol. 8)
Prize	*Prize Essay* (*Inquiry Concerning the Distinctness of the Principles of Natural Theology and Morality*) (1764) (Ak., vol. 2)

Progress	*What Real Progress Has Metaphysics Made in Germany since the Time of Leibniz and Wolff?* (1793/ 1804) (Ak., vol. 20)
Prol	*Prolegomena to Any Future Metaphysics That Will Be Able to Come Forward as a Science* (1783) (Ak., vol. 4)
Refl	*Reflections* (Ak., vols. 14–19, 23)
Religion	*Religion within the Boundaries of Mere Reason* (1793) (Ak., vol. 6)
Soemmering	*From Soemmering's* On the organ of the soul (1796) (Ak., vol. 12)
Subtlety	*The False Subtlety of the Four Syllogistic Figures* (1762) (Ak., vol. 2)
TP	*On the Common Saying: That May Be True in Theory, But It Is of No Use in Practice* (1793) (Ak., vol. 8)

English Translations

English translations are according to *The Cambridge Edition of the Works of Immanuel Kant,* edited by P. Guyer and A. Wood (Cambridge: Cambridge University Press, 1992–).

Kant, Immanuel (1999). *Critique of Pure Reason.* Trans. Paul Guyer and Allen W. Wood. Cambridge: Cambridge University Press.

Kant, Immanuel (1999). *Practical Philosophy.* Trans. Mary J. Gregor and Allen W. Wood. Cambridge: Cambridge University Press.

Kant, Immanuel (2000). *Critique of the Power of Judgment.* Trans. Paul Guyer and Eric Matthews). Cambridge: Cambridge University Press.

Kant, Immanuel (2001). *Lectures on Metaphysics.* Trans. Karl Ameriks and Steve Naragon. Cambridge: Cambridge University Press.

Kant, Immanuel (2003). *Theoretical Philosophy, 1755–1770.* Trans. David Walford and Ralf Meerbote. Cambridge: Cambridge University Press.

Kant, Immanuel (2004). *Lectures on Logic.* Trans. Michael J. Young. Cambridge: Cambridge University Press.

Kant, Immanuel (2004). *Metaphysical Foundations of Natural Science.* Trans. Michael Friedman. Cambridge: Cambridge University Press.

Kant, Immanuel (2010). *Notes and Fragments.* Trans. Paul Guyer, Curtis Bowman, and Frederick Rauscher. Cambridge: Cambridge University Press.

Kant, Immanuel (2010). *Theoretical Philosophy after 1781.* Trans. Henry Allison, Peter Heath, Gary Hatfield, and Michael Friedman. Cambridge: Cambridge University Press.

Kant, Immanuel (2011). *Anthropology, History, and Education.* Trans. Günter Zöller and Robert B. Louden. Cambridge: Cambridge University Press.

Kant, Immanuel (2013). *Lectures on Anthropology.* Trans. Robert B. Louden, Allen W. Wood, Robert R. Clewis, and G. Felicitas Munzel. Cambridge: Cambridge University Press.

Other Works and Secondary Literature

Abela, Paul (2006). "The Demands of Systematicity: Rational Judgment and the Structure of Nature". In Graham Bird (ed.) *A Companion to Kant*. Oxford: Blackwell. 408–22.

Allais, Lucy (2009). "Kant, Non-Conceptual Content and the Representation of Space". *Journal of the History of Philosophy* 47: 383–413.

Allais, Lucy (2015). *Manifest Reality: Kant's Idealism and His Realism*. Oxford: Oxford University Press.

Allison, Henry E. (2000). "Where Have All the Categories Gone? Reflections on Longuenesse's Reading of Kant's Transcendental Deduction". *Inquiry* 43(1): 81–90.

Allison, Henry E. (2004). *Kant's Transcendental Idealism* (2nd ed.). New Haven: Yale University Press.

Allison, Henry E. (2015). *Kant's Transcendental Deduction: An Analytical-Historical Commentary*. Oxford: Oxford University Press.

Ameriks, Karl (1978). "Kant's Transcendental Deduction as a Regressive Argument". *Kant-Studien* 69: 273–87.

Ameriks, Karl (2000). *Kant's Theory of Mind* (2nd ed.). Oxford: Clarendon Press.

Anderson, R. Lanier (2014). *The Poverty of Conceptual Truth*. Oxford: Oxford University Press.

Appiah, K. Anthony (2017). *As If: Idealization and Ideals*. Cambridge, MA: Harvard University Press.

Aristotle (c.350 BCE/2016). *Aristotle's "De Anima"*. Trans. with commentary Christopher Shields. Oxford: Clarendon Press.

Armstrong, David (1968). *A Materialist Theory of the Mind*. London: Routledge.

Augustine of Hippo (397–8/2008). *Saint Augustine: Confessions*. Trans. Henry Chadwick. Oxford: Oxford University Press.

Austin, John L. (1962). *How to Do Things with Words*. Oxford: Clarendon Press.

Bar-On, Dorit (2004). *Speaking My Mind: Expression and Self-Knowledge*. Oxford: Oxford University Press.

Baumgarten, Alexander G. (1739/2011). *Metaphysica*. Ed. and trans. Günter Gawlick and Lothar Kreimendahl. Stuttgart-Bad Cannstatt: Frommann-Holzboog.

Beck, Lewis W. (1978/1986). "Did the Sage of Königsberg Have No Dreams?" In Lewis W. Beck, *Essays on Kant and Hume*. New Haven/London: Yale University Press. 38–60.

Bennett, Jonathan (1966). *Kant's Analytic*. Cambridge: Cambridge University Press.

Bird, Graham (2000). "The Paralogisms and Kant's Account of Psychology". *Kant-Studien* 91: 129–45.

Bird, Graham (2006). *The Revolutionary Kant*. Chicago: Open Court.

Blackwell, Richard J. (1961). "Christian Wolff's Doctrine of the Soul". *Journal of the History of Ideas* 22(3): 339–54.

Boyle, Matthew (2009). "Two Kinds of Self-Knowledge". *Philosophy and Phenomenological Research* 78(1): 133–64.

Brandt, Reinhardt (1999). *Kritischer Kommentar zu Kants "Anthropologie in pragmatischer Hinsicht"*. Hamburg: Meiner.

Brandt, Reinhardt (2003). "The Guiding Idea of Kant's Anthropology and the Vocation of the Human Being". In Brian Jacobs and Patrick Kain (eds.) *Essays on Kant's Anthropology*. Cambridge: Cambridge University Press. 85–104.

Breitenbach, Angela (2009). *Die Analogie von Vernunft und Natur*. Berlin/New York: De Gruyter.

Breitenbach, Angela (2014). "Biological Purposiveness and Analogical Reflection". In Ina Goy and Eric Watkins (eds.) *Kant's Theory of Biology*. Berlin/New York: De Gruyter. 131–48.

Brook, Andrew (1994). *Kant and the Mind*. New York/Cambridge: Cambridge University Press.

Buchdahl, Gerd (1967). "The Relation between 'Understanding' and 'Reason'". *Proceedings of the Aristotelian Society* 67: 209–26.

Buchdahl, Gerd (1969). *Metaphysics and the Philosophy of Science: The Classical Origins – Descartes to Kant*. Oxford: Basil Blackwell.

Buchdahl, Gerd (1971). "The Conception of Lawlikeness in Kant's Philosophy of Science". *Synthese* 23(1): 24–46.

Callanan, John (2008). "Kant on Analogy". *British Journal for the History of Philosophy* 16(4): 747–72.

Carl, Wolfgang (1989). *Der schweigende Kant. Die Entwürfe zu einer Deduktion der Kategorien vor 1781*. Göttingen: Vandenhoeck & Ruprecht.

Carl, Wolfgang (1992). *Die Transzendentale Deduktion der Kategorien in der ersten Auflage der "Kritik der reinen Vernunft": Ein Kommentar*. Frankfurt a. M.: Klostermann.

Carl, Wolfgang (1997). "Apperception and Spontaneity". *International Journal of Philosophical Studies* 5: 147–63.

Carl, Wolfgang (1998). "Ich und Spontanität". In Marcelo Stamm (ed.) *Philosophie in Synthetischer Absicht*. Stuttgart: Klett-Cotta. 105–22.

Carl, Wolfgang (2014). *The First-Person View*. Berlin: De Gruyter.

Carruthers, Peter (2001/2016). *Stanford Encyclopedia of Philosophy*, s.v. Higher-order Theories of Consciousness. http://plato.stanford.edu/entries/consciousness-higher

Cary, Philip (2000). *Augustine's Invention of the Inner Self*. Oxford: Oxford University Press.

Cassam, Quassim (1993). "Inner Sense, Body Sense, and Kant's 'Refutation of Idealism'". *European Journal of Philosophy* 1: 111–27.

Cassam, Quassim (1997). *Self and World*. Oxford: Oxford University Press.

Castañeda, Hector-Neri (1967). "On the Logic of Self-Knowledge". *Noûs* 1(1): 9–21.

Chignell, Andrew (2007). "Belief in Kant". *Philosophical Review* 116(3): 323–60.

Chignell, Andrew (2014). "Modal Motivations for Noumenal Ignorance: Knowledge, Cognition, and Coherence". *Kant-Studien* 105(4): 573–97.

Chignell, Andrew (2017). "Can't Kant Cognize Himself?" In Anil Gomes and Andrew Stephenson (eds.) *Kant and the Philosophy of Mind*. Oxford: Oxford University Press. 138–57.

Ciami, Mario (1995). "Über eine wenig beachtete Deduktion der regulativen Ideen". *Kant-Studien* 86: 308–20.

Cohen, Alix (2009). *Kant and the Human Sciences: Biology, Anthropology and History*. London: Palgrave Macmillan.

Cohen, Hermann (1885). *Kants Theorie der Erfahrung*. Berlin: Dümmler.

Coliva, Annalisa (2016). *The Varieties of Self-Knowledge*. London: Palgrave Macmillan.

Collins, Arthur W. (1999). *Possible Experience: Understanding Kant's Critique of Pure Reason*. Berkeley/London: University of California Press.

Cramer, Konrad (1985). *Nicht-reine synthetische Urteile a priori. Ein Problem der Transzendentalphilosophie Immanuel Kants*. Heidelberg: Carl Winter.

Descartes, René (1641/1996). *Descartes: Meditations on First Philosophy*. Ed. and trans. John Cottingham. Cambridge: Cambridge University Press.

De Vleeschauwer, Herman J. (1976). *La Déduction transcendentale dans l'œuvre de Kant*. 3 vols. New York: Garland.

DeWitt, Janelle (2018). "Feeling and Inclination". In Kelly Sorensen and Diane Williamson (eds.) *Kant and the Faculty of Feeling*. Cambridge: Cambridge University Press. 67–87.

Düsing, Klaus (1997). *Selbstbewusstseinsmodelle: Moderne Kritiken und systematische Entwürfe zur konkreten Subjektivität*. München: Fink.

Düsing, Klaus (2010). "Apperzeption und Selbstaffektion in Kants 'Kritik der reinen Vernunft'. Das Kernstück der 'transcendentalen Deduktion' der Kategorien". In Norbert Fischer (ed.) *Kants Grundlegung einer kritischen Metaphysik. Einführung in die "Kritik der reinen Vernunft"*. Hamburg: Meiner. 139–53.

Dyck, Corey (2006). "Empirical Consciousness Explained: Self-Affection, (Self-) Consciousness and Perception in the B Deduction". *Kantian Review* 11: 26–54.

Dyck, Corey (2009). "The Divorce of Reason and Experience: Kant's Paralogisms of Pure Reason in Context". *Journal of the History of Philosophy* 47: 249–75.

Dyck, Corey (2014). *Kant and Rational Psychology*. Oxford: Oxford University Press.

Dyck, Corey (2016). "The Scope of Inner Sense: Development of Kant's Psychology in the Silent Decade". *Con-textos Kantianos* 3: 326–44.

Dyck, Corey and Wunderlich, Falk (eds.) (2017). *Kant and His Contemporaries*. Cambridge: Cambridge University Press.

Emundts, Diana (2007). "Kant über innere Erfahrung". In U. Kern (ed.) *Was ist und was soll sein: Natur und Freiheit bei Immanuel Kant*. Berlin: De Gruyter. 191–205.

Emundts, Diana (2010). "The Refutation of Idealism and the Distinction between Phenomena and Noumena". In Paul Guyer (ed.) *Cambridge Companion to Kant's "Critique of Pure Reason"*. Cambridge: Cambridge University Press. 168–89.

Emundts, Dina (2017). "Kant's Ideal of Self-Knowledge". In Ursula Renz (ed.) *Self-Knowledge: A History*. Oxford: Oxford University Press. 183–98.

Engstrom, Stephen (2009). *The Form of Practical Knowledge*. Cambridge, MA: Harvard University Press.

Evans, Gary (1982). "Self-Identification". In John McDowell (ed.) *Varieties of Reference*. Oxford: Oxford University Press. 205–66.

Falduto, Antonio (2014). *The Faculties of the Human Mind and the Case of Moral Feelings*. De Gruyter: Berlin.

Falkenstein, Lorne (1995). *Kant's Intuitionism: A Commentary on the Transcendental Aesthetic*. Toronto: University of Toronto Press.

Ferrarin, Alfredo (2015). *The Powers of Pure Reason*. Chicago: Chicago University Press.

Fichte, Johann Gottlieb (1794/1997). *Grundlage der gesamten Wissenschaftslehre als Handschrift für seine Zuhörer*. Hamburg: Meiner.

Finkelstein, David H. (2003). *Expression and the Inner*. Cambridge, MA: Harvard University Press.

Förster, Eckart (1987). "Is There a Gap in Kant's Critical System?" *Journal of the History of Philosophy* 25: 533–55.

Frank, Manfred (1991). *Selbstbewußtsein und Selbsterkenntnis: Essays zur analytischen Philosophie der Subjektivität*. Stuttgart: Reclam.

Frank, Manfred (2007). "Non-Objectal Subjectivity". *Journal of Consciousness Studies* 14(5–6): 152–73.

Frank, Manfred (2011). *Ansichten der Subjektivität*. Frankfurt a. M.: Suhrkamp.

Freitag, Wolfgang (2018). "Wittgenstein on 'I Believe'". *Grazer Philosophische Studien* 95(1): 54–69.

Freitag, Wolfgang and Kraus, Katharina (2020). "An Expressivist Interpretation of Kant's 'I think'". *Noûs*. https://doi.org/10.1111/nous.12350

Friedman, Michael (2013). *Kant's Construction of Nature: A Reading of the Metaphysical Foundations of Natural Science*. Cambridge: Cambridge University Press.

Frierson, Patrick (2009a). "Kant on Mental Disorder 1: An Overview". *History of Psychiatry* 20: 267–89.

Frierson, Patrick (2009b). "Kant on Mental Disorder 2: Philosophical Implications". *History of Psychiatry* 20: 290–310.

Frierson, Patrick (2014). *Kant's Empirical Psychology*. Cambridge: Cambridge University Press.

García-Carpintero and Torre, Stephen (eds.) (2016). *About Oneself. De Se Thought and Communication*. Oxford: Oxford University Press.

Geiger, Ido (2003). "Is the Assumption of a Systematic Whole of Empirical Concepts a Necessary Condition of Knowledge?" *Kant-Studien* 94: 273–98.

Geiger, Ido (2009). "Is Teleological Judgment (Still) Necessary? Kant's Arguments in the Analytic and in the Dialectic of Teleological Judgment". *British Journal for the History of Philosophy* 17: 533–66.

Gennaro, Rocco (1999). "Leibniz on Consciousness and Self-Consciousness". In Rocco Gennaro and Charles Huenemann (eds.) *New Essays on the Rationalists*. Oxford: Oxford University Press. 353–71.

Ginsborg, Hannah (2006). "Empirical Concepts and the Content of Experience". *European Journal of Philosophy* 14: 349–72.

Ginsborg, Hannah (2008). "Was Kant a Nonconceptualist?" *Philosophical Studies* 137: 65–77.

Ginsborg, Hannah (2017). "Why Must We Presuppose the Systematicity of Nature?" In Michela Massimi and Angela Breitenbach (eds.) *Kant and the Laws of Nature*. Cambridge: Cambridge University Press. 71–88.

Goldman, Avery (2007). "Critique and the Mind: Towards a Defense of Kant's Transcendental Method". *Kant-Studien* 98(4): 403–17.

Goldman, Avery (2012). *Kant and the Subject of Critique: On the Regulative Role of the Psychological Idea*. Bloomington: Indiana University Press.

Golob, Sacha (2014). "Kant on Intentionality, Magnitude, and the Unity of Perception". *European Journal of Philosophy* 22(4): 505–28.

Gouaux, Charles (1972). "Kant's View on the Nature of Empirical Psychology". *Journal of the History of the Behavioral Sciences* 8: 237–42.

Green, Gareth (2010). *The Aporia of Inner Sense*. Leiden/Boston: Brill.

Grier, Michelle (1993). "Illusion and Fallacy in Kant's First Paralogism". *Kant-Studien* 83: 257–82.

Grier, Michelle (1997). "Kant on the Illusion of a Systematic Unity of Knowledge". *History of Philosophy Quarterly* 14: 1–28.

Grier, Michelle (2001). *Kant's Doctrine of Transcendental Illusion*. Cambridge: Cambridge University Press.

Grüne, Stefanie (2009). *Blinde Anschauung: Die Rolle von Begriffen in Kants Theorie sinnlicher Synthesis*. Frankfurt a. M.: Klostermann.

Grüne, Stefanie (2017). "Givenness, Objective Reality, and A Priori Intuitions". *Journal of the History of Philosophy* 55(1): 113–30.

Grünewald, Bernward (2009). *Geist – Kultur – Gesellschaft: Versuch einer Prinzipientheorie der Geisteswissenschaften auf transzendentalphilosophischer Grundlage*. Berlin: Duncker & Humblot.

Guyer, Paul (1979). *Kant and the Claims of Taste*. Cambridge: Cambridge University Press.

Guyer, Paul (1987). *Kant and the Claims of Knowledge*. Cambridge: Cambridge University Press.

Guyer, Paul (1990). "Reason and Reflective Judgment: Kant on the Significance of Systematicity". *Noûs* 24: 17–43.

Guyer, Paul (2003). "Kant on the Systematicity of Nature: Two Puzzles". *History of Philosophy Quarterly* 20(3): 277–95.

Haag, Johannes (2007). *Erfahrung und Gegenstand: Das Verhältnis von Sinnlichkeit und Verstand*. Frankfurt a. M.: Klostermann.

Habermas, Jürgen (1991). "Vom pragmatischen, ethischen und moralischen Gebrauch der praktischen Vernunft". In Jürgen Habermas, *Diskursethik – Philosophische Texte Band 3*. Frankfurt a. M.: Suhrkamp.

Hanna, Robert (2001). *Kant and the Foundations of Analytical Philosophy*. Oxford: Oxford University Press.

Hanna, Robert (2005). "Kant and Nonconceptual Content". *European Journal of Philosophy* 13: 247–90.

Hatfield, Gary (2006). "Empirical, Rational, and Transcendental Psychology: Psychology as Science and as Philosophy". In Paul Guyer (ed.) *The Cambridge Companion to Kant*. Cambridge: Cambridge University Press. 200–27.

Heidegger, Martin (1929/1990). *Kant und das Problem der Metaphysik*. Frankfurt a. M.: Klostermann. (English translation: Richard Taft (trans.) (1990) *Kant and the Problem of Metaphysics*. Bloomington: Indiana University Press.

Heidemann, Dietmar H. (1998). *Kant und das Problem des metaphysischen Idealismus*. Berlin: De Gruyter.

Heidemann, Dietmar H. (2001). "Innerer und äußerer Sinn. Kants Konstitutionstheorie empirischen Selbstbewusstseins". In Volker Gerhardt, Rolf-Peter Horstmann and Ralph Schumacher (eds.) *Kant und die Berliner Aufklärung. Akten des IX. Internationalen Kant-Kongresses*, Vol. 2. Berlin/ New York: De Gruyter. 305–13.

Helfer, Martha (1996). *The Retreat of Representation: The Concept of Darstellung in German Critical Discourse*. Albany, NY: State University of New York Press.

Heller-Roazen, Daniel (2007). *The Inner Touch: Archaeology of a Sensation*. New York: Zone Books.

Henning, Tim (2010). "Kant und die Logik des 'Ich denke'". *Zeitschrift für philosophische Forschung* 64(3): 331–56.

Henrich, Dieter (1967). *Fichtes ursprüngliche Einsicht*. Frankfurt a. M.: Klostermann.

Henrich, Dieter (1969). "The Proof-Structure of Kant's Transcendental Deduction". *Review of Metaphysics* 22(4): 640–59.

Henrich, Dieter (1976). *Identität und Objektivität: Eine Untersuchung über Kants transzendentale Deduktion*. Heidelberg: Winter.

Henrich, Dieter (1994). *The Unity of Reason: Essays on Kant's Philosophy*. Cambridge, MA: Harvard University Press.

Heßbrüggen-Walter, Stefan (2004). *Die Seele und ihre Vermögen: Kant's Metaphysik des Mentalen in der "Kritik der reinen Vernunft"*. Paderborn: Mentis.

Hölder, Alfred (1873). *Darstellung der Kantischen Erkenntnistheorie mit besonderer Berücksichtigung der verschiedenen Fassungen der transscendentalen Deduction der Kategorien*. Tübingen: Laupp.

Hoppe, Hansgeorg (1983). *Synthesis bei Kant: Das Problem der Verbindung von Vorstellungen und ihrer Gegenstandsbeziehung in der "Kritik der reinen Vernunft"*. Berlin/New York: De Gruyter.

Horstmann, Rolf-Peter (1989). "Why Must There Be a Transcendental Deduction in Kant's *Critique of Judgment*?". In Eckart Förster (ed.) *Kant's Transcendental Deductions: The Three "Critiques" and the "Opus Postumum"*. Stanford, CA: Stanford University Press. 157–79.

Horstmann, Rolf-Peter (1993). "Kants Paralogismen". *Kant-Studien* 83: 408–25.

Horstmann, Rolf-Peter (2018). *Kant's Power of Imagination*. Cambridge: Cambridge University Press.

Howell, Robert (1992). *Kant's Transcendental Deduction*. Dordrecht: Kluwer.

Howell, Robert (2001). "Kant, the 'I Think', and Self-Awareness". In Cicovacki, Predrag (ed.) *Kant's Legacy: Essays in Honor of Lewis White Beck*. Rochester, NY: University of Rochester Press. 117–52.

Hudson, Hud (1994). *Kant's Compatibilism*. Ithaca, NY: Cornell University Press.

Hume, David (1740/1978). *A Treatise on Human Nature*. Eds. Lewis A. Selby-Bigge and Peter H. Nidditch. Oxford: Oxford University Press.

Husserl, Edmund (1900/1975). *Logische Untersuchungen. Erster Band: Prolegomena zur reinen Logik*. In Elmar Holenstein (ed.) *Husserliana XVIII*. The Hague: Nijhoff.

Husserl, Edmund (1928). *Vorlesungen zur Phänomenologie des inneren Zeitbewußtseins*. Ed. Martin Heidegger. Halle: Niemeyer.

Husserl, Edmund (1931/1988). *Cartesian Meditations*. Trans. Dorion Cairns. Dordrecht: Kluwer.

Indregard, Jonas Jervell (2017). "Self-Affection and Pure Intuition in Kant". *Australasian Journal of Philosophy* 95(4): 627–43.

Indregard, Jonas Jervell (2018). "Consciousness as Inner Sensation: Crusius and Kant". *Ergo* 5(7): 173–201.

Jacob, Pierre (2019). *Stanford Encyclopedia of Philosophy*, s.v. Intentionality. https://plato.stanford.edu/entries/intentionality

Jankowiak, Tim (2014). "Sensations as Representations in Kant". *British Journal for the History of Philosophy* 22(3): 492–513.

Jorgensen, Larry M. (2011). "Leibniz on Memory and Consciousness". *British Journal for the History of Philosophy* 19(5): 887–916.

Kannisto, Toni (2016). "*Positio contra complementum possibilitatis* – Kant and Baumgarten on Existence". *Kant-Studien* 107(2): 291–313.

Kaplan, David (1989). "Demonstratives". In Joseph Almog, John Perry and Howard Wettstein (eds.) *Themes from Kaplan*. New York: Oxford University Press. 481–563.

Keller, Pierre (1995). "Personal Identity and Kant's Third Person Perspective". *Idealistic Studies* 24(2): 123–46.

Keller, Pierre (1998). *Kant and the Demands of Self-Consciousness*. Cambridge: Cambridge University Press.

Kemp Smith, Norman (1930). *A Commentary to Kant's "Critique of Pure Reason"*. London: Macmillan.

Kitcher, Patrica (1984). "Kant's Real Self". In Allen Wood (ed.) *Kant on Self and Nature*. Ithaca, NY: Cornell University Press. 113–47.

Kitcher, Patricia (1990). *Kant's Transcendental Psychology*. Oxford: Oxford University Press.

Kitcher, Patricia (1999). "Kant on Self-consciousness". *Philosophical Review* 108 (3): 345–86.

Kitcher, Patricia (2011). *Kant's Thinker*. Oxford: Oxford University Press.

Kitcher, Philip (1986). "Projecting the Order of Nature". In Robert Butts (ed.) *Kant's Philosophy of Physical Science*. Dordrecht: Reidel. 201–35.

Klemme, Heiner (1996). *Kants Philosophie des Subjekts*. Hamburg: Meiner.

Korsgaard, Christine (2008). *The Constitution of Agency*. Oxford: Oxford University Press.

Korsgaard, Christine (2009). *Self-Constitution: Agency, Identity, and Integrity*. Oxford: Oxford University Press.

Kraus, Katharina (2016). "Quantifying Inner Experience? – Kant's Mathematical Principles in the Context of Empirical Psychology". *European Journal of Philosophy* 24(2): 331–57.

Kraus, Katharina (2018). "The Soul as the 'Guiding Idea' of Psychology: Kant on Scientific Psychology, Systematicity, and the Idea of the Soul". *Studies in History and Philosophy of Science* 71: 77–88.

Kraus, Katharina (2019a). "The Parity and Disparity between Inner and Outer Experience in Kant". *Kantian Review* 24(2): 171–95.

Kraus, Katharina (2019b). "Rethinking the Relationship between Empirical Psychology and Transcendental Philosophy in Kant". *International Yearbook of German Idealism* 15: 47–76.

Kraus, Katharina (forthcoming). "Kant's Argument against Psychological Materialism in the *Prolegomena*". In Peter Thielke (ed.) *Kant's "Prolegomena": A Critical Guide*. Cambridge: Cambridge University Press.

Kraus, Katharina and Sturm, Thomas (2017). "'An Attractive Alternative to Empirical Psychologies Both in His Day and Our Own'? A Critique of Frierson's *Kant's Empirical Psychology*". *Studi Kantiani* 30: 203–23.

Kriegel, Uriah (2009). *Subjective Consciousness: A Self-Representational Theory*. Oxford: Oxford University Press.

Kulstad, Mark A. (1991). *Leibniz on Apperception, Consciousness and Reflection*. Munich: Philosophia Verlag.

Land, Thomas (2014). "Spatial Representation, Magnitude, and the Two Stems of Cognition". *Canadian Journal of Philosophy* 44(5–6): 524–50.

Land, Thomas (2015a). "No Other Use Than in Judgment? Kant on Concepts and Sensible Synthesis". *Journal of the History of Philosophy* 53(3): 461–84.

Land, Thomas (2015b). "Non-Conceptual Readings of Kant's Transcendental Deduction". *Kantian Review* 20(1): 25–51.

Leary, David E. (1978). "The Philosophical Development of the Conception of Psychology in Germany, 1780–1850". *Journal of the History of the Behavioral Sciences* 14: 113–21.

Lee, Seung-Kee (2012). "Logical Forms, Indeterminacy, and the Subjective Unity of Consciousness in Kant". In Piero Giordanetti, Riccardo Pozzo and Marco Sgarbi (eds.) *Kant's Philosophy of the Unconscious*. Berlin: De Gruyter. 233–70.

Leibniz, Gottfried Wilhelm (1686/1989). "Discourse on Metaphysics." In Gottfried Wilhelm Leibniz, *Philosophical Essays*. Eds. and trans. Daniel Garber and Roger Ariew. Indianapolis: Hackett Publishing. 35–68.

Leibniz, Gottfried Wilhelm (1714a/1989). "The Principles of Philosophy, or, the Monadology". In Gottfried Wilhelm Leibniz, *Philosophical Essays*. Eds. and trans. Daniel Garber and Roger Ariew. Indianapolis: Hackett Publishing. 213–25.

Leibniz, Gottfried Wilhelm (1714b/1989). "Principles of Nature and Grace". In Gottfried Wilhelm Leibniz, *Philosophical Essays*. Eds. and trans. Daniel Garber and Roger Ariew. Indianapolis: Hackett Publishing. 206–13.

Leibniz, Gottfried Wilhelm (1765/1996). *New Essays on Human Understanding*. Eds. and trans. Peter Remnant and Jonathan Bennett. Cambridge: Cambridge University Press.

Lewis, David (1979). "Attitudes *De Dicto* and *De Se*". *Philosophical Review* 4: 513–43.

Locke, John (1690/1975). *An Essay on the Human Understanding*. Ed. Peter H. Nidditch. Oxford: Clarendon Press.

Longuenesse, Béatrice (1998). *Kant and the Capacity to Judge*. Princeton: Princeton University Press.

Longuenesse, Béatrice (2005). *Kant on the Human Standpoint*. Cambridge: Cambridge University Press.

Longuenesse, Béatrice (2007). "Kant's 'I think' versus Descartes' 'I am a Thing that Thinks'". In Béatrice Longuenesse and Daniel Garber (eds.) *Kant and the Early Moderns*. Princeton: Princeton University Press. 9–31.

Longuenesse, Béatrice (2012). "Two Uses of 'I' as Subject". In Simon Prosser and François Récanati (eds.) *Immunity to Error through Misidentification*. Cambridge: Cambridge University Press. 81–103.

Longuenesse, Béatrice (2017). *I, Me, Mine*. Oxford: Oxford University Press.

Lycan, William (1996). *Consciousness and Experience*. Cambridge, MA: MIT Press.

Makkreel, Rudolf (1990). *Imagination and Interpretation in Kant: The Hermeneutical Import of the Critique of Judgment*. Chicago: University of Chicago Press.

Makkreel, Rudolf (2001). "Kant on the Scientific Status of Psychology, Anthropology, and History". In Eric Watkins (ed.) *Kant and the Sciences*. New York: Oxford University Press. 185–204.

Makkreel, Rudolf (2003). "The Cognition–Knowledge Distinction in Kant and Dilthey and the Implications for Psychology and Self-Understanding". *Studies in History and Philosophy of Science* 34: 149–64.

Maly, Sebastian (2011). *Kant über die symbolische Erkenntnis Gottes*. Berlin: De Gruyter.

Mariña, Jacqueline (2011). "Transcendental Arguments for Personal Identity in Kant's Transcendental Deduction". *Philo* 14(2): 109–36.

Marshall, Colin (2010). "Kant's Metaphysics of the Self". *Philosophers' Imprint* 10 (8): 1–21.

Meyer, Jürgen Bona (1870). *Kants Psychologie*. Berlin: Verlag von Wilhelm Hertz.

McLaughlin, Peter (2014). "Transcendental Presuppositions and Ideas of Reason". *Kant-Studien* 105(4): 554–72.

McLear, Colin (2011). "Kant on Animal Consciousness". *Philosophers' Imprint* 11 (15): 1–16.

McLear, Colin (2014). "The Kantian (Non)-Conceptualism Debate". *Philosophy Compass* 9(11): 769–90.

McLear, Colin (2015). "Two Kinds of Unity in the *Critique of Pure Reason*". *Journal of the History of Philosophy* 53(1): 79–110.

McNulty, M. Bennett (2015). "Rehabilitating the Regulative Use of Reason: Kant on Empirical and Chemical Laws". *Studies in History and Philosophy of Science* 54: 1–10.

Melnick, Arthur (2009). *Kant's Theory of the Self*. New York: Routledge.

Merritt, Melissa (2018). *Kant on Reflection and Moral Virtue*. Cambridge: Cambridge University Press.

Merritt, Melissa and Valaris, Marco (2017). "Attention and Synthesis in Kant's Conception of Experience". *Philosophical Quarterly* 67(268): 571–92.

Michel, Karin (2003). *Untersuchungen zur Zeitkonzeption in Kants "Kritik der reinen Vernunft"*. Berlin: De Gruyter.

Mischel, Theodore (1967). "Kant and the Possibility of a Science of Psychology". *Monist* 51: 599–622.

Mohr, Georg (1991). *Das sinnliche Ich. Innerer Sinn und Bewußtsein bei Kant*. Würzburg: Königshausen & Neumann.

Mudd, Sasha (2017). "The Demand for Systematicity and the Authority of Theoretical Reason in Kant". *Kantian Review* 22(1):81–106.

Munzel, Felicitas (1999). *Kant's Conception of Moral Character: The "Critical" Link of Morality, Anthropology, and Reflective Judgment*. Chicago: Chicago University Press.

Nassar, Dalia (2016). "Analogical Reflection as a Source for the Science of Life: Kant and the Possibility of the Biological Sciences". *Studies in History and Philosophy of Science* 58: 57–66.

Natorp, Paul (1912). *Allgemeine Psychologie nach kritischer Methode*. Tübingen: Mohr (Siebeck).

Nayak, Abhaya C. and Sotnak, Eric (1995). "Kant on the Impossibility of the 'Soft Sciences'". *Philosophy and Phenomenological Research* 55: 133–51.

Neiman, Susan (1994). *The Unity of Reason: Rereading Kant*. Oxford: Oxford University Press.

O'Neill, Onora (1989). *Constructions of Reason: Explorations of Kant's Practical Philosophy*. Cambridge: Cambridge University Press.

Paton, Herbert J. (1936). *Kant's Metaphysics of Experience*. London: George Allen & Unwin Ltd.

Pendlebury, Michael (1995). "Making Sense of Kant's Schematism". *Philosophy and Phenomenological Research* 55(4): 777–97.

Perry, John (1979). "The Problem of the Essential Indexical". *Noûs* 13(1): 3–21.

Peters, Julia (2018). "Kant's *Gesinnung*". *Journal of the History of Philosophy* 56(3): 497–518.

Pippin, Robert (1976). "The Schematism and Empirical Concepts". *Kant-Studien* 67: 156–71.

Pippin, Robert (1982). *Kant's Theory of Form*. New Haven/London: Yale University Press.

Pollok, Konstantin (2001). *Kants "Metaphysische Anfangsgründe der Naturwissenschaft": Ein kritischer Kommentar*. Hamburg: Meiner.

Pollok, Konstantin (2017). *Kant's Theory of Normativity: Exploring the Space of Reason*. Cambridge: Cambridge University Press.

Powell, Thomas (1990). *Kant's Theory of Self-Consciousness*. Oxford: Oxford University Press.

Reininger, Robert (1900). *Kants Lehre vom inneren Sinn und seine Theorie der Erfahrung*. Wien/Leipzig: Braumüller.

Rosefeldt, Tobias (2000). *Das logische Ich*. Berlin: PHILO.

Rosefeldt, Tobias (2003). "Kant's Self: Real Entity and Logical Identity". In Hans-Johann Glock (ed.) *Strawson and Kant*. Oxford/New York: Oxford University Press. 141–54.

Rosefeldt, Tobias (2017). "Subjects of Kant's First Paralogism". In Anil Gomes and Andrew Stephenson (eds.) *Kant and the Philosophy of Mind*. Oxford: Oxford University Press. 221–44.

Rosenberg, Jay (2005). *Accessing Kant: A Relaxed Introduction to the "Critique of Pure Reason"*. Oxford: Oxford University Press.

Sartre, Jean-Paul (1943/1948). *Being and Nothingness*. Trans Hazel E. Barnes. New York: Philosophical Library.

Schechtman, Marya (2014). *Staying Alive: Personal Identity, Practical Concerns, and the Unity of a Life*. Oxford: Oxford University Press.

Schmidt, Claudia (2008). "Kant's Transcendental and Empirical Psychology of Cognition". *Studies in History and Philosophy of Science* 39(4): 462–72.

Schmitz, Friederike (2015). "On Kant's Conception of Inner Sense: Self-Affection by the Understanding". *European Journal of Philosophy* 23(4): 1044–63.

Schönrich, Gerhard (1991). "Kant und die vermeintliche Unmöglichkeit einer wissenschaftlichen Psychologie". *Psychologie und Geschichte* 2: 130–7.

Schulting, Dennis (2012). *Kant's Deduction and Apperception: Explaining the Categories*. London: Palgrave Macmillan.

Searle, John R. (1969). *Speech Acts: An Essay in the Philosophy of Language*. Cambridge: Cambridge University Press.

Sellars, Wilfrid (1968). *Science and Metaphysics: Variations on Kantian Themes*. London: Routledge & Kegan Paul.

Sellars, Wilfrid (1978). "The Role of Imagination in Kant's Theory of Experience". In Henry Johnstone (ed.) *Categories: A Colloquium*. University Park, PA: Pennsylvania State University Press. 231–45.

Serck-Hanssen, Camilla (2009). "Kant on Consciousness". In Sara Heinämaa (ed.) *Psychology and Philosophy*. Berlin: Springer. 139–57.

Serck-Hanssen, Camilla (2011). "Der Nutzen von Illusionen: Ist die Idee der Seele unentbehrlich?". In Bernd Dörflinger and Günter Kruck (eds.) *Über den Nutzen von Illusionen: Die regulativen Ideen in Kants theoretischer Philosophie.* Hildesheim: Olms. 59–70.

Shabel, Lisa (1998). "Kant on the 'Symbolic Construction' of Mathematical Concepts". *Studies in History and Philosophy of Science* 29(4): 589–621.

Shabel, Lisa (2007). "Kant's Philosophy of Mathematics". In Paul Guyer (ed.) *The Cambridge Companion to Kant and Modern Philosophy.* Cambridge: Cambridge University Press. 94–128.

Shoemaker, Sidney (1968). "Self-Reference and Self-Awareness". *Journal of Philosophy* 65: 555–67.

Shoemaker, Sidney (1994). "Self-Knowledge and 'Inner Sense'". *Philosophy and Phenomenological Research* 54: 249–314.

Simmons, Allison (2011). "Leibnizian Consciousness Reconsidered". *Studia Leibnitiana* 43(2): 196–215.

Sorensen, Kelly (2002). "Kant's Taxonomy of the Emotions". *Kantian Review* 6: 109–28.

Sorensen, Kelly and Williamson, Diane (eds.) (2018). *Kant and the Faculty of Feeling.* Cambridge: Cambridge University Press.

Stang, Nicholas (2016). *Kant's Modal Metaphysics.* Oxford: Oxford University Press.

Stephenson, Andrew (2015). "Kant on the Object-Dependence of Intuition and Hallucination". *Philosophical Quarterly* 65(260): 486–508.

Stephenson, Andrew (2017). "Imagination and Inner Intuition". In Anil Gomes and Andrew Stephenson (eds.) *Kant and the Philosophy of Mind.* Oxford: Oxford University Press. 104–23.

Strawson, Galen (2011). *Locke on Personal Identity: Consciousness and Concernment.* Princeton: Princeton University Press.

Strawson, Peter (1959). *Individuals: An Essay in Descriptive Metaphysics.* London: Routledge.

Strawson, Peter (1966). *The Bounds of Sense.* London: Routledge.

Sturm, Thomas (2001). "Kant on Empirical Psychology: How Not to Investigate the Human Mind". In Eric Watkins (ed.) *Kant and the Sciences.* New York: Oxford University Press. 163–84.

Sturm, Thomas (2009). *Kant und die Wissenschaften vom Menschen.* Paderborn: Mentis.

Sturma, Dieter (1985). *Kant über Selbstbewußtsein: Zum Zusammenhang von Erkenntniskritik und Theorie des Selbstbewußtseins.* Hildesheim: Georg Olms Verlag.

Tetens, Johann Nicolaus (1777). *Philosophische Versuche über die menschliche Natur und ihre Entwickelung.* Leipzig: Weidmann.

Thiel, Udo (1994). "Hume's Notion of Consciousness and Reflection in Context". *British Journal for the History of Philosophy* 2: 75–105.

Thiel, Udo (1996). "Between Wolff and Kant: Merian's Theory of Apperception". *Journal of the History of Philosophy* 34: 213–32.

Thiel, Udo (1997). "Varieties of Inner Sense. Two Pre-Kantian Theories". *Archiv für Geschichte der Philosophie* 79(1): 58–79.

Thiel, Udo (2001). "Kant's Notion of Self-Consciousness in Context". In Volker Gerhardt, Rolf-Peter Horstmann and Ralph Schumacher (eds.) *Kant und die Berliner Aufklärung. Akten des IX. Internationalen Kant-Kongresses*, Vol. 2. Berlin/New York: De Gruyter. 468–76.

Thiel, Udo (2011). *The Early Modern Subject: Self-Consciousness and Personal Identity from Descartes to Hume.* Oxford: Oxford University Press.

Thiel, Udo (2017). "Kant and Tetens on the Unity of the Self". In Corey Dyck and Falk Wunderlich (eds.) *Kant and His Contemporaries.* Cambridge: Cambridge University Press. 59–75.

Thiel, Udo (2018). "Feder und der Innere Sinn". In Hans Peter Nowitzky, Udo Roth and Gideon Stiening (eds.) *Johann Georg Heinrich Feder (1740–1821): Empirismus und Popularphilosophie zwischen Wolff und Kant.* Berlin: De Gruyter. 55–86.

Thöle, Bernhard (1991). *Kant und das Problem der Gesetzmäßigkeit der Natur.* Berlin: De Gruyter.

Tolley, Clinton (2013). "The Non-Conceptuality of the Content of Intuitions: A New Approach". *Kantian Review* 18(1): 107–36.

Tolley, Clinton (2016). "The Difference between Original, Metaphysical, and Geometrical Representations of Space". In Dennis Schulting (ed.) *Kantian Nonconceptualism.* London: Palgrave. 257–85.

Tolley, Clinton (2017). "Kant on the Place of Cognition in the Progression of Our Representations". *Synthese.* https://doi.org/10.1007/s11229-017-1623-5

Tugendhat, Ernst (1979). *Selbstbewußtsein und Selbstbestimmung: Sprachanalytische Interpretationen.* Frankfurt a. M.: Suhrkamp.

Vaihinger, Hans (1892). *Kommentar zu Kants "Kritik der reinen Vernunft".* Stuttgart.

Vaihinger, Hans (1911). *Die Philosophie des Als Ob: System der theoretischen, praktischen und religiösen Fiktionen der Menschheit auf Grund eines idealistischen Positivismus. Mit einem Anhang über Kant und Nietzsche.* Berlin: Reuther & Reichard.

Valaris, Markos (2008). "Inner Sense, Self-Affection and Temporal Consciousness in Kant's *Critique of Pure Reason*". *Philosophers' Imprint* 8(4): 1–18.

Van Cleve, James (1999). *Problems from Kant.* Oxford: Oxford University Press.

Vogel, Jonathan (1993). "The Problem of Self-Knowledge in Kant's 'Refutation of Idealism': Two Recent Views". *Philosophy and Phenomenological Research* 53: 875–87.

Warren, Daniel (2001). *Reality and Impenetrability in Kant's Philosophy of Nature.* New York: Routledge.

Washburn, Michael C. (1976). "Did Kant Have a Theory of Self-Knowledge?" *Archiv für Geschichte der Philosophie* 58: 40–56.

Watkins, Eric (2005). *Kant and the Metaphysics of Causality.* Cambridge: Cambridge University Press.

Watkins, Eric (2009). *Kant's "Critique of Pure Reason": Background Source Materials*. Cambridge: Cambridge University Press.

Watkins, Eric (2013). "Kant on *Infima Species*". In Alfredo Ferrarin, Claudio La Rocca and Margit Ruffing (eds.) *Kant und die Philosophie in weltbürgerlicher Absicht: Akten des XI. Internationalen Kant-Kongresses*. Berlin: De Gruyter. 283–96.

Watkins, Eric (2016). "Kant on Materialism". *British Journal of the History of Philosophy* 24 (5): 1035–52.

Watkins, Eric (2019). "Kant on Real Conditions". In Violette L. Waibel and Margit Ruffing (eds.) *Natur und Freiheit: Akten des XII. Internationalen Kant-Kongresses*. Berlin: De Gruyter. 1133–40.

Watkins, Eric and Willaschek, Marcus (2017a). "Kant's Account of Cognition". *Journal of the History of Philosophy* 55(1): 83–112.

Watkins, Eric, and Willaschek, Marcus (2017b). "Kant on Cognition and Knowledge". *Synthese*. https://doi.org/10.1007/s11229-017-1624-4

Waxman, Wayne (1991). *Kant's Model of the Mind: A New Interpretation of Transcendental Idealism*. New York/Oxford: Oxford University Press.

Weinberg, Shelley (2008). "The Coherence of Consciousness in Locke's 'Essay'". *History of Philosophy Quarterly* 25(1): 21–39.

Westphal, Kenneth (2004). *Kant's Transcendental Proof of Realism*. Cambridge: Cambridge University Press.

Willaschek, Marcus (1992). *Praktische Vernunft: Handlungstheorie und Moralbegründung bei Kant*. Stuttgart/Weimar: J. B. Metzler.

Willaschek, Marcus (2009). "Der eigenen Wille". In Jan-Christoph Heilinger, Colin G. King and Héctor Wittwer (eds.) *Individualität und Selbstbestimmung*. Berlin: Akademie-Verlag. 191–212.

Willaschek, Marcus (2010). "The Primacy of Pure Practical Reason and the Very Idea of a Postulate". In Andrews Reath and Jens Timmermann (eds.) *Kant's "Critique of Practical Reason": A Critical Guide*. Cambridge: Cambridge University Press. 168–96.

Willaschek, Marcus (2018). *Kant on the Sources of Metaphysics: The Dialectic of Pure Reason*. Cambridge: Cambridge University Press.

Wittgenstein, Ludwig (1958). *The Blue and Brown Books*. Oxford: Blackwell Publishing.

Wolff, Christian (1720/1997). *Vernünftige Gedanken von Gott, der Welt und der Seele des Menschen, auch allen Dingen überhaupt*. In *Gesammelte Werke* I 2. Hildesheim: Olms.

Wolff, Christian (1732/1968). *Psychologia empirica*. In *Gesammelte Werke* II 5. Hildesheim: Olms.

Wolff, Christian (1734/1994). *Psychologia rationalis*. In *Gesammelte Werke* II 6. Hildesheim: Olms.

Wolff, Michael (2006). "Empirischer und transzendentaler Dualismus. Zu Rolf-Peter Horstmanns Interpretation von Kants Paralogismen". *Deutsche Zeitschrift für Philosophie* 54: 265–75.

Wolff, Robert Paul (1973). *Kant's Theory of Mental Activity*. Gloucester, MA: Peter Smith.

Wood, Allen (2018). "Feeling and Desire in the Human Animal". In Kelly Sorensen and Diane Williamson (eds.) *Kant and the Faculty of Feeling*. Cambridge: Cambridge University Press. 88–106.

Wuerth, Julian (2010). "The Paralogisms of Pure Reason". In Paul Guyer (ed.) *The Cambridge Companion to Kant's "Critique of Pure Reason"*. Cambridge: Cambridge University Press. 210–44.

Wuerth, Julian (2014). *Kant on Mind, Action, and Ethics*. Oxford: Oxford University Press.

Wunderlich, Falk (2005). *Kant und die Bewußtseinstheorien des 18. Jahrhunderts*. Berlin/New York: De Gruyter.

Wundt, Wilhelm (1888). "Selbstbeobachtung und innere Wahrnehmung". *Philosophische Studien* 4: 292–309.

Wundt, Wilhelm (1902). *Grundzüge der physiologischen Psychologie*. Leipzig: Wilhelm Engelmann.

Young, J. Michael. 1982. "Kant and the Construction of Arithmetical Concepts." *Kant-Studien* 73: 17–46.

Zahavi, Dan (2005). *Subjectivity and Selfhood: Investigating the First-Person Perspective*. Cambridge, MA: MIT Press.

Zuckert, Rachel (2017). "Empirical Scientific Investigation and the Ideas of Reason". In Michela Massimi and Angela Breitenbach (eds.) *Kant and the Laws of Nature*. Cambridge: Cambridge University Press. 89–107.

INDEX

actuality *(Wirklichkeit)*, 126
adjacency, sheer, 54, 63, 72
affection, 32–3, 53
   inner/outer, 38, 45, 50–1, 62, 65
   transcendental/empirical, 48–9
Allison, Henry A., 34, 38, 44, 49, 52,
   54–5, 62–3, 67, 71–2, 88, 90, 98,
   111, 116, 118–19, 138, 140, 146,
   158–9, 185, 197–8, 203, 211, 213
Ameriks, Karl, 5, 33–4, 44, 88, 138–9,
   161–2, 164, 166
Analogies of Experience, 136, 186–7,
   203, 245
analogy, 2, 173, 194–6, 209–15
   inference by, 202
   thought by, 203–5
Anderson, R. Lanier, 231–3, 235
*Anth (Anthropology from a Pragmatic
   Point of View)*, 34, 36, 42, 52–3, 62,
   79, 102, 152, 228–9, 238–9, 244–7,
   260, 262, 268, 274–6
Anticipations of Perception, 136, 156
appearances, inner/outer, 33–4
   and form of intuition, 33
   and sensation (matter) of intuition,
   33
   sum total of, 235
Appendix to the Dialectic of Pure
   Reason, 10, 171, 174, 179, 183, 188,
   196, 199, 204, 206, 223
apperception, 30, 36, 83–4, 185
   analytic/synthetic unity of, 90–1, 119
   and self-ascription, 94, 98–105
   and self-consciousness, 97
   and the form of reflexivity, 9, 81–129
   empirical, 61–2, 97
   expressivist reading of, 81–129

logical reading of, 92–4, 98–105
   psychological reading of, 93–8
   transcendental (original) unity of, 59,
   86–92, 102
apprehension, 56–60, 65, 118
Aristotle, 17, 260
"as if" *(als ob)*, 184, 208, 226
association, principles of, 59, 193
attention *(attentio)*, 76, 78–80, 244
   and abstraction, 78
   and distraction, 78
   and self-affection, 78
Augustine of Hippo, 27
Austin, John Langshaw, 122, 128

Baumgarten, Alexander, 17, 25, 27,
   29–30, 134, 139–40, 154, 161, 184,
   261
belief *(Glaube)*, 166, 219, 225
   doctrinal *(doktrinaler)*, 189
Boyle, Matthew, 249–50
Breitenbach, Angela, 236
Brook, Andrew, 6, 44, 59, 96, 98–9, 104
Buchdahl, Gerd, 180, 191, 220

Carl, Wolfgang, 3, 18, 29, 31, 67, 86, 88,
   96, 98, 100, 125, 128, 137, 141, 146
category(ies), 25, 68–72, 74, 112
   and schematization, 74
   objective validity, 22, 47–8
   of relation, 80, 131, 134, 208–15
   pure, 143, 196
   schematization of, 196–9
   transcendental deduction of, 85–92,
   115
causality, 53, 209–15
   principle of, 73, 210–1, 228

298

90, 96–8, 100, 107, 112, 117, 119,
123, 125, 127–8, 138, 142, 144, 146,
154, 157, 159–62, 164–5, 232, 250

mark (*Merkmal*), 68, 109, 119, 135, 149,
231–3
memory, 193, 271
mental act, first-order, 11, 80, 86, 252,
254, 257–8
mental activity, 6, 44, 251–3
mental state, 20, 43–4, 209–10,
228, 254
Merritt, Melissa, 79, 245, 247, 263
metaphysics
critique of, 131, 137
rationalist, 137, 172, 259
methodological reading, 190–4
*MFNS (Metaphysical Foundations of
Natural Science)*, 107, 155, 207,
213, 222
MM (Metaphysics of Morals), 40, 260,
275, 277
model passage (*CpR* B67–68), 50
Mohr, Georg, 5, 18, 33–4, 38, 45, 49, 65,
70, 77, 183

nature, 37, 85, 179–80, 184, 205–6,
233–4, 247, 271
inner/outer, 206–9, 214, 216, 235–40
neo-Kantianism, 5
normative, 173, 182, 217, 223, 225–6
concept of a person as, 231–41,
266–7, 270–6
noumenal interpretation of the idea of
the soul, 172, 181–2, 187–90, 193
noumenon, noumenal, 97–8, 139, 162,
172, 208, 263

O'Neill, Onora, 247, 258, 273
object, 4, 7–9, 19, 20–2, 25, 51, 66, 89, 219
in general, 89–91, 110, 113, 234–5
in the idea, 200–2, 208
of empirical cognition, 8, 64, 91,
112–13, 135–6, 223
of (possible) experience
(*Gegenstand*), 8–9, 20, 26, 73, 76,
130, 133, 145, 200, 235–6
of perception, 126, 133
of the senses (*Erscheinung*), 8, 127, 130

of thought (*Gedankending*), 8–9, 104,
130–1, 133, 138–50
opinion (*Meinung*), 218–9
organism, 173–4, 236–7, 259–60

paralogisms of pure reason, 31, 131,
138–43, 152
First Paralogism, 132, 143–5, 147
Third Paralogism, 161–7
paralogistic inference, 144–5
parity of inner and outer experience,
3–6, 151, 216
part–whole relation, 173, 198–9, 205,
209, 216, 222, 236, 252, 272
Paton, Herbert James, 44, 46, 62, 67–8,
88, 111, 116
perception, 37–8, 66, 141
a priori temporal conditions of, 65–74
and attention, 76–7
and empirical consciousness, 44–6,
58, 75–8
and intuition, 46
inner/outer, 44, 60–5
interactive model of, 49–65
persistence, 153–63, 186–7, 213
person, 1–2, 10–1, 132, 251–76
and idea of the soul, 256–61
and individuality, 42, 218, 236, 242,
269–70, 277–9
character of a, 229, 239–40, 261–4
concept of a, 160–1, 218, 236, 241–4,
270–6
practical, 261–2, 267, 278–9
psychological, 160–1, 171, 251,
255–6, 261–70
personal identity, 11, 28, 153–67, 187,
208, 264–5, 267–70
capacity for being conscious of one's,
29, 261–2
personhood (personality), 1, 30, 132
practical/psychological, 261–4
phenomenology (philosophical
movement), 5, 107
phenomenon, phenomenal, 231–40
Pippin, Robert, 46, 51, 67, 197–8
Pollok, Konstantin, 25, 71, 157, 175, 182
possibility, formal/real, 136
Postulate of the Immortality of the
Soul, 209, 262, 278